SOCIAL CLEAVAGES AND POLITICAL CHANGE

Social Cleavages and Political Change

Voter Alignments and U.S. Party Coalitions

JEFF MANZA

AND

CLEM BROOKS

OXFORD

UNIVERSITY PRESS

OXFORD
UNIVERSITY PRESS

Great Clarendon Street, Oxford OX2 6DP
Oxford University Press is a department of the University of Oxford.
It furthers the University's objective of excellence in research, scholarship,
and education by publishing worldwide in

Oxford New York

Athens Auckland Bangkok Bogotá Buenos Aires Calcutta
Cape Town Chennai Dar es Salaam Delhi Florence Hong Kong Istanbul
Karachi Kuala Lumpur Madrid Melbourne Mexico City Mumbai
Nairobi Paris São Paulo Singapore Taipei Tokyo Toronto Warsaw

and associated companies in Berlin Ibadan

Oxford in a registered trade mark of Oxford University Press
in the UK and certain other countries

Published in the United States
by Oxford University Press Inc., New York

British Library Cataloguing in Publication Data
Data available

Library of Congress Cataloging in Publication Data
Manza, Jeff.
Social cleavages and political change: voter alignments and US
party coalitions / Jeff Manza and Clem Brooks.
Includes bibliographical references and index.
1. Party affiliation–United Sates. 2. Social classes–United
States. 3. Voting–United States. I. Brooks, Clem. II. Title.
JK2271.M28 1999   324.9730929–dc21   99-15986

ISBN 0-19-829492-1

1 3 5 7 9 10 8 6 4 2

Typeset by J&L Composition Ltd, Filey, North Yorkshire
Printed in Great Britain
on acid-free paper by
Biddles Ltd
Guildford and King's Lynn

ACKNOWLEDGEMENTS

Our investigation of the impact of social cleavages on voter alignments and party coalitions in the United States has been several years in the making, and we have benefited from the help of many people along the way. Our most profound debt is to Michael Hout, who has been a source of advice and inspiration throughout this project. We began our collaboration as first-year graduate students in Mike's course on statistical methods at the University of California–Berkeley a full decade ago. Over the years Mike has been a wonderful teacher, mentor, collaborator, and friend. We hope the final product lives up to the high standards upon which he has continually insisted.

A number of friends and colleagues have given us valuable advice on this project. As we began our work, Philip Converse and Paul Sniderman usefully advised us to limit the project into something more manageable than called for by our original ambitions. We received useful advice concerning specific parts of the manuscript from (in alphabetical order) David Brady, Ann Branaman, Steven Brint, Terry Clark, Geoff Evans, Bill Form, Joseph Gerteis, Andrew Greeley, David Grusky, John Goldthorpe, John R. Hall, Jerome Karabel, Kevin Leicht, Scott Long, Paul Nieuwbeerta, Eric Plutzer, Whitney Pope, Robert Robinson, Art Stinchcombe, Laura Stoker, David Weakliem, and Richard Wood. Bill Domhoff kindly read the penultimate version of the manuscript on short notice and provided his usual generous and incisive comments. We received research assistance from Marcus Britton, Roblyn Rawlins, Quynh Tran, and Michael Sauder. Our thanks to all.

We have presented versions of various chapters to a number of scholarly audiences. Early versions of Chapters 3, 4, 5 and 7 were presented to audiences at three different meetings of the American Sociological Association in 1994, 1996, and 1997. Chapter 3 was presented to the 1995 meetings of Social Science History Association. Chapter 6 was presented to a conference on Class and Politics at the Woodrow Wilson Center in Washington, DC, organized by Seymour Martin Lipset and Terry Clark in April 1996. A version of the entire argument was presented to colloquia at the Survey Research Center at the University of California–Berkeley and the departments of sociology at the University of Chicago, the University of Wisconsin–Madison, Northwestern University, Stanford University, New York University, the Ohio State University, the University of Minnesota, and Temple University in the 1997–1998 academic year. The valuable feedback we received from colleagues and audience members at these various forums has improved the overall quality of our work, and in some cases led us to reformulate our ideas.

We have benefited from institutional resources provided by the departments of sociology at SUNY–Stony Brook, Indiana University, Pennsylvania State University, and Northwestern University, as well as the Population Research Institute at Penn State and the Institute for Policy Research at Northwestern. Over the course of our work on this book, we have both moved to new institutions, and we thank our colleagues at Indiana and Northwestern for their support during and after these moves. At Northwestern, Robert Nelson kindly loaned Manza his office and otherwise eased the transition during a particularly intense writing phase. On the personal front, we are grateful that Amy Hafter and Ruth Kelly have been willing to put up with this project, and our children (Dana Hafter-Manza, Zoë Hafter-Manza, and Amanda Brooks-Kelly) have delightfully grown up alongside it. We thank them all for their patience and good cheer.

The Introduction and Chapters 1, 2, 8, 9, and 10 appear here for the first time. Earlier versions of many of the analyses in Chapter 4 appeared in the *American Journal of Sociology* (volume 103, 1997), Chapter 5 in the *American Journal of Sociology* (volume 103, 1998), and Chapter 6 in the *American Sociological Review* (volume 62, 1997), respectively, although the text and interpretations in the chapters presented here have been substantially expanded and rewritten. Parts of Chapters 3 and 6 appeared in *Social Forces* (volume 79, 1997) and the *American Sociological Review* (volume 62, 1997), and Chapter 7 in the *European Sociological Review* (volume 15, 1999), respectively; both the analyses and text of those chapters have been reworked and rewritten for this volume. We thank the editors and anonymous referees of these publications for their thoughtful comments on earlier versions of our work.

Jeff Manza
Evanston, Illinois

Clem Brooks
Bloomington, Indiana

December 1998

CONTENTS

FIGURES

TABLES

Introduction

The impact of social divisions on political life has long been a central concern of political sociology. For much of the formative decades of the field, research on social movements, party systems, public opinion, and voting behavior examined the social bases of political life. The reasons for this interest are not hard to discern. In capitalist democracies, politics, like other arenas of social life, is shaped by inequalities in the amount of power and status enjoyed by different groups. How such factors affect political contests and outcomes tells us much about the nature of democratic polities in specific national contexts.

In recent years, however, there have been numerous claims in the social science literatures on political behavior that postindustrial economic, social, and cultural trends have reduced the import of social factors. In this book we investigate this claim. More specifically, we consider the role of social group divisions on voting behavior and party coalitions produced by the distribution of votes in national elections in America since the 1950s. While our empirical focus is on the United States, the general approach we develop could readily be applied to other countries.

A central assumption that motivates much of the sociological research on political behavior, including our own, is that the structure of electoral coalitions ultimately—if indirectly—has an impact on both the policy agendas and electoral strategies pursued by major political parties. Interpretations of major electoral change—such as the Republican triumph of 1896, the New Deal era Democratic sweeps of the 1930s, or even Richard Nixon's capture of the presidency for the Republicans in 1968 (which began a period of Republican dominance at the presidential level)—often focus on underlying shifts in the group bases of the party coalitions. Where the votes come from, why, and with what impact are central questions in the scholarly analysis of historical and contemporary political behavior.

Interest in the social bases of U.S. electoral coalitions is, of course, not limited to professional social scientists. Candidates for political

office and their consultants and advisors frequently develop strategies
to reach out to (or target) distinct social voting blocs (such as women,
minorities, union members, evangelical Christians, or self-employed
businesspersons). The core of the Democratic Party's electorate has
long been thought to consist of African-American and other minority
voters, the poor, unionized workers, Catholics, and Jews. Conversely,
Republicans have often been viewed as drawing disproportionate
strength from the bulk of the educated middle classes, Protestants,
business owners, and white suburbanites.

The classical works of American political sociology and political
behavior in the 1950s and 1960s were informed by such assumptions.
Studies of the linkages between social group memberships and voting
behavior led to the development of a distinctive 'sociological approach'
to voting behavior, due to the presumed importance it attached to social
characteristics in shaping individual voting decisions.[1] From the 1950s
to the present (the time period covered by our research), signs of
growing electoral instability in the United States and elsewhere have
encouraged many scholars to infer that the traditional social group
bases of political behavior and party coalitions are breaking down.
Some possible manifestations of this instability can be seen in the
independent presidential campaigns of George Wallace (1968) and H.
Ross Perot (1992, 1996), the increasing proportions of independent
voters in the electorate, the rise of split-ticket voting, and the emergence
cross-cutting ideological conflicts that appear to be increasingly central
to electoral politics. One outcome is said to be a new type of political
order characterized by issue-driven conflicts and a much looser attachment of voters to parties. Terms such as 'realignment' and 'dealignment'
have come into wide use as a way of characterizing these trends.

In the course of trying to explain the hypothesized rise of electoral
instability, many analysts have suggested that a sociological approach is
increasingly irrelevant to understanding a postindustrial polity. In one
recent review of contemporary political behavior research, for example,
Russell Dalton and Martin Wattenberg declare that the 'sociological
model' of voting is producing rapidly diminishing intellectual returns.
For these authors,

When all the evidence is assembled, one of the most widely repeated findings
of modern electoral research is the declining value of the sociological model
of voting behavior. . . . [T]he evidence is seldom in dispute. . . . The decline of
sociologically based voting is most apparent for the class and religious
cleavages, but a similar erosion of influence can be observed for most other
sociological characteristics.

Elsewhere in their review, Dalton and Wattenberg argue that 'there has been an attenuation of the specific linkage between social class and electoral politics', that 'the religious cleavage is following the same pattern of decline as social class', and finally that 'despite repeated proclamations of an emerging gender gap, gender remains a minor factor in voting behavior'.[2]

The recent controversies concerning the sociological approach to studying political change frame this study. If the critics of the sociological approach are correct, social divisions in American society are shrinking toward political irrelevance. However, if social divisions have not disappeared, critics of the sociological approach may have missed some important sources of change and stability in U.S. national politics. This is especially true because the size of major social groups and their political alignments tend to change slowly and thus cumulate over time, leading to potentially significant long-term consequences.

We thus present here the first systematic book-length reassessment and restatement of the sociological approach toward American politics in more than twenty years.[3] We argue that many of the criticisms of the sociological approach are overstated. More specifically, we develop a new way of thinking about some of the major social cleavages in the American political system as well as a strategy for examining the political effects of those cleavages in presidential elections. Our reformulation makes use of sounder conceptualizations of the major social cleavages in American society and methodological innovations to develop a new and more comprehensive understanding of the linkages between social group memberships and voting behavior. On the basis of these analyses, we conclude that despite significant changes in the American political landscape, social cleavages as a whole remain an important source of voter alignments and the composition of the Democratic and Republican Party coalitions.

The new analyses presented in this book start from three simple premises. First, studies concerned with the effects of social cleavages should use adequate measures of each cleavage. For example, class analysts should employ a theoretically sound, multi-category class schema that takes into account changes in the class structures of the United States and other democratic capitalist societies in the second half of the twentieth century. For too long analysts have employed simplistic two-class models (e.g. blue collar versus white collar) of class structure in their research. As we show in Chapter 3, such a representation of class structure fails to capture many recent changes and thus leads researchers to underestimate the political effects of class. Similarly, analysts of religion and politics should take into account the divisions *among* Protestants as well as between Protestants, Catholics, Jews, and other religious groups. While most specialists in the study of religious politics have made such distinctions in their work, many general analysts of social cleavages have failed to incorporate these distinctions.

Second, analyses of the relationship between social group memberships and voting behavior should employ statistical models that allow researchers to distinguish between trends that influence all groups from those that influence only some groups. For example, it only makes sense to infer that Catholics are becoming less supportive of Democrats in presidential elections if declines in support among Catholics are greater than that of other religious groups. Otherwise, Catholics remain in the same *relative* alignment as before. As our analyses in Chapter 4 show, Catholics did become less supportive of the Democratic Party after 1964 but only in tandem with other major denominational groups in the American electorate. By focusing on such relative voting trends, we are able to distinguish between trends that apply only to specific groups versus those trends that apply to the electorate as a whole. Only when there is clear evidence of the former does it make sense to say that a group has changed its political alignment.

Third, research on the social group foundations of political behavior should also take into account the size of different groups and group-based turnout rates. The size of the groups making up a cleavage can change over time, occasionally in dramatic ways. For example, our analyses show that liberal Protestants shrank from nearly a quarter of the population in 1960 to just over 13% by 1992, and that nonskilled workers declined from 34% of the employed population in 1960 to just 23% by 1992. Such changes can affect the shape of party coalitions and, ultimately, election outcomes.

Changes in the turnout rates of different groups may also influence the shape of party coalitions. One notable example is that of African-American voters. Historically voting at much lower rates that whites (in large part because of their effective disfranchisement in the South prior to 1965), blacks had by the 1980s increased their turnout rates significantly relative to whites. Similarly, women also had historically lower rates of turnout than men, but those differences eroded steadily from the 1950s to the 1970s and have even reversed themselves slightly in the 1980s and 1990s. As a result, blacks and women have provided a more important bloc of votes in recent elections than in earlier periods. Our analyses in Chapter 7 are designed to take both group size and turnout into account.

Our approach produces a number of new findings, many of which challenge the conventional wisdom about group-based voting alignments and party coalitions. The most significant findings and interpretations presented in this study include:

- Of the four major social cleavages we investigate, the race cleavage is approximately twice the size of the religious cleavage, with the class cleavage less than the religious cleavage and the gender cleavage the smallest;
- The dramatic growth of the race cleavage has not led to the overall decline of other important social cleavages;
- The class cleavage fluctuated from the 1950s through 1992 with class differences declining considerably in 1996;
- Professionals have moved from being the most Republican class in the 1950s to the second most Democratic class by the late 1980s and the most Democratic class in 1996;
- The self-employed became significantly more Republican, and nonskilled workers less Democratic, in the 1980s, with nonskilled workers shifting even further towards the center in 1996;
- Liberal Protestants moved from being the most Republican religious group in the 1960s to a centrist position by the 1990s;
- Conservative Protestants have not realigned with the Republican Party, in large part because they have always preferred Republican candidates;
- The gender gap has been growing slowly since the 1960s, rather than starting in the 1980 election, as many analysts have assumed, and is a product of the increased proportion of women in the paid labor force.

Having uncovered a series of significant political trends, we also seek to develop explanations for those trends. These analyses consider two broad kinds of factors: sociodemographic and attitudinal. Sociodemographic factors include changes in the composition of a group, such as the racial, gender, class, or educational levels of group members. The attitudinal factors we find most significant include issues concerning personal economic interests, social provision and the welfare state, and social issues such as gender equality and civil rights of African-Americans.

PLAN OF THE BOOK

To develop the larger context within which our research is situated, we begin with an intellectual history of the study of social cleavages and political alignments (Chapter 1). Our strategy for reformulating the sociological approach to political behavior appears in Chapter 2. These chapters lay the foundation for our empirical investigations in the rest of the book.

In Chapter 3 we take up the question of class politics. We begin by showing that differences in class-based political alignments were surprisingly robust from the early 1950s through 1992. This result calls into question the large literature which hypothesizes that class differences narrowed during this period. But we also find a complex pattern of change, with some classes moving away from, and others toward, the political center. In the second half of the chapter, we consider the sources of trends and differences between the 'old' and 'new' middle classes (or, more specifically, professionals, managers, and the self-employed). We document and explain two significant but heretofore largely ignored trends among these groups: the realignment of professionals from the Republican to Democratic parties and the emerging alignment of the self-employed with the Republican Party. Our detailed investigations of each of these trends ask whether class interests (as opposed to non-class factors) can account for these trends. The trend among professionals toward the Democrats since the 1960s has been driven by their increasingly liberal attitudes on social issues, not class-related factors. Conversely, however, the self-employed have embraced the Republicans in part because of class-related concerns with taxes and the size of government. The chapter also examines the dynamics of working-class politics. Our results suggest that nonskilled workers' support for the Democrats eroded in the 1980s because of their perceptions of personal and national economic decline under the Carter Administration in the late 1970s and subsequent improvement in their perceptions of personal well-being under Reagan in the 1980s.

In Chapter 4, we consider the effects of religion on voting behavior. In recent years, changes in the traditional patterning of the religious cleavage in American politics have sometimes been viewed as a product of the rise of the Christian Right. This development is thought to have significantly increased Republican voting among evangelical Christians. By contrast, our analyses demonstrate that only one group—liberal Protestants—has actually changed its alignment in recent elections. Other religious groups fluctuate in their patterns of support for the major parties but exhibit no clear trend. Our analysis of the trend among liberal Protestants shows that, like professionals, they have shifted away from the Republican Party because of their growing liberalism on social issues. We also explore more systematically the surprising absence of a trend among Catholics. Although most analysts have proclaimed that Catholics are becoming increasingly conservative, our analysis shows that while they have become more conservative on economic issues (which pushes them in a Republican direction), they have become less conservative on social issues (pulling them back in a Democratic direction).

In Chapter 5, we consider the widely discussed 'gender gap'. Our analyses show that the gender gap has been emerging steadily since the 1950s, rather than suddenly appearing in 1980 as many analysts have supposed. To explain this finding, we explore a variety of possible explanations: social-psychological differences between men and women, the growing autonomy of women, the increase of feminist consciousness among women, and rising labor-force participation rates among women. Our analyses suggest that most of the rising gender cleavage is due to the steadily increasing proportion of women in the workforce, although we also find that in recent elections feminist consciousness has a significant, independent effect.

The subject of the racial cleavage in American politics has been widely explored, and the results of our own investigations are largely consistent with the thrust of earlier research. Chapter 6 opens with a discussion of those issues. Following this overview, we turn to a consideration of whether the growth and persistence of the race cleavage since the early 1960s has altered other social cleavages. A number of analysts have suggested that racial divisions in American politics are attenuating class divisions because white voters are becoming more unified in their opposition to government programs that are seen as disproportionately benefiting blacks. Such propositions concern the interrelationships between, and relative magnitudes of, each of the major social cleavages. We explore the possibility that cleavages may be 'cross-cutting' by examining whether changes in one cleavage lead to changes in the others. We find that while the race cleavage has increased since 1960 and the religious cleavage has declined slightly, the class cleavage has fluctuated without any clear trend and the gender cleavage has increased. Overall, the results of this chapter demonstrate that there is no evidence of systematic decline in the effects of social groups on political behavior, even when we take into account the impact of the racial cleavage.

In Chapter 7, we assess the contributions of class, racial, religious, and gender groups to the Democratic and Republican Party coalitions since the 1950s. We examine how changes in the size of particular groups, as well as changes in their loyalty to the parties, have led to significant changes in the sources of votes for Democratic and Republican presidential contenders. We conclude that these changes have evolved slowly over a relatively long period of time. In conjunction with changes in group-based alignments, changes in size (and to a lesser extent, turnout rates) have produced some important trends in the contributions of group to the two parties' coalitions. The most important of these trends are the dramatic decline of liberal Protestants in the Republican Party, the decline of unskilled workers in the Democratic coalition, and the rise of professionals and managers in both coalitions (with professionals growing disproportionately in the Democratic coalition and managers in the Republican coalition). By the 1990s, both parties—but especially the Republican Party—received fewer votes from people outside the labor force, primarily because of the rising labor force participation of women.

In Chapter 8, we examine social group cleavages in the 1996 election. Although the election was unusual in that the Democratic candidate (Bill Clinton) captured nearly half the votes cast for the first time in twenty years, most of the trends and patterns of alignment observed in earlier elections continued to hold. However, we also find evidence for two important new developments: the further growth of, and changes in, the gender cleavage, coupled with a sharp decline of the class cleavage. We consider the implications of these new developments in light of the overall stability of the total social cleavage.

While our main focus is on major party voting (and nonvoting), the rise of third party candidates is an important phenomenon in its own right. In Chapter 9, we consider the relationship of social groups to the major third party candidacies since World War II: George Wallace and H. Ross Perot. What social groups supported these candidates? To what extent did the Wallace campaign, with its explicit appeals to white voters resistant to civil rights legislation, differ in terms of its social bases of support from the support received by the Perot campaigns? Did the 1996 rerun of the Perot candidacy sharpen the social bases of support and/or opposition to the Texas billionaire?

Finally, in the concluding chapter we assess the theoretical and political significance of our results. Given the changes in the patterns of group alignment and contributions to the Democratic and Republican parties, we explore some of the emerging political opportunities and dilemmas faced by both parties. We then return to the theoretical framework developed in Chapter 2. We use that framework to explain the historical evolution and comparative magnitude of the race, religious, class, and gender cleavages in U.S. politics since the 1950s.

1

The Sociological Tradition in Political Behavior Research

Scholarly interest in the relationship between social cleavages and political alignments can be traced to recurring political predictions (especially in the European context) that the interests of a growing working class might provide the foundation for an 'electoral road to socialism'. These predictions were based on the assumption that class interests inevitably lead voters to favor the political party most likely to advance those interests. The 'class politics' thesis became the object of social science inquiry when political change did not unfold in the ways predicted by the theories put forward by Marxists and other social democratic intellectuals.

The implications of extending the franchise to the working class in late nineteenth-century Europe were widely debated. In the infamous introduction to the 1895 edition of Marx's *The Class Struggles in France, 1848–50*, published at the very end of his life, Friedrich Engels hailed the steady growth in the votes received by the German Social Democratic Party (SPD), arguing that this signaled the inevitable electoral triumph of socialism. Engels wrote that 'the two million voters [the SPD] sends to the ballot box . . . form the most numerous, most compact mass, the decisive "shock force" of the international proletarian army. This mass already supplies over a fourth of the votes cast; and . . . [i]ts growth proceeds as spontaneously, as steadily, as irresistibly, and at the same time as tranquilly as a natural process. All government intervention has proved powerless against it.'[1] Conservative opponents of the socialist movement were also keenly interested in the political effects of the extension of the franchise. For example, in the debates in Britain in the 1860s over reform proposals to extend the franchise to all male voters—irrespective of their property endowment—one of the bitterest opponents of the pending legislation, a Conservative member of Parliament, Robert Lowe, declared:

Look at this tremendous machinery: if you only arm it with the one thing it wants—the Parliamentary vote . . . the working classes . . . are the lever. But

they must have a fulcrum before they can act . . . .Give them the vote in a
number of boroughs and it is supplied to them. . . . There appears great danger
that the machinery which at present exists for strikes and trade unions may be
used for political purposes . . . [the working classes] therefore have in their
hands the power, if they know how to use it, of becoming masters of the
situation, all the other classes being, of necessity, powerless in their hands.[2]

Although they disagreed sharply over the likely consequences of a
working-class franchise, nineteenth-century conservatives and socialists
generally expected there to be a close correspondence between class
location and voting behavior.

   Questions about the social bases of voter alignments in the United
States were raised in three different historical contexts. First, there was
the 'why no socialism?' question. The early extension of the franchise,
combined with paltry vote totals for the socialist parties, led theorists to
speculate about the existence of cross-pressures weakening the links
between social forces and vote choice in the United States. In his widely
discussed 1906 book, *Why Is There No Socialism in the United States?*
the German sociologist Werner Sombart advanced his famous thesis
that because of the economic success of American capitalism and the
prospects for upward social mobility, 'all socialist utopias came to
nothing on roast beef and apple pie.' Sombart also emphasized the
importance of the frontier myth in which land provided a unique exit
option for workers, as well as the institutional advantages of the major
parties in undermining the socialist vote among the American working
class. In his 1928 book, *Theory of the Labor Movement*, the institutional
economist Selig Perlman argued that class consciousness among the
American working class did not develop as in Europe because of the
absence of feudal legacies, the early extension of the franchise, and
successive waves of immigration, all of which were said to undermine
classwide solidarity. For Sombart and Perlman, such internal divisions
within the American working class marked it as distinct from European
labor movements and limited the development of a class-based politics
in the United States.[3]

   The second source of interest in the relationship between social
groups and voting came from a non-class source: the clear evidence
of an 'ethnoreligious' cleavage in American politics that could be traced
to early nineteenth-century controversies over the disestablishment of
official state churches. The well-established Protestant denominations,
such as the Congregationalists, were generally aligned with the Federalist Party (which supported the idea of state churches), while members
of lower status churches challenging the hegemony of the traditional

churches were more likely to line up with the Jeffersonian Democratic-Republicans. Electoral divisions between liturgical denominations supporting the Whigs and pietist denominations supporting the Jacksonian Democratic Party characterized much of the antebellum period (1828–60). After the Civil War, party competition in the North and Midwest was increasingly structured along both religious and ethnic lines as higher status and earlier immigrant groups increasingly aligned with the Republican Party and lower status religious and immigrant groups (especially Catholics from Southern and Eastern Europe) aligned with the Democrats.[4]

Gender provided the third context in which the role of social divisions in shaping electoral behavior was debated. The debate over the extension of the franchise (finally granted to women in 1920 with the adoption of the 19th Amendment to the Constitution) generated considerable speculation about the possibility that a distinct 'women's vote' would emerge. Many feminists hoped—and some male politicians feared—that newly enfranchised women voters would back candidates supporting a wide range of 'maternalist' social policies such as protective wage and hour laws, expansive health and housing policies, and other types of social provision for indigent women and families. The appearance of women voters in the electorate raised the possibility that one of the parties might succeed in providing an organizational vehicle for the promotion of such policies and come to represent 'women's interests'.[5]

Not surprisingly, the failure of a 'class' or 'gender' vote to fully materialize motivated some of the earliest voting studies. Prior to the advent of survey research, the best available voting data sources were aggregate, district-level data, which could be combined with U.S. Census data to paint a crude picture of electoral coalitions based on social group membership. Indeed, the earliest voting research (dating to the 1910s) utilized ecological techniques to infer the voting patterns of different classes or 'income groups' by linking information about the social characteristics of small areas derived from census data to electoral results in specific voting districts.[6] The inherent limitations of these data and methods forced analysts to limit their attention to social cleavages in conducting empirical voting studies.[7]

POSTWAR VOTING STUDIES

It was not until the 1930s and 1940s and the advent of the modern election survey that scholars began to go beyond ecological approaches to develop individual-level analyses of the sources of voting behavior.[8] The innovations of survey researchers eventually made it possible to systematically test the impact of different kinds of social cleavages in multivariate models incorporating other political and ideological factors influencing voter alignments.

The Columbia School and the Social Bases of Political Behavior

In the early post-World War II period, the most influential and pioneering work in what was then referred to as 'electoral sociology' was done by Paul Lazarsfeld and his colleagues at Columbia University's Bureau of Applied Social Research.[9] During the 1940 presidential election campaign, Lazarsfeld, Bernard Berelson, and Hazel Gaudet conducted a panel study of voters in Erie County, Ohio. Their goal was to investigate how voters choose a preferred candidate during presidential elections and whether (and when) they changed their minds during the campaign.[10] However, they found only a modest amount of vote switching during the campaign (54 of their 600 panel members changed their candidate preference during the campaign), a finding that implied most voters had relatively stable political preferences.[11] Where did these preferences come from? In their 1948 book, *The People's Choice*, Lazarsfeld and his colleagues developed an 'Index of Political Predisposition' to account for voter preferences. The initial index was based on three components: (1) 'socioeconomic status' (operationalized by an interviewer-coded evaluation of the respondent's living situation), (2) religion, and (3) urban or rural residence. Respondents were classified from 1 (high SES level, Protestant, and rural residence) to 6 (low SES, Catholic, urban) to predict vote intention. Of the respondents placed in category 1, 74% reported an intention to vote Republican, while 83% of the respondents in category 6 intended to vote Democratic.[12]

In their follow-up study of the 1948 election based on a panel survey of voters in Elmira, New York, Berelson, Lazarsfeld, and William McPhee identified nineteen distinct social characteristics that could be used to predict an individual's vote. As in the first study, the results suggested that voter preferences were largely stable during the election. The key finding of the second Columbia study, anticipated but not empirically assessed in *The People's Choice*, was the importance of social networks of friends, family members, and coworkers in structuring the political preferences of voters. These relatively homogenous groups were viewed as reinforcing voters' initial preferences over the course of the campaign.[13] Although the point was often forgotten in subsequent polemics directed against the early Columbia School,[14] the bulk of the actual research in both volumes was concerned with accounting for the ways in which voters made use of information received during the campaign. By focusing on the importance of reference groups and social networks, the Columbia School introduced an important set of theoretical ideas into the study of voting behavior. However, owing to the absence of suitable national survey data measuring social networks and employing a longitudinal design, it is only in recent years that these ideas have begun to be systematically deployed in the study of political behavior.[15]

Extending the Columbia School Model: Lipset

The wide-ranging work of the political sociologist Seymour Martin Lipset—onetime collaborator with Paul Lazarsfeld—provided additional grounds for focusing on the importance of social cleavages in electoral behavior.[16] In the essays gathered together in his seminal 1960 work, *Political Man*, Lipset developed what he would later characterize in the 1981 postscript to the reissue of the book as an 'apolitical Marxist' approach to explaining the social origins of democracy, fascism, communism, and the political coalitions of modern political parties in democratic polities. Lipset focused his investigations on the distinctive social bases of ideologies, social movements, and political parties that shape the larger political phenomena (fascism, communism, democracy) he sought to explain. Democratic societies are said to be those with a large and stable bloc of middle-class citizens. Fascism and communism, by contrast, are traced to the authoritarian politics of key groups or classes, including workers (Lipset's famous formulation of the thesis of 'working-class authoritarianism'), small business owners and other economically threatened middle-class segments. In his chapter on the 'democratic class struggle' in the United States, Lipset claimed that 'in every election since 1936 . . . the proportion voting Democratic increases sharply as one moves down the occupational or income ladder'.[17] *Political Man* also helped to popularize the thesis of 'cross-cutting cleavages': the idea that individual voters may be pulled in more than one direction by virtue of diverse social group memberships.[18]

Lipset's most systematic theoretical work on the problem of political cleavages appeared in the introduction to a 1967 collection of essays on European party systems, co-authored with the Norwegian political sociologist Stein Rokkan.[19] Lipset and Rokkan characterized the structure of contemporary political divisions as a reflection of a complex set of historical processes triggered by two revolutions, a *national* revolution and an *industrial* revolution. The social cleavages produced by these twin revolutions were portrayed as having led to stable patterns of group-based political conflict, expressed through modern party systems. Among the most important of these cleavages were those based on class divisions (emerging out of the industrial revolution), and religion, ethnicity, and language (products of national revolutions). Lipset and Rokkan argued, however, that not all possible social divisions necessarily lead to full-blown cleavages embodied in party systems. The precise articulation and relative magnitude of each of these cleavages vary from country to country, depending on local political history, institutional structures, and party systems.[20] But once established, cleavages were seen as providing a predictable and enduring basis for political conflict expressed through the ballot box. In their famous and oft-quoted summary statement, Lipset and Rokkan asserted that 'the party systems of the 1960s reflect, with but few significant exceptions, the cleavage structure of the 1920s'.[21]

The Michigan School and the Social-Psychological Tradition

The most influential approach of the post-World War II period in the emerging field of political behavior was that of the 'Michigan School'. In their 1960 masterpiece, *The American Voter* (*TAV*), University of Michigan influentials Angus Campbell, Philip Converse, Warren Miller, and Donald Stokes sought to develop a general theory of voting.[22] Although often seen as simply substituting a 'psychological' approach for the 'sociological' approach of the Columbia School, the Michigan approach (as reflected in *TAV*) is better viewed as seeking a more nuanced, multilevel understanding of the relationship between social cleavages, political psychology, and voting behavior.[23] *TAV* viewed the mechanisms of voting through the metaphor of a funnel. Social-structural variables, including class origins and occupation, were seen as operating at the large end of the funnel, leading to the social-psychological attributes (primarily partisan identification and political attitudes) at the narrow end of the funnel that ultimately predicted vote choice. Emphasizing a lack of ideological consistency and low levels of political sophistication on the part of most Americans, the Michigan School viewed the direct influence of social cleavages on vote choice as modest. Only a handful of citizens were sufficiently informed about the candidates and the parties to make voting decisions on the basis of their class location or other social attributes. Instead, they argued, party identification (inherited in childhood and reinforced in adulthood) was the main source of the vote.[24]

The Michigan approach quickly became dominant in voting behavior research after the publication of *TAV*. Both institutional and intellectual factors contributed to its ascendancy. The Michigan School controlled the primary means of (intellectual) production for election studies. The National Election Study (NES) has been run out of the University of Michigan's Survey Research Center since 1948 (and its sub-unit, the Center for Political Studies, since 1970). This institutional power ensured that data of interest to adherents of the Michigan approach would continue to be collected. But more important, the Michigan model provided a way of moving beyond the conceptual limitations of early cleavage-based approaches to studying voting behavior. They noted that in no case did the members of a social group give all of their votes to one party: there were always numerous defectors. The Michigan approach provided one way of accounting for these defections. Social-psychological factors mediated the relationship between social group membership and vote choice, often causing voters to switch away from voting their class or other group interest.[25] The social-psychological approach thus pointed the way to a broader multi-causal theory, while raising the possibility that the effects of group cleavages depended on causal processes that could blunt (or enhance) their political effects.

The Michigan approach has recently been given a vigorous restatement by original *TAV* author Warren Miller and second-generation Michigan scholar J. Merrill Shanks, in their 1996 work *The New American Voter*.[26] Miller and Shanks attempt to revive the funnel metaphor in an examination of contemporary voting patterns. As in the original, social group memberships are said to influence other, more proximate causes in the chain of causality leading ultimately to voters' choices of candidates. They identify six levels of causal factors (ranging from socioeconomic factors, partisan and policy preferences, economic assessments, and candidate and partisan evaluations), each of which is affected by (but does not itself influence) a prior factor. Although their analyses provide some evidence of stability in the causes of voting in the United States, they also report a significant set of changes in voter attitudes and party attachments. These are said to stem from persistent generational differences (which in turn reflect different socialization experiences).

Economic Models of Voting Behavior

The third of the major postwar approaches—increasingly influential in
other political science subfields—seeks to apply an economic model to
the study of voting behavior and political outcomes.[27] Tracing its origins to Anthony Downs's influential 1957 work, *An Economic Theory of
Democracy*, economic models of political behavior emphasize the ways
in which voters evaluate the expected utility of choices they are offered
by candidates and parties. Downs's original thesis started with the
assumption that 'citizens act rationally in politics. This axiom implies
that each citizen casts their vote for the party he believes will provide
him with more benefits than any other.'[28] In this view, 'groups' are
aggregates of self-interested actors, and group-based voting is explained
in terms of the similar calculations made by individual members.

How might we view class voting (or other cleavage-based voting)
from an economic perspective? In their 1954 review essay, 'The Psychology of Voting,' Lipset, Lazarsfeld, and their colleagues provide one
possible interpretation, arguing that

The most impressive single fact is that in virtually every economically developed country the lower-income groups vote mainly for parties of the left, while
higher-income groups vote mainly for parties of the right. Our explanation for
this is simple economic self-interest. The leftist parties represent themselves as
instruments of social change in the direction of equality; the lower-income
groups will support them in order to become economically better-off, while the
higher-income groups will oppose them in order to maintain their economic
advantages.[29]

Since left parties seeking to represent the numerically large working-
class groups do not win every election, however, it is necessary to move
beyond the simple notion of economic utility implied by crude material
calculation. Economic voting analysts have sought to answer this question by distinguishing between 'egocentric' voting (choices based on
personal financial prosperity) and 'sociotropic' voting (choices based
on perceptions of national prosperity).[30] The concept of sociotropic
evaluations enables economic theories of voting to acknowledge
symbolic sources of utility that are independent of calculations about
personal well-being.[31]

Another set of distinctions introduced by economic analysts of
voting concerns the differences between *retrospective* and *prospective*
evaluations of candidates and parties. In Downs's original formulation,
voters are portrayed as primarily making decisions based on the
expected economic consequences of the policies offered by parties

and candidates. Voters make prospective assessments on the basis of which party is likely to provide greater benefits in the future. Conversely, other analysts have emphasized the importance of retrospective evaluations, in which voters punish or reward the incumbent candidate or party based on an assessment of past economic performance.[32] Both retrospective and prospective assessments of individual voters can be made on the basis of either individual self-interest or national (sociotropic) interests.[33]

One especially interesting application of economic voting models to social group voting trends emphasizes the different impact of economic changes on the perceptions of different groups of voters. Economic strains such as inflation and unemployment may affect social groups in different ways. Inflation has relatively fewer effects on the income shares of poorer households, but more significant negative consequences for upper-income groups (whose savings may be eroded). Conversely, rising unemployment hurts the poor but has only modest consequences for the affluent.[34] Some scholars have sought to demonstrate that class differences in voting can be accounted for by the responses of voters to economic conditions. In these arguments, workers will tend to vote for parties that adopt policies to reduce unemployment, while the affluent will favor parties that promote policies to reduce inflation.[35] More generally, cleavage-based voting is equivalent to economic voting when the basis for groups' differing patterns of political choice stem from divergent preferences on matters relating to economic policies of the party in office.

Group Affect Models

A very different approach to analyzing the role of groups in shaping political behavior has emphasized the importance of subjective identification or 'group consciousness'. These group affect models differ from the Michigan School approach by refining the notion of the social group beyond simple objective group memberships (such as one's religion, class, gender, race, or region of residence). According to advocates of this approach, the underlying causal process is not to be found in the objective social attributes of voters, but rather in the degree to which people identify with, or develop positive affect toward, a particular group. If objective group membership does not also involve a subjective component, it can be expected to have much less influence over attitudes and behavior.

The earliest versions of this social psychological thesis can be traced to the idea of the 'reference group': the group(s) toward which an individual orients herself, irrespective of actual group membership.[36] In his landmark 1949 work, *The American Soldier*, Samuel Stouffer and his associates introduced the notion of 'relative deprivation' in attempting to explain why various groups of soldiers expressed satisfaction or dissatisfaction with their situations. They assumed that the sense of deprivation was always relative to that of some other group. The most systematic early theoretical statement of 'reference group theory' was developed in Robert Merton and Alice Rossi's 1950 essay on the subject, and expanded by Merton in the 1957 edition of *Social Structure and Social Theory*. Merton built upon Stouffer's original empirical work to develop a general theory of the reference group. He distinguished between a membership group and a reference group, noted that individuals may have multiple, overlapping reference groups, analyzed the different nature and social functions of positive and negative reference groups, and distinguished between individual versus group-based reference categories.[37]

The classical concept of the reference group has been revived in the more recent literature on the social psychology of group consciousness. Several different conceptions of groups have been elaborated.[38] The core distinctions are: (1) *group identification*, including self-awareness of one's membership in a group and/or a psychological attachment to the group;[39] (2) *group consciousness*, an individual's awareness of her group's relative position in society and support for collective action in support of the group's interests;[40] (3) *group affect*, the positive or negative evaluations that an individual attaches to a group;[41] and (4) *group heuristics*, the use of positive or negative evaluations of groups to make larger political attributions (e.g. towards candidates or parties).[42] Underlying these concepts is the general assumption that some degree of 'group consciousness is a necessary condition for groups to exert their power on individual voter decision-making'.[43]

Social-psychological theories have often demonstrated that group affect has large, direct effects on individual behavior.[44] In this study, however, our primary focus is on objective group memberships rather than on subjective group consciousness. Since our interest is historical—and with trying to make sense of how social, economic, and political changes since the 1960s have altered the relationship between social groups and political behavior—the fact that almost all group consciousness measures did not become available on the NES until 1972 severely limits use of such measures.[45] Moreover, given that the debates over changes in the political impact of social cleavages focus primarily on the linkages of objective group memberships and voting behavior, we do not investigate the group affect thesis here.

THE DECLINE OF CLEAVAGE-BASED ALIGNMENTS?

Since the early 1960s, there have been a number of major changes in the nature of political campaigns, party organizations, and policy conflicts in the United States. One of the most dramatic changes has been the rising importance of television advertising and the vast increase in the amount of money spent on political campaigns. In addition to the growing centrality of the mass media, there is some evidence that many of the principal organizational vehicles that have historically connected citizens to the political process have decayed. Included among these are the two major parties, unions, and civic organizations of various kinds. A number of objective political indicators suggest that these broader political changes have altered citizens' views of politics. For example, turnout has fallen, increasing numbers of voters identify themselves as independents rather than as partisans of either party, 'split-ticket' voting has steadily increased, and levels of public cynicism and distrust about the political process or specific political institutions have grown dramatically. Such facts have suggested the possibility that the U.S. and similar polities are undergoing a profound transformation in which traditional political alignments are becoming increasingly irrelevant as sources of political behavior.[46]

One central proposition of many arguments about the decline of traditional political forces is the claim that social cleavages are declining in importance. Writing in the early 1980s, for example, Lipset argued that:

The basic political division of industrial society was materialistic, a struggle over the distribution of wealth and income. But postindustrial politics is increasingly concerned with *non-economic* or *social issues*—a clean environment, a better culture, equal status for women and minorities, the quality of education, peaceful international relations, greater democratization, and a more permissive morality, particularly as affecting familial and sexual issues. These concerns have produced new bases for political cleavage which vary from those of industrial society and have given rise to a variety of 'single issue' protest movements. Since the existing political parties have found it difficult to link positions on the new issues to their traditional socioeconomic bases of support, party loyalties and even rates of voter participation have declined in a number of countries, including the United States. In effect, crosspressures deriving from differential commitments to economic and social values have reduced the saliency of loyalty to parties, tied largely to the structural sources of cleavage—class, ethnicity, religion, region. (Italics in the original)[47]

Summarizing the results of a collaborative set of national studies of changes in the role of social cleavages in shaping voter alignments, the political scientist Mark Franklin similarly concludes that

while social structure does appear to have been an important determinant of partisanship in most countries in the 1960s (explaining more than 16 percent of variance in left voting in eleven countries) by the 1980s there were only five countries left where this was still true. Even more telling, while in the 1960s there were eight countries in which more than 20 percent of the variance was explained by social structure . . . by the 1980s only Norway and Italy were left in this position. This widespread reduction in variance explained by social structure has gone far enough in some countries to vitiate the fundamental assumption upon which the expected linkage between social cleavages and party strengths is based.[48]

The recent international scholarship on the decline of social cleavages has offered a number of dramatic labels to characterize the new environment. It is said that there has been a 'declining political significance of class', a 'loosening up of the electorate', increasing numbers of 'voters beginning to choose' leading to an 'opening up' of the electorate (or a shift from 'closed class to open elections'), the emergence of a 'new politics' rooted in ideas and values rather than social cleavages, and even a 'liberation from the straightjacket of traditional cleavage politics'.[49] As group-based loyalties decline, the argument asserts, voters are becoming capable of making meaningful choices between parties and candidates rather than behaving on the basis of social group memberships (the crude 'straightjacket' of social cleavages). The Dutch political scientist Cees Van Eijk and his colleagues argue, for example, that 'the decline of cleavage politics means that electorates are free to react to completely unexpected developments (such as global warming or the liberalization of Eastern European societies) in ways that are impossible to anticipate. The most salient feature of the political landscape that emerges with the end of cleavage politics is precisely the fact that it has no clear universal features.'[50]

Explanations for the Declining Significance of Social Cleavages

Four general theories have been put forward to account for this alleged decline in the influence of social cleavages on voting behavior: (1) changes in social structure, especially increased levels of affluence, upward social mobility, and declining marital homogamy; (2) increased levels of education and 'cognitive mobilization' in the electorate, which potentially provide voters with the tools to make judgments independent of social group loyalties; (3) the rise of new value and issue conflicts; and (4) changes in the party systems and the patterning of macro-level electoral alignments. We examine each of these theses briefly.

Changing Social Structure Thesis. The most basic set of arguments advanced in support of the declining significance of social cleavages thesis starts from analyses of changes in the social structure of post-industrial capitalist democracies. Growing societal affluence after World War II in these countries is sometimes said to have reduced the pressures that gave rise to cleavage-based voting alignments in the first place. In the case of the class cleavage, for example, growing affluence may have either reduced the relative gap between the classes or provided significant parts of the working class with a greater material stake in a low-tax and low-spending government.[51] In turn, this may have enabled conservative parties to make inroads into the working classes. One other outcome of this process is that the proportion of the working population of all capitalist democracies employed in white-collar service-sector employment has risen sharply throughout the postwar period, including very rapid growth in professional and managerial occupations.[52] As significant numbers of voters have moved from working-class origins into white-collar jobs, the structural incentives for parties to pursue economically egalitarian policy agendas may be declining.

One difficulty with such arguments is that they provide a very one-sided picture of recent economic change. Existing side-by-side with the growth of white-collar employment is increasing inequality, at least in the United States. Here, wage inequality has grown since the early 1970s, reaching its highest level since the Great Depression by the mid–1990s.[53] On balance, the empirical evidence suggests that, in recent decades, the benefits of economic change and growth have not been shared by all. Moreover, changes in the occupational structure alone do not necessarily affect the association between class location and political preference. Those remaining in the working class may be just as supportive of the Democratic Party (relative to other classes), even if there are fewer of them.

Arguments about social-structural changes in the other three social cleavages (race, religion, and gender) examined in this book have also been made, although with less clear implications. Consider first the case of race. The passage of civil rights legislation and the corresponding growth of a new black middle class since the early 1960s prompted a debate about the 'declining significance of race'.[54] Although almost all of the economic gains blacks made relative to whites were achieved between the early 1960s and the late 1970s, the claim that a narrowing of the gap between black and white Americans on a number of social and political indicators over the entire period from the 1950s to the 1990s remains plausible. These developments suggest that the political divisions between whites and blacks should have narrowed or, alternatively, that growing economic divisions among African-Americans would be accompanied by growing political diversity. Conversely, however, rising political conflicts over race-targeted social programs (notably affirmative action) might provide the foundation for a deepening of electoral differences with white voters.[55]

The case of gender reveals a similar pattern of modest narrowing of some social-structural differences between men and women alongside other social trends that have produced new types of gender inequalities. Women, including those with small children, have become much more likely to hold full-time jobs in the 1990s than they were in the 1950s. Whereas only 37% of women of prime working age (25–54 years-old) were in the paid labor force in 1950, by 1994 75% of the same group were in the labor force.[56] The gender 'wage gap' between men and women has also declined somewhat, particularly among younger cohorts where women are increasingly gaining access to occupations (including opportunities in lower- and middle-level management and the professions) previously monopolized by men.[57] However, increasing gender equality in terms of labor-force participation has not necessarily altered (and indeed may have exacerbated) other kinds of inequalities. Most notable here is the uneven distribution of household labor within families, the inequalities produced by rising divorce rates, and the growing number of single-parent families headed by women.[58]

Finally, in the case of religion, a 'declining significance of denominationalism' thesis has been advanced. This thesis asserts that the boundaries between religious denominations in the United States have weakened during the period since World War II; this is attested to by rising rates of 'denominational switching' (persons raised in one religious denomination converting to one or more other religions as an adult), religious intermarriage, and declining overt tensions between denominations.[59] A narrowing of the economic and status differences between Catholics and Protestants has also been hypothesized as contributing to declining political differences between the major religious groups in American society.[60] At the same time, however, rising political controversies between conservative churches of various denominations and secular institutions raises the specter of increasing conflict over religious values and beliefs. The strong growth of conservative churches in recent decades may fuel such conflicts.[61]

Cognitive Mobilization Theories. The second broad category of arguments that have been advanced to explain the declining influence of social cleavages on voter alignments has hypothesized that an increasingly better-educated citizenry is capable of making political decisions independently of the constraints of social attributes.[62] This approach has sometimes been characterized as a process of 'cognitive mobilization', and it explicitly endorses the idea that citizens are better able to engage in what Ronald Inglehart has characterized as 'elite-directing' politics. The influence of class, religious, and other types of social group memberships is said to have become less important in this new environment.

The hypothesized rise of voters' cognitive capacities has been attributed to two factors. First, there has been a general increase in educational levels in American society, particularly as younger, better-educated cohorts displace older, less well-educated cohorts. For example, the proportion of the general population with a college degree rose from 8% in 1960 to 22% by 1996, with corresponding changes at other levels of educational attainment. Education potentially provides voters with a set of tools for evaluating the policy and issue stands of candidates and parties.[63] The second factor is the vast increase in the amount of information available to voters with the growth of new types of mass media. It is, in principle, easier for voters to obtain politically relevant information today than in the 1950s.[64]

The cognitive mobilization approach represents a double departure from the classical *TAV* model. First, it offers a direct challenge to the claim that most voters remain incapable of making informed, issue-driven distinctions between candidates and political parties. For example, Philip Converse's famous 'black/white' model of voters—in which most citizens are seen as lacking the capacity and necessary information to make political judgments—is correspondingly seen as placing unrealistic requirements on the nature of judgment and political belief systems.[65] Second, it suggests that there are two types of voters: social group voters and independent voters. The Michigan model suggested that only better informed voters were likely to vote consistently

on the basis of their social interests. Political learning approaches
reverse these claims, arguing that it is the independent voter who is
better informed (and presumably better educated).[66]

The most prominent application of the cognitive learning approach
as a general theory of political change in the United States is developed
by the political scientists Norman Nie, Sidney Verba, and John Petrocik
in *The Changing American Voter*. Nie and his colleagues attempt to
show that voter attitudes and capacities for ideological reasoning and
decision-making were transformed during the protest era of the 1960s.
They hypothesize that emerging and increasingly visible partisan conflicts over 'new' issues and increasingly clear candidate stances led to a
more sophisticated, ideologically consistent and issue-driven electorate.
Subsequent research, however, has cast doubt on these claims. Voters
do not appear more sophisticated in their use of ideological labels, and
many of Nie et al.'s key measures have been shown to have serious
flaws.[67]

Increasing Value Conflict.   A related approach to theorizing the declining significance of social group cleavages asserts that value conflicts
provide an alternative and increasingly important source of political
division. The revival of interest in values as a source of political conflict
has been a particularly notable feature of recent work in political
sociology and political culture. The 'postmaterialist' thesis of Ronald
Inglehart and his colleagues—which hypothesizes that a clash between
'materialist' and 'postmaterialist' values has displaced social group
conflicts as the principle source of political division in advanced industrial societies—is probably the most well known. Other prominent
recent statements would include the widely discussed 1995 book by
Ben Wattenberg, *Values Matter Most*, which argues that Americans'
latent traditional beliefs about family, sexuality, morality, and crime
have become increasingly salient and even partisan issues.[68] Seymour
Martin Lipset's most recent explication of his theory of 'American
exceptionalism' is based on claims about the greater centrality of
value-oriented conflicts within the U.S. in comparison to other polities.[69]

There are two distinct, yet complementary, versions of the value
conflict thesis. One emphasizes the growth of a 'second left' rooted in
concerns about 'quality of life' issues such as protecting the environment and individual freedoms. The other emphasizes the growth of a
'new right,' rooted in concerns about family and religious values, opposition to liberal abortion policies, and conservatism on other social

issues involving normative principles. Underlying these ideological positions are two latent dimensions along which citizens and parties place themselves. As a result, when left-of-center parties, including the Democratic Party, embrace liberal stands on 'social' issues, they create opportunities for Republican strategists to recruit working-class voters. As right-of-center parties, including the Republican Party, embrace the Christian Right, they open space for the Democrats to appeal to educated middle-class voters who are less supportive of religious conservatism.

The 'two lefts' thesis formalizes these claims, hypothesizing that during the same period in which close linkages between the working class and the Democratic Party have eroded, growing numbers of middle-class voters have turned to the Democrats out of concerns about noneconomic social issues. In the words of Everett Carll Ladd, this is 'liberalism turned upside down'. A large share of support for the Democratic Party is thus said to come from affluent middle-class voters. (We discuss and evaluate these theories in Chapter 3.) Similar processes—made even more dramatic as a result of electoral systems that do not hinder third parties as much as in the United States—can be found in other postindustrial capitalist democracies. Here, left parties find middle-class voters receptive to 'green' political messages. Thus, as the coalitions of left parties shift toward middle-class voters, there is an alteration of the class-specific character of their political appeals.[70]

The most general version of the 'two lefts' hypothesis has been advanced by Ronald Inglehart and his associates.[71] In a series of books and articles based on an extensive set of cross-national surveys fielded in ten or more countries in every year since 1973, Inglehart has set forth an ambitious and comprehensive attempt to understand what he calls the 'New Politics' from the standpoint of changing values among mass publics.[72] Inglehart's work has been widely influential, and it constitutes a key point of departure in the scholarly debates over the possible role of value conflict in displacing social cleavages as a factor governing voter alignments.

Inglehart hypothesizes that in recent decades political changes in the 'advanced industrial societies' can be traced to a shift in 'the values of Western publics . . . [from] an overwhelming emphasis on material well-being and physical security toward greater emphasis on the quality of life'.[73] Among the key changes he identifies are the decline of political conflict based around traditional left/right and social class cleavages, the rise of new social movements and green political parties, a growing focus on individual autonomy and lifestyle issues, and the increasing vulnerability of bureaucratic welfare states. Inglehart argues that older cohorts with predominantly materialist values are being displaced by younger generations with increasingly postmaterialist values. This value shift, along with the hypothesized increase in the cognitive skills of younger, better educated cohorts (as discussed in the previous section), is said to account for changes in political life since the 1960s. Over time, this value change has slowly transformed the political system, leading to a 'new politics' that is exemplified by social movements and new parties (as well as traditional parties responding to the new environ-ment) pursuing postmaterialist goals.

While the two lefts model emphasizes the increasing involvement of middle-class voters in left party coalitions, the 'two rights' model emphasizes the role of conservative cultural values in shifting workers and small business owners into a right-wing coalition with the tradi-tional bastions of the Republican Party. In the American context, the two rights model can trace its origins to the search for a mass base for McCarthyism in the 1950s.[74] More recent scholarship has focused on two dimensions of a new social base for the right: the appearance of a 'new' Christian Right and the re-politicization of religious values; and the rising importance of racial attitudes and the possibility of a backlash among whites against social programs targeted at African-Americans.[75] Both aspects of this new right have led analysts to explore the role of conservative cultural values in the creation of a new set of cross-cutting ideological divisions that dampen class and other social influences on American politics.

Macro-Political Forces.   Finally, some analysts have looked to the role of macro-political factors in explaining why social cleavages are declin-ing. Two broad sets of arguments have been developed. The first type of macro-level argument asserts that there has been a recent decline in the political effects of traditional social cleavages as a result of the social, economic, and cultural changes associated with the rise of a global, postindustrial economy.[76] The rapidity of economic and cultural change associated with the rise of postindustrialism has been said to undermine the prospects for class solidarity and stable class-based electoral alignments.[77] According to this argument, the ongoing pene-tration of market forces into the domain of the culture and the spread of new communications technologies that enhance the pace of cultural change lead to a decentering of the self and a proliferation of new identities distinct from traditional social categories.[78]

The second macro-level argument examines the role of political parties. In its most forceful variant, developed by the political scientists

Adam Przeworski and John Sprague in their analysis of the history of social democratic parties in Western Europe, political parties face a perpetual electoral dilemma that progressively weakens their ability to appeal to group-based interests. The dilemma is straightforward. No party, including social democratic parties seeking to represent the working class, has a single group constituency that consists of more than half the electorate. As a consequence, parties are forced to make appeals beyond their core groups. In the process, they inevitably weaken group-specific patterns of support and lose votes among their traditional base.[79]

In the long-dominant two-party system in the United States, the vote trade-off appears at first glance much more limited than in the multiparty systems of Western Europe studied by Przeworski and Sprague. Because voters have no realistic alternatives to the two main parties, opportunities for defection are correspondingly much more limited. However, high rates of nonvoting serves as a de facto exit option for voter dissatisfaction in the American political system. Thus, while rates of class voting are typically lower in the United States than in other postindustrial capitalist democracies, rates of class *non*voting are much higher. Falling turnout compels the major parties to further concentrate their appeals on those citizens who are likely to vote. In this way, nonvoting, especially among poor and working-class voters, may encourage the Democratic Party in particular to make appeals to constituencies whose class character is more diffuse.[80]

Many observers have also speculated that another major source of party-driven dealignment is the political shift of the Democratic Party from a position endorsing unions, modest redistribution, and the welfare state to, by the 1990s, a position that downplays unions, promotes a balanced budget and reduced government expenditures, and, under the leadership of Bill Clinton, brought 'welfare as we know it' to an end.[81] The old 'Tweedledum and Tweedledee' image of the parties has never seemed more apt than at the present to many contemporary intellectuals, especially those on the left. These analysts typically explain this shift as reflecting the increasing importance of money in politics and the need for aspiring politicians to secure extraordinary sums to win office and to ensure re-election. The well-developed political action committee (PAC) system has not, of course, simply turned elected officials into naked servants of their campaign contributors. But it has encouraged certain types of policy initiatives and ideological stances while discouraging others. The largess available from corporate PAC sources in Congress and many state legislatures has been important in transforming both parties, but especially the Democratic Party,

into more corporate-oriented parties increasingly incapable of mobilizing voters from below.[82]

If voters indeed perceive the two parties as becoming virtually indistinguishable on major policy issues, this scenario would have profound
consequences for analyzing electoral behavior. Not only would the
impact of social cleavages on political behavior likely shrink precipi-
tously, *any* political cleavage requiring that voters perceive policy differences would eventually disappear. Have voters' overall perceptions of
party differences in fact undergone such a decline? We examine the
evidence for this proposition in Figure 1.1. The data presented in this
figure are from the entire National Election Studies series. They indicate
the proportion of voting-age adults who answer 'yes' when asked 'Do
you think there are important differences in what the Republicans and
Democrats stand for?'[83]

These data provide little support for claims about a decline in public
perceptions of party-based differences. Indeed, despite a short-term
drop in perceptions of party differences between 1968 and 1976, the
overall trend is toward an increase in such perceptions. Moreover, this
increase has occurred during the past two decades, the time during
which the economic and socially conservative wings of the Republican
Party gained national prominence during and after the election of
Ronald Reagan.[84]

Why have voters not perceived changes in the parties in the same way
as many intellectuals and political analysts? There are two important
reasons. First, while on some important issues the parties have grown
more similar, on other issues they have in fact grown further apart.
Consider for example the well-known case of race.[85] In the 1950s and
1960s, many liberal Republicans supported civil rights legislation
opposed by Southern Democrats. Today, there are much stronger
inter-party conflicts over racial questions than intra-party conflicts.
The welfare state provides another instructive example. Although the
two parties did agree on the reform of the welfare program in 1996,
across a range of other issues (Medicare, Social Security, national
health insurance), the parties have grown further apart. No longer
are there many Republicans prepared to champion these programs.
Second, the disappearance of 'liberal' Republicanism and the decline
of the Southern Democrats are also crucial. For many decades, party
discipline on most issues was low because Northern Democrats and
liberal Republicans, on the one hand, and Southern Democrats and
conservative Republicans, on the other, were sometimes more likely to
find common ground. Increasingly, those cross-party alliances have

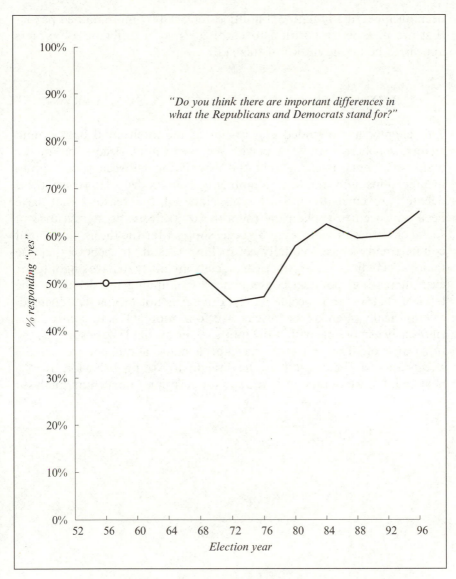

"Do you think there are important differences in
what the Republicans and Democrats stand for?"

FIG 1.1. Perceptions of differences between the Democratic and
Republican Parties among voting-age respondents, 1952–96
Note: Question not asked in the 1956 survey; the value for
1956 is an interpolation (see open circle).

been disappearing in national politics, replaced by more unified parties that are in a better position to enforce partisan differences.[86] Voters appear to be taking notice of this shift.

THE STATE OF THE DEBATE: A SUMMARY

This chapter has provided a snapshot of the intellectual background against which this study proceeds. We have summarized some of the main arguments asserting that the association between social group memberships and political alignments has eroded. However, these debates are currently inconclusive. None of the reasons that have been advanced to explain the (hypothesized) declining significance of social cleavages provide unambiguous support for the thesis. Important countertrends suggest equally compelling reasons to believe that the major social divisions in American society are likely to have ongoing (or even increasing) political consequences. Continuing the debate at the level of rhetoric and speculative hypotheses is not productive. Instead, as empirically oriented social scientists, our approach is to confront, as rigorously as possible within the limits of the available data sources, the full range of arguments that have been made about changes in the effects of social cleavages as they relate to voting behavior. In the next chapter, we outline our strategy for carrying out such an analysis.

2

Social Cleavages and American Politics

This chapter introduces the concepts and strategies of inquiry we employ in the rest of this study. It considers a range of methodological and statistical issues involved in our study of social cleavages. We also present the theoretical interpretations that we use as a guide to analyzing patterns of change over time.

THE CLEAVAGE CONCEPT

The concept of a 'cleavage' has been used by scholars to identify enduring conflicts within the electorate. Despite the concept's long intellectual pedigree, there has been little agreement in the social science literature as to precisely what type of division merits the label of a cleavage. Given its centrality in this study, we clarify our use of the concept and the differences between cleavages and other types of social divisions or ideological conflicts.

Social Cleavages and Political Divisions

The cleavage concept can be traced to the intersection of Marxist and Weberian social theory. Marx's class-centered model of history and social change, and Weber's distinction between classes, status groups, and organizations in capitalist societies locate the primary source of political division in social structures. Weber built upon the Marxian legacy by expanding the definition of social cleavage to encompass the idea of the status group (*stand*) and, more importantly, by calling attention to the role of organizational and institutional factors (such as parties and states) in shaping the emergence and actual impact of cleavages.[1]

As noted in the previous chapter, Seymour Martin Lipset and Stein Rokkan use the cleavage concept in their landmark 1967 theoretical statement to describe the political conflicts that emerged out of the transformations of social structure during the industrial and national revolutions of the eighteenth–twentieth centuries. They viewed cleavages as a product of the social-structural changes produced by these twin revolutions. However, they argue that these divisions only take on political significance when some social groups develop clear perceptions of the differences and conflicts between themselves and other social groups, and these differences come to be institutionalized in the political system. By defining cleavages in this way, Lipset and Rokkan (and other authors who follow in their footsteps) distinguish cleavages rooted in social-structural divisions from other types of political conflicts or divisions.[2]

Other theorists have used the cleavage concept more broadly to refer to any type of enduring political conflict. Robert Dahl, for example, employs the concept of 'political cleavage' to refer to persistent and frequently intense issue conflicts that come to define a political system. Some use the cleavage concept broadly but distinguish social-structural cleavages from ideological or value-based cleavages. Erik Allardt and Pertti Pesonen distinguish between what they refer to as 'structural' (class) and 'nonstructural' (ideological) cleavages. Douglas Rae and Michael Taylor distinguish between 'ascriptive' or 'trait' cleavages (essentially social structural in our sense), 'attitudinal' cleavages, and 'behavioral' cleavages (such as voting).[3] Although most of these authors pay some attention to differences among cleavages, the inclusive definitions tend to become somewhat vague inasmuch as they are used to describe virtually the entire universe of political divisions found in a particular society.

Partly as a result of this problem, recent scholarship has tended to return to the original meaning of the concept, defining cleavages as patterns of political alignment arising out of social-structural divisions. For example, the introduction to a recent cross-national study of changes in the impact of social cleavages on voting argues that

The term 'cleavage' simply refers to issues, policy differences or political identifications related to certain long-standing conflicts in a particular society. Certain authors tend to emphasize the attitudinal or ideological content of issues that are involved and are less concerned with their relation to social groups. Most students of political sociology and electoral behavior, however, are strongly concerned with the other aspect. In their thinking, political cleavages are basically seen as reflecting broadly based and long-standing social and economic divisions within society, and the cleavage structure is thought of in terms of social groups and of the loyalties of members to their social groups. In this book we shall be using the term in this latter meaning, prefering to use the words 'issues,' 'policy differences,' or 'ideological concerns' when we want to talk about conflicts of the other sort.[4]

Such a definition usefully restricts the concept of cleavage by differentiating it from other types of political conflicts.

Limiting cleavages to conflicts that grow out of social divisions addresses some of the ambiguities of the concept. Nevertheless, several questions remain with respect to *which* divisions, *what* form they take, and *how* the wide variability that is observed in comparative studies might be explained. Alan Zuckerman has suggested that it is possible to distinguish between approaches to social cleavages that view 'social divisions [as] a necessary and a sufficient condition for the emergence of political cleavages', and those which view 'social divisions as a necessary but not a sufficient condition for the emergence of political cleavages'.[5] In contrast to the first approach, this second approach calls attention to the institutional and organizational factors that mediate the effects of social cleavages. We believe that the second approach is an appropriate starting point for theorizing the variability and significance of social cleavages in the realm of politics.

Social Cleavages: A Theoretical Model

In developing our theoretical interpretation, we build from Stefano Bartolini and Peter Mair's multilevel approach to understanding electoral change in European democracies since the late nineteenth century.[6] The analytical problem, as they put it, is that 'the concept of cleavage lies in its intermediate location between the two main approaches of political sociology: that of social stratification and its impact on institutions and political behavior, on the one hand, and that of political institutions and their impact on social structure and change, on the other. . . . The concept of cleavage is often either reduced "down" to that of "social cleavage" or "up" to that of "political cleavage."' Their proposed solution to this dilemma is to suggest that any social cleavage capable of shaping political behavior will simultaneously exist on three different levels. First, it has an 'empirical' component rooted in social structure. Second, it has a 'normative' component, in that the social groups making up a cleavage field adopt conflicting forms of consciousness. Third, it has a macro-institutional component, expressed through 'individual interactions, institutions, and organizations, such as political parties, which develop as part of the cleavage'.[7]

According to Bartolini and Mair's definition, types of political divisions that exist at only one of these three levels should not be viewed as full-fledged social cleavages. Social-structural divisions based on class inequalities, for example, may or may not become important political factors in different societies.[8] It is only when class divisions simultaneously develop a normative component and are institutionalized through the party system that they can properly be characterized as a 'cleavage'. In the absence of one or more components, political divisions will tend to either remain latent (failing to affect voters) or short-lived (failing to lead to enduring divisions). For instance, social-structural inequalities and normative grievances shared by a group can be expected to have little impact on political behavior and voter alignments if there is no opportunity to express such components within a polity (if, e.g., political parties do not differentiate themselves on the issue in question).[9] By contrast, the absence of social-structural components limits the durability of a purely political division. Political-institutional conflicts coupled with group conflict tend to be short-lived if there are no deep-seated socioeconomic inequalities associated with the conflict between groups. We consider each level of cleavage in greater detail below.

Social Structure. 'Social' cleavages are grounded in the social structure of a given society. Because social structures change slowly, social cleavages tend to endure once they are established. Social-structural divisions give rise to groups of people with shared interests or statuses. Social-structural changes can either take the form of changes in the relative size of particular groups within a cleavage or changes in the internal composition of the group, irrespective of its relative size. If, for example, the proportion of working-class voters declines, the overall impact of the class cleavage on party coalitions may decline even if the voting behavior of those who remain in the working class is unchanged. Conversely, the working class may change internally in ways that alter its political alignment. The social-structural divisions that have the strongest political impact across a number of different national contexts are religion, class, race and ethnicity, and language. Gender is also of increasing importance, albeit with wide variation across different national contexts.

Group Identification and Conflict. The second level can be characterized as the cleavage 'field', in which two or more distinct groups exist whose members recognize themselves as in conflict. Group identification is a necessary condition for social-structural divisions to become social cleavages; without some recognition of group boundaries, social or economic inequalities are unlikely to emerge in the organizational and institutional settings in which political conflicts occur.

Macro-Political Conflict. The third condition for the emergence of a social cleavage is that political parties or social movements explicitly draw upon structurally-based group conflicts as a way of mobilizing some segment of the population for political action. The two-party system in the United States tends to discourage direct group-based appeals. Rather than seeking to capture and consolidate a distinct segment of the electorate and then enter into multi-party parliamentary bargaining (the typical pattern in European polities), a two-party system encourages both parties to seek an electoral majority on the basis of broad appeals to all groups. Yet even in a two-party system, parties frequently make explicit appeals to social groups, even if such appeals are often filtered through vaguely worded policy proposals or symbolic appearances before organizations representing specific groups.

SOCIAL CLEAVAGES AND AMERICAN SOCIETY

Using the theoretical interpretation outlined above, we can identify four major social cleavages in American politics in the postwar period: race, religion, class, and gender. Table 2.1 summarizes the four cleavages in terms of social structure, group identification/conflict, and organizational and institutional factors.

Race Cleavage

Political divisions among voters arising out of race can be traced back to the Civil War and Reconstruction. As a result of the legacies of slavery, racial segregation, and the persistence of white racism (and the economic and social inequalities it has fostered), African-Americans

TABLE 2.1. *The level of development of major social cleavages in postwar United States*

Level of development (high/intemediate/low) in terms of	Race	Religion	Class	Gender
Organizations/institutions	High	High	Low	Emerging
Group identity/conflict	High	Intermediate	Intermediate	Intermediate
Social structure	High	Declining	High	Intermediate

developed a powerful sense of group identity, while many whites have conversely developed a sense of identity in opposition to blacks and other minorities. The struggles around racial issues since the Civil War created far-reaching normative conflicts between black and white Americans, and also among white Americans. In electoral politics, enfranchised black voters developed an alignment with the Republican Party that lasted from Reconstruction until the New Deal, while Southern white voters were overwhelmingly aligned with the Democratic Party. The New Deal altered this historic pattern, as Northern black voters aligned with the Democratic Party (although most Southern blacks remained disfranchisement until the 1960s). In the 1940s, the Democratic Party took some tentative steps toward an embrace of its new black constituency, although the reluctance of many Democratic leaders to alienate Southern white voters (and thus risk the 'Solid South') placed limits on this embrace. When the party adopted its first significant civil rights plank in 1948, it led to a revolt by Southern conservatives and the third party presidential bid of Strom Thurmond.

By the 1950s, black voters had developed a clear allegiance to the Democratic Party, although significant numbers of black voters still voted for Eisenhower and, in 1960, Richard Nixon. The far-reaching consequences of the Civil Rights movement, the passage of the Civil Rights Act and the Voting Rights Act, and the explicit anti-integration appeals of the 1964 Barry Goldwater campaign were decisive for sharpening the political alignment of black voters with the Democratic Party. First, these developments eroded the last vestiges of the 'party of Lincoln' legacy of the Republican Party among black voters. Second, in presidential politics (and eventually in congressional and subnational politics as well) they brought about the end of the Solid South. This had the consequence of greatly diminishing the influence of Southern racial conservatives within the Democratic Party and insuring that the Democratic platform would never again fail to endorse a civil rights agenda.

The black/white racial division has been especially powerful in American politics by virtue of its simultaneous strength at all three cleavage levels. It is grounded in social-structural differences between white and black Americans and reinforced at the normative level by ideological and policy conflicts over civil rights and affirmative action policies. The parties have, since 1964, increasingly adopted policy agendas with significant racial content, diverging on civil rights issues, affirmative action, and other social policy issues. As a result, the racial cleavage exemplifies the most fully developed social cleavage in U.S. politics.

Religious Cleavage

Of the four cleavages we examine, the religious cleavage is the least well-developed at the level of social structure. Unlike race, gender, and often class, one can change one's religious identity. Yet, through most of American history, adherents of different denominations have been born into their religious faith, and have maintained at least a nominal allegiance to it throughout their lives. Further, religious groups have differed, historically, in terms of social status and economic prestige. Members of the elite mainline Protestant denominations, especially Episcopalians, Presbyterians, and Congregationalists (United Church of Christ), have long been overrepresented within the American political elite as well as in business, the military, and academe. The massive immigration of Catholics and (to a lesser extent) Jews from Southern and Eastern Europe in the late nineteenth and early twentieth century produced group-based conflicts between the affluent, established Protestant denominations and the challenging newcomers. These conflicts, and the legacies they created, lasted well beyond World War II. There is more recent evidence, however, that these social-structural divisions among religious groups are eroding. For example, rates of denominational switching have risen, there is much more intermarriage among religious groups, and members of subordinate religious groups face less prejudice when seeking entry to elite educational institutions and occupations.

Religious group differences have historically been particularly well-established at the level of normative conflict. Hostility from the dominant Protestant culture to both Roman Catholics and Jews provided one enduring source of normative conflict. Among the major Protestant denominations, further divisions along doctrinal lines have been significant. 'Fundamentalist' Protestant denominations have periodically struggled to reorient American society and culture away from the more secular tendencies of the mainline Protestant groups. More recently, some analysts have argued that the normative religious cleavage has increasingly shifted toward a religious versus secular divide, although this is a claim that remains controversial.

At the organizational level, the religious cleavage in American politics can be traced back to the founding of the Republic, especially in the conflicts over the maintenance of state churches. In the late nineteenth century, the major parties made explicit appeals to different ethno-religious groups. In the 1960 (Kennedy/Nixon) presidential contest, religious differences (raised by Kennedy's Catholicism) were made especially significant. More recently, explicit religious appeals have reappeared in American politics. In the 1992 presidential campaign, for example, Republican convention delegates applauded former candidate Pat Buchanan's calls for a 'religious war' against the allegedly irreligious Democrat Bill Clinton and his party. While conflicts over religious themes have continued throughout the Clinton presidency, issues relating to religious conflicts—the teaching of evolution versus creation, a proposed flag-burning amendment, and 'family values'— have also been prominent in many subnational elections during this period.

Class Cleavage

Like any capitalist society, a basic set of class differences can readily be observed in the United States. Although there are (as we note in the next chapter) a variety of ways to characterize the class structure, there can be no doubt about its significance at the level of social structure. In terms of collective action and conflict, class divisions are also readily apparent. Although unionization levels are low, American workers have at times been as militant on the shopfloor as any working class in the developed capitalist world. Further, there are two sides to the class struggle, and in the U.S. employers have generally been better organized and more capable of taking collective action against workers and labor organizations than employers anywhere else in the advanced capitalist world. Growing income inequality is just one manifestation of the persistence of the class divide at the level of social structure in the United States.

Differences in attitudes and perceptions based on class divisions have never been as sharp in the United States as in other capitalist democracies. Normative conflicts between classes are thus generally much weaker than in other countries. It is at the organizational level that the class cleavage in American politics has been weakest. Comparatively low levels of unionization in the United States and the unique absence of a significant labor or social democratic party has meant that the class cleavage was not as central to the founding and development of the modern American party system as in other capitalist democracies. To be sure, the Democratic Party has historically drawn disproportionate support from workers and farmers, while the Republicans have similar support from business owners and the middle classes. But these divisions have rarely been large enough to define the main contours of the party system.

Gender Cleavage

The nature of gender inequalities in social, economic, and political life are also well understood. Women are underrepresented in most of the high-prestige occupations (and overrepresented in low-prestige occupations), they earn lower wages (even in comparison with men in the same occupation), they are less likely to hold political office, and inside families they are more likely to handle a disproportionate share of the household chores (the 'second shift'). The appearance of a mass women's movement since the late 1960s has politicized these inequalities and made them the object of both normative conflict and institutional struggles over public policy.

Over the past three decades, the gender cleavage has become increasingly important for national party organizations. Since the conflicts over the Equal Rights Amendment in the 1970s, both the Democratic and Republican Parties have been increasingly forced to take sides on controversial issues relating to gender equality and family policy. While both parties have nominally endorsed the general principle of equal opportunity for working women, the Republican Party has also simultaneously defended traditional gender roles. Further, on other issues related to gender, such as abortion/reproductive rights, parental leave, and sexual harassment in the workplace, there is clear evidence of divergence between the parties (with the Democrats more willing to embrace pro-feminist positions).

Other Potential Social Cleavages

Some readers will no doubt be surprised that region (primarily the South/non-South divide) is not one of the central social cleavages we consider. Regional political divisions are sometimes listed alongside race, religion, and class as major social cleavages in American politics.[10] Other analysts might also propose that political divisions arising out of urban/suburban or metropolitan/nonmetropolitan residence be considered as well.[11]

Regional divisions have been of crucial historical importance for American political history, although regional identity and conflict appear to be declining since World War II. But while the Southern political economy may have been clearly distinct from the rest of the country, at least through the 1960s, there are practical reasons for not treating region as a central social cleavage in the investigations which follow. At the level of presidential politics, the regional divide began to erode far earlier than in congressional elections and state-level politics. Eisenhower did not perform as well in the South as he did in other parts of the country, but in both 1952 and 1956, he carried a number of Southern states. In 1956, Eisenhower received only 5% less of the popular vote in the South than in the nation as a whole. In 1960, Richard Nixon did virtually as well in the South as in the rest of the country, and by 1964, Barry Goldwater did significantly better in the South than in the rest of the country. Since 1964 Republican presidential candidates have generally done as well or better in the South (with the exception of the two Jimmy Carter campaigns of 1976 and 1980). In any analysis of presidential elections, treating 'region' as a core social cleavage runs the risk of misrepresenting what has clearly remained an important factor in subnational politics.

Use of the cleavage concept to understand urban versus suburban and/or metropolitan versus nonmetropolitan residence-based divisions requires a number of problematic assumptions. In the case of the urban/suburban divide, it is fairly clear that many key social-structural and ideological divisions of interest are antecedent to place of residence in the causal chain linking residential divisions to voting behavior. More affluent citizens are often attracted to suburban enclaves as a way of exiting from urban areas, just as many whites of all classes seek to escape cities with large minority populations. Thus, it is not suburban residence per se that produces an urban/suburban cleavage, but other social factors embedded in the class and race cleavages that cause some citizens to choose to live in suburbs the first place.

A better case can be made for metropolitan versus nonmetropolitan residence as a social cleavage, especially in that a major component of domestic policy debates (over agricultural subsidies and programs) are explicitly directed at one recognizable social group (farmers) in rural areas. But the interests of farm owners (and farm laborers) are partially subsumed by our conceptualization of the class cleavage (see Chapter 3). Further, since the size of the farming population has become very small in the period covered by this study, it is hardly necessary to establish it as a separate social cleavage.

Subjective Social Group Memberships

We examine 'objective' group memberships in this study. As we discussed in the previous chapter, there has been a considerable literature
arguing that objective group membership alone is inadequate to define
group membership. However, our focus here is on objective group
memberships, for both substantive and practical reasons. While
objective group membership provides a more conservative estimate
of the full impact of group membership on political behavior, limiting group members to those who identify with (or exhibit affect
toward) the group may exaggerate that impact. Our focus is also
appropriate in light of the null hypothesis in contemporary scholarly
debates over social cleavages, namely, that the political impact of
such cleavages has declined over time. Instead of limiting group
membership to group identifiers, our strategy will be to use group
identification as a control variable in multivariate models that seek to
account for the trends we observe over time. This strategy enables us
to determine whether the relationship between objective and subjective membership has changed over time, and also whether the real
causal factor behind group membership lies in subjective identification.[12] Our solution to this trade-off is a reasonable one, especially in
view of our findings about the surprisingly large impact of objective
group memberships and the direct effects of such memberships on
political behavior.

THE CONCEPTS OF REALIGNMENT AND
DEALIGNMENT REVISITED

Scholarly debates over social cleavages and political change in the
United States have often centered on questions of political realignment.
Since the appearance of V. O. Key's pair of path-breaking articles
introducing the concept in the late 1950s, the realignment controversy
has been the subject of continual debate in political behavior research.[13]
Although it has many critics, we argue that realignment concepts can,
with some reformulation, provide a useful vocabulary for analyzing
political change among social groups.

In this study, we distinguish between two different conceptions of
'realignment': (1) electorate-wide realignments in the overall level of
support given to one of the two major parties; and (2) realignments
pertaining to specific groups of voters making up the electoral coalitions

of the parties. Realignment processes are also distinct from 'de-alignment'. Whereas realignment refers to the processes by which voters move from support for one party to the other, dealignment refers to the processes by which voters move away from consistent support for any party.[14] As with realignments, dealignments can also occur at the level of specific groups. In this study, we ask a series of questions about the patterns of group-specific 'realignment' and 'dealignment' in American politics. More specifically, we are interested in whether particular races, classes, genders, or religious groups have realigned or dealigned.

In the realignment literature, a distinction has often been made (going all the way back to Key) between 'critical' realignments (which happen over a single election cycle) and 'secular' realignments (which take place over a series of elections). In this study, we find evidence of both group-specific critical and secular realignments. An example of the former is the case of the self-employed, who moved decisively into the Republican camp relative to other voters beginning in a single (critical) 1980 election. Examples of secular realignment can be found in the case of professionals and women, both of whom become more Democratic relative to other classes and men respectively only over a long series of elections.

Finally, we utilize the concept of electoral 'shifts' to characterize significant increases or decreases in a group's support for the party it consistently backs. Among the most important examples of shifts are those of unskilled workers and blacks. The strengthening of support among black voters for the Democratic Party (relative to whites) begins in 1964. This shift can be described as 'critical' inasmuch as it can be traced to a single election, but it is not a realignment since blacks were already in the Democratic camp before 1964. Unskilled workers similarly experienced a critical shift during the 1980 election, when their high levels of support for the Democratic Party eroded (and have not recovered since that time).

All of these group-specific cases of political change may occur independently of changes in the levels of support for the major parties among the entire electorate. Several groups have shifted toward the Democrats (blacks, women, professionals, liberal Protestants), yet for most of the period under investigation Republicans have dominated the presidential elections. How can this be the case? The answer lies in our theoretical focus on the alignment of individual groups within a given cleavage relative to the other groups in the field. As a result, our approach distinguishes changes in group alignments from changes affecting all voters. For instance, while women are becoming more

Democratic than men since 1960, in many of these elections women have none the less given a majority of their votes to the Republican candidate. The gender gap has increased because men have moved even faster toward the Republican Party.

ANALYTICAL STRATEGIES

To carry out the research agenda outlined above, we have made a series of decisions about methodological issues pertaining to our choice of presidential elections as the primary dependent variable, the types of statistical models we employ, and the sources of data and the measurement limitations they impose. All of these decisions are consequential, not mere 'backstage' operations, and hence necessitate some clarification and justification at the outset of the study.

Why Presidential Elections?

We focus our attention in this book on presidential elections, and more specifically on the general election, which is usually a two-party contest. Critics might reasonably point to the restricted choices available to voters in general elections and the importance of candidate-specific factors in a presidential race, which inevitably distorts voters' decision-making. Taken in combination, such considerations might be expected to significantly reduce the effects of social group membership on voting behavior. Some analysts might prefer us to concentrate on party identification, congressional elections, or public opinion to analyze the political consequences of social cleavages for national politics.

We believe firmly, however, that an examination of elections—and specifically presidential elections—is preferable to the alternatives given the questions we investigate in this study. First, elections are ultimately decided by votes rather than party identification. Party identification (and the Democratic advantage in partisanship) has changed only very slowly since the 1960s, but the Republicans won five out of the six presidential elections from 1968 to 1988 and gained control of Congress in 1994. They did so because they won elections. By focusing on voting, we thus seek to capture the most fundamental component of political change among major social groups. Second, electoral change tends to occur in voting behavior first. Party identification tends to change much more slowly and tends to follow, not precede, changes in presidential voting.[15]

We limit our investigation in this book to presidential elections (as opposed to congressional or state and local elections) largely for practical reasons. The complexities involved in analyzing presidential elections in the manner we do in this book would make the task of incorporating analyses of congressional elections (not to mention state or local elections) overwhelming for a single volume. The general approach we develop in this book could, however, readily be extended to a study of subnational elections. A comparison of the differences vis-à-vis presidential voting might well prove revealing.

Statistical Models

Our strategy of analysis builds directly from the questions we ask. We are interested in political change over a relatively long time frame (approximately forty years). We thus need to assess the evidence for significant patterns of change, especially trends, during the time period under investigation. To test for the existence of trends, we use models that enable us to measure change in the *relative* alignments of each of the major groups making up our four main cleavages. By relative—or alternatively, *group-specific*—change, we refer to a situation in which one group changes faster (or slower) than the other group(s) defining a particular cleavage.

In practice, this means that we must be able to distinguish election-specific forces that affect all groups in a cleavage from those factors affecting only some groups. In any election, candidate-specific (or party-specific) factors will affect all voters negatively or positively, thereby influencing the outcome of the contest. For example, in 1964, Republican Barry Goldwater lost votes among almost all social groups in comparison to Richard Nixon's campaign in 1960. Similarly, in 1972, George McGovern was deeply unpopular among all key groups in comparison with previous Democratic presidential candidates, as was Walter Mondale in 1984. In such cases, groups that had previously provided higher levels of support for their party's presidential candidates reduced their support. But before we can conclude that any particular group is altering its pattern of support for one of the two major parties, we have to examine that group in relation to all other groups making up that cleavage. For instance, only if working-class voters have become less supportive of Democratic candidates *relative* to other classes can we safely conclude that class-based political change, perhaps even realignment, has taken place.

The nature of these questions imposes two key requirements on the measurement of cleavages. First, it is necessary for our measures to distinguish between changes that affect all categories of a cleavage variable equally (which we term 'absolute' change) and changes that have differential effects on certain categories of a cleavage variable (which we term 'relative' change). Using the class cleavage as an example, when support for Democratic candidates among all classes declines at the *same* rate, the absolute level of support for Democrats declines but the *relative* differences in Democratic support among classes remain stable. If the Democratic candidate receives 50% of the total vote in election A and 40% of the total vote in election B, and 60% of the vote of skilled workers in election A and 50% of their vote in election B, the relative alignment of skilled workers is unchanged in the two elections, in spite of the significant (10%) fall off in gross Democratic support among that group. Measures failing to distinguish between absolute and relative types of change in voting behavior can lead to serious biases; they provide no way of differentiating shifts in party or candidate popularity that reflect preferences among all classes from shifts that stem disproportionately from losses or gains among particular social groups.

The second assumption of our approach is that suitable measures should be compatible with multivariate analyses incorporating relevant control variables. Individuals are always members of multiple groups, some of which may be cross-cutting (e.g. Black managers) or reinforcing (white conservative Protestants). In the former case, the effects of either race or class will tend to be muted by the other, while in the latter case the effects of one attribute will combine with the other, disposing the voter to support the same party.[16] Surprisingly, as we point out in several of the substantive chapters, many scholarly studies of the class, gender, and religious cleavages in American politics (as well as in cross-national, comparative analyses) have often employed bivariate models that cannot incorporate additional variables. Such models are not only unrealistic but provide no basis for answering inherently multivariate questions about the simultaneous impact of multiple social cleavages on political alignments. Moreover, in the current study, we want to know not only whether the relationship between vote choice and a given social cleavage has changed over time but also whether these changes are related to changes in other sources of voter alignments. We seek, in other words, to determine whether one single set of changes underlies trends in specific social cleavages.

Guided by the two preceding assumptions, our measurement approach allows us to detect a series of important voting trends relating to specific groups within each of the four cleavage fields. However, once we have established these trends (or nontrends), we also seek to explain their origins. For these analyses, we use a regression decomposition strategy that enables us to make causal inferences. Our decomposition substitutes year-specific sample means for the causal factors measured by our statistical model. We compare the impact of each of these factors using over-time differences in these means between a given pair of elections; we then develop estimates of the contribution of each source of political change to the total change in voter alignment experienced by a particular social group. For instance, in our causal analysis of the sources of professionals' dramatic change in alignment (presented in Chapter 3), a decomposition allows us to examine the respective roles of shifts in demographic composition, changing attitudes toward civil rights-related issues, and changes in class-related factors (such as class identification and egocentric, economic evaluations). It is also worth noting that, because our decompositions use the coefficients from our multivariate models, they again take into account causal factors that affect all social groups equally (these are measured by the residual, main effects of each election in the analysis).

Data and Measures

Because we are interested in historical trends, this study relies on the biennial survey of the American electorate conducted by the Survey Research Center and its Center for Political Studies at the University of Michigan. This survey, the National Election Study (NES), is an extraordinary record of American society and politics, stretching back over nearly four decades. These data are unique in containing a reasonably full battery of questions about each respondents' sociodemographic characteristics, measures of attitudes on policy issues and political conflicts, and a precise battery of questions about voting, turnout, and party identification.[17] Fielded in two parts (the first wave is carried out right before a national election while the second wave is fielded immediately after the election), the NES contains the most reliable data on the main dependent variable of interest to us in this study, vote choice. As a survey instrument that has been widely used by political scientists and political sociologists, it has made possible an impressive range of scholarly investigations over the years.[18]

Despite the advantages of the NES as a source of historical data, however, there are also certain limitations that should be noted at the outset of this study. Perhaps most importantly, the NES does not contain a consistent set of questions measuring attitudes on policy issues until 1972. Because of the importance of using identically worded survey items for over-time analysis, our explanatory analysis using these items focuses on the post-1972 period. Since most of the key group-specific trends have occurred (or reach maturation) since 1972, the lack of suitable data prior to that time is not a decisive limitation for the study.

The NES series also has some limitations in the level of detail relating to race, religion, and class. In the case of the racial cleavage, we limit our analysis to white and black voters. Because of rapid growth of Hispanics and Asians, by the mid-1990s they made up more than 13% of the population of the United States (although a smaller proportion of the electorate). However, due to the relatively small size of the NES ($N < 2,500$ in most elections), there were not enough Latino or Asian voters in the sample to permit meaningful analyses until very recently.[19]

In the case of the religious cleavage, the NES did not distinguish among Protestants until 1960 and did not distinguish between Northern and Southern Baptists until 1972. Although some authors have studied the religious cleavage using a single, undifferentiated Protestant category, we follow most analysts in arguing that a more fine-grained distinction among Protestants is necessary given the sharp doctrinal differences among the major Protestant denominations. Because of these limitations in the NES series, many of our analyses of the religious cleavage start in 1960. We are, however, able to develop an informative comparison between Catholics and Protestants (taken as a whole) from 1952 on. This comparison helps us to better understand the unusual effect of the candidacy of Catholic John Kennedy in the 1960 presidential election.

There are also limitations of the NES data for measuring the major class categories used in this study. In principle, we would prefer to operationalize class using detailed information about each respondent's employment situation, rather than simple occupational titles. However, the lack of information about respondents' employment situations simply makes it impossible to operationalize a class schema of the type developed, for example, by the sociologist Erik Olin Wright.[20] Instead, we have relied on occupational titles to assign respondents to classes. We have carefully recoded the occupational variables for each year to maximize over-time comparability. The lack of information about other aspects of the employment relationship (as well as periodic changes in the list of occupational titles) obviously leads to measurement error.

However, because most of this error is random in nature, it will have no effect on our analysis of changes in the class cleavage, unless it is also correlated with time.[21]

In the next seven chapters, we apply the concepts and strategies outlined in this chapter to explore various aspects of the relationship between social divisions in American society and the construction of party coalitions in presidential elections. We begin with an analysis of the evolution of the class cleavage.

3

Class

Does class still matter? As we noted in Chapter 1, the 'class' question has long been central to sociological research on politics and political behavior. Part of the explanation for this emphasis is that many socio-logical studies of voting have started from the assumption that all social cleavages are in large part a product of material inequalities. Scholars of U.S. politics have generally agreed that, outside the South, the New Deal party system rested in large measure on economic class divisions. This conventional wisdom also asserts that since the 1950s, electoral class divisions—alongside the New Deal party system itself—gradually began to erode with postwar societal affluence. This decline is often viewed as accelerating in the 1960s as a result of intense social conflicts over issues such as civil rights, gender equality, and the environment. The idea of the 'Reagan Democrat' (working-class supporters of Republican presidential candidates) and the 'new class' liberal (educated middle-class Democrats) gained currency in both journalistic and scholarly accounts of this period.

In this chapter we re-examine such widely held assumptions about the role of class divisions in American electoral politics. We begin with a historical overview of class politics. We pay particular attention to the different ways in which class has been conceptualized in earlier research. These concepts, as we will see, usually lead to the finding that class divisions are either insignificant or declining in importance over time. Next, we present an alternative approach for studying class voting. This approach builds from recent research on conceptualizing class in other social science subfields. In contrast to almost all of the existing political behavior literature, we employ a structural, multi-category class scheme that is not based on simple income groups, a blue-collar/white-collar distinction, or subjective class identification. We then discuss the statistical models and indices we use to measure overall and group-specific trends in class voting.

Following these preliminaries, we turn to our two main empirical questions. First, to what extent has the class cleavage declined over the period from 1952 to 1992? Second, to what extent, and why, have individual classes shifted their political allegiances? We find little evidence that class divisions have narrowed in this period, but we do find evidence of significant shifts in the alignment of particular classes, especially among professionals, the self-employed, and nonskilled workers. In the remainder of the chapter, we examine the factors driving the shifts among these realigning classes. We show that the sources of change among these classes are different. Professionals have become more Democratic relative to the rest of the electorate because of their increasingly liberal attitudes on social issues. The self-employed have embraced Republican candidates since 1980 because of lower levels of economic satisfaction under Jimmy Carter and higher levels of economic satisfaction under Ronald Reagan, as well as declining support for the welfare state. Satisfaction with the economy in the 1980s and declining support for the welfare state are behind the changes in political alignments among nonskilled workers.

We should emphasize one point at the outset. The most important way in which class matters in U.S. electoral politics is through the longstanding differences in turnout rates between classes.[1] Managers and professionals vote at far higher rates than the working class, thereby altering the shape of the electorate. This class turnout gap is much larger in the United States than in other capitalist democracies; in some countries with very high turnout rates (such as the Netherlands), there is no class gap at all.[2] When comparative class voting analysts argue that class matters less in American politics than in Western Europe, however, they typically focus on class differences in the choice of candidates or parties, rather than turnout. Our focus in this chapter is on the effects of class on voting; we investigate the impact of turnout in Chapter 7.

THE 'DEMOCRATIC CLASS STRUGGLE' IN AMERICAN POLITICAL HISTORY

Seymour Martin Lipset noted in *Political Man* that 'The Democrats from the beginning of their history have drawn more support from the lower strata of society, while the Federalist, Whig, and Republican parties have held the loyalties of the more privileged groups.' Later, he suggests that 'it often comes as a shock, especially to Europeans, to be reminded that the first political parties in history with "labor" or "workingman" in their names developed in American politics in the

1820s and 1830s'.[3] Yet most commentators, including Lipset, have emphasized an unusual patterning of class and party in the United States. The absence of an electorally powerful labor or social democratic party has meant that class divisions are not as politicized in the same way as in other countries. This issue has been at the core of the debates over 'American exceptionalism'.

A number of unique features of American political institutions and political history have combined to produce these outcomes. With respect to institutional factors, legislative election rules influence the shape of a national party system: countries with proportional representation (PR) systems tend to produce multi-party systems, while single-member district systems tend to produce two-party systems.[4] In the single-member district system of U.S. politics, third parties have usually faced nearly insurmountable obstacles to establishing a lasting political presence. Among the many third party movements in American political history are a large number that sought to organize themselves on a class basis. The most notable of these include the populist movement of the late nineteenth Century and various left-wing parties between the 1890s and World War II.[5]

Other historical factors have hindered the development of working-class political parties. The unique and crucial role of the South contributed to the factors generating political fragmentation and undermining class politics in the United States. The disfranchisement of African-Americans and many working-class white voters in most Southern states in the late nineteenth and early twentieth centuries produced shriveled, conservative, white electorates and discouraged political action by social or labor movements in that region.[6] Uncompetitive elections in most parts of the South meant that Southern political elites had no incentive to respond to whatever popular pressures might emerge. Further, the almost complete hegemony of the Democratic Party through the late 1940s in the South made a class-based alignment of voters and parties impossible. The opposition of powerful Southern politicians—whose long congressional seniority, and resulting domination of commitee chairmanships, was virtually assured by the region's electoral system—to virtually all state-building reform proposals (except those that addressed their special concerns) made it very difficult for a Democratic Party beholden to their support to pursue a pro-labor agenda.[7]

The timing of working-class enfranchisement in the United States was also significant. The early extension of the franchise (albeit only to white men) meant that struggles for voting rights were not linked to demands for a broad program of social insurance, union rights, or socialist or social democratic party-building, as in many parts of Europe. This precluded the typical European outcome, where working-class political parties gained broad followings and a foothold in the polity that was based initially on popular demands for the franchise.[8]

During the late nineteenth and early twentieth centuries, unions suffered political defeats at the hands of hostile employers, the courts, and in many cases direct government intervention on the side of employers during strikes. These defeats hindered the emergence of any significant class-wide organization of the U.S. working class until the 1930s, or after the consolidation of the modern party system.[9] The sociologist Kim Voss has demonstrated with particular force that by the 1880s, the American labor movement had developed political ideologies and organizational capacities similar to those of their European counterparts. But the successful organization of U.S. employers against the Knights of Labor crippled the labor movement at the very point when workers' movements elsewhere were beginning to mature. The absence of a broad-based labor movement in turn limited the ability of workers to organize themselves effectively in the political sphere.[10]

In sum, at no point in the late nineteenth or early twentieth centuries were American workers able to build stable ties to a labor-based political party comparable to those in Western Europe, Canada, or Australia. And no socialist or social democratic party was able to successfully penetrate the two-party system. To be sure, prior to the 1930s there were ideological and institutional forces in American politics which could (and occasionally were) able to generate class-related political demands. Yet these divisions were never translated into durable voting cleavages along class lines. The 'system of 1896', the electoral era of Republican dominance at the national level between 1896 and 1932, was characterized by declining electoral competitiveness and, in most parts of the country, regional political monopolies for one or the other of the major parties.

The New Deal: A Turning Point?

The economic and political crisis brought on by the Great Depression of the 1930s loosened many of the institutional and organizational barriers to the emergence of a class-based political order at the national level. Growing numbers of industrial workers and poor farmers came to be aligned with the Democratic Party during this period. With the strike waves of 1933–34 and 1937 and the concomitant growth of organized labor, renewed third party movements on the left, and the appearance of other class-based social movements (such as the unemployed workers' movement of the 1930s), there were good reasons for contemporary observers to think that class forces were gaining political importance. The Democratic victories in the 1932–36 elections, including the election and re-election of Franklin Roosevelt, were unprecedented. And the resulting bundle of New Deal domestic reform policies adopted by the Democratic majority between 1933 and 1938 drew sharp programmatic lines between the parties for the first time in the twentieth century.[11] The Democratic Party pushed through the Social Security Act, the National Labor Relations Act, banking and security reform measures, a variety of job-creation schemes (the most important of which was the Works Progress Administration), tax reform, and other measures which cumulatively defined a sweeping reform agenda. By 1938 (at the end of the reformist phase of the New Deal), the U.S. was the most generous social spender in the capitalist world, and by a substantial margin.[12] It also provided, through the National Labor Relations Act, as systematic a governmental framework for encouraging unionism as existed anywhere in the world.

Most scholarly assessment of the social bases of the New Deal coalition from the 1930s through the late 1940s have claimed to find unprecedented levels of class polarization. Although the study of individual-level political behavior was very much in its infancy, contemporary social science research generally supported these conclusions (though often noting that the class divide did not appear to be nearly as large as journalistic accounts suggested). The most famous of these studies were those of Paul Lazarsfeld, Bernard Berelson and their collaborators (discussed in Chapter 1). The work of the sociologist W. F. Ogburn and his collaborators provided another example. On the basis of ecological studies of income and voting, they concluded that individuals living in working-class neighborhoods were significantly more likely to vote for Roosevelt in the 1930s than were the middle class and the rich.[13] In a 1943 book introducing the phrase 'democratic class struggle' into the political sociological lexicon, political scientists Dewey Anderson and Percy Davidson utilized electoral rolls in Northern California which contained information about each voter's occupation to test theories about political alignments and change during the New Deal. Their analysis showed that Democratic Party affiliation in the 1930s was disproportionately concentrated among voters with working-class occupations, while those in professional and managerial occupations were more likely to register as Republicans.[14]

Postwar scholarship has generally supported the conclusion that class polarization increased during the New Deal, although the limited ecological and survey data available for the period has made clear resolution of the issue difficult.[15] A number of arguments and pieces of evidence have been assembled. The spectacular failure of the *Literary Digest* poll in 1936 to predict Roosevelt's landslide victory has been construed by several analysts as indicating that class differences had increased (hence the significance of the unrepresentative character of the *Literary Digest* readership). The early survey data indicated large gaps in Democratic alignment between affluent and working-class voters. The apparent rise in importance of economic concerns and class-based differences in attitudes toward New Deal social programs also appear to have become key factors influencing political behavior.[16]

Class Politics Since the New Deal

If the politics of the New Deal were class politics, the conventional wisdom has been that in the period since the early 1950s, electoral class divisions have retreated in importance. Numerous studies employing a dichotomous manual/nonmanual conception of the class divide have reported evidence of a declining association between class and party.[17] At least ten different scholars have deployed a variant of a single graph, originally developed by Seymour Martin Lipset for the expanded 1981 edition of *Political Man*. The graph shows the declining association between class (manual vs. nonmanual) and vote (left parties vs. right parties) in several countries, including the United States.[18] A handful of scholars have also found evidence of declining class voting using more sophisticated conceptualizations of class structure.[19] Summarizing the conventional wisdom, David Lawrence asserts that, 'the overall pattern since 1952 is for there to be a rather modest association between class and vote choice, and the pattern of change since the high point of the New Deal system is certainly one of decline.'[20]

To be sure, not all analysts have accepted these characterizations. Writing in the early 1970s, Richard Hamilton's exhaustive examination of class politics in the United States concluded by noting that class divisions may actually tend to increase (or offset other declines) with the erosion of ethnic ties connecting members of ethnic groups to political parties. In his analyses of the social bases of partisanship from the 1950s through the early 1970s, David Knoke argued that 'class associations with party preferences did not undergo any substantial change over the two decades' he examined, and that his class index 'fluctuates within the range of 10 to 20 percent, without evident direction'.[21] William Form's varied investigations of the political behavior of American workers emphasized the growing complexities of intra-class divisions, but always in an overall context of persisting class differences between U.S. workers and other classes.[22] More recently, Warren Miller and Merrill Shanks's updating of the multicausal model of voting developed by the Michigan School identifies some grounds for expecting that social structural divisions will continue to have significant political consequences.[23]

WHAT IS THE CLASS CLEAVAGE?

Conceptualizing Class

To develop a systematic exploration of changes in the class cleavage, we must first re-examine the question of how to properly conceptualize class divisions. In political analyses the concept of class is most useful in analyzing instances of collective action in which 'class-in-itself' becomes a 'class-for-itself', in Marx's famous formulation.[24] However, such direct forms of class mobilization are very rare in the context of electoral politics. This is especially true in the United States during the post-World War II period. Our conceptualization of class in the rest of this chapter thus refers to a more limited, structural conception, defining clusters of actors in similar economic locations rather than a group of actors with a highly developed consciousness of those interests.

In the study of U.S. political behavior, voting analysts have operationally defined 'class' typically in one of three distinct ways. The most common approach is to distinguish blue-collar from white-collar workers. The assumption underlying this model is that the principal class distinction in capitalist societies is 'between the middle class as a whole and the lower or working class'.[25] It is relatively easy to see the limitations of such an assumption. First, there are important sources of class divisions within both the middle class(es) and the working class(es) that cannot be identified with a two-class model. For example, it is very difficult to place routine white-collar employees working in service industries. While such workers do not have manual employment, they hardly enjoy the benefits of the employment relations typical of professional or managerial occupations. Further, important changes in the class structures of capitalist societies since World War II are difficult to identify with such a model.[26]

The second common approach is to distinguish classes on the basis of their income. The use of income groups as proxies for classes is typical in most journalistic reporting of election results, but can also be found in many scholarly works as well. The basic logic is straightforward. Higher-income people have different material interests than lower-income people. They are better able to fend for themselves in the market, and thus should have much less use for government-provided social provision or progressive taxation. Conversely, lower-income people should be expected to have the opposite interests. The difficulty with using income as an indicator of class membership, however, is that it is often the case that people with the same income will have quite different long-term economic interests. The part-time school teacher, the semi-skilled factory worker, the college student working part-time as a computer programmer, and the self-employed artist may all report the same income on their tax returns. But as salaried, hourly, or self-employed workers, they have different sources of income (growing out of different employment relations) and ultimately very different life chances.

The third approach is the one that most contemporary sociologists use, although it is less common in voting studies. Here class is defined in terms of occupational location and/or employment situation. There are both gradational and relational conceptions of class in this tradition.[27] Through the 1970s, the dominant approach in class analysis was gradational: class analysts placed occupations on a single continuum, ranked by the prestige attributed to each job.[28] While gradational approaches have been used extensively in studies of social mobility, their relevance to the study of political behavior is less clear.

In relational approaches, different clusters of occupations are viewed as having similar—though not identical—employment situations and/or life chances. Rather than generating a scale of all occupations, relational approaches define classes in terms of either market or production relations. The result is a set of categorical distinctions among actors based on their employment situation. Although a variety of different class schemes can be found in the literature, most share several common starting points. One widely shared assumption is that there are important class differences between those who are self-employed versus those who work for someone else. It is, of course, also useful to distinguish among the self-employed (for example, between those who do and do not have employees). Unfortunately, few repeated surveys have sufficient information to make such distinctions. Among employed persons, most relational voting analysts make several additional distinctions: (1) between those who possess significant educational credentials or knowledge-based skills from those who do not; (2) between those who work as salaried employees and are in positions of trust vis-à-vis their employers, and those who are not; and (3) between those who, in their employment situation, possess some type of organizational assets and those who do not.[29]

A well-designed relational class scheme has several advantages over income group or blue-collar/white-collar definitions of class structure. It captures many of the long-term differences in life chances that go beyond current income level to determine individual class locations. Over-time changes in the class structures of capitalist societies are also more visible than with simple blue-collar/white-collar or income group distinctions.

We thus employ a multi-category class scheme rooted in a relational conception of class structure. We distinguish between six class locations and one residual category for those respondents without an occupational class location. This 'class map' is based on information about the respondents' occupation and employment situation, available in each year of the NES series. We have coded each respondent into one of the following class locations:

- *Professionals* (both salaried and self-employed, including lawyers, physicians, engineers, teachers, scientists, writers, editors, and social workers);
- *Managers and administrators* (including all non-retail sales managers);
- *Owners, proprietors, and other non-professional self-employed persons* (including farm owners);
- *Routine white-collar workers* (retail sales, clerical, and the white-collar service workers);
- *Skilled workers and foremen* in all industries;
- *Nonskilled workers* in all industries (including farming and services); and
- *Non-full-time labor-force participants* (homemakers, retirees, students, and the disabled working less than twenty hours a week).

It is important to note at the outset that within each of these categories there is considerable variation in respondents' income and type of job. In the chapter appendix, we list some of the principal occupations coded into each class category.

Professionals and managers constitute the elite employed classes in this scheme. We also include self-employed professionals here, on the grounds that the distinction between being employed and self-employed is often blurred for many professional occupations. Professionals possess recognizable credentials and licenses that entitle them to engage in certain types of income-generating activities foreclosed to others. Their credentials are generally transferable from one context to another, providing them with a degree of employment security that is rare for non-professionals.[30] The manager category constitutes a more diffuse grouping of individuals who typically possess either firm-specific organizational assets or transferable managerial and/or administrative skills or knowledge. Many members of managerial occupations also possess valuable experiential assets which may be transferred from one firm to another, although rarely with the same degree of flexibility as that of professionals.

Some analysts have grouped professionals and managers together into a single class category: for example, John Goldthorpe's 'service class'; Anthony Heath's 'salariat'; or Barbara and John Ehrenreich's 'professional-managerial class'.[31] However, we prefer to place professionals and managers in different class locations for three reasons. First, professionals and managers derive their incomes from different sources: for professionals, it is the application of specialized knowledge within occupational monopolies; managers, on the other hand, are typically located within less-sheltered corporate hierarchies (especially in the current era of corporate downsizing since the late 1970s). Second, mobility studies have often found different patterns between the two groups, reflecting different life chances.[32] Finally, our own earlier work showed increasingly sharp differences in the voting behavior of professionals and managers, providing indirect support for this decision.[33]

Our self-employed category includes all non-professional respondents working on their own account, whether or not they employ additional workers. This category is potentially extremely heterogeneous, as it would include both Bill Gates (the founder and major stockholder of the enormous computer software firm Microsoft) as well as the independent hot dog vendor working the streets of any large city. However, in practice this diversity is much more restricted than these extreme cases would suggest. There are few large entrepreneurs or street vendors in the NES sample. Most of our self-employed respondents are, in fact, small proprietors of one sort or another, including farm owners. They share, in spite of potentially large differences among them, several common attributes. They all face direct exposure to market pressures, and they share a similar relationship to the government (which offers extremely limited benefits and protections for self-employed persons).

The routine white-collar category includes all respondents who are working in white-collar jobs with few opportunities for advancement. These include secretaries, clerks, all other types of routine office jobs, and other non-professional white-collar jobs. Many, though not all, of these jobs are typically paid on an hourly (rather than salaried) basis. Although a wide variety of job titles are subsumed by this category, the combination of modest skill assets and lack of advancement opportunities are sufficient to appropriately define them as a distinct class.

We identify two discrete working-class categories. The first is limited to skilled craft workers in all branches of industry, as well as foremen and other manual workers with supervisory responsibilities. This group constitutes a relatively privileged segment of the working class; members have either the skills or the experience to find or maintain decent-paying jobs even in periods of economic downturn. The second, broader category includes all workers employed in semi- or unskilled jobs. These are jobs that can typically be learned in a matter of days (or even hours). As a result, the workers in these jobs have a much lower degree of economic security, lower wages, and more limited life chances than workers in skilled working class jobs.[34]

Finally, we also include in the analyses a broad category of respondents who are not working full time in the labor force. This is a substantial segment of the electorate who, on grounds of empirical completeness, must be included in the analyses.[35] But it is also a heterogeneous category. Its two largest components are homemakers and the aged. Homemakers should, in principle, be placed in the class location of their spouses, but we have insufficient information about the employment situation of spouses in the NES data to adopt this strategy. The placement of the aged in the class structure also requires a trade-off. The crucial problem is whether to place retirees in the class location of their (former) working life, or alternatively, to place them in a separate class of retirees. The logic of the latter approach is that upon retirement, all persons are removed from concrete employment relations that would ordinarily define class location. Further, retirees have some very important common interests, most notably the maintenance of public health and pension benefits (the Medicare and Social Security programs). On the other hand, there are important divisions among retirees, especially between those who have private pension benefits and/or significant savings versus those who do not. As a result of these processes, employment-based class divisions carry over into retirement, suggesting that it is appropriate to treat retirees as members of the same class as they occupied as during their working years. But in our own investigations,

we are compelled to treat retirees as members of separate class because
of lack of sufficient information about their employment situation during their working years (i.e. prior to their participation in the NES
survey). Since we will not be conducting any direct analyses of retirees
or other persons employed less than 20 hours a week, for purposes of
simplification we combine them into a single (residual) category.[36]

One Further Difficulty: Working Women in the Class Structure[37]

An important analytical problem all class analysts have to address is the
placement of women in the class structure. This is most problematic in
the case of working women. Consider the case of a female sales clerk
married to a lawyer. Should she be placed in a class location on the
basis of her own work, or should she be placed in the class location of
her husband? (Note that the somewhat rarer case of men working in
lower class positions than their wives raises the same issues.) The
'conventional' view holds that since women often do not have either
the same level of long-term commitment to the labor market, or (as is
more typically asserted in the recent literature) because of workplace
gender inequalities, it makes sense to define both adult members of a
family as belonging to the same class.[38] One alternative to the conventional approach is to place working women in the class structure on the
basis of their own job rather than that of their husbands. This approach
has been utilized in some recent work on social mobility and status
attainment.[39] The justification is that working women are presumed to
have their own trajectory in the workforce, as a result influencing their
subsequent behavior (such as voting).

We adopt this second approach here. There is a practical reason for
this decision, given that the NES series does not contain enough detail
about spousal employment to permit coding according to spouse's class.
But there are substantive reasons as well, in view of the fact that rising
divorce rates and other social trends that have loosened women's
economic dependence on men. As a result, their own employment
situation may be of greater consequence than allowed by the conventional view. The empirical results presented in Chapter 5 offer a powerful confirmation of this position.

Class Voting Analyses: A Preview

The analyses presented in the rest of the chapter address two related,
but different, questions. The first question asks whether there have been

changes in the overall pattern of class divisions in presidential elections. This question concerns the class cleavage as a whole. It is a question that engages one of the main controversies of the existing sociological literature on class voting trends. The second question is concerned with the factors that account for the largest shifts in class alignment from the 1950s to the 1990s. Here, we are concerned with questions of causal mechanisms. To what extent are these shifts related to class-related factors as opposed to non-class factors? This latter question has been posed much less frequently in the scholarly literature on class politics.

DATA AND MEASURES

Our analyses of class voting trends examine the period from 1952 through 1992. The 1952 NES is the first survey of sufficient size to allow us to employ our multi-category class scheme. It is, of course, unfortunate that we cannot examine 1948 (the first year of the NES, and a year of high class voting in many studies), but the small sample size of that survey (N = 404) and inadequate information about respondents' occupation precludes our use of it.[40]

Statistical Models

Throughout our analysis, the dependent variable is major party vote choice, coded as a dichotomy, with '1' for Democratic and '0' for Republican vote choice. Our model of trends in class voting uses a series of constraints to measure class-specific patterns of change in voter alignments. These constraints relate to the structure or timing of class-specific voting trends.[41]

Our model implies that five of our seven classes (professionals, managers, the self-employed, skilled workers, and nonskilled workers) have experienced shifts in political alignment. The vote choices of the remaining categories (routine white-collar, and non-full-time labor force participants) vary over time in tandem with election-to-election fluctuations, but without necessarily implying class-specific trends. We measure voting trends among professionals as emerging steadily since the 1964 right turn on civil rights represented by Republican candidate Barry Goldwater's opposition to federal civil rights programs and laws.[42] The model identifies the shift among the self-employed and nonskilled workers as occurring during and after the 1980 election. We measure the structure of these two trends as reflecting a single, one-step movement away from Democratic candidates starting in the 1980 and continuing through the 1992 elections.[43] Political commentators have searched for the social bases of the 'Reagan Democrats', viewing the 1980 election as indicating the successful emergence of the fiscally and socially conservative wing of the postwar Republican Party. Our modelling of the post-1980 vote trends locates this phenomenon among nonskilled workers and the self-employed. We also impose substantively meaningful restrictions on the two remaining class-specific trends. Both skilled workers' and managers voting trends are constrained as occurring during the 1952 through 1972 elections.[44]

Measuring the Class Cleavage and Class-Specific Changes in Political Alignment

Once we have established that our model of class-specific voting trends provides a satisfactory description of the NES data, we use an index to measure changes in the magnitude of the class cleavage as well as trends affecting individual classes. In contrast to most previous attempts to measure the class cleavage, the index we employ allows for more than two classes (or two parties); it can be derived for bivariate or multivariate models; and it can be used for categorical data models that use powerful maximum-likelihood estimation.[45] The principal assumption behind this index is that the magnitude of the class cleavage at a given point in time is best measured as the average difference between the political alignments of all classes from the electorate-wide mean. As discussed in Chapter 2, class-specific political alignments are, then, the *relative* tendency to favor a given party's candidate over others. We formalize this assumption by taking the standard deviation of the estimates for each class-specific pattern of vote choice as our measure of the overall class cleavage.[46] For purposes of identification, we use a normalizing strategy in which the logistic coefficients for the seven class categories sum to zero at each election.

In addition to the standard deviation measure of the overall class cleavage, we also obtain a class-specific voting score for each class in a given election. While some identifying constraint is necessary to derive scores for each class, the zero-sum constraint has some useful, presentational advantages. When a class-specific score is positively signed, it indicates a greater tendency to favor Democratic candidates (relative to the mean of zero); conversely, negative scores indicate support for Republican candidates (again relative to the mean). As a result, we can thus observe not only whether a particular class supports a given party relative to the average support received by that party (among all classes), but also the degree to which there are trends affecting the alignment of a specific class. We present our findings about changes in the overall class cleavage and in class-specific trends in political alignments using a series of graphical displays.

ANALYSES I: THE CLASS CLEAVAGE, 1952–1992

Our first task is to investigate the patterns of change in the class cleavage during the 1952 through 1992 period. In Table 3.1, we compare three competing models of change in the class cleavage. Model 1 provides us with an instructive baseline, given that it assumes that there are no class-by-year interactions. By contrast, model 2 implies extensive trends, and constrains these trends to all follow the same, linear pattern. Finally, model 3 represents the approach described in the previous section, where some classes (professionals, managers, and skilled workers) experience steady changes in alignment while other classes (nonskilled workers and the self-employed) experience sharp changes in alignment during a single election.

TABLE 3.1. *Fit statistics for logistic regression models[a] of change in class and presidential vote choice[b], 1952–1992* (N = 11,861)

Models	Fit statistics	
	$-2LL$ (d.f.)	BIC
1. Null trend: Class and Election Year Main Effects	15877.90 (11844)	−95,231
2. Total class realignment All Classes * Year$_{1952-1992}$	15789.23 (11838)	−95,263
3. Class-specific changes in vote choice Professionals * Year$_{1964-1992}$ Managers * Year$_{1952-1972}$ Skilled Workers * Year$_{1952-1972}$ Self-Employed × Year$_{\geq 1980}$ Nonskilled Workers × Year$_{\geq 1980}$	15789.83 (11839)	−95,272

[a] Linearly constrained interaction effects designated by '*'; non-linearly constrained interaction effects designated by 'x'. BIC for null model (including only a constant) is −94,834.
[b] Dependent variable is coded '0' for the Republican, and '1' for the Democratic Presidential candidate.

To compare these models, we use the -2 log-likelihood statistic ($-2LL$) and the Bayesian Information Criterion (BIC). The fit of model 2 readily improves over the fit of model 1 according to both $-2LL$ and BIC. In turn, BIC provides strong evidence for preferring model 3 over model 2, given that the -9 BIC difference between the models favors model 3.[47] Because models 2 and 3 do not have a nested inter-relationship, the $-2LL$ statistic cannot be used to directly compare models. However, while the two models' $-2LL$ are virtually identical, model 3 consumes one less degree of freedom than model 2. This means that our alternative model is preferred on grounds of parsimony, thereby corroborating the direct comparison enabled by the BIC index. Taken as a whole, these results demonstrate the utility of constraining the structure and timing of class-specific changes in voter alignments.

Using Figure 3.1, we use our results to display the magnitude of the class cleavage from 1952 through 1992. With the single exception of the 1964 election, there is little over-time change in the class cleavage. Whereas 1964 marks a high point in the cleavage's magnitude, corresponding to a .56 value on the logit scale, the corresponding values in other elections vary slightly about .40. Instead of implying a pattern of decline, these results show considerable over-time stability in the class cleavage. Moreover, the results also show that the magnitude of the class cleavage is far from negligible. For instance, in a close election in which the Democratic and Republican candidates each receive approximately 50% of the popular vote, the .40 logit index score translates into .10 on the more familiar probability scale. This means that the average difference between each of the seven classes and the electorate-wide mean is .10. The average difference between a given pair of classes is thus predicted as being a substantial 20%, much larger than the 0% we would find if the class cleavage had disappeared.

Our next order of business is to examine the class-specific trends among each of the seven classes. We use the graphical displays in Figure 3.2 to summarize these trends. The lines in Figure 3.2's panels represent the class-specific trends (or non-trends) for each of the seven class categories. As discussed earlier, the zero-sum normalization we employ tells us how a particular class votes at a given point in time relative to how all classes voted, thereby distinguishing between voting trends affecting all classes versus those affecting only specific classes.

The results displayed in Figure 3.2 reveal the following class-specific trends: (1) a dramatic turn from Republican to Democratic vote choice among professionals; (2) a steeper Republican trend among the self-employed, but applying to the more recent period beginning with the

Class 65

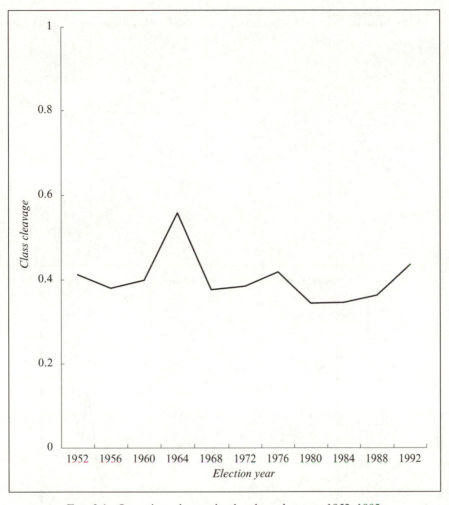

FIG. 3.1. Over-time change in the class cleavage, 1952–1992

1980 election; (3) an equally sharp drop in support for Democratic candidates among nonskilled workers in the 1980 to 1992 period; (4) a decay in Democratic Party support among skilled workers from 1952 through 1972, with a partial recovery since 1972; (5) a similar pair of trends among managers, whose level of Republican candidate support increased between 1952 and 1972, while moving back towards the political center since 1972; and (6) a slight trend towards the Democratic Party among routine white-collar employees since 1972. Finally, the voting behavior of non-labor-force participation shows considerable

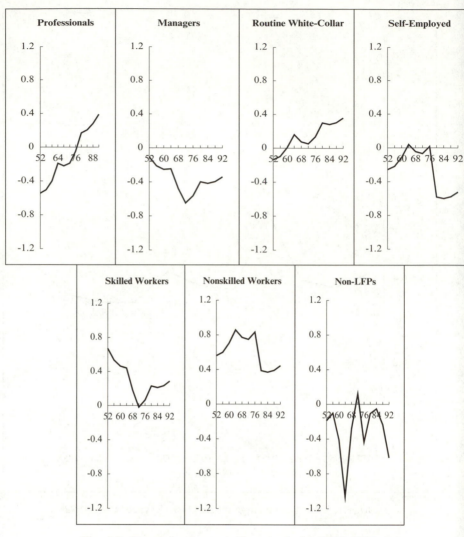

Fig. 3.2. Trends in class-specific vote choice, 1952–1992

volatility relative to the mean; however, despite considerable election-to-election variability, this segment of the electorate is generally aligned with the Republican Party.

Of these voting trends, the changes experienced by professionals, the self-employed, and nonskilled workers are the largest and most signific-ant. Professionals have moved from being the most Republican of any class in the 1950s to the second most Democratic class in recent elections. The approximately linear trajectory of professionals' trend (relative to the overall mean) suggests that it has been a steady process, not contingent on one or a handful of elections.[48]

The self-employed have moved from a modest Republican alignment into a much deeper pattern of GOP support since 1980. In contrast to professionals, the forces behind this change resulted in a sharp change during a single election.

Voting trends among the two working-class categories show declines over time in support for Democratic candidates relative to the rest of the electorate. But there are some important differences. Skilled workers lowered their Democratic support relative to other classes from 1952 through 1972, but they have begun to swing back towards their earlier, pro-Democratic position since 1972. The structure and timing of non-skilled workers' trend, by contrast, show a sharp, one-time movement away from the Democrats in 1980, similar to the trend among the self-employed. As with the self-employed, this relative shift away from the Democrats has continued since 1980. The result for the nonskilled challenges some of the expectations from the literature on economic stagnation among nonskilled workers. We discuss this puzzle in more detail in the next section.

ANALYSES II: EXPLAINING CLASS-SPECIFIC VOTING TRENDS

In this section, we analyze the causal factors behind the trends among professionals, the self-employed, and nonskilled workers. Before turning to our analyses of the sources of these class-specific trends, however, we first examine some of the main theoretical arguments about each class that might account for these changes. These literatures motivate our choice of variables in the multivariate analyses.

The Politics of Professionals: Theoretical Debates

Why might professionals be shifting towards the Democrats relative to other classes in recent elections? Classical sociological theories of the political alignments of the educated middle classes generally emphasized their ideological conservatism.[49] Since the late 1960s, however, it has become increasingly clear that the much discussed 'new' social movements (e.g. women's, environmental, and gay and lesbian) have drawn their support primarily from members of the educated middle classes.[50] This has led to the development of a number of theoretical arguments about the receptiveness of various middle-class segments to liberal (or even radical) political appeals.[51] Some of these interpretations have emphasized the interests of the professional middle classes in support for the public sector, while others point to changing values. Subsequent empirical research has focused on factors that dispose middle-class actors to join social movements or adopt liberal policy attitudes. Our analysis here (and in an earlier study comparing the voting behavior of U.S. professionals and managers[52]), extends this debate to the institutional arena of voting behavior in national elections.

Unquestionably the most controversial interpretation of liberal and radical political tendencies in the middle class is the so-called 'New Class' thesis.[53] New Class theorists hypothesize that growing segments within the educated middle classes are receptive to liberal or left-wing ideas and are disposed to participate in struggles for social change on the basis of their material interests in, or ideological commitment to, protecting and expanding the public and nonprofit sectors of the economy. These sectors are said to provide members of the New Class with their primary source of power and employment opportunities with the result of placing them in a distinct class.

Variations on the New Class thesis suggest two complementary explanations of middle-class political behavior: a materialist interpretation and a symbolic interpretation. The materialist interpretation implies that support for state-building outcomes—and hence the most consistent support for Democratic candidates—should come from those segments of the middle class that would benefit most from these types of developments: people employed in the public and nonprofit sectors.[54] The symbolic interpretation implies that Democratic voting among middle-class voters is largely rooted in pro-state and/or anti-market attitudes, which may or may not be directly linked to employment sector.[55] Such attitudes, rather than material interests *per se*, might explain any propensity for left political alignments among professionals.[56]

The other major approach to explaining liberal trends among the educated middle classes focuses on changes in attitudes towards social issues as a source of political cleavage. Probably the most prominent version of this argument is that of Ronald Inglehart and his collaborators, which we discussed in Chapter 1. Inglehart argues that the materialist concerns of earlier generations are increasingly being replaced by 'post-materialist' value orientations.[57] Postmaterialist social issues include support for civil liberties, quality of life considerations (such as protection of the environment), tolerance of cultural, racial, and ethnic diversity, and gender equality. The increasing prominence of such issues has led Inglehart and a number of other analysts to hypothesize the possible emergence of a 'second' left, whose liberal views on social issues (rather than on 'traditional' materialist or economic concerns) disposes them to support liberal or left political parties. This 'two lefts' thesis distinguishes sharply between working-class support for economic egalitarianism and middle-class support for social issue liberalism.[58]

The Politics of the Self-Employed: Theoretical Debates

Theoretical work on the political alignments of the self-employed has involved fewer controversies in recent years than the debates over the educated middle classes. In comparison with most employed persons, the self-employed face direct exposure to market pressures. It has long been assumed that such pressures tend to elicit distinctive political attitudes and behavior, usually in a conservative, anti-statist direction. Many interpretations of right-wing movements have suggested that these movements draw disproportionate support from a 'frustrated' petty-bourgeoisie whose members are often among the first to suffer from economic downturns. This thesis was common, for example, in the case of early research on the social bases of fascist and other reactionary political movements in Europe.[59] A number of scholars have applied similar insights to the self-employed in the United States. It can be found in some interpretations of the rise of McCarthyism and other right-wing movements.[60] During the New Deal, some of the most bitter opposition to the Roosevelt Administration's domestic reform agenda came from small business (though not farmers).[61] More recently, Clarence Lo's study of the tax revolt in California notes the early role played by small business leaders who became activists in the campaign to win passage of Proposition 13.[62]

But the politics of the self-employed in the United States have not been as straightforward as these discussions imply. C. Wright Mills captured these contradictions well in his mid-century writings. Mills noted that 'the small entrepreneurs seem to be more often on the side of business . . . [and] small businessmen are shock troops in the battle against labor unions and government controls . . . [b]ut they do not look to it [i.e. big business] as the solver of their problems; for this, strangely enough, they look to government'.[63] This ambiguity appeared to be reflected in their political behavior. Through the late 1970s, the voting pattern of the self-employed in national elections was generally thought to be in the center relative to other classes (a picture which is confirmed in our analyses of relative voting trends; see Figure 3.2 above). Writing in 1975, Richard Hamilton pointed to this as evidence that 'independent businessmen' were a sufficiently heterogeneous group to defy assumptions about their conservatism found in the literature. Hamilton noted that while the ranks of the self-employed include affluent individuals who were likely to be politically conservative, there were also large numbers of self-employed persons from working-class origins with marginal incomes who were politically more sympathetic to the Democratic Party.[64] Further, he argued, for these actors the possession of a small amount of property does not differentiate them from employed persons in the same industry. At the time Hamilton wrote there was little reason to doubt his conclusions about the politics of the self-employed. And since the early 1970s, there is further evidence of an infusion of economically marginalized individuals within the ranks of the petty-bourgeoisie (although this claim has not been without controversy).[65]

However, our finding of a deepening Republican alignment implies the existence of something more than a simple change in composition among the self-employed. Why would the self-employed swing so decisively towards the Republican Party from 1980 onwards? One possibility is suggested by the nature of the ideological appeals of Ronald Reagan to this group. In his explicit contrast between what he characterized as hardworking entrepreneurs and a slothful public sector, it is conceivable that Reagan mobilized class-based attitudes toward public policy and the parties among the self-employed. We explore this and other possibilities in the analyses which follow.

The Politics of Nonskilled Workers: Theoretical Debates

As we noted above, at the heart of theories of American exceptionalism is the question of to what extent, and why, the U.S. working class is politically more conservative than working classes elsewhere in the world.[66] We evaluate three specific theses in the course of this investigation. First, we consider versions of the classical embourgeoisement argument, which argues that the political commitment of the working class to a left or liberal political agenda erodes with improvements in absolute economic circumstances. The embourgeoisement argument might thus help to account for Republican voting trends if there was evidence of material improvement among U.S. workers.

But the recent stratification literature suggests this is clearly not the case, at least for nonskilled workers. Income stagnation (or even decline) has been the experience of large sectors of the U.S. working class since the 1970s.[67] But economic stagnation appears to have produced very modest evidence of a political backlash among U.S. workers.[68] Why might this be the case? Even if the objective evidence suggests that a crude version of the embourgeoisement thesis must be wrong, there is a related subjective version that must be considered. Perceptions of economic well-being may have become partially independent of objective economic circumstances. We consider this possibility by examining changing responses to perceptions of personal well-being among nonskilled workers from the 1970s to the 1990s.[69]

A second classical thesis we explore is the theory of 'working-class authoritarianism', popularized in Lipset's famous chapter in *Political Man* by that title. Lipset advanced the thesis that the working classes of the democratic countries are left on economic matters, but generally conservative and intolerant on social and cultural issues.[70] Other researchers have since demonstrated that intolerance is a consequence of low education, not working-class occupation per se.[71] The working-class authoritarianism thesis has been revived more recently, however, by a number of analysts investigating the impact of racial attitudes on working-class political behavior.[72] To the extent that the Democrats have come to be viewed as the party that has promoted affirmative action and other race-targeted social programs, they may be losing support disproportionately from the ranks of the white working class. We consider this possibility by including a number of measures of attitudinal conservatism on social issues in our models.

Finally, we consider the possibility of working-class alienation from the Democrats in particular, and government in general. Some analysts have emphasized working-class alienation from political life as a key source of declining voter turnout and decreasing support for the Democrats.[73] One factor that may mediate these linkages are unions, by providing members with information and the motivation to participate in electoral politics. The decline of union membership may itself be a source of working-class disaffection with both the Democratic Party and declining enthusiasm for government programs.

Explaining Class-Specific Political Change Since the 1960s

We can now begin to address some of these debates as they bear on class-based political alignments. Our examination requires that we analyze a range of new independent variables in our analyses. These variables fall into one of three categories: (1) those that concern *class-related* interests or attitudes; (2) those that involve other (i.e. non-class) sociodemographic attributes; and (3) those concerning attitudes towards *social issues* (especially relating to the 'two lefts' and 'working-class authoritarianism' theses). We list each of these variables in Table 3.2, along with the sample means for professionals, the self-employed, and nonskilled workers. The sociodemographic covariates employed in the analysis are treated as dummy variables: gender (female = 1), race (African-American = 1), cohort (sixties = 1), education ($\geq$ BA = 1), region (South = 1), and employment sector (public/nonprofit = 1). The social composition of each of the three class categories has changed

TABLE 3.2. *Class-specific sample means for independent variables in the analyses*

Independent variable (measurement)	Professionals		Self-Employed		Nonskilled Workers	
	1972	1992	1972	1980–92	1972	1980–92
Household income (1992 dollars)	51,324	51,068	47,974	49,488	34,282	32,426
Union (ref. = not a member)	.11	.16	.00	.04	.34	.30
Economic satisfaction (ref. = better off)						
Same as year age	.41	.36	.46	.29	.43	.25
Worse off than year ago	.13	.18	.25	.28	.29	.30
Class consciousness (ref. = middle class)						
Working-class identification	.26	.28	.46	.47	.74	.73
Welfare state attitudes (continuous)						
higher scores → more support	3.01	2.73	2.46	1.90	3.55	2.91
Age (years)	37.94	40.62	48.96	46.44	42.43	41.24
Race (ref. = white/other)						
African-American	.11	.08	.14	.04	.25	.17
Gender (ref. = male)						
Female	.39	.47	.36	.29	.48	.38
Region (ref. = non-South)						
South	.21	.23	.39	.31	.34	.26
Employment sector (ref. = private)						
Public/nonprofit	.63	.31	.04	.00	.09	.11
Education (years)	15.39	15.82	11.50	13.23	11.25	12.21
Racial attitudes (continuous)						
higher scores → support for						
civil rights	.79	1.04	.46	.74	.66	.84
Gender attitudes (continuous)						
higher scores → more						
egalitarianism	4.10	5.27	3.64	4.43	3.17	4.25
Political alienation (ref. = don't care)						
care about outcome of election	.67	.87	.79	.78	.68	.79

over time, and these changes may also be relevant to some of the trends we observe.

Class-related factors are measured in two ways. First, we examine both objective and subjective economic factors. The objective measure is household income, coded as a continuous variable scaled to constant (1992) dollars. The subjective economic measure is an item asking respondents to assess their current economic situation in comparison to the past year. We analyze this item as two dummy variables for 'same as' and 'worse off than a year ago', with the reference category for each being 'better off than a year ago'. Negative or positive economic assessments can provide individuals with reason to vote against an incumbent President, or alternatively for the party in power during periods of (actual or perceived) economic growth.[74] For example, during a period of perceived economic stagnation the incumbent President's party may be blamed for poor economic performance and lose votes. During a period of perceived economic growth, the party in possession of the presidency may be ascendant. These perceptions may also vary by class. We are especially interested, given the timing of the trend among the self-employed and nonskilled workers, in perceptions during the Carter Administration leading up to the 1980 election.

The next variable in our analyses—views towards social provision—also concerns class-related factors. The NES item we use refers to an ideal-typical attribute of the modern welfare state: the provision of jobs and a guaranteed standard of living.[75] This is the only identically worded question concerning welfare state attitudes in the NES series that pre-dates 1980. This is a crucial consideration for investigating trends among the self-employed and nonskilled workers, but the item has other virtues. Endorsements of, as well as opposition to, the welfare state have a clear class content. For nonskilled workers, a welfare state guarantee of employment and a minimal standard of living potentially provides an alternative to the normal pattern of economic insecurity they face in capitalist societies. By tightening labor markets, full-employment policies may also bid up wages by reducing competition among workers for jobs (especially at the low-end of the labor market). Conversely, for the self-employed such policies are likely to raise the costs of doing business (if they employ others) and also impose higher tax burdens. For professionals, there is no clear class-wide logic to support for, or opposition to, welfare state programs. For those professionals in welfare-related fields (education, medicine, social services, etc.), support for such programs may be linked to class interests. But for other types of professionals (e.g. those in private law practice, business services, or more commercial fields like computers), welfare state programs provide few direct benefits. In each case an important question is whether and to what extent such attitudes have changed over time, possibly affecting their political alignments.

Our final indicator of class-related factors is union membership. Being a union member exposes voters to (pro-Democratic) political messages at election time. Unions may also organize political meetings or other gatherings in which partisan loyalties are reinforced. Union membership in the United States has declined significantly over the course of the past four decades, especially in the period from the 1960s through the mid-1990s.[76] This decline has occurred disproportionately among blue-collar workers, and it may thus account for some of the fall-off in Democratic voting among nonskilled workers. Conversely, rising union membership among professionals may have the reverse effect on that class.

To examine the effects of attitudes towards social issues, we analyze two items that have been consistently asked in the NES since 1972: attitudes towards civil rights for racial minorities and attitudes towards gender equality. The civil rights item is a three-category item asking whether the civil rights movement is moving too fast, about right, or too slow, while the gender equality item is a 7–point scale asking whether women and men should have equal roles in the family and workplace. We analyze both items as continuous variables. Changes in the marginal distributions of these items are large and move in a liberal direction across the electorate. But some classes may be changing faster than others, suggesting a possible association between social issue attitudes, voting trends, and specific classes. The 'two lefts' theory predicts that liberal social issue attitudes have strengthened among professionals faster than the rest of the population, and may thus be the primary source of increased Democratic voting among that group. Working-class authoritarianism theories, by contrast, suggest that the working class may be moving away from the Democratic Party as a result of its increasing embrace of liberal positions on social issues such as civil rights, gay and lesbian rights, and gender equality. The final item in our analyses concerns political alienation. We use this item to examine the possibility that perceptions of alienation are disproportionately concentrated among skilled or nonskilled workers, thereby accounting for a loosening of their traditional political alignments.

Results

We now turn to an analysis of the factors responsible for voting trends among professionals, nonskilled workers, and the self-employed. All of these trends occurred during the 1972–1992 period. Given that professionals' voting trend is approximately linear, we choose the 1972 and 1992 elections as the end-points of our comparison. The self-employed and nonskilled workers, however, experienced an abrupt shift towards the Republican Party during the 1980 election that has continued to affect their voting patterns. For these two classes we thus treat the entire 1980 through 1992 elections as the period with which to compare to the 1972 election.

In Table 3.3, we present the coefficients for our explanatory model of vote choice during the 1972 through 1992 elections. We use these coefficients and the sample means presented in Table 3.1 to make causal inferences about the sources of our three main voting trends of interest. In general, the coefficients of our model closely follow the findings of past studies of sources of change in the presidential vote.[77] However, two sets of coefficients deserve special commentary. First, we find clear evidence that class-related variables have significant effects on presidential vote choice. The effects of union membership, egocentric economic evaluations, and attitudes toward the welfare state are all quite large. For instance, the 1.03 coefficient for the second category of the economic evaluation item indicates that people who viewed their economic situation as worse than a year ago were more than one logit more likely to favor the Democratic over the Republican candidate than people who viewed their economic situation as better than a year ago.[78]

The coefficients for the social issue attitudes items are also noteworthy. While voting analysts rarely treat such issues as important sources of political behavior, our results show that they do have a significant impact. Greater support for civil rights for African-Americans and gender equality leads to greater support for Democratic candidates. Also of note, the impact of these attitudes is considerably larger for professionals than for other voters. These results provide evidence that social issues of this type—relating broadly to civil rights—have greater salience for the most highly educated segment of the middle class.[79] As discussed below, this has the effect of magnifying the causal impact of changing attitudes toward these issues on the political alignments of professionals.

We present the results of our explanatory analyses in Table 3.4. The estimates in the table's columns represent the effect (in logits) that

TABLE 3.3. *Logistic regression coefficients[a] (s.e. in parentheses) for explanatory model of vote choice, 1972–1992* (N = 3,971)

Independent variables	Coefficients	(s.e.)
Constant	−1.53*	(.32)
Class categories (reference = non-labor-force participant)		
Professionals	−2.04*	(.44)
Managers	−.02	(.15)
Routine white-collar employees	.21	(.12)
Self-employed	.04	(.16)
Skilled workers	.20	(.17)
Nonskilled workers	.13	(.14)
Class-related independent variables		
Household income (in 1,000s of dollars)	−.01*	(<.01)
Union membership (reference = non-member)	.65*	(.11)
Economic satisfaction (category 1)	.37*	(.09)
Economic satisfaction (category 2)	1.03*	(.10)
Class consciousness (working-class identification = 1)	.07	(.08)
Welfare state attitudes	.29*	(.02)
Other sociodemographic variables		
Age (years)	<.01	(.01)
Race (African-American = 1)	1.81*	(.20)
Gender (women = 1)	.14	(.08)
Region (South = 1)	.05	(.09)
Employment sector (Public/nonprofit = 1)	−.01	(.12)
Education (years)	−.04*	(.02)
Social issue variables		
Racial attitudes	.43*	(.07)
Gender attitudes	.10*	(.02)
Political alienation		
Care about outcome of election	.14	(.08)
Interactions		
Economic satisfaction (category 1) × 1980	−.33	(.21)
Economic satisfaction (category 2) × 1980	−1.12*	(.18)
Professionals × racial attitudes	.77*	(.19)
Professionals × gender attitudes	.33*	(.08)
Fit statistics		
−2LL (d.f.)	4404.38	(3945)
BIC	−28,287	

[a] An asterisk next to a coefficient indicates significance at the .05 level (2–tailed test).
[b] Dependent variable is coded '1' for Democratic and '0' for Republican vote choice.

change in a row-specific factor is predicted as having on vote choice for a particular class. The last row's estimates are the sum of the row-specific effects on vote choice for each factor. By dividing each estimate by its appropriate column total, we thus arrive at a summary measure of the relative causal importance of a given factor (presented in parentheses). To illustrate the meaning of these results, consider the example of professionals and gender. The .01 in the first column indicates that the increasing proportion of women in the professions has raised the log-odds of professionals as a whole favoring the Democratic candidate by .01. The .01 figure in parentheses (calculated by dividing .01 by the total predicted logit change, .75) summarizes the contribution of this change to explaining professionals' overall shift during the 1972 to 1992 period. The 1% figure tells us that the increasing presence of women in the professions has had a positive but very small impact on changes in the political alignment of that class.

Table 3.4's estimates show that the key to professionals' realignment is their increasingly liberal views of social issues. The .80 estimate for the combined effect of change in professionals' attitudes toward social issues represents 107% of the total predicted change in vote choice. The

TABLE 3.4. *Logistic regression decomposition[a] for explaining change in vote choice among professionals, self-employed, and nonskilled workers*

Independent variables	Professionals (1972 vs. 1992)	Self-employed (1972 vs. 1980–92)	Nonskilled workers (1972 vs. 1980–92)
Δ **Class−related factors**	**−.02 (−.03)**	**−.32 (.84)**	**−.36 (1.06)**
Δ Household income	.00 (.00)	−.02 (.05)	.02 (−.06)
Δ Union membership	.03 (.04)	.03 (−.08)	−.03 (.09)
Δ Economic satisfaction	.03 (.04)	−.17 (.45)	−.16 (.47)
Δ Class consciousness	.00 (.00)	.00 (.00)	.00 (.00)
Δ Welfare state attitudes	−.08 (−.11)	−.16 (.42)	−.19 (.56)
Δ **Other sociodemographic factors**	**−.06 (−.08)**	**−.26 (.68)**	**−.19 (.56)**
Δ Age	.00 (.00)	.00 (.00)	.00 (.00)
Δ Race	−.05 (−.07)	−.18 (.47)	−.14 (.41)
Δ Gender	.01 (.01)	−.01 (.03)	−.01 (.03)
Δ Region	.00 (.00)	.00 (.00)	.00 (.00)
Δ Employment sector	.00 (.00)	.00 (.00)	.00 (.00)
Δ Education	−.02 (−.03)	−.07 (.18)	−.04 (.12)
Δ **Social issue attitudes**	**.80 (1.07)**	**.20 (−.53)**	**.19 (−.56)**
Δ Racial attitudes	.30 (.40)	.12 (−.32)	.08 (−.24)
Δ Gender Attitudes	.50 (.67)	.08 (−.21)	.11 (−.32)
Δ **Political alienation**	**.03 (.04)**	**.00 (.00)**	**.02 (−.06)**
Σ TOTAL LOGIT Δ IN VOTE CHOICE	**.75 (1.00)**	**−.38 (.99)**	**−.34 (1.00)**

[a] Entries in columns are the predicted change in the log-odds of Democratic vote choice attributable to a row-specific factor (entries in parentheses are the proportion of the total predicted change in vote choice attributable to the row-specific factor).

latter proportion exceeds 100% because had only these attitudinal
changes occurred, professionals' shift towards the Democrats would
in fact have been somewhat larger. However, the negative effects of all
sociodemographic changes (see Table 3.2 for these marginal changes)
pushed professionals slightly in the direction of Republican Party
support. Both class-related and political alienation factors, it should
be noted, have a positive, but minimal (−3% and 4%, respectively)
bearing on explaining professionals' changing voting behavior.[80]

Like professionals, the self-employed have become more liberal in
their views of social issues (see Table 3.2). In fact, had only these
changes occurred, the self-employed would have experienced a .20 logit
shift towards support for Democratic presidential candidates. As a
result, the estimate for the effects of social issue attitudes in explaining
the Republican voting trend among the self-employed is negatively
signed (−.53). Both class and sociodemographic factors have, however,
pushed the self-employed further into a Republican alignment (with
political alienation factors having no impact whatsoever). Of the two,
class-related factors have greater causal importance. Higher levels of
economic dissatisfaction under Democratic President Carter's Administration, and higher levels of economic satisfaction during the Reagan–
Bush Administrations account for nearly half of the voting trend;
growing resistance to the welfare state accounts for 42% of this trend.
The declining proportion of African-American owned businesses is the
most important of the sociodemographic factors (accounting for fully
47% of the trend).

The results in Table 3.4 suggest that the historical context and causal
sources of the trend is similar for nonskilled workers. Higher levels of
economic dissatisfaction under a Democratic presidential administration coupled with higher rates of economic satisfaction during the
subsequent Reagan–Bush Administrations are predicted as lowering
the log-odds of favoring Democratic candidates by −.16. Our analyses
also reveal the existence of a separate, ideological basis for Republican
Party support in that declining support for the welfare state among
nonskilled workers explains over 50% of their post-1980 voting shift.
While both these latter factors relate to class politics, it is also worth
noting that social issue attitudes have been of consequence here as well,
but in the opposite direction from that predicted by the working-class
authoritarianism thesis. Trends in these attitudes limit what would have
otherwise been an even larger shift among nonskilled workers towards
the Republican Party. Finally, alienation factors have little bearing on
nonskilled workers' voting trends, given that increasing interest in the

outcome of elections would have actually raised nonskilled workers' log-odds of voting Democratic by a modest .02 logits.

These results about working-class political change come as something of a surprise. They imply a divorce between objective economic realities and subjective perceptions of economic improvement among working-class individuals. They help to explain why there has not been more working-class grievances or mobilization during difficult economic times.

CONCLUSION

The analyses we have presented here support several conclusions. With respect to the overall class cleavage in voting, we observe 'trendless fluctuation' but no evidence of monotonic decline through 1992. This result challenges the conventional wisdom about class politics in the United States. However, within this overall pattern of trendless fluctuation, we find several classes increasing or weakening their traditional alignment. And one class (professionals) has realigned entirely over the course of the past forty years.

Liberal trends in attitudes towards social issues have led to professionals' increasing support for Democratic presidential candidates. Many previous studies have largely ignored or downplayed the significance of social issue liberalism. Steven Brint's informative study of the politics of American professionals, for instance, while reporting greater levels of social liberalism among professionals, places much greater emphasis on conservative counter-trends during the 1980s in describing their political behavior. An earlier study by Mary Jackman goes even further, arguing that liberal attitudes among all voters are superficial, implying that 'liberal' trends in public attitudes toward black civil rights and women's rights are largely illusory.[81] Our analyses suggest a different conclusion: social issues are of causal importance and have propelled professionals into a new political alignment.

Our results for the self-employed and nonskilled workers suggests a picture of similar causal sources of their respective voting trends. For each class, the main factor behind the shift away from the Democrats is a perception of poor economic performance under Carter and increased economic well-being under Reagan. This perception appears to have extended through 1992. However, the evidence that neither the self-employed or the working class are moving in a more conservative direction because of that party's increasing commitment to social issue liberalism (as the working-class authoritarianism and small business conservatism theories predict) is not without controversy. For example, in an analysis of the present state of the Democratic Party, Robert Kuttner claims that 'to the extent that liberal positions on social issues have any effect, they push white working-class voters to the Republican column'.[82] We find no evidence for such assertions. In fact, nonskilled workers have turned away from support for the welfare state at a faster rate than the rest of the population, suggesting that the Republicans' ideological criticisms of the federal government's social welfare responsibilities have resonated among some important segments of the electorate.

Social Issue Cleavages Versus Class Cleavages

One final issue is worth addressing. When juxtaposed with our findings about the persistence of class politics, the powerful effects of attitudes toward social issues raises an important question about the inter-relationship of these two sources of political change. For example, the postmaterialist thesis is consistent with our findings about the growth of social issue liberalism, but Inglehart and his collaborators have repeatedly insisted that the rising political salience of such issues dis-places class-related political concerns. If true, the social issue displace-ment hypothesis would mean that the class cleavage should show a decline once the effect of social issues are taken into account.

We can readily extend the current analyses to answer this question. Since we want to know what effect social issue attitudes have had on the class cleavage, we must rely on the 1972–1992 NES data. (Limiting the analyses to this period, as we have noted, is a function of the relevant NES items being unavailable before 1972.) As an additional check on the choice of the six most recent elections, however, we also repeat our presentation of the change in the total class cleavage (not controlling for social issues) for the entire 1952 to 1992 period. These twin sets of estimates allow us to evaluate whether the estimate of the total class cleavage obtained using only the data from the 1972–1992 election studies leads to a biased portrait of the 1972–1992 period when com-pared to the portrait derived from our analyses of the entire 1952–1992 dataset.

Figure 3.3 presents the results of these analyses. Each of the figure's three trend lines represent measures of the class cleavage. The solid line for the entire 1952 through 1992 series is the class cleavage not con-

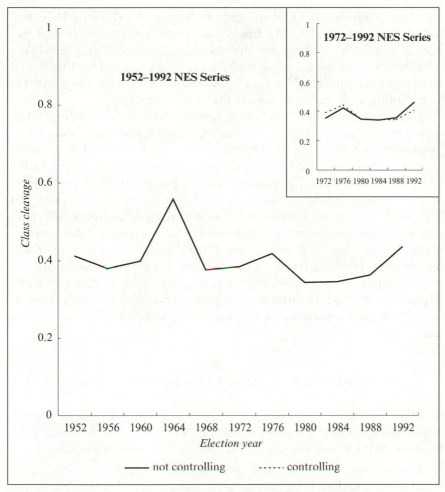

1952–1992 NES Series

Class cleavage

Election year

1972–1992 NES Series

——— not controlling ⋯⋯ controlling

FIG. 3.3. Over-time change in the class cleavage, controlling vs. not controlling for attitudes toward social issues

trolling for social issues, and it serves as the baseline for comparison. In the smaller, embedded chart, we present the twin estimates of the total class cleavage for the more recent, 1972–1992 period. As before, the solid line represents the class cleavage not controlling for the social issue cleavage. The second, dotted line in the embedded chart represents the trend estimates for the class cleavage when social issues have been measured in the model.

The two trend lines in the embedded chart are similar, with the main difference being that when social issues are taken into account, the class cleavage is estimated as being slightly larger in 1972 and 1976 and slightly smaller in 1992. Adding social issues to the model thus has the effect of slightly flattening out the class cleavage during the 1972–1992 period, but the magnitude of the class cleavage during this period is largely unchanged.[83] There is thus no evidence for a declining trend in class voting once social issues are taken into account.[84]

These analyses thus yield a potentially significant finding: class divisions and social issue attitudes do not have a zero-sum relationship with one another. The postmaterialist thesis is thus only partially correct. Changes in the social issue cleavage have had an effect on the class cleavage since 1972, but only by flattening out what would have otherwise been a slight, net increase in the class cleavage during this period. With the exception of professionals, social issues affect all classes in the same way, and controlling for the social issue cleavage does not decrease the magnitude of the class cleavage. The rising importance of social issues and the growth of social liberalism are clearly important and politically relevant phenomena in their own right. However, their rise has little relationship to class politics and cannot be used to explain either the magnitude or the stability of the total class cleavage.

APPENDIX: OCCUPATION AND CLASS

In this chapter, we use information available in the NES about respondents' occupation to create our class categories. Within the constraints of the existing data, we have coded the class categories as follows:

- *Professionals (salaried and self-employed)*: architects, aerospace engineers, materials engineers, mining engineers, chemical engineers, civil engineers, agricultural engineers, industrial engineers, mapping scientists, computer systems analysts, lawyers, statisticians, physicists, chemists, geologists, food scientists, forestry scientists, physicians, dentists, registered nurses, dieticians, speech therapists, college professors, teachers, librarians, artists, social scientists, social workers, clergy, lawyers, judges, laboratory technicians, mapping technicians, air traffic controllers, and computer programmers;
- *Managers and administrators*: chief executives, financial managers, personnel managers, purchasing managers, advertising managers, educational administrators, health managers, properties managers, postmasters, funeral directors, accountants, underwriters, financial

officers, management analysts, purchasing agents, wholesale buyers, construction inspectors, wholesale sales representatives, sales engineers, insurance sales, real estate sales, business agents, compliance officers, and protective services administrators;

- *Owners and proprietors*: all self-employed persons in non-professional occupations, including farm owners;
- *Routine white-collar workers*: apparel sales, shoe sales, motor vehicles sales, television sales, appliance sales, hardware sales, parts sales, counter clerks, street sales, news vendors, auctioneers, sales support, computer operators, secretaries, stenographers, typists, interviewers, hotel clerks, reservation agents, receptionists, correspondence clerks, library clerks, file clerks, records clerks, book keepers, payroll clerks, billing clerks, calculating machine operators, duplicating machine operators, office machine operators, telephone operators, communications equipment operators, postal clerks, mail carriers, messengers, dispatchers, shipping clerks, meter readers, eligibility clerks, bill collectors, bank tellers, teachers' aides, and general office clerks;
- *Skilled workers and foremen in all industries*: automobile mechanics, automobile mechanic apprentices, bus mechanics, truck mechanics, aircraft engine mechanics, small engine repairers, automobile body repairers, aircraft mechanics, heavy equipment mechanics, farm equipment mechanics, industrial machinery repairers, machinery maintenance operations, equipment repairers, data processing equipment repairers, household appliance repairers, telephone line installers, telephone repairers, air conditioning mechanics, musical instruments repairers, office machine repairers, elevator insulators, millwrights, construction trades supervisors, brickmasons, tile setters, stonemason apprentices, carpenters, drywall installers, electricians, electrical power installers, painters, plasterers, plumbers, pipefitters, concrete fitters, insulation workers, roofers, structural metal workers, and earth drillers;
- *Nonskilled (unskilled and semiskilled) workers in all industries*: cooks, housekeepers, child care workers, private household cleaners, launderers, auditors, maids, generators, elevator operators, pest control workers, cleaners, personal service occupations supervisors, barbers, recreation attendants, ushers, public transportation attendants, baggage porters, farm workers, agricultural supervisors, agricultural inspectors, forestry and logging workers, fixers, drillers, dressmakers, shoe repairers, butchers, bakers, machine operators, welders, production testers, truck drivers, parking lot attendants, rail vehicle operators, sailors, longshore operators, construction

laborers, garbage collectors, stock handlers, machine feeders, material handlers, vehicle washers, service station workers, and hand packers;

- *Non-full-time labor force participants*: homemakers, retirees, students, and all other persons working less than 20 hours a week.

4

Religion

In the history of social science research on the social bases of political behavior, class has undoubtedly received more attention than religion. This is true even for the United States, despite its unusually high rates of religious adherence and diverse array of faiths. So strong was the assumption that religion did not affect political behavior in the early days of survey research that when Paul Lazarsfeld informed George Gallup that his 1940 study of voters in Erie County, Ohio showed that religious differences were associated with voting preferences even after controlling for class and other sociodemographic attributes, Gallup expressed utter disbelief.[1] Under the sway of the dominant secularization model, the earlier generation of American historians and social scientists saw little benefit in extensive study of contemporary religious influences on politics.[2]

It was not until the 1970s and early 1980s that a substantial amount of systematic empirical work on religion and voting behavior in the U.S. began to appear. A series of dramatic religious mobilizations around the world prompted increasing scholarly interest. These events include the fundamentalist Islamic revolution in Iran, the active role of the Catholic Church in the Solidarity movement in Poland in 1980–81, the appearance of 'liberation theology' movements in Latin America, and, in the U.S., the rising visibility of politically active conservative Christian organizations such as the Moral Majority. Over the past twenty years, there has been a substantial outpouring of scholarship (and scholarly controversies) about the association between religious group memberships, beliefs, and practices and voting behavior during the past fifteen years.[3]

In this chapter, we present our own contribution to these debates. Our methodological innovations – which extend the approach developed in Chapters 2 and 3 on class voting to the religious cleavage – and empirical applications lend support for some of the major hypotheses about trends in the religion/politics relationship in the existing social science literature, while challenging others. Our discussion is in four parts. We begin with an overview which situates the contemporary American religious cleavage in comparative and historical perspective. The second part develops our conception of religion as a social cleavage. We then provide an overview of the recent debates, focusing on four theses about possible changes in the religious political cleavage and the political behavior of specific religious groups in the electorate. These theses frame our empirical investigations, presented in the final part. We first consider trends in presidential vote choice and turnout between 1960 and 1992, and then perform a more detailed examination of trends among Catholics, liberal Protestants, and conservative Protestants.

AMERICAN RELIGIOUS EXCEPTIONALISM

Viewed from a comparative perspective, the United States has long appeared exceptional in the degree and level of religiosity found among citizens.[4] The French aristocrat Talleyrand claimed in the late eighteenth century to have uncovered an astounding 32 denominations among Americans, but only one sauce. Since that time, the number of sauces has (fortunately) increased, but so too has the diversity of religious expression.[5] Foreign observers have long claimed to find evidence of unusual levels of religiosity that defied Enlightenment theories of religious decline. Both Tocqueville and Weber argued that the American case showed that secularization was not an inevitable outcome of social development.[6] Tocqueville's famous argument about the strength of voluntary associations rooted in religious organizations emphasized their importance for maintaining the vitality of American democracy. Whatever its virtues for holding civil society together, religion has frequently been deployed as a weapon in partisan political conflicts as well.[7]

In comparison with other developed capitalist democracies, post-World War II survey research confirmed that religiosity among U.S. citizens was unusually high.[8] Americans routinely claim higher levels of church membership and attendance at religious services, are more likely to believe in God, and claim that religion is of considerable importance in their lives than citizens in other postindustrial capitalist democracies.[9] They are much more likely to hold fundamentalist beliefs, such as God performing miracles (a belief held by 80% of Americans).[10] Summarizing a range of cross-national survey data, Seymour Martin Lipset reports cross-national opinion polls taken by Gallup and others. . . . indicate Americans are the most churchgoing in Protestantism and the most fundamentalist in Christendom. One comparative survey shows 94 percent of Americans expressing faith in God, as compared with 70 percent of Britons and 67 percent of West Germans. In addition, 86 percent of Americans surveyed believe in heaven; 43 percent say they attend church services weekly. The corresponding numbers for British respondents are 54 percent accepting the existence of heaven and only 14 percent indicating they attend church weekly. For West Germans, the numbers are also distinctly lower than for Americans, at 43 percent and 21 percent respectively. . . . And it should be noted that the historical evidence indicates that religious affiliation and belief in America are much higher in the twentieth century than in the nineteenth, and have not decreased in the post-World War II era.[11]

The unusual nature of American religious pluralism also provides a key to explaining institutional differences with other countries. The typical European pattern—in which a single state-sanctioned religious body dominated the religious landscape—never developed in the United States.[12] Here, the absence of an absolutist state and an accompanying state church has resulted in the flourishing of an unprecedented range of denominations and sects. The remarkable history of denominational schisms and religious sectarianism has long interested sociologists of religion. Striking cleavages among Protestant denominations, as well as among Catholics, Jews, and other religious traditions, continue and may even be intensifying.[13] While there are periodic moves towards ecumenism among leading religious organizations, the long-term outcome of denominational change has been a continual expansion of the options for religious practice available to most Americans.[14]

Religion and Political Behavior: Historical Background

The 'new political history' of religion that developed in the 1960s and 1970s established quantitative historical evidence of the importance of religious cleavages for voting behavior and the formation of party coalitions throughout the nineteenth century.[15] 'Ethnoreligious' cleavages, as they came to be known in this literature, reflected both ethnic differences in the churching of immigrant groups as well as broader denominational differences. They provided a source of political division that was well understood by both contemporary actors and later analysts.[16] Controversies over the disestablishment of official state churches provided the earliest source of religious political division,

beginning virtually at the founding of the Republic.[17] Supporters of
state churches, especially the Congregationalists, were generally aligned
with the Federalist Party, while members of lower status churches
challenging the hegemony of the traditional churches were more likely
to line up with the Jeffersonian Democratic-Republicans. The antebellum period (1828–60) appears to have been loosely characterized by the
alignment of voters from 'liturgical' or 'ritualist' religious traditions
with the Democratic Party of Andrew Jackson, and voters from pietist
or evangelical denominations with first the Whig Party and later the
Republican Party.[18]

In the period after the Civil War, party competition in the North and
Midwestern parts of the country was even more decisively structured by
ethnic and religious divides. Up until 1896, the Republican Party
received very strong support from Episcopalians, Congregationalists,
New School Presbyterians, Methodists, and black Protestants; while the
Democrats drew support most heavily from Catholics, and less
broadly from Lutherans and Unitarian-Universalists.[19] In the 'system
of 1896', Republican domination of the North and Midwest involved
strong support from nearly all Protestant denominations.[20] (The post-
Reconstruction South, of course, was a very different matter; Democratic dominance in that region through World War II made religious
differences of little consequence.[21])

With the coming of the New Deal, many analysts assumed that the
sharp ethnoreligious cleavages in the North would decline in strength as
class factors increased in importance. But it appears instead that the
growth of class divisions during the New Deal developed alongside, not
in place of, traditional religious cleavages. Roosevelt generally performed better among all religious groups than Democratic candidate
Al Smith did in 1928, leaving largely unchanged relative levels of support
from most key religious groups.[22] The core of the Democratic coalition
continued to be defined by working-class Catholic and Jewish voters in
the North and Midwest and white voters of all religions (but disproportionately Baptist and Methodist) in the South. The greatly weakened
Republican coalitions of the 1930s and 1940s, by contrast, continued to
receive disproportionate support from Northern mainline Protestants.[23]

The early post-World War II period was one of unusual stability in
the religious world, but by the late 1960s and early 1970s important
changes were taking place in nearly every major religious denomination.[24] The mainline Protestant denominations had been experiencing a
relative membership decline (in which they were losing religious market
share) for many decades, and beginning in the late 1960s this decline

accelerated. Long associated with the political and economic status quo, these denominations were deeply influenced by the great moral crusades of the period: the Civil Rights Movement and the demand for racial justice, protests against the war in Vietnam, and the women's movement. A growing split between liberal Protestant clergy supporting the CRM and other 1960s movements and a more conservative laity generated intra-denomination (and intra-church) tensions.[25] The evangelical Protestant churches also reacted sharply—but very differently—to the social and cultural movements of the period. Reacting against the liberalizing trends of the period, many leaders of evangelical churches organized or promoted new Christian political movements and discourses which sought to defend 'traditional values'.[26] Among Catholics, internal reforms associated with the Second Vatican Council in the mid-1960s produced profound transformations within the Church, as have rapidly changing social practices among Catholics (and all Americans) which fundamentally challenge Church teachings on issues such as sex, abortion, and other 'social' issues.[27] In addition to the changes within the major religious traditions, there also appeared during this period numerous new religious movements, of dizzying variety, as well as the growth of more established religious groups outside the mainstream (such as the Mormon Church).[28]

The transformation of the major religious traditions in the United States during the 1960s and 1970s suggests that there have likely been significant changes in the alignments of religious voters with political parties. Indeed, as we will outline in more detail below, analysts of religious voting behavior have hypothesized a whole series of changes affecting the political consequences of religion and also several specific denominations. Have these changes indeed occurred? And if so, how have they affected the political alignments of religious voters? This chapter offers a detailed assessment of the impact of religious change during the past three decades.

WHAT IS THE RELIGIOUS CLEAVAGE?

There are three distinct religious cleavages that have been analyzed with reference to voter alignments. The first and most basic cleavage is between voters who are connected to a church and those who are unchurched, or alternatively between those for whom religion is very important versus those who are less involved in religious practices. Attendance at religious services may be important for several reasons:

(1) it provides a context for reinforcing religious beliefs and ethical precepts; (2) it may reinforce group identities, especially as exemplified in ethnically-rooted churches found earlier in the twentieth century; and/or (3) it provides a context for connecting religious beliefs to the larger world, including politics.

This 'religiosity' cleavage has been shown to be especially powerful in many countries in Western Europe. In these countries, a single church has dominated the religious marketplace and has typically been aligned with (and supported by) the political regime. As a result, high levels of religiosity are usually associated with conservative voting.[29] In the United States, some analysts have indeed speculated that the increasing numbers of persons without religious affiliations—and the overrepresentation of seculars in highly visible positions in the media, the universities, and high and middle-brow culture—provide a visible target for those with strong religious orientations.[30] Here, the religiosity cleavage is defined in terms of seculars versus those with religious attachments. Some have argued in very strong language that such a cleavage is in fact emerging.[31]

A second major religious cleavage that scholars have identified concerns the nature of the religious beliefs held by individuals. Probably the most salient division here is between religious traditionalists, who believe in the literal truth of the Bible, and religious modernizers, who adopt a context-bound interpretation of the teachings of the Bible.[32] Traditionalists— once politically engaged—may seek to apply narrowly defined biblical concepts to solve social problems, while modernizers adopt more flexible, context-bound interpretations of the Bible.[33] The most famous example in the twentieth century was the infamous 1925 Scopes 'monkey' trial, in which the teaching of Darwinian evolutionary theory in the public schools was litigated. Recently, the teaching of Darwinian theories of evolution in the public schools has again become a significant issue dividing religious conservatives from seculars and religious liberals.[34]

The third, and most commonplace, way in which political sociologists have treated the religious cleavage in the United States is to conceptualize differences arising from denominational memberships. For example, Catholic voters may, by virtue of their exposure to a particular religious culture, have a different worldview and, hence, political preferences than Jews or Protestants. Divisions among Protestant denominations have also been noted, as have differences between members of Judeo-Christian and non-Judeo-Christian faiths. As we have discussed above in Chapter 2, there is frequently a social-structural foundation to such divisions.

In this chapter, we focus on the relationship of denominational divisions (including a threefold division of the Protestant denominations) and voting behavior. We will, however, evaluate the effects of religiosity (measured as regular attendance at religious services) as a possible mediating factor that may strengthen the denomination/vote association.[35] Regular church attendance (the religiosity cleavage) may reinforce the consequences of denominational group membership (the denominational cleavage).[36] Moreover, the effects of religiosity may vary by denomination. It is possible, for example, that being Jewish inclines voters towards political liberalism (and Democratic Party support) with or without regular synagogue attendance, whereas among Catholics attendance at religious services may increase the political consequences of religious group membership.[37] Our analysis of church attendance allows us to examine these possibilities.

One of the most important limitations of our analyses, however, stem from our focus on these long-term historical trends. This broad historical focus makes it difficult to test theories of increasing doctrinal conflict. Suitable measures for making meaningful distinctions among voters along doctrinal lines are only available beginning with the 1980 NES (interestingly, the very period in which a resurgent Christian Right reappeared in national politics). Although there appears to be some evidence of the increasing importance of religious beliefs relative to denominational divisions since 1980,[38] we cannot test such a proposition over the entire period in which we are interested.[39]

RECENT DEBATES OVER RELIGION AND POLITICAL BEHAVIOR

Four specific scholarly controversies over religion and voting behavior have shaped recent discussions of religion and politics in the United States, and these debates frame the analyses developed in this chapter. The first controversy concerns whether or not the overall impact of denominational cleavages on voter alignments in presidential elections has declined. Here, debates over theories of secularization and the decline of denominationalism are most relevant. The other three controversies center on hypotheses about trends among particular groups of religious voters. A second set of debates concerns the oft-discussed mobilization of evangelical Protestants and the extent to which they have increased both their turnout and support for Republican candidates. Third, there are debates about whether Catholic voters have

moved away from traditional support for the Democratic Party towards
a more neutral posture. Finally, some scholars have postulated that
mainline or liberal Protestants have become less supportive of the
Republican Party. In this section, we examine the research literatures
that have generated each of these hypotheses before turning to our own
analyses.

Secularization: Religious Decline?

The classical sociological theory of religion is generally referred to as
the 'secularization' model. Indeed, it is probably accurate to claim, as
Rodney Stark has suggested, that 'during the past century, only one
social science thesis has come close to universal acceptance among
Western intellectuals—that the spread of modernization spells doom
for religious and mystical belief.'[40] Although a number of different
social processes are subsumed under the secularization label, the basic
assumptions underlying the model of secularization are that one or
more of three processes have occurred in modern societies: (1) a decline
in the importance of religion in the lives of individuals; (2) a decline in
the social and political influence of religion in relation to other institutions; and (3) the retreat of religion into private realms (what is sometimes referred to as the 'privatization' thesis).[41]

The theory of secularization would seem to, to poorly describe the
American case. First, there is no clear trend toward declining church
attendance as is found in many other countries. In fact, just the
opposite trend—toward rising church attendance—appears to have
occurred over the past one hundred and fifty years. In the most
rigorous examination of the historical data on church attendance
and religious organizations, the sociologists Roger Finke and Rodney
Stark have demonstrated a sharp increase in church attendance since
the founding of the Republic.[42] Reviewing the survey data on church
attendance available for the period since World War II, Andrew
Greeley demonstrates that, other than a dip in the late 1960s and
early 1970s concentrated primarily among Catholics, there is no
evidence of any fall-off in attendance at religious services. But also
such findings have been challenged. In particular, there is a debate over
the degree of over-reporting of religious attendance in routine social
surveys. C. Kirk Hadaway and his colleagues have recently argued that
Americans significantly over-report church attendance, and imply that
this over-reporting is increasing over time.[43] These issues remain unre-
solved.

Secularization theory also argues that religion matters less in individuals' lives, and hence implies a decline in the import of religion on political life. We cannot systematically address, much less resolve, the secularization debate in this chapter. But since the secularization thesis does imply claims about the likely consequences of religion for political behavior, we can consider those claims in light of the voting data.

Declining Significance of Denominations?

One of the more stimulating corollaries of the secularization model is the view that specific interdenominational conflicts are losing their power, but religion (and religious differences) in general remain robust. This implies that divisions within denominations have become as significant as the divisions between them. The strong version of this argument has been advanced most forcefully by Robert Wuthnow. It argues that religious conservatives of all denominations are aligning themselves against liberals of all denominations and actively secular persons.[44] Other scholars have also emphasized the possibility that religious values may transcend denominational boundaries to create new ecumenical coalitions.[45]

Wuthnow emphasizes three pieces of evidence in support of the declining significance of denomination hypothesis. First, there has been a decline in interdenominational tensions. This is most obvious in the case of Protestant/Catholic and Protestant/Jewish relations. For much of American history, anti-Catholicism and anti-Semitism provided a powerful glue holding together the diverse array of Protestant groups.[46] Interdenominational social divisions, especially those based on class, ethnicity, and region, marked the divide between the established mainline Protestant bodies and lower status Protestant churches, Catholics, and Jews. Other expressions of denominational identity—parades and other public events, the discourses of religious leaders and the publications of denominational bodies—regularly included denunciations of other religious traditions or other rhetorics of distinction. But since World War II, Wuthnow argues, there has been a clear decline in these tensions. Most obviously, public expressions of explicitly anti-Catholic or anti-Jewish sentiment have largely disappeared—albeit with periodic but roundly denounced exceptions—from public life.[47]

Second, there has been an increase in 'denominational switching' (or what is sometimes referred to as 'religious mobility'). Denominational switching occurs when people born into one denomination move to other denominations as adults. The diverse array of religious options available in the U.S. make switching relatively easier here than in other countries. Wuthnow cites Gallup data suggesting that while in the mid-1950s only 1 in 25 adults switched from the faith of their childhood, fully 1 in 3 reported being in a different religious denomination in the mid-1980s.[48] Finally, there is evidence of increasing religious intermarriage. The most careful and rigorous recent research shows that there have been significant trends toward declining marital homogamy among religious groups.[49] The increased likelihood of marriage outside of one's own denomination implies the break-up of the social boundaries that once characterized different religious communities.

With respect to religious influences on political behavior, the declining significance of denominationalism implies that the older, denominationally-based voting cleavages should have contracted. Increasing numbers of religious conservatives, as well as religious liberals and secular people, cross over denominational lines to participate in broad ecumenical organizations and social movements in the pursuit of moral and political objectives.[50] Wuthnow argues that

As denominational boundaries have generally diminished in influence, a new division has risen in importance. At the national level, much evidence suggests that this division, as we have seen in previous chapters, can best be characterized simply as a division between self-styled religious liberals and religious conservatives. According to national studies, the population divides itself almost evenly between these two categories, with various gradations of extremity and moderation in each one. Each of the major religious groupings for which large enough numbers can be obtained also seems to reflect this division. Lutherans, Baptists, Methodists, and Roman Catholics all have about equal numbers of religious liberals and religious conservatives among their members.[51]

According to this model, we should thus expect to find (1) declining political differences between denominations and (2) rising importance of ideological differences between religious conservatives and liberals.

A few researchers have examined the evidence for over-time changes in the religious cleavage as a whole and found support for declining voting differences, in line with the predictions of the denominational decline thesis.[52] Most of these studies, however, have only considered the Protestant/Catholic comparison. For example, in their ongoing series on changes in the social bases of American political behavior, Paul Abramson, John Aldrich, and David Rohde present evidence of declines in the political importance of region, union membership, class, and religious cleavages. Their measure of religious voting is based primarily on a dichotomous conceptualization: the percentage of Catholics who voted Democratic minus the percentage of Protestants who voted Democratic. Using this measure—with its clear parallels to the Alford class voting measure—Abramson et al. find that the religious political cleavage among white voters declined from a high in 1960 (.48) to a low in 1980 (.10), rising again somewhat through 1992 (.20).[53] Using a related pair of contrasts, Edward Carmines and Harold Stanley find a similar picture of decline in the religious cleavage in their analyses of the 1972 through 1988 presidential elections.[54]

However, evaluation of the evidence for religious decline in the overall religious cleavage has not yet been systematically tested at the national level using a more differentiated conception of denominational identities than the simplified Protestant vs. Catholic dichotomy would suggest. Without such an investigation, dichotomous approaches are potentially misleading, for growing divisions *among* Protestants are undetectable in analyses employing an undifferentiated 'Protestant' category. One of the few existing historical studies that we have found that attempts to estimate the overall size of the religious cleavage over an extended time-period with a multi-model of Protestant denominations is Paul Lopatto's 1985 study, *Religion and the Presidential Election*. Lopatto examines changes among five religious groups (liberal Protestants, moderate Protestants, conservative Protestants, Catholics, and Jews), using a simple percentage deviation from the 'normal' vote for each group. This leads him to find evidence of election-by-election fluctuation, with some additional evidence of an overall decline in levels of religious voting in the later elections in his series. However, his study only goes through 1980, and his approach is further limited in that it cannot control for other factors that may suppress or exaggerate the impact of denominational membership.[55]

In short, then, evidence for the overall decline in the significance of religion on voting remains inconclusive. The first part of the analyses in this chapter attempts to establish the evidence in a more systematic fashion than has been previously attempted.

The Christian Right Thesis

The second widely debated thesis about religion and politics in both the mass media and among political analysts concerns the possibility of a political realignment among conservative Protestant voters. The sudden emergence of the 'Christian Right' (CR) in the late 1970s as a factor in U.S. politics, and the visible role of some early CR groups such as the Moral Majority in the 1980 elections seemed to herald a new type of political conflict in which conservative religious values were becoming increasingly influential within the political system. Media coverage of the CR has frequently portrayed its rise as a threat to secular, democratic institutions.[56]

Perceptions of CR influence were fueled by Ronald Reagan's 1980 election (and even larger victory in 1984), the 1980 recapture of the Senate by the Republicans for the first time in nearly thirty years, and the intense media attention given to early CR leaders such as Jerry Falwell and Pat Robertson. A common assumption is that the Republicans were able to win the presidency and regain the Senate in part because the CR was able to mobilize evangelical voters and signal their willingness to pursue a conservative religious policy agenda.

In the relatively brief period since 1980, however, the varying fortunes of the CR have prompted a cyclical pattern of dismissal and then rediscovery of religious conservatism as a political force. The initial search for a mass base to the CR in the 1980s unearthed both very modest support for groups such as the Moral Majority and little evidence that the CR mobilized a significant group of voters.[57] Indeed, by the late 1980s, many informed observers were emphasizing the decline of the CR, at least as a force in national politics.[58] Much of this decline was organizational—for example, many CR groups that relied on direct-mail fundraising appeals had gone bankrupt by the mid-1980s—but organizational decline was often assumed to be connected to electoral decline as well.

In the 1990s, the cycle of debates over the CR appears to have come around yet again. The rapid growth of the Christian Coalition, an organization that grew out of Pat Robertson's 1988 presidential bid, revived scholarly interest in, and respect for, the political power of the CR. The Coalition has emphasized state and local politics, working up to the national level by gaining influence with the state-level Republican Party.[59] In 1995, the Coalition distributed some 30 million voter guides in the 1994 midterm elections and 45 million for the 1996 presidential elections; a careful recent survey found that some 20% of all Americans report having relied upon such literature in making voting decisions.[60] With the renewed prominence of the CR in politics, a new spate of studies appeared, many advancing arguments or evidence of a recent shift of evangelical voters with the Republican Party.[61]

Three questions frame any serious investigation of the influence of the CR on political outcomes. First, is there a recognizable bloc of voters who were influenced by the CR and who changed their vote accordingly? Second, did that bloc shift to the Republican Party faster than other blocs of religious voters, or in our terms, was there a *relative* shift or realignment among evangelical Christians? As discussed in earlier chapters, this is a particularly important issue given that voting trends among religious groups that affect all voters are indications of a spurious association between religion voting, and time.

The third issue concerns the mobilization of evangelical voters. Historically, low turnout rates among evangelical voters have been a widely noted phenomenon, frequently attributed to their lower average education levels and the other-worldly concerns of their religious beliefs.[62] CR organizations, however, sought, to change this by articulating connections between beliefs and the corresponding positions taken by politicians and the major political parties. Subsequent claims of success in achieving higher levels of electoral mobilization of evangelicals by Christian Right groups have often been accepted as true in much of the media coverage of the CR. Surprisingly, however, this issue has rarely been systematically examined by social scientists. To the extent that it has been examined, the general conclusion has been that evangelical voters did increase their turnout in 1980 and thereafter.[63] Our analyses develop a systematic reconsideration of this issue as well.

The Catholic Dealignment Thesis

The possibility that Catholics voters are shifting away from alignment with the Democratic Party towards a more centrist posture is a third widely debated issue among analysts of religion and politics. Virtually all social scientists who have studied this question have reached such conclusions.[64] Abramson, Aldrich, and Rohde even characterize the shift among Catholic voters as 'precipitous'.[65] Key to the interpretation of rapidly shifting Catholic voters is the assumption that Catholics were once overwhelming Democratic. Writing in the early 1980s, the journalist E. J. Dionne bluntly summarized this position, suggesting that 'loyalty to the Democratic Party has been something on the order of a theological commitment for a large share of America's Catholic community'.[66] In more recent elections, however, significantly smaller proportions of Catholic voters have supported Democratic presidential candidates. Based on such evidence, most analysts of Catholic voting behavior have concluded that Catholics are now a 'swing' constituency susceptible to election-specific economic conditions or candidate-centered appeals.[67]

The most common explanation that has been offered for this hypothesized shift among Catholics is one of personal economic interests. Catholics have become progressively more affluent over time, gaining and even surpassing Protestants on a number of measures of socioeconomic attainment. Such processes are hypothesized as causing Catholics to shift to the right as a consequence. As two analysts of religion and politics have put it,

Once firmly embedded in the Democratic coalition due to lower class and minority religious status, many Catholics have moved rapidly up the socio-economic ladder and into the cultural mainstream. Although the 'new ethnic' Catholics, such as blacks and Hispanics, still resemble old ethnocul-tural communities, such as the Irish and Italians, and vote heavily Demo-cratic, white Catholics now closely resemble other Americans, and have consequently drifted away from the Democrats, particularly at the Presidential level.[68]

Indeed, the most systematic review of the evidence suggest that by the 1980s Catholics had reached parity with mainline Protestants in terms of average income, and were rapidly closing the gap in terms of access to positions of power and influence.[69] As Catholic voters have gained affluence, relocated to the suburbs, and lost their minority political status, their support for government programs as a vehicle for achieving social equality (associated with the Democratic Party) is said to have declined.

A second set of interpretations hypothesizes that Catholic voters were disproportionately opposed to the increasingly liberal social issue agenda adopted by the Democratic Party since the 1960s. This approach is especially popular with conservative political comment-ators who have seen Catholic voters as a Democratic constituency ripe for the picking by Republicans seeking to drive a wedge through the New Deal coalition.[70] This interpretation has much in common with the 'two lefts' interpretation that we have examined elsewhere in the book (see Chapters 1 and 3), with Catholics being a core part of the traditional, 'old left' wing of the Democratic coalition.

The Liberal/Mainline Protestant Dealignment Thesis

The final hypothesis we consider in this chapter concerns the 'mainline' or 'liberal' Protestant denominations. The members of these denom-inational families, especially Episcopalians, Congregationalists (after 1957, the United Church of Christ), and Presbyterians, have long been overrepresented among the American political elite and in busi-ness, academe, and the military establishment.[71] Reflecting their social and cultural power in American society, the 'Protestant establishment', as E. Digby Baltzell once characterized them, have long been viewed by many social scientists as a solidly Republican constituency.

In recent years, however, the stability of the political alignments of mainline Protestant denominations has been questioned. Several analysts have found evidence of a shift of mainline Protestants away from the Republican Party and towards the political center. Other scholars have denied there is any evidence of changing political alignments among mainline Protestants.[72] As with the CR and Catholic analyses, we re-examine these issues through an over-time analysis that distinguishes electorate-wide shifts from religious group-specific changes in political behavior.[73]

Scholars who have reported trends among mainline Protestants have tended not to offer causal explanations for those trends. Nevertheless, a number of plausible starting points do exist in the literature on the mainline denominations. One possible account would emphasize rising levels of social issue liberalism among these groups. The receptivity of many mainline Protestant religious leaders to politically liberal messages on issues relating to the Vietnam war and issues of racial and gender inequality suggests one possible explanation for the relative shift away from the Republican Party. Second, some analysts have emphasized changes in the demography of the mainline Protestant groups, in which more conservative church members are defecting from, or not joining, strict denominations. Left behind is a group of adherents in the mainline churches who are more in tune with the messages of the clergy.[74]

THE CONTEMPORARY RELIGIOUS LANDSCAPE

In view of both past research and our focus on the political consequences of denominational membership, our first task is to develop a 'religious map' that is suitable for our empirical analyses. This task is critical given the strength of religious pluralism in the United States. Devising a strategy for handling the broad array of Protestant denominations is a key challenge in creating such a map. On the one hand, there are far too many denominations for survey researchers to try to treat each individually. On the other hand, the continuing reliance of some voting analysts on simplified schemes that fail to draw any distinctions among Protestant voters are not satisfactory.[75]

While a wide range of different schemes have been proposed, we adopt one of the most widely used multicategory schemes for dividing Protestant denominations. It is based on a denominational typology

devised by Rodney Stark and Charles Glock in the 1960s and employed
by a number of analysts since that time.[76] This scheme distinguishes
between 'liberal', 'moderate', and 'conservative' Protestants on the
basis of doctrinal positions associated with denominational membership. The scheme further distinguishes Catholics, Jews, those with no
religious identification (including atheists), and people belonging to
other religions. Full details of our adaptation of the Stark/Glock
scheme are provided in the chapter appendix.[77]

Using these distinctions, we arrive at the following seven mutually
exclusive and exhaustive categories:

- Liberal Protestants
- Moderate Protestants
- Conservative Protestants
- Catholics
- Jews
- Other religions
- No religion

We caution that this scheme does not capture all of the denominational
diversity in the U.S. during the period we are investigating.[78] There will
accordingly be some random measurement error in this (or any other
similar) typology. Nevertheless, it substantially improves over cruder
schemes that treat Protestants as a single homogenous category. The
major alternative approach in the recent literature makes a simpler
distinction between 'mainline' and 'evangelical' Protestant denominations.[79] In these schemes most of the denominations characterized as
'moderate' in our scheme are grouped with 'liberal' Protestants to
create a single 'mainline' Protestant category, contrasted with a slightly
enlarged category of 'evanagelical' Protestants. The latter is somewhat
more inclusive than our corresponding 'conservative' Protestant category. In our analyses below, we also report results that reproduce this
mainline/evangelical distinction, to compare it with our threefold
Protestant categories.

With regard to the non-Protestant categories in our scheme, 'other
religion' is a residual category for the remaining religious groups coded
by the NES. It includes Mormons, Greek and Russian Orthodox, and
religious bodies outside the Judeo-Christian tradition such as Muslims,
Buddhists, and others. In general, these groups are too small as a
proportion of the NES samples to permit analysis of trends. Moreover,
the major scholarly controversies have concerned the larger religious
groups incorporated into our six main categories.[80]

In the Catholic category, we include both Roman Catholics and (the very small group of) Greek Rite Catholics. There are some important doctrinal differences between the two groups, and also among Roman Catholics, but these differences have no substantive bearing on our analysis.[81] Similarly, we include Orthodox, Conservative and Reform Jews in the single Jewish category. While there are significant differences separating Orthodox Jews from other Jews, there are none the less other concerns (e.g. combating anti-Semitism, Israel, and economic liberalism) that have brought all segments of American Jewry into close alignment with the Democratic Party since the New Deal.[82]

The 'no religion' category is especially interesting, both because it has grown from 1%–2% of the population in the 1950s to approximately 10% of the population today (as we show in more detail in Chapter 7) and because the composition of the group has shifted as well.[83] Three types of respondents are included in the 'none' category: avowed atheists, agnostics, and those who simply report no religious identity. Among the latter, however, are a significant number who believe in God, the idea of a heaven, and pray regularly. Indeed, Greeley reports that some 40% of those with 'no religion' are biblical literalists.[84] Some analysts of the 'no' religion category have hypothesized that there are in actuality two distinct groups: 'cultural' nones and 'structural' nones.[85] The cultural nones are seculars who consciously reject religion for reasons having to do with personal beliefs. Structural nones, by contrast, are respondents who believe in God but do not identify with a particular church. Cultural nones can be expected to be critical of the influence of the CR within the Republican Party, and would thus seem to be disposed to favor the Democratic Party. But, the existence of a significant proportion of 'structural' nones among the no religion category suggests a countervailing tendency within this group. Our analyses allow us to explore whether changes in the composition of the nones has altered their partisan balance over time.

We employ this denominational scheme to develop estimates of change in the relationship between religion and political behavior. For the rest of this book, when speaking of the 'religious political cleavage' we will refer to this scheme.

Change in the Religious Cleavage versus Change among Specific Religious Groups

Our analysis of the religious cleavage addresses two distinct types of trends involving religious voters: at the level of specific religious groups, and for the religious cleavage as a whole. This precisely parallels the approach to modelling trends in class voting that we developed in Chapter 3. In the first instance, we are looking at how each of our seven religious groups have shifted *relative* to one another. In the second, our concern is with the religious cleavage as a whole, and the issue of whether the overall differences among religious groups have declined.

As with class voting, changes at these two levels may co-vary, but that need not always be the case. If, for instance, Catholics fall out of a Democratic alignment while conservative Protestants shift towards support for Republican candidates, these two group-specific changes may cancel one another out. Such a scenario implies that the size of the religious cleavage would be largely unchanged, despite some important shifts in the alignments of religious groups not captured by the overall trends. While the declining religious cleavage thesis encompasses all seven religious groups, the claims about change among Catholics, liberal Protestants, and conservative Protestants are primarily concerned with specific groups of religious voters. As with class voting, and in line with the four sets of debates about religious voting outlined above, we consider the evidence for changes at both levels.

DATA AND MEASURES

NES Data: Religious Measures

Our analyses in this chapter focus primarily on the period from 1960 to 1992; we begin with 1960 due to the limitations in the NES denominational coding scheme prior to that election. In addition to the historical period covered by these nine elections studies, we also supplement our analyses with data from the 1952 and 1956 NES surveys to consider trends among Catholic voters in greater detail. This enables us to situate the unique 1960 Catholic vote for John Kennedy into proper historical context.

There are some important problems and limitations of the NES series on religion—in addition to the failure to distinguish among Protestants prior to 1960—that are worth mentioning. First, there are two problems with the religious attendance variable. Like most other national surveys, the NES items tend to lead to over-reporting of the level of religious attendance. In particular, many respondents who, in fact, virtually never attend religious services report occasional attendance. (Interestingly, the introduction of a more detailed question about attendance at religious services in the 1992 NES increased the proportion of respondents reporting no attendance from 14% to 34%.[86]) This over-reporting of religious attendance among non-attenders is important because if they are treated as attenders we may underestimate the effects of attendance. Our approach to handling this issue is to distinguish regularly attending respondents from everyone else. In analyses that include an attendance variable, we include a dummy variable that captures this contrast.[87]

A second problem is the failure of the NES prior to 1972 to distinguish the Southern Baptist Convention from other Baptist groups. As the largest single Protestant denomination, the SBC has a long and distinctive history which diverges significantly from northern Baptists, who have experienced a much greater degree of modernization and liberalization than SBC churches. The large size of the SBC makes it imperative that analysts properly place it within the scheme. Two strategies can be found in the existing literature. Some analysts lump all Baptists together, placing them in an 'evangelical' or 'conservative' Protestant category.[88] Other analysts have attempted more fine-grained distinctions among Baptists, either by placing northern Baptists in the 'mainline' or 'moderate' category after 1972, or making some kind of ad hoc adjustment that attempts to distinguish among Baptists (such as coding all Baptists living in the South in the 'Southern Baptist' category).[89]

Our approach to the Baptist problem is to seek a middle ground. Most of our analyses place all Baptists in our 'conservative' Protestant category, affording over-time consistency. However, it is possible that by placing northern Baptists in the conservative Protestant category, we miss a trend among Southern Baptists. To test this possibility, we have created a separate Southern Baptist dummy variable for use in analyzing trends since 1972. This enables us to test for the existence of a conservative trend that would be missed by not distinguishing among Baptists. We summarize these coding details in the chapter appendix.

Other Independent Variables

Our analyses seek to measure both the overall religious cleavage and changes involving specific religious groups. Both are estimated with and without controls. The latter estimates add age, education, region, gender, household income, and church attendance to the model to determine whether change in these variables is related to change in the religious political cleavage (or in the behavior of specific groups).

Education and income, in particular, are relevant as measures of the growth of affluence and status among religious voters (and thus have particular relevance to the Catholic dealignment thesis). Age (years), education (years), and income (dollars) are measured as continuous variables, while region is a dummy variable ('1' for South, '0' otherwise). To estimate the effect of household income for the entire 1960 through 1992 period, we have scaled income to 1992 dollars for each election year in the analyses. We also include a dummy variable for regular church attendance in the model (coded '1' for regular attendance and '0' otherwise). As noted above, in the course of evaluating statistical models, we test whether church attendance has a greater impact for some religious groups.

Statistical Models

As before, our approach to modelling the religious cleavage is to the compare a series of competing models to arrive at a preferred model of change in the relationship between religious group membership and vote choice/turnout. Our simplest model serves as a baseline for subsequent comparisons. In this model, vote choice is predicted as a function of religious group membership and election year. However, because this model does not include any religion by election interactions, it assumes that trends in presidential vote choice affect all religious groups equally.[90]

Our evaluations of model fit yield a preferred model of change in religious voting. This model implies three main voting trends affecting liberal Protestants, conservative Protestants, and Catholics. The model constrains the trend of liberal Protestants to follow a linear evolution over the course of the nine elections. By contrast, the other trends—affecting conservative Protestants and Catholics—take place only during a pair and a single election, respectively. As discussed below, this means there is evidence for long-term changes affecting liberal Protestants, but not Catholics or conservative Protestants.[91]

An Index of the Religious Political Cleavage

Using the coefficients of our preferred models of presidential vote choice and turnout for the 1960 through 1992 period, we construct an index of change in the religious political cleavage. By summarizing the information contained in the model's coefficients, this index provides us with a measure of the magnitude of the religious cleavage at a given election. Because it is measured in standard deviations, this enables us to directly compare the magnitude of the cleavage at various elections, thereby gauging the evidence for over-time trends.

Our measure of the religious cleavage in presidential vote choice is calculated as the average deviation of a given religious category from the overall mean. This index—which is essentially identical in structure to our index of class voting introduced in Chapter 3—is summarized in equation 4.2, where the βs are the coefficients of the model,[92] and the t subscript for the index indicates that there is a single score for each of the election years:

$$\text{Religious Cleavage Index}_t = \sqrt{\frac{\sum_{p=1}^{P}(\beta_p^R + \beta_{pt}^T + \beta_p^{RT})^2}{P}} \qquad (4.2)$$

Scores for this index measure the magnitude of the religious cleavage for a given election in deviations from the mean. When the voting behavior of religious groups diverges, the standard deviation of the group-specific coefficients increases; conversely, when the voting behavior of religious groups converges, the index score approaches zero. By examining whether these scores increase or decrease over time, we test whether a decline (or alternatively, an increase) has occurred in the religious political cleavage.

We use a series of graphical displays to present scores under our religious cleavage index. The first set of displays present a pair of index scores, one of which is the result of modeling *only* the effect of religion on vote choice, the second of which adds our controls to the model. The first set of scores are thus derived from the coefficients of our model incorporating no controls; the second set of scores are derived from the coefficients of the model with controls. Using the graphical displays, we can observe whether change in our five control variables has affected the magnitude of, and trends in, the religious political cleavage. Using household income as an example, this comparison tells us whether changes in economic affluence have had the effect of narrowing the denominationally-based religious cleavage.

In addition to analyzing changes in the religious cleavage, we also consider the contribution of each of the specific religious groups in the analysis to this cleavage. In our second set of figures, we thus present our measures of religious group-specific voting behavior for each of the seven groups in the analyses. This measure is the (normalized) logit coefficient for the category in question, and because the coefficients sum to zero, scores indicate a tendency for a particular religious group to vote Democratic (a positive sign) or Republican (a negative sign) in a given election. By graphing group-specific voting behavior by election year, we can thus determine whether the groups in the analyses have moved together from election-to-election (implying stability in the religious cleavage), or whether one or more groups has moved disproportionately towards support for one of the parties, thus showing evidence of a change in political alignment.

ANALYSES

Our analyses are presented in four stages. In the first stage, we analyze presidential vote choice, voter turnout, and party identification using our seven-category scheme for the entire 1960 through 1992 period. Our goal here is to weigh the evidence for political trends in the behavior of specific groups as well as in the overall religious cleavage. In the second stage of the analyses, we examine in more detail the surprising evidence for the absence of trends among Catholic voters found in our initial estimates. The third stage examines the causes of liberal Protestants' movement away from the Republican Party. The fourth stage uses a measure that more precisely distinguishes Southern from Northern Baptists. This allows us to search for any additional evidence for political trends among conservative Protestants after 1992 that might have been missed in the first round of analyses.

The Religious Political Cleavage and Group-Specific Trends Since 1960

Our first set of analyses examines the evidence for change in the religious cleavage and in the political behavior of the seven specific groups. In Table 4.1, we present fit statistics for our competing models of presidential vote choice in the 1960 through 1992 period. Model 2, which includes a Catholic-by-1960 election interaction, results in an improvement in fit over the baseline model (model 1), which includes only the main effects of religion and election year.[93] Model 3 contains an additional term for a linear voting trend among liberal Protestants, and it also results in an improvement over model 2's fit (the −11 BIC improvement of model 3 over model 2 represents strong evidence for this trend). Model 4, which adds a single parameter relating to conservative Protestants' voting behavior in the 1976 and 1980 elections

TABLE 4.1. *Fit statistics[a] for logistic regression models of religious groups and presidential vote choice[b], 1960–1992* (N = 8,568)

Models	Fit statistics	
	-2 log-likelihood (d.f.)	BIC
1. Election Years, Religious Categories	10944.09 (8553)	$-66,510$
2. Kennedy Effect for Catholics	10894.14 (8552)	$-66,551$
3. Liberal Protestants * Election Year	10874.54 (8551)	$-66,562$
4. Carter Effect for Conservative Protestants	10861.50 (8550)	$-66,566$
5. Religious Categories x Election Year	10803.42 (8505)	$-66,216$
6. Model 4 + Household Income,[c] Years of Education, Age, Region, Gender, Church Attendance, Attendance x Religious Categories, and Attendance x Year$_{1992}$	10499.41 (8536)	$-66,801$

[a] Degrees of freedom are presented in parentheses; BIC for null model (including a constant only is $-65,829$. Linearly constrained interactions designated by '*'; unconstrained interactions designated by 'x'.

[b] Dependent variable is coded '1' for choice of the Democratic presidential candidate, '0' for the Republican presidential candidate; (African-American voters are excluded from the analyses).

[c] Scaled to constant 1992 dollars.

(what we call in Table 4.1 the 'Carter' effect), in turn provides a better fit to the data.

In model 5, we test whether model 4's three religious group-by-year interactions are sufficient to capture all sources of change in the inter-relationship of religion and voting behavior. Model 5 allows the religious categories to interact freely with election year. We readily select model 4 over model 5, demonstrating that there is no evidence for additional trends among the seven religious groups. While model 4 is thus our preferred model of religious voting not controlling for socioeconomic changes, model 6 adds covariates for church attendance, income, education, age, and gender, as well as interactions for church attendance by religious group, and church attendance with the 1992 election.[94] Model 6 is thus our preferred model with controls.

In Table 4.2, we present the coefficients from our two preferred models of change in the religious cleavage. The three statistically significant coefficients for liberal Protestants by year, Catholics by 1960, and conservative Protestants by 1976/1980 are of particular interest. For Catholics, the 1.20 coefficient indicates that the log-odds of Catholics choosing the Democratic candidates was much greater in 1960 than all other elections in the series. Similarly, conservative Protestants were disproportionately likely to favor born-again Baptist Jimmy Carter in

TABLE 4.2. *Logistic coefficients[a] (s.e. in parentheses) for initial trend and preferred models of religious groups and presidential vote choice[b], 1960–1992* (N = 8,568)

Independent variables	Initial trend coefficients (s.e.)	Preferred coefficients (s.e.)
Constant	−.33* (.16)	1.30* (.26)
Election years (reference = 1960)		
1964	.89* (.11)	.94* (.11)
1968	−.19 (.12)	−.07 (.12)
1972	−.64* (.11)	−.50* (.11)
1976	−.09 (.11)	.09 (.12)
1980	−.52* (.13)	−.34* (.13)
1984	−.49* (.11)	−.34* (.12)
1988	−.30* (.13)	.00 (.13)
1992	.16* (.12)	.62* (.14)
Religious categories (reference = other religion)		
Liberal Protestants	−.51* (.17)	−.92* (.22)
Moderate Protestants	−.19 (.14)	−.42* (.20)
Conservative Protestants	−.16 (.14)	−.61* (.20)
Catholics	.64* (.14)	.14 (.20)
Jewish	1.80* (.21)	1.66* (.26)
No religion	.94* (.16)	.41* (.21)
Religion by time interactions		
Liberal Protestants * Year(linear)	.11* (.02)	.11* (.02)
Catholics x Year$_{1960}$	1.20* (.21)	1.22* (.22)
Conservative Protestants x Year$_{1976/1980}$	.49* (.14)	.46* (.14)
Region (reference = Northeast)		
South	—	.13 (.07)
Midwest	—	.11 (.07)
West	—	.20 (.08)
Gender (reference = male)	—	.14* (.05)
Household income[c] (continuous, in 1,000s)	—	−.01* (.01)
Years of education (continuous)	—	−.05* (.01)
Age (continuous)	—	−.01* (.01)
Regular church attendance (reference: less than regularly)	—	−1.11* (.28)
Church attendance by religion, time interactions:		
Regular attendance x liberal Protestants	—	1.01* (.30)
Regular attendance x moderate Protestants	—	.40 (.30)
Regular attendance x conservative Protestants	—	.70* (.30)
Regular attendance x Catholics	—	1.13* (.29)
Regular attendance x Jewish	—	1.11 (.61)
Regular attendance x Year$_{1992}$	—	−.47* (.15)

[a] An asterisk indicates significance at the .05 level (2-tailed test).
[b] Dependent variable is coded '1' for choice of Democratic presidential candidate, '0' for Republican presidential candidate; (African-American voters are excluded from the analyses).
[c] Scaled to constant 1992 dollars.

1976 and 1980 in comparison to the much lower levels of support they gave to Democratic candidates in other presidential elections.

The three coefficients representing these three voting trends are virtually unchanged in the first versus second columns, indicating that the additional variables in the model (including controls) do not explain these religious group-by-year changes. Given that they pertain to one or two elections respectively, the Catholic and conservative Protestant voting 'trends' are, however, less consequential for long-term changes in the religious cleavage than the liberal Protestant trend, which spans the entire 1960 to 1992 period. Catholics' and conservative Protestants' unusual support for Democratic candidates are instead the products of specific elections in which these two groups gave unusually high levels of support to a political candidate from their religious group. By contrast, the trend among liberal Protestants is clearly not explained by candidate-centered factors of this sort. The cumulative effects of this trend are, moreover, substantial: the .11 coefficient for liberal Protestants indicates that since 1960, the tendency to favor the Democratic over the Republican presidential candidate has increased by .11 logits per year, amounting to a .99 total increase since 1960 in the log-odds of Democratic vote choice. Whereas liberal Protestants were once the most supportive of Republican candidates of *any* religious group, they now give the least support to Republican candidates among the three Protestant groups.

How have these group-specific changes in presidential vote choice affected the overall religious cleavage? The charts displayed in Figure 4.1 provide a graphical illustration. In the figure's right-hand panel, we present our twin sets of estimates for trends in the religious cleavage in presidential voting. The solid line shows the trend according to model 4 (without controls), and the dotted line shows the trend according to model 6 (with controls). Model 6's trend line is slightly higher at each election since 1968, indicating that the combined effect of the five control variables has been to actually suppresses the total effect of religion on vote choice during these elections. With regard to trends, the critical finding conveyed by Figure 4.1's right-hand panel is that both sets of estimates show a *decline* in the religious political cleavage. This decline of the religious cleavage between 1960 and 1980 is substantial, and the fact that the trend estimates for models 4 and 6 are parallel during most of the series is especially important. It reveals that change in the five covariates cannot explain most of the decline in the voting difference among the seven religious groups.

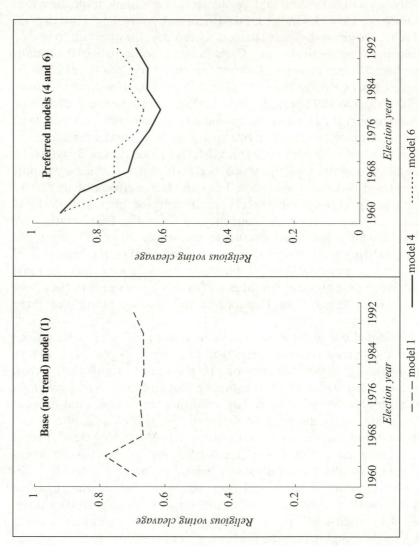

FIG. 4.1. Maximum likelihood estimates of the religious political cleavage under models 1, 4, and 6, 1960–1992

In Figure 4.1's left-hand panel, we present for purposes of comparison estimates of trends in the religious cleavage according to model 1, the model without any religion by year interactions. While model 1's fit to data is, of course, much worse than either models 4 or 6, its coefficients nevertheless contain useful information. These estimates show us what trends in religious voting would have looked like had liberal Protestants' long-term (and Catholics' and conservative Protestants' short-term) trends *not* occurred. Model 1's dashed trend line shows no net change from 1960 to 1992, revealing that the decline in the religious cleavage established in the preferred models is due entirely to the three category-specific trends.

In Figure 4.2, we examine how the presidential voting behavior of the specific religious groups in the analyses has contributed to the decrease in the magnitude of the religious cleavage. Figure 4.2's six panels display the group-specific trend estimates. As before, the solid lines represent the trend according to model 4, and the dotted lines represent the trends according to model 6. The three main groups of interest are liberal Protestants, Catholics, and conservative Protestants, given that the results have already established the existence of year by category interactions for these groups.

The first panel shows that the voting trend among liberal Protestants has been steep relative to changes in the average presidential choice of all voters. Once the most Republican of all religious groups, liberal Protestants have moved to within close proximity of the x-axis, marking the point at which their probability of voting for the Democratic candidate is predicted as being .5. This suggests a considerable movement away from their earlier political alignment, and the nearly perfect congruence of the two trend lines again reveals that liberal Protestants' voting trend is not explained by the socioeconomic attributes measured in model 6.

The trend for Catholics is mostly captured in a single step from disproportionately high support for Kennedy in 1960 to much lower support for Democratic candidates in the remaining elections. Insofar as they remain above the x-axis, however, Catholics continue to be in a (weak) Democratic political alignment relative to the average religious voter, and the trend lines for the two preferred models are nearly congruent. Given that the current series goes back no further than the 1960 election, we utilize data from the 1952 and 1956 elections in the next stage of the analyses to more fully measure any evidence of a shift away from the Democratic Party among Catholics since the 1950s.

With the partial exception of two elections, conservative Protestants have consistently favored Republican candidates by a large margin. The

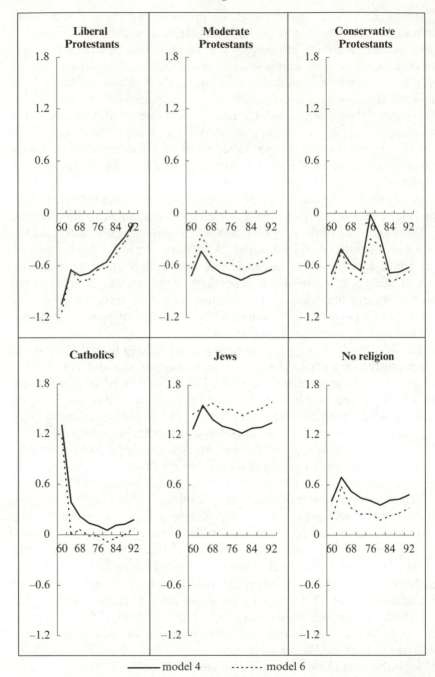

FIG. 4.2. Maximum likelihood estimates of religious group-specific presidential
vote choice under preferred models 4 and 6, 1960–1992

trend estimates for models 4 and 6 are very similar. They are suggestive of a Republican voting trend *only* if one were to take the 1976 election as the baseline for assessing political change among this segment of the electorate.[95]

Jewish voters remain by far the most Democratic of religious groups, and our analyses show that their level of support has varied little (with the exception of the 1964 election) relative to the electorate-wide mean. Our results are consistent with the findings of other scholars who have found little evidence of any rightward shift among Jewish voters in spite of some effort by the Republican Party in recent years to attract Jewish support.[96]

Respondents with no religious affiliation are consistently Democratic throughout the 1960 through 1992 period, although at a lower rate than Jews. While this result is perhaps not surprising in recent elections, the Republican Party's open embrace of traditional values during the past two decades cannot *per se* explain their support for Democratic candidates over the entire period. Accordingly, we find no evidence to support claims that this segment of the electorate is becoming more Democratic over time. In fact, the high-water mark of nones' relative support for the Democratic Party came in 1964, in reaction to the Goldwater candidacy. This finding has some very important consequences for understanding changes in the two parties' electoral coalitions since 1960. As those with no religious affiliation have become more numerous in American society, they have become a larger part of *both* the Democratic and Republican electoral coalitions. Our analyses in Chapter 7 document this conclusion.

The two residual categories in the analysis—moderate Protestants and 'other' religions—are aligned with the Republican Party. Moderate Protestants are slightly more Republican in their voting behavior than conservative Protestants, and the defection of liberal Protestants from the GOP has left moderates as the most consistently Republican of the three Protestant groups since 1976.[97] The 'other religion' category's voting behavior shows significant volatility from election to election. While they remain aligned with the Republican Party, their support for Republican candidates is considerably more variable than that of moderate and conservative Protestants.

Trends in Turnout and Party Identification

We now analyze group-specific trends in voter turnout and party identification. This allows us to consider in greater detail liberal Protestants' voting trend, as well as the evidence for a political mobilization involving conservative Protestants. We present in Table 4.3 fit statistics for evaluating competing models of trends in the relationship between religious group membership and voter turnout. Model 2's improvement in fit over model 1 provides evidence that conservative Protestants were more likely to vote in the years in which Democrat Jimmy Carter was running for the presidency. However, the failure of model 3 to improve the fit of model 2 also shows that voting trends involving conservative Protestants were limited to the 1976 and 1980 elections.[98] Likewise, the failure of model 5 to improve over the fit of model 2 establishes that there are no more significant turnout trends among specific religious groups. Given that the control variables in model 6 result in a significant improvement in fit over model 2, model 6 is our preferred model of religious and voter turnout.

The coefficients of our preferred model (see Table 4.4) show that Jewish voters enjoy the highest rate of turnout among the seven groups. The next largest coefficient is for Catholics, with liberal and moderate Protestants following close behind. The small coefficients (.18 and .19) for conservative Protestants and seculars are not statistically significant, indicating that turnout rates among these two groups are not distinguishable from the 'other religion' category. While

TABLE 4.3. *Fit statistics[a] for logistic regression models of religious groups and voter turnout[b] 1960–1992* (N = 11,885)

Models	Fit statistics	
	−2 log-likelihood (d.f.)	BIC
1. Election Years, Religious Categories	12611.92 (11870)	−98,765
2. Carter Effect for Conservative Protestants	12601.70 (11869)	−98,766
3. Model 2 + Conservative Protestants x Year	12597.70 (11862)	−98,704
4. Model 2 + Preferred Model of Partisan Choice	12596.31 (11867)	−98,752
5. Model 2 + Religious Categories x Election Year	12542.30 (11822)	−98,384
6. Model 2 + Household Income,[c] Years of Education, Age, Region, Gender, Church Attendance	11143.84 (11861)	−100,14

   [a] Degrees of freedom are presented in parentheses; BIC for null model (including a constant only) is −98,519. Linearly constrained interactions designated by '*'; unconstrained interactions designated by 'x'.
   [b] Dependent variable is coded '1' for voted and '0' for did not vote; (African-American voters are excluded from the analyses).
   [c] Scaled to constant 1992 dollars.

TABLE 4.4 *Logistic regression coefficients[a] (s.e. in parentheses) for preferred models of religious groups and voter turnout[b] 1960–1992* (N = 11,885)

Independent variables	Preferred coefficients (s.e.)
Constant	−2.55* (.22)
Election years (reference = 1960)	
1964	−.55* (.13)
1968	−.80* (.12)
1972	−1.04* (.12)
1976	−1.18* (.12)
1980	−1.29* (.13)
1984	−1.00* (.12)
1988	−1.17* (.13)
1992	−.98* (.12)
Religious categories (reference = other religion)	
Liberal Protestants	.50* (.14)
Moderate Protestants	.59* (.14)
Conservative Protestants	.19 (.14)
Catholics	.64* (.13)
Jewish	1.01* (.24)
No religion	.18 (.15)
Religion by time interactions:	
Conservative Protestants x Year$_{1976/1980}$	.48* (.13)
Region (reference = Northeast)	
South	−.33* (.07)
Midwest	.10 (.07)
West	.06 (.08)
Regular church attendance (reference: less than regularly)	.68* (.05)
Gender (reference = male)	−.24* (.05)
Household income[c] (continuous, in 1,000s)	.02* (.01)
Years of education (continuous)	.19* (.01)
Age (continuous)	.03* (.01)

[a] An asterisk indicates significance at the .05 level (2-tailed test).
[b] Dependent variable is coded '1' for voted and '0' for did not voted.
[c] Scaled to constant 1992 dollars.

conservative Protestants are as unlikely as any other religious group to actually vote, the 1976 and 1980 elections are an exception. In these two elections, our model predicts their log-odds of voting increased by .48. The same force that elicited unusually high levels of Democratic Party support among conservative Protestants—the candidacy of a 'born-again' presidential candidate—also led to higher than average voting rates among this segment of the electorate.

In similar fashion to the earlier presentation of the presidential vote choice results, we summarize in Figure 4.3's panels our findings for religious voter turnout.[99] Five of the six trend lines are essentially flat, with 'other religion' showing a net increase in the likelihood of voting, and conservative Protestants experiencing a temporary, but sharp, boost in turnout in 1976 and 1980. Most importantly for the CR thesis, there is no evidence of increasing participation by conservative Protestants at the ballot box since 1980.

In Table 4.5, we consider religious group-specific trends in party identification during the 1960 to 1992 period. The OLS model whose coefficients we present includes our control variables, as well as an additional (linearly constrained) interaction for Southern residence and election year; the latter coefficient $(-.14, \text{s.e.} = .02)$ represents the well-known break-up of the solid, Democratic South. In addition to the main effects of religious group membership, we also estimate a series of interactions with time; these are all linear interactions with election year (coded '1' for 1960, '2' for 1964, . . . , and '9' for 1992) with the exception of Catholics, whose category is constrained to interact solely with the 1960 election (during which time their Democratic identification was unusually high).

The only two statistically significant religious group-by-year coefficients are for Catholics and liberal Protestants. This implies that trends in party identification among the five remaining religious groups are fully captured by the changes expressed in the election year (or region by year) coefficients. The main finding of interest relates to the trend for liberal Protestants. The statistically significant .10 coefficient translates into a sizable shift in party identification between 1960 and 1992— nearly a full point change (.90) on the seven-point scale in the direction of Democratic identification. This trend in party identification provides additional evidence that liberal Protestants' voting trend represents a *partisan* shift in political alignment, not merely a shift in voting patterns.

CATHOLIC VOTING BEHAVIOR SINCE 1952

Before any firm conclusions about change in Catholics' political alignment can be drawn, it is necessary to examine the period prior to the highly unusual 1960 (Kennedy) election. To test the hypothesis that Catholics have moved over time from consistently strong to weak Democratic Party support, we need to determine whether Catholics'

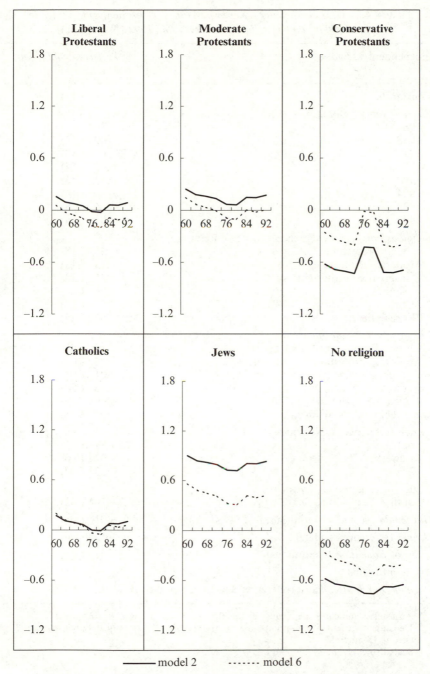

FIG. 4.3. Maximum likelihood estimates of group-specific religious voter turnout under preferred models 2 and 6, 1960–1992

TABLE 4.5. *OLS coefficients[a] (s.e. in parentheses) for analyzing trends in partisanship[b] among religious voters, 1960–1992* (N = 8,568)

Independent variables	Preferred coefficients (s.e.)
Constant	5.31* (.23)
Election years (reference = 1960)	
1964	.36* (.11)
1968	.09 (.12)
1972	.01 (.12)
1976	.02 (.14)
1980	−.12 (.16)
1984	−.08 (.16)
1988	−.25 (.18)
1992	.04 (.19)
Religious categories (reference = other religion)	
Liberal Protestants	−.45* (.18)
Moderate Protestants	−.14 (.18)
Conservative Protestants	.25 (.18)
Catholics	1.70* (.23)
Jewish	1.59* (.28)
No religion	.53 (.29)
Religion by time interactions	
Liberal Protestants * Year(linear)	.10* (.03)
Moderate Protestants * Year(linear)	.02 (.03)
Conservative Protestants * Year(linear)	.01 (.03)
Catholics x $Year_{1960}$	−.55* (.20)
Jewish * Year(linear)	.08 (.05)
No religion * Year(linear)	.05 (.05)
Region (reference = Northeast)	
South	1.32* (.12)
Midwest	.02 (.06)
West	.22* (.07)
Region by time interactions	
South * $Year_{1960–1992}$	−.14* (.02)
Household Income[c] (continuous, in 1,000s)	−.01* (.01)
Gender (reference = male)	.10* (.04)
Years of Education (continuous)	−.08* (.01)
Age (continuous)	−.01* (.01)
Regular church attendance (reference: less than regularly)	−.32* (.05)

[a] An asterisk indicates significance at the .05 level (2-tailed test); R^2 for model is .13.
[b] Dependent variable is a 7–point scale ranging between '1' (strong Republican) and '7' (strong Democrat.
[c] Scaled to constant 1992 dollars.

support in the 1950s for Democratic candidates (relative to other voters) was similar to their support for Kennedy over Nixon in 1960. If so, it would indicate that Catholics' 1964–1992 voting behavior represents a fundamental shift in their alignment with the Democratic Party (rather than a single election spike towards the Democratic Party in 1960).

To test this hypothesis, we present in Table 4.6 fit statistics for models of Catholic vote choice for the entire 1952 through 1992 period. Limitations in the information available on Protestant denominations prior to 1960 make it impossible to distinguish among Protestant voters, so for these analyses we treat them as the (homogeneous) reference category in our regressions.[100] While this limitation would be problematic for obtaining estimates during the post-1960s period of the analyses (during which time liberal Protestants diverge substantially in their vote choice, thus leading to greater political heterogeneity among Protestants), it should not introduce any bias into our estimates of the *Catholic* vote in the 1950s. Because our earlier analyses of presidential voting showed that all three Protestant denominational groups were very similar in their high levels of Republican Party support in the 1960s, they can be expected to show similarly homogeneous voting patterns in the 1950s.

Corroborating our earlier finding, model 2 (which adds a single interaction for Catholics in the 1960 election) improves over the fit of

TABLE 4.6. *Fit statistics[a] for logistic regression models of presidential vote choice[b] among Catholics vs. Protestants, 1952–1992* (N = 10,673)

Models	Fit Statistics	
	-2 log-likelihood (d.f.)	BIC
1. Election + Religion[c] Main Effects	13768.36 (10661)	$-85,117$
2. Kennedy Effect for Catholics (Catholics x Year$_{1960}$)	13710.82 (10660)	$-85,166$
3. Catholics x Year$_{1952/1956}$	13708.98 (10659)	$-85,159$
4. Catholics x Year	13692.72 (10651)	$-85,100$

[a] Degrees of freedom are presented in parentheses; BIC for null model (including only a constant) is $-84,531$. Linearly constrained interactions designated by '*'; unconstrained interactions designated by 'x'.

[b] Dependent variable is coded '1' for choice of Democratic presidential candidate, '0' for Republican Presidential candidate; (African-American voters are excluded from the analyses).

[c] Religious categories in the 1952–1992 analyses are: (homogeneous) Protestants and Catholics.

model 1 (which includes only terms for the main effects of religion and election year). In model 3, we add a second interaction for Catholics' vote choice in 1952 and 1956 to test whether their voting patterns in the 1950s differed from the remainder of the series. The clear lack of improvement in fit of model 3 over model 2 provides no support for this hypothesis.[101] Model 4's additional parameters (which allow the dummy variable for Catholics to interact freely with election year) also do not improve model 2's fit. These results establish a critical fact: Not only was Catholic support for the Democratic candidate in 1960 unusually high, their tendency to favor Democratic candidates in all other elections (relative to the corresponding preference of Protestant voters) shows no distinctive net trend (either towards or away from the Democratic Party) during the entire 1952 to 1992 period.[102] With the exception of 1960, Catholics' vote choice has fluctuated in tandem with rest of the electorate but without any shift in alignment away from (or towards) the Democratic Party since the 1950s. These results also imply that the post-1960 decline in the religious political cleavage is entirely a product of liberal Protestants' dealignment from the Republican Party.

Liberal Protestants' Voting Trend

Of the group-specific trends we have investigated, the trend for liberal Protestants is of greatest consequence for the religious cleavage. Whereas political change among Catholics and conservative Protestants is limited to one or two elections, liberal Protestants' changing voting behavior has steadily moved them from being the most Republican of any religious group to being nearly as likely to be Democratic in their presidential preference.

   Using the 1972 through 1992 NES surveys,[103] we explore some of the factors that might explain liberal Protestants' voting trend. The items we use for these analyses measure an array of potentially relevant causal factors that may account for the phenomenon at hand. We summarize these items in Table 4.7, along with their sample means for the election years defining the end-points of the trend: 1972 and 1992. Most of these means show net changes for the 1972–1992 period. But to determine whether these changes actually explain liberal Protestants' trend, we must first estimate their coefficients from a multivariate model. Once we have obtained these coefficients, we use a regression decomposition to derive estimates of the contribution of each item in the analyses to explain the liberal Protestant trend. These estimates are presented in Table 4.8.

TABLE 4.7. *Sample means for liberal Protestants, 1972 vs. 1992*

Independent variable (measurement)	1972	1992
Region (categorical: reference cat. = all other regions)		
South	.19	.25
Gender (categorical: reference cat. = Male)		
Female	.57	.49
Age (continuous)	45.98	50.39
Years of education (continuous)	13.37	14.02
Household income (continuous)	45,026.00	46,587.00
Church attendance (categorical: reference cat. = less than regularly)		
Regularly	.36	.33
Economic satisfaction (categorical: reference cat. = better off than year ago)		
Same as year ago	.49	.28
Worse off than year ago	.15	.39
Welfare state (continuous: higher scores indicate support for welfare state)	2.49	2.34
Gender equality (continuous: higher scores indicate support for egalitarianism)	3.80	4.87
Abortion (categorical: reference cat. = all else)		
Unconditional pro-choice position	.30	.59
Civil Rights Movement (categorical: reference cat. = moving too fast)		
Moving about right	.47	.63
Moving too slow	.07	.15

The estimates in the first column of this table are the change in presidential vote choice from 1972 to 1992 that is predicted using the regression coefficients and the change in the item's sample mean. The estimates in the second column (in parentheses) are the proportion of the total (predicted) change in vote choice among liberal Protestants attributable to a row-specific factor. Using the results for gender as our example, the −.01 estimate indicates that on the basis of a decrease in the proportion of female liberal Protestants since 1972, we predict a very slight shift towards support for Republican candidates among liberal Protestants as a whole. The accompanying −.03 estimate in parentheses shows that the explanatory power of gender as a causal factor is low. In fact, the estimate is negatively signed because the actual (as well as the predicted) overall change in liberal Protestants' vote choice is towards Democratic candidates (and thus is positively signed).

TABLE 4.8. *Logistic regression decomposition for explaining trend in vote choice among liberal Protestants, 1972–1992*

Independent variable	Estimates[a]
Region	.00 (.00)
Gender	−.01 (−.03)
Age	−.01 (−.03)
Years of education	−.04 (−.11)
Household income	−.02 (−.06)
Church attendance	.01 (.03)
Economic satisfaction	.11 (.31)
Welfare state attitudes	−.05 (−.14)
Gender attitudes	.07 (.20)
Abortion attitudes	.15 (.43)
Civil Rights attitudes	.14 (.40)
Σ LOGIT CHANGE IN PARTISAN VOTE CHOICE, 1972–1992	.35 (1.00)

[a] Column entries are the predicted change in the log-odds of Democratic vote choice attributable to a row-specific factor; figures in parentheses are the proportion of the total logit change attributable to a row-specific factor.

Taken together, the first six factors relating to sociodemographic and church attendance do not explain the liberal Protestant trend. In fact, they predict a turn towards support for Republican candidates during this period. Lower rates of personal economic satisfaction during Republican presidential administrations, by contrast, have a positive impact on Democratic vote choice, explaining just over 30% of the trend. The next factor, relating to attitudes towards the welfare state, is negatively signed. This indicates that declining liberal Protestant support for the welfare state would have by itself intensified their alignment with the Republican Party.

The main part of the causal story is summarized in the last three rows of Table 4.8. These results show that liberal Protestants have become increasingly liberal in their views of social issues relating to gender, abortion, and race; attitudinal change on these issues explains an impressive 103% of the trend. The fact that this proportion exceeds 100% shows that, by itself, the expansion of socially liberal attitudes would have resulted in a slightly larger trend toward the Democrats. Of these three factors, abortion attitudes explain the largest share (43%) of the (predicted) trend, but gender attitudes (20%) and views of the civil rights movement (40%) also have had a very substantial impact.

Conservative Protestants and Southern Baptists

Our final set of analyses return to the case of conservative Protestants and the CR thesis. Our results for the analyses of the 1960 through 1992 period found no evidence of a mobilization or realignment among denominationally conservative Protestants. However, to maintain consistency over the entire time-series we placed all Baptists in the conservative Protestant category. It is, however, possible that Southern Baptists—the largest evangelical denomination in the United States— did in fact undergo a shift to the right. This shift could be undetectable in our analysis of the conservative Protestant category if, for instance, Southern Baptists were moving further towards the Republican Party at the same time that their Northern counterparts were moving away from the GOP. These divergent trends would thus cancel one another out leaving the 'conservative Protestant' category trendless. To test this hypothesis, we use the NES's more detailed information on religious denomination (available for the 1972 through 1992 surveys) to distinguish among conservative Protestants and between Northern and Southern Baptists. Using a dummy variable coded '1' for Southern Baptists (and '0' for the remainder of the 'conservative' Protestant category), we analyze the evidence for trends in presidential vote choice within the larger category of conservative Protestants.

The results summarized in Table 4.9 provide no evidence for the hypothesis of a Southern Baptist shift. The −1 BIC improvement of

TABLE 4.9. *Fit statistics[a] for logistic regression models of presidential vote choice[b] among conservative Protestants, 1972–1992 (N = 1,419)*

Models	Fit statistics	
	−2 log-likelihood (d.f.)	BIC
1. Election Year	1764.20 (1413)	−8,491
2. Southern Baptist[c] Main Effect	1755.42 (1412)	−8,492
3. Southern Baptist * Year	1755.10 (1411)	−8,486
4. Southern Baptist x Year	1747.35 (1407)	−8,464

[a] Degrees of freedom are presented in parentheses; BIC for null model (including only a constant) is −8,465. Linearly constrained interactions designated by '*'; unconstrained interactions designated by 'x'.
[b] Dependent variable is coded '1' for choice of Democratic presidential candidate, '0' for Republican Presidential candidate; (African-American voters are excluded from the analyses).
[c] Dummy variable coded '1' for Southern Baptists, '0' for Northern Baptists and other conservative Protestants.

model 2 (adding to model 1 a term for the main effect of the Baptist variable) provides weak but positive evidence that Southern Baptists' vote choice differed from the rest of the conservative Protestant category during the 1972 through 1992 period. The coefficient for Southern Baptist dummy variable (.39, s.e. = .13) is, however, positively signed, indicating that Southern Baptists were in fact slightly *more* likely than other conservative Protestants to favor Democratic candidates from 1972 through 1992. With respect to political change, either a linear trend parameter for Southern Baptists (model 3), nor a set of unconstrained interactions of (Southern) Baptist with election (model 4) improve over model 2's fit. In short, there is no evidence of the 'right-turn' among Southern Baptists predicted by the CR thesis.

CONCLUSION

The results of this chapter give modest support to arguments that the religious political cleavage has experienced a small decline in magnitude. Yet our analyses also show that the explanation for this development is not consistent with either secularization models or theories of the declining significance of denominationalism. Rather, it is the striking changes among one important group of Protestants—liberal Protestant denominations—that has driven these changes. Growing affluence within historically disadvantaged churches, the rise of denominational switching, and increasing rates of religious intermarriage have not resulted in changes to the underlying political alignments of the major denominations.

Scholars using dichotomous or trichotomous measures of the religious cleavage have also concluded that declines in the religious cleavage are due to the growing political similarity of Catholics and Protestants. But these formulations do not capture the full story. Our analyses using a seven-category scheme show that the religious cleavage has narrowed precisely because of the growing political *heterogeneity* of Protestant denominations. Instead of being a function of conservative Protestants' behavior (which shows no net trends) or the behavior of all Protestants, the decline in the religious cleavage is a function of changes in the voting behavior of liberal Protestants, who have fallen out of the earlier, Republican political alignment they shared with moderate and conservative Protestants towards a more neutral alignment.

Second, we find no evidence for a political realignment or mobilization among denominationally conservative Protestants. Ironically, the only trend we find for presidential vote choice and turnout among conservative Protestants (relative to the mean) relates to their higher than expected levels of turnout and support for (Democrat) Jimmy Carter in 1976 and 1980.[104] This does not mean that a 'new' Christian Right cannot be identified, but that its base cannot be located denominationally.[105] Rates of voter turnout among this group are notable not because of any trend towards greater participation, but rather because of their comparatively low (and relatively unchanging) turnout level. Given that conservative Protestants were in a Republican alignment prior to the rise of conservative evangelical activists, the challenge for these activists continues to be one of leading conservative Protestants to the ballot box in the first place.

Third, our results suggest that claims about the dealignment of Catholic voters have been significantly overstated. We conclude that with the exception of the unusual 1960 election, Catholics have maintained above-average support for the Democratic Party since 1952, once we factor into the analysis the decline in the popularity of Democratic presidential candidates among all religious groups during this period. Our results for Catholics also show that taking 1960 as a baseline would yield a misleading portrait of political trends. This is because the Catholic vote for Kennedy was high in 1960 not because it was a continuation of the pattern from the elections of the 1950s, but instead because Catholics became momentarily more Democratic in their party identification and presidential voting preferences.

Finally, we have shown that the single most important source of change in the relationship between religious group membership and political behavior involves liberal Protestants and their eroding support for Republican candidates. Given the historical period covered by our analyses, our findings present a highly consistent portrait of the mechanisms explaining this voting trend. Since the 1960s, liberal Protestants have been under pressure from a clergy that has grown considerably more receptive to calls for a variety of social changes. These included past opposition to the Vietnam war and concern with civil rights and civil liberties, as well as more recent struggles to bring women into the clergy and to allow participation of gays and lesbians. Further, since the pivotal Goldwater campaign of 1964—coinciding with the origins of liberal Protestants' voting trend—socially conservative activists have made considerable inroads into the Republican Party.

Opposition to the increasingly conservative Republican agenda appear to have pushed liberal Protestants away from their traditional alignment with the Republican Party.

Overall, however, the religious cleavage has been surprisingly robust. Conservative Protestants, despite being less affluent than liberal Protestants, remain staunchly Republican in their political alignment, whereas Catholics, despite relative economic gains, have occupied a consistently (moderate) Democratic alignment in relation to other voters. Jewish voters, most notably, have remained Democratic Party stalwarts. These results imply that modernizing forces and institutional changes affecting churches and religious denominations may not necessarily alter the religious cleavage to the degree predicted by the classic secularization model.

APPENDIX: MAJOR DENOMINATIONAL CODING SCHEME

- Liberal Protestants
    Congregational/United Church of Christ
    Episcopalian/Anglican
    Methodist (except Nazarene/Free Methodist)
    Unitarian/Universalist
- Moderate Protestants
    Presbyterian
    Lutheran (except Missouri Synod Lutheran)
    Evangelical and Reformed Protestants
    Reform, Dutch Reformed, or Christian Reformed
    African Methodist Episcopal Church
    Protestants n.e.c.
    'Christian' n.e.c.
- Conservative Protestants
    Baptists (including Southern Baptists and Primitive/Free Will Baptists)
    Pentecostal/Assemblies of God
    Holiness/Church of God
    Plymouth Brethren
    Seventh Day Adventist
    Missouri Synod Lutheran
    Fundamentalist, n.e.c.
    Church of the Nazarene

- Catholics
    Roman Catholic Church
    Greek Rite Catholic
- Jewish:
    Conservative
    Reformed
- Other:
    Christian Scientist
    Jehovah's Witnesses
    Mennonite Church
    Mormon Church
    Eastern Orthodox
    Non-Judeo Christians (Buddhist, Hindu, Muslim, etc.)
    Quaker
    Salvation Army
- None
    Agnostic, Atheist
    No Preference

5

Gender

The existence of a clear and persistent gender cleavage in recent national elections is a relatively unique feature of American politics. No similar 'gender gap' has developed in other democratic polities.[1] The size of the gender gap has often been larger than the margin of victory for Democratic candidates in recent presidential or congressional elections. For both Democratic and Republican political strategists, the gender gap has become a matter of intense concern. After decades of slowly increasing their initially lower levels of participation in national elections, women voters since 1980 have participated at higher rates than men.[2]

Not surprisingly, then, appeals designed to attract the 'women's vote' have become commonplace in recent elections. A couple of recent examples of gender-centered strategic maneuvering, reported by the *New York Times* in late 1996 exemplify the major parties' keen interest in the gender gap:

Seeking to insure a strong turnout from a crucial voting bloc, President Clinton made a special appeal to women today by highlighting Government efforts to fight breast cancer and telling a rally audience in Virginia that the election is 'not about party, it's about you.' . . . Clinton stressed the health care, education and child-based themes that have been central to his campaign and that have a particular resonance with women.[3]

Republican governors today were given a sobering presentation of their party's troubles with female voters, and told that a more compassionate tone and a focus on education were the cure. The presentation, at the closing session of a three-day meeting of the Republican Governors' Association, came from Haley Barbour, the Republican national chairman, who said that according to the party's own research, Bob Dole and Republican Congressional candidates fared even worse among women on Election Day than had been suggested by exit polls taken by the news media.[4]

As these reports suggest, the partisan implications of the gender gap are straightforward: Republicans seek ways to narrow the gender gap, while Democrats regularly court additional support from women voters.[5]

The gender gap has also been used by women's political groups and feminist social movement organizations as a means of gaining leverage and influence within both parties. The possibility that a distinct 'women's vote' has emerged provides an important source of momentum for policy initiatives which can be tied to that vote.[6] While claims about such a vote have frequently been exaggerated, they have served as a powerful weapon for women's groups in appealing to political elites. For example, in the aftermath of the 1980 election a number of feminist analysts and activists argued that Reagan lost votes among women because of his opposition to the ERA. The implication was clear: adopt policy stances supported by women's groups or lose significant votes.[7]

The logic of group cleavages outlined in Chapter 2 suggests, however, that political analysts and strategists are mistaken to assume a one-to-one correspondence between gender differences in voting and the overall outcome of elections. The simple percentage difference in support provided by men and women for Democratic (or Republican) candidates is often independent of the total vote received by either party's candidates. For example, a 20-point gender gap in a two-candidate race in which women split their vote 50/50 while 70% of men voters choose the Republican candidate results in both a very large gender gap as well as a Republican landslide. It is thus misleading to think that the existence of an increasing gender gap in national elections will, by itself, produce significant partisan advantage for the Democrats. None the less, the growth of the gender cleavage is important because it has reshaped the group foundations of the major party coalitions, a point developed in more detail in Chapter 7.

In this chapter our focus is on the origins and development of the gender gap in the political alignments of women and men. In the course of our discussion, we tackle three questions. First, *when* did the current gender gap emerge, and how has it evolved over time? Second, why did a gender gap emerge, and why has it grown? Not surprisingly, a number of theories have been developed to explain this phenomenon. We describe these theories as a necessary prelude to our empirical analyses of the gender gap in presidential voting. Finally, building from the results of those analyses, we advance a theory of the gap emphasizing the centrality of rising labor force participation rates among women.

WHAT IS THE 'GENDER GAP' IN
AMERICAN POLITICS?

Recent elections have been accompanied by extensive commentary on the magnitude and causes of the gender gap in voting; as the political scientist M. Kent Jennings has put it, trying to explain the gender gap has become a veritable 'national pastime'.[8] Not surprisingly, the precise nature of the gap is the subject of considerable debate. Indeed, there are at least five recognizable and distinct political gender gaps that have been discussed by scholars, political analysts, and journalists.

First, there have been extensive discussions about turnout differences between men and women—a subject we address separately in Chapter 7. Second, there is a gender gap in the arena of officeholding.[9] Women are significantly less likely to run for (and consequently hold) political office. The number of elected female officeholders at all levels of government has, however, increased to the point that women now hold 20% of all state legislative offices. Women have also gone from very marginal influence on the two major parties to having increasingly significant access to positions of influence within each party's hierarchy. All recent presidents have appointed several women to their cabinets, although none has come close to having as many women as men. Despite such advances, however, women hold a mere 10% of all seats in Congress, and the struggle for equal representation will thus be likely to continue into the foreseeable future.

A third gender gap lies in the contrasting views of men and women across a range of policy issues. Two types of attitudinal differences between men and women have been the focus of scholarly attention. In comparison to women, men have traditionally been more willing to use force to resolve international conflicts, and to support an aggressive military posture (especially vis-à-vis the Soviet Union and its' allies prior to the fall of Communism).[10] Such differences may lead to greater female support for presidential candidates advocating more moderate defense policies.[11] Other analysts have focused on domestic policy concerns, especially the comparatively greater support of women for social provision than men.[12] Women are often viewed as more likely to support programs that aim to provide a safety net for poor families and their children or measures that promote equality.[13]

The gender gap that is the primary subject of this chapter is, however, the persistent difference in vote choice between men and women. These differences have been found in both congressional and presidential elections. In congressional races, post-election surveys have typically found wide variation in the size of the gender gap in different campaigns.[14] Most of the existing literature, however, has focused on recent presidential campaigns. In spite of this interest, there have been few scholarly attempts to develop systematic empirical understandings of the historical *origins* of the gender gap in voting have been undertaken. Most past research investigates only one or a small number of elections, with virtually none going back before the 1970s (and the emergence of the contemporary women's movement).

WHEN DID THE GENDER GAP EMERGE?

To understand the gender gap, we must first develop an analysis of its historical origins. Discussions about the possibility of a distinct 'women's vote' date to the struggle over enfranchisement (1920).[15] But most studies have taken the 1980 election as the beginning of a distinct gender cleavage in national politics; indeed, we have found no fewer than twenty analysts who date the origins of the gap to this election.[16] A number of historical events lend initial support for this interpretation. In 1980, reversing decades of Republican support for women's rights, Ronald Reagan's presidential campaign attacked the Equal Rights Amendment (which had been supported by Gerald Ford in 1976), endorsed 'traditional' values (including a renewed emphasis on protecting and sanctioning intact two-parent families with a male breadwinner and a female housewife/mother), and strongly opposed the right of women to choose an abortion (including support for a Constitutional amendment which would have banned virtually all abortions). Reagan also endorsed a very aggressive military posture which spoke openly of a campaign to 'roll back' Communism (rather than simply 'containing' it), which many analysts hypothesized as further alienating women voters. Moreover, in the 1990s the Reagan wing of the Republican Party had emerged triumphant, with most Republicans in national politics supporting a conservative social issue agenda. The distance between the Republican and Democratic Parties on many issues of special concern to women widened from the 1970s to the 1990s at the same as the gender gap emerged as a significant factor in American political life. These considerations imply that increasing numbers of women began voting for the Democratic Party because the Republican Party had abandoned its previous support for policies of importance to women.[17]

This is the conventional wisdom concerning the historical origins of the gender gap.[18] There is, to be sure, plenty of room for different explanations for why a gender gap emerged in 1980. In this chapter, however, we begin by challenging the view that the gender gap emerged in 1980. Instead, we believe it is more fruitful to view the emergence of the gender gap as a gradual process which had its origins in the 1950s. Figure 5.1 summarizes the direction in which our argument proceeds. The figure's left-hand panel shows the changing size of the gender gap using raw data from the National Election Studies (and the Voter News Service data for the 1996 Presidential election). The estimates suggest that the gender gap has grown over much of the NES series, but election-to-election fluctuations make the underlying trends hard to discern. The estimates in Figure 5.1's right-hand panel bring the under-lying pattern of political change into sharper focus.[19] These estimates reveal a growing trend since 1952 which peaked but did not begin in 1980.

   Systematic analysis of the historical evidence suggests that much of the debate about the gender gap has been miscast. Rather than 1980 representing a sharp departure from the past, it was merely the dra-matic culmination of a long process through which women voters became progressively more Democratic *relative* to men. Instead of asking what made 1980 a critical election for the emergence of the gender gap, we must accordingly examine the factors behind the long historical trend that had by 1980 produced a gender gap.

THEORIZING THE GENDER GAP

The classical works of political behavior in the first two decades after World War II offered a portrait of women voters as consistently more conservative than men. Maurice Duverger's influential 1955 book *The Political Role of Women* presented evidence that when the voting pat-terns of men and women diverged in Norway, France, and Germany, women were more likely to support conservative parties. Other scholars reported similar findings in countries such as Australia, Greece, Finland, Switzerland, Britain, and Italy.[20] In the United States, evidence of the greater support of women for Republican candidates had been presented as early as 1924.[21] Columbia School analysts Bernard Berelson and Paul Lazarsfeld made the argument that women voters were likely to remain in a conservative alignment in 1945, and pollster Louis Harris's 1954 book *Is There a Republican Majority?* included women in that majority.[22] Summarizing the conventional

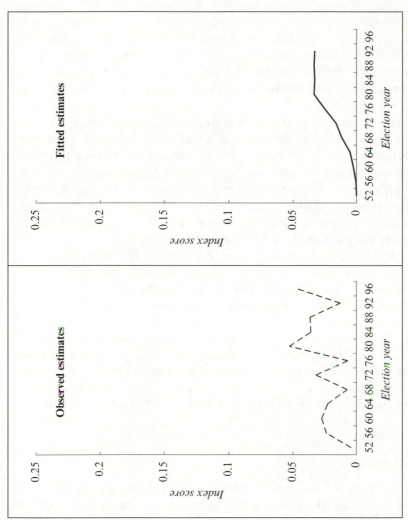

Fig. 5.1 The emergence of the gender gap in presidential elections, 1952–1996
Note: Index scores are calculated by taking the standard deviation of the observed or
fitted probabilities of Democratic vote choice among women and men.

wisdom in 1960, Lipset asserted in *Political Man* that 'Women, particularly housewives, are less involved in the intra-class communications structure, see fewer politically knowledgeable people with backgrounds and interests similar to their own, and are therefore more likely to retain the dominant conservative values of the larger culture'.[23] Gabriel Almond and Sidney Verba similarly suggested that 'Wherever the consequences of women's suffrage have been studied, it would appear that women differ from men in their political behavior only in being somewhat more frequently apathetic, parochial, conservative, and sensitive to the personality, emotional, and esthetic aspects of political life and electoral campaigns'.[24]

The resurgence of women's liberation and second wave feminist movements beginning in the late 1960s and early 1970s, coupled with the accumulation of evidence that women were now turning out to vote at levels comparable to men (but supporting different candidates) had by the early 1980s led to renewed efforts to rethink the fundamental assumptions of the scholarly classics of the 1940s and 1950s. How could women begin to vote differently than men if they were apathetic or simply following the lead of their husbands?

The newer literature has suggested four distinct explanations for the gender gap. First, there are approaches which emphasize differences in the gender socialization of men and women. These differences are seen as shaping men's and women's basic values and orientations. Second, there are approaches that stress the growing autonomy of women fueled by high divorce rates and increasing economic opportunities. Third, a number of analysts have emphasized the role of rising levels of feminist consciousness among women since the 1960s. Finally, there are approaches emphasizing the importance of the increasing participation of women in the paid labor-force as a factor influencing their political outlooks.[25]

Gender Socialization Models

The first set of theories emphasizes the importance of the different patterns of socialization experienced by women and men in shaping core values, political orientations, and behavior. Two distinct strands of such gender-centered social-psychological research can be identified. First, there are approaches that emphasize the importance of childhood socialization.[26] Although often disagreeing on particulars, these interpretations share an emphasis on gender differences in political behavior as stemming from sex roles learned during childhood socialization. In the influential argument of Carol Gilligan, 'the moral imperative that emerges repeatedly in interviews with women is an injunction to care, a responsibility to discern and alleviate the "real and recognizable trouble" of this world. For men, the moral imperative appears rather as an injunction to respect the rights of others and thus to protect from interference the right to life and self-fulfillment.'[27] There is some evidence suggesting that when it comes to economic issues, women are more likely to endorse 'sociotropic' concerns (i.e. concerns about the economic health of the nation) while men are more likely to express 'egocentric' concerns relating to their own (or their family's) economic well-being.[28]

By contrast, a second set of adult socialization approaches emphasize the ways in which the effects of childhood socialization are mediated by adult roles.[29] The most important of these is the experience of motherhood and parenting—activities that continue to be disproportionately carried out by women (despite some evidence of increased co-parenting).[30] In their roles as mothers, Sara Ruddick argues that women develop a 'maternal' mode of thinking. Maternal thinking is shaped by the caring work performed by mothers, and women are said to project this thinking into their conceptualization of the larger society.[31]

As the party that has, since the New Deal, stood for a greater governmental role in insuring the well-being of individuals and families, the Democratic Party may be seen as more attractive to women who have been socialized to value nurturing activities. To be sure, the political context in which elections are contested will have much to do with whether or not deeply rooted gender ideologies are activated.[32] Applied to the gender voting cleavage, socialization approaches imply that as the Republican Party—beginning with Goldwater in 1964, but especially since 1980—adopted an anti-government posture, women's greater concerns with protecting children and the weakest members of society have caused them to turn towards the Democrats.

A second way of linking socialization processes to voting emphasizes differences between men and women in their attitudes towards the use of force. As noted earlier, the largest consistent policy conflicts between men and women are over issues concerning militarism and the use of force to solve foreign policy conflicts or domestic social problems. A number of analysts have argued that the gender gap in voting reflects these differences in policy preferences. Women voters are said to be attracted to presidential candidates advocating more moderate approaches to the use of force.[33] However, it is not clear whether these

arguments can explain the gender gap in voting. One important
problem is that they cannot account for the trends in gender voting
differences. The most careful assessments have suggested that while
there is an attitudinal gap between men and women on force/military
issues, that gap has been stable since the 1960s.[34] Second, there is also
considerable variability (and frequent convergence) in the major parties' national and domestic security policy stances over the forty-year
period from the 1950s to the 1990s.[35] Third, it has been well-established
that foreign and defense policy issues generally have low salience for
most voters. In view of these considerations, we do not pursue analyses
of the 'force' hypothesis in this chapter.

Gender socialization approaches usually share the view that political
differences between men and women are derived from general patterns
of sex-role differentiation, rather than the social or economic interests
of subsets of women. As a consequence, sociodemographic group memberships should not lead to divergent political behavior among women.
Defending this inference, Jean Bethke Elshtain argues that

The gender gap is real and it concerns what political scientists like to call
'moral issues,' which traditionally have been the purview of women and, for
that reason, often in the past labeled 'social questions,' not properly political
ones.. . . [O]n questions of conscriptions, militarization, nuclear weapons,
capital punishment, and environmental safeguards, statistically significant differences show up between the categories 'all men' and 'all women.' These
differences cut across class and education and hold whether the woman in
question is employed or not.[36]

Similarly, David O. Sears and Leonie Huddy argue that political
divisions among women 'go back in large part, if not completely, to
political socialization in earlier life', and that their empirical work
suggests that 'interest-related differences were dwarfed by differences
based on predispositions, as in much earlier research'.[37] The socialization model of the gender gap would thus be challenged, albeit indirectly,
by evidence that differences among women and also between women
and men are related to economic interests.

The Growing Autonomy of Women

A second possible source of the growing gender gap is the increase in
women's autonomy brought about by changes in family structures,
especially rising divorce rates. One proponent of this thesis, Susan
Carroll, suggests that 'the autonomy explanation emphasizes that
unmarried women may express different political views and choices

from those of married women or men because unmarried women are able to make independent assessments of their political interests, unconstrained and undominated by the political interests of individual men'.[38] Some early commentators on gender politics asserted that married women tend to follow the political leads of their husbands because of their lack of economic independence. Rather than viewing this subordination as a natural state of affairs, feminist scholars have argued that the routine functioning of the sexual division of labor tends to reinforce gender inequalities.[39] The interdependence of men and women in marriage may give them common material interests and thus lead to similar political preferences. As Carroll puts it, 'the wife and husband . . . have a common interest in the rate of inflation, the condition of the stock market, the husband's veteran benefits, and the availability of public transportation.'[40] Such common interests may override other sources of division between men and women to produce electoral convergence within families.[41]

However, changes in marriage patterns since the 1960s have reduced this dependence. Women are postponing marriage, are much more likely to become divorced, and a small but increasing number of women are choosing not to marry at all.[42] The average age of first marriage for women rose from 20.3 in 1960 to 24.4 by 1992.[43] Approximately half of all marriages can be expected to end in divorce, so while there were only 35 divorced persons for every 1,000 married adults in 1960, by 1992 there were 152.[44] The overall percentage of unmarried women increased from 37% in 1960 to 47% in 1992 as a result of these changes.

A plausible argument can be made that currently divorced, widowed, or single women will have different material interests (and ultimately voting preferences) than those of married women. For example, the economic consequences of divorce disproportionately hurt women.[45] Such inequalities may encourage women to support the Democrats as the party that has been more supportive of social provision. Some analysts have indeed developed arguments centered on the rising independence or autonomy of women as a possible source of the gender gap. Kathleen Frankovic reports that 'sex differences in support for Ronald Reagan in 1980 were smallest in two adult, one male, one female households. Consensus within a household in the course of living together does appear to minimize sex differences.' Carroll's analyses attempt to show that the gender gap in the 1980 and 1982 national elections can be attributed to the growing number of women who are psychologically and/or economically independent from a husband. Unmarried women were significantly less likely to back Ronald Reagan than married women.[46]

The political role of increased independence among women is related to—and possibly confounded by—the existence of a 'marriage gap' that has developed in recent elections. This division is one in which married persons (of both genders) are significantly more Republican than unmarried persons.[47] The existence of a marriage gap suggests that both men and women are propelled towards a Democratic alignment (relative to married persons) by virtue of living outside of marriage.[48]

Feminist Consciousness

The third mechanism we consider in this chapter concerns the rise of feminist consciousness as a factor influencing the vote choice of women. The revival of a large and diverse women's movement in the 1960s profoundly influenced all spheres of social life in the United States. In mass politics, however, figuring out the precise impact of the women's movement on voter alignments is complex. Most women—certainly after the initial phase of grassroots mobilization of the early 1970s—had either little or no direct personal involvement with women's organizations. But almost all women (and men) are aware of the goals of the women's movement, and a number of scholars have argued that changing attitudes towards that movement may have contributed to the growth of the gender gap. For example, Pamela J. Conover argues that much of the gender differences in policy attitudes can be traced to the greater prevalence of feminist identities among women. Another recent study of presidential voting reports that net of controls for partisanship, political ideology, and sociodemographic factors, feminist women were significantly more supportive of Democratic Presidential candidates in 1972, 1984, and 1988 than their non-feminist counterparts. A number of other scholars have reported similar findings.[49]

There is evidence of increasing feminist identities among women. Since 1972, the National Election Study has asked respondents to rate their views of the women's movement using a 0–100 point 'thermometer' where degrees reflect positive or negative feelings. These data provide evidence for change in feminist identities among women. In 1972, women's 'warmth' average rating of the 'women's liberation movement' was 45 degrees in 1972. By 1976, women's mean climbed to 54, continuing upwards to 59 in 1984. In 1988, a differently-worded NES item referring to 'feminists' yielded a lower average rating of 53 among women, while in 1992 another different question wording (asking about the 'women's movement') yielded a thermometer mean of 65. In spite of these wording changes, the 1972–84 data provide clear evidence of a 'warming' trend in the attitudes of women with respect to feminist identity.

How and in what ways might identification with the women's movement influence voting? At one level, the answer is obvious: the Democrats have often embraced the policy goals of women's movement organizations, while the Republicans (for most of the period we are examining) have not. But at another level, it is not so simple. Men can also endorse feminist policy goals, and on many surveys they have been shown to be as, or more, supportive of key feminist policy goals such as reproductive rights or gender equality.[50] Such complexities in attitudes relating to gender issues calls into question whether there are sufficient differences between women and men's views of the women's movement to explain the gender gap.

Women's Rising Labor Force Participation and the Gender Gap

The final approach to explaining the gender gap we consider comes from interpretations stressing the political importance of the increasing proportion of women in the paid labor force. Labor force participation (LFP) rates for women have risen throughout the twentieth century, but especially in recent decades. Between 1950 and 1994, the proportion of women of prime working years (25 to 54) in the paid labor force increased from 37% to 75%. Perhaps even more striking, 67% of women with children were employed, a figure larger than that of all women (59%).[51]

Why might women's participation in the labor force influence their political views? Most fundamentally, the growing participation of women in the workforce has not abolished wage inequalities between men and women. Women's wages have remained significantly below those of men overall, despite recent improvements for some women.[52] Job segregation by sex remains a central factor of the employment structure in the United States, with women being concentrated in jobs paying lower wages than jobs primarily controlled by men.[53] Direct exposure to these inequalities may thus dispose women voters to be more supportive of Democratic presidential candidates.

A number of scholars have also hypothesized that paid work exposes voters to discussions of candidates, policy debates, and other information about political campaigns that are less available to those without work (e.g. housewives).[54] While information per se may not explain the gender gap, it may nevertheless enable working women to develop independent political perspectives. The same employment-related factors that increase turnout may provide women with a context for translating their individual concerns into a larger political worldview. Issues such as workplace gender inequality, sexual harassment, wage inequalities, and job segregation may cause women voters to support the Democrats as the party more likely to promote public policies that would challenge traditional male dominance in the workplace.[55]

Other analysts have argued that employment enhances women's support for feminist goals.[56] These approaches hypothesize that employment provides women with life experiences that call into question traditional gender role ideologies. In the 1950s, many social scientists assumed that women worked only during those periods of the life-course when it did not interfere with the raising of children.[57] However, the labor market activity of most women today differs substantially from that mid-century portrait. Far fewer women are willing (or able) to completely disrupt their work lives to raise children, and many women take much shorter leaves when they do stop working to raise children.[58] If the growth of career-oriented employment patterns reduces women's acceptance of traditional values, this may dispose them to turn away from the contemporary Republican Party.

Summary: Theoretical Approaches to the Gender Gap

The existing literature on gender politics suggests four distinct causal mechanisms that may explain the origins and development of the gender cleavage in U.S. politics. The *gender socialization* thesis emphasizes the divergent core values of men and women. The socialization processes discussed by adherents of this approach are said to be experienced by all women and men, thus implying that the gender gap is present within all sociodemographic categories. Evidence to the contrary thus calls the socialization thesis into question. The *women's autonomy* thesis predicts that women who are economically and psychologically independent of men should be the most likely to differ politically. We test this claim by examining the effects of marital status and level of education, two proxies for women's autonomy. The *feminist consciousness* thesis predicts that women who identify with the women's movement should be the most likely to vote Democratic. Finally, the labor force participation thesis predicts that working women should be the most likely to be Democratic, and that the growth of the gender gap in electoral politics in turn reflects the increasing proportion of such women in the electorate as a whole.

ANALYSES

As in the previous chapters, our analyses use data from the 1952–92 NES series. As before, our dependent variable, partisan vote choice, is coded '1' for the Democrat and '0' for the Republican candidate in presidential elections. Table 5.1 summarizes the variables we use to measure the potential causes of the gender gap. Gender is coded as a dichotomy (women = 1; men = 0). Since a number of analysts have found a relationship between class divisions and the gender gap,[59] we utilize three measures of class: objective class location, subjective class identification (working-class identification = 1; 0 otherwise), and household income (scaled to 1992 dollars). We use the same measure of objective class location (distinguishing professionals, managers, owners and proprietors, routine white-collar workers, foremen and skilled

TABLE 5.1. *Coding of independent variables in the analyses*

Independent variable	Coding
Variables in the 1952–1992 analyses	
Partisan vote choice (dichotomy)	GOP voter = 0; Democratic voter = 1
Gender (dichotomy)	men = 0; women = 1
Linear year covariate (continuous)	1952 = 1, 1956 = 2, . . . , 1992 = 11
Class location (categorical; reference = non-labor force participant)	dummies for professionals, managers, routine white-collar, self-employed, skilled workers, and nonskilled
Subjective class identification (dichotomy)	all else = 0; working-class = 1
Labor force participation (dichotomy)	non-participant = 0; participant = 1
Years of education (continuous)	1 year = 1, 2 years = 2, . . . , 17+ years = 17
Marital status (dichotomy)	not married = 0; married = 1
Household income (continuous)	scaled to constant 1992 dollars
Race (dichotomy)	all else = 0; African American = 1
Region (categorical; reference = Northeast)	3 non-redundant dummy variables for residence in South, Midwest, or West
Cohort (categorical; reference = all else)	3 non-redundant dummies for fifties, sixties, and seventies generations
Variables in the analyses of recent elections	Likert item: women should stay at home = 1, . . . , should have an equal role = 7
Gender role attitudes (continuous)	
Views of social services (continuous)	Likert item: cut spending/services = 1 , . . . , increase spending/services = 7
Views of women's movement (continuous)	Feeling Thermometer Score: 0–100°

workers, nonskilled workers) used in previous chapters. We also use a
new dichotomous variable to analyze the effects of labor force participation (employed more than 20 hours a week = 1). The class and LFP
variables enable us to test hypotheses about the role of work as a factor
shaping women's political attitudes and behavior.

To assess the possibility that generational shifts are related to the
emergence of the gender gap,[60] we analyze the impact of generational
membership on vote choice. This is measured by three dummy variables
for fifties, sixties, and seventies cohorts. Fifties cohort membership is
defined as respondents born between 1933 and 1944; sixties cohort is
defined as respondents born between 1945 and 1962; and the seventies
cohort is defined as respondents born since 1963. We evaluate the
women's autonomy thesis with a marital status variable, coded as a
dichotomy (married = 1), and controls for years of education. We also
control for race (African-Americans = 1), and region (three dummy
variables for South, Midwest, and West residence).

We use three scales to examine the possible roles of differences in
policy attitudes and feminist consciousness in accounting for the gender
gap. Unfortunately, these variables are only available for our analyses of
recent presidential elections (1980–1992). However, as will become
clearer in the course of our analyses, the results also have implications
for the earlier years in which we cannot measure these variables. The
first item is a seven-point scale measuring support for social services in
which respondents indicate their preference for increasing social service
spending or cutting spending by decreasing social services. The other
two items measure attitudes that relate to the feminist consciousness
thesis. Both are seven-point Likert items, which we treat as continuous
variables. The first of these is a gender equality item asking whether
women and men should have equal roles in the family and the workplace. In this item, response category '1' indicates the greatest support
for the view that 'women's place is in the home', and '7' indicates the
greatest support for the view that 'women should have an equal role
with men in running business, industry, and government'. The second
item is a feeling thermometer that asks respondents to rate how warmly
they feel towards the women's movement. Scores on the thermometer
range from 0° to 100°, with higher thermometer scores indicating more
favorable views of the women's movement.[61]

Following the same approach developed earlier in the book, we
conceptualize the gender gap in presidential elections as the average
difference between men and women's major party vote choice. When
women and men's vote is similar (i.e. both support the Democratic or

Republican candidate at the same rate), the gap declines, but when their vote diverges, the gap expands. Since the actual size of the gender gap varies from election-to-election, the task at hand is to determine whether over-time variation in its magnitude represents an emerging trend.[62]

To develop our estimates of the size and evolution of the gender gap, we must first choose a suitable model. Continuing the approach developed earlier, we compare the fit of a series of competing models to the NES data for the 1952–1992 elections. Our simplest (baseline) model posits no change in the size of the gender gap; it includes variables only for the main effects of election year. It thus serves as a useful baseline for comparisons with models that posit trends in the gender gap.

The model we ultimately select as the best description of the data shows an emerging gender gap from 1952 to 1980.[63] However, between 1980 and 1992, the magnitude of the gender gap remains stable. Once we establish the evidence for this model, we consider whether our explanatory variables can explain away the gender gap.

The Evolution of the Gender Gap, 1952–1992

When did the gender gap emerge, and how has it evolved over time? Our analyses in Table 5.2 provide answers to these questions. The models considered in the table present contrasting pictures of the gender gap. Model 2 implies that the gender gap is a product of the 1980–88 elections. This model improves over the fit of model 1 (which hypothesizes unrealistically that there is no gender gap during the entire period). There is thus ample evidence for a gender gap. Model 3, in turn, provides a better fit, showing that the gender gap was also operating in the 1992 election.[64]

Models 4–6 suggest a divergent picture of the gender gap as emerging over the course of the entire 1952–1992 period. Of these three, model 6 is the best-fitting, and its fit is also preferable to model 3.[65] This model also has the same number of parameters as model 3, although its −2*LL* statistic is smaller. Using Raftery's BIC index for comparing non-nested models, the BIC test provides positive evidence (BIC improvement = −2) favoring model 4. Model 5 tests the hypothesis that the growth of the gender gap during the 1952–1992 period is best captured by an exponential function. Its fit is virtually identical to the fit of model 4, making comparisons using the BIC test inconclusive.[66]

What does model 6 tell us about the timing and development of the gender gap? As displayed earlier in the right-hand panel of Figure 5.1,

TABLE 5.2. *Fit statistics and select coefficients for logistic regression models[a] of the emerging gender gap in presidential elections[b], 1952–1992* (N = 13,081)

Models	Fit statistics −2LL (d.f.)	Coefficients $\beta_{\text{women*(year')}^2}$ (s.e.)
1. Election Year	17683.97 (13070)	—
2. Model 1 + Gender Gap I: Women x Year$_{1980/84/88}$	17665.95 (13069)	—
3. Model 1 + Gender Gap II: Women x Year$_{1980/84/88/92}$	17660.73 (13069)	—
4. Model 1 + Gender Gap III: Women * Year	17658.73 (13069)	—
5. Model 1 + Gender Gap IV: Women * (Year)^2	17659.16 (13069)	—
6. Model 1 + Gender Gap V: Women * (Year')^2	17656.82 (13069)	.006† (.0001)
7. Model 6 + Gender Gap VI: Women x Year	17642.82 (13060)	—

[a] Linearly constrained interaction effects are designated by '*', unconstrained interaction effects by 'x'; a '†' next to a logistic regression coefficient indicates significance at the .05 level (2-tailed test).

[b] Dependent variable is coded '0' for the choice of the Republican and '1' for the choice of the Democratic presidential candidate.

women's small but steady relative movement away from Republican presidential candidates led to growing voting differences between women and men. In 1980, those voting differences peak, remaining at the same level through 1992. The .006 coefficient from Table 5.2 for the gender gap indicates that between 1952 and 1980, women's log-odds of Democratic vote choice has increased by .29. The significance of this growth must be gauged relative to changes experienced by all voters (as captured by the election year coefficients in the model). In 1952, the predicted probabilities of Democratic vote choice among women and men are predicted as being .42. In 1972, these probabilities are .37 and .34, and in 1980 .47 and .4. In the 1980 through 1992 elections, these analyses predict a stable but substantial 7% gap between men and women voters. Taken together, these results direct our attention to the causal factors that can explain these cumulative changes in the voting behavior of women relative to men.

Explaining the Gender Gap

We evaluate competing explanations of change in the gender gap in Table 5.3. The models in this table add to the preferred model from

TABLE 5.3. *Fit statistics and select parameter estimates for logistic regression models^a explaining the emerging gender gap in presidential elections^b, 1952–1992* (N = 11,410)

Models	Fit statistics $-2LL$ (d.f.)	Coefficients $\beta_{women*(year')^2}$ (s.e.)
1. Base Model: Election Year, Women * (Year')^2	15370.90 (11398)	.005† (.001)
2. Model 1 + Class Location, Class Identification, Household Income, Cohort, Marital Status, Education, Race, and Region	14286.17 (11381)	.005† (.001)
3. Model 2 + Significant Two-Way Interactions: Women x Marital Status, Women x Fifties Generation	14275.20 (11379)	.005† (.001)
4. Model 1 + Women x Labor-Force Participation	15356.23 (11397)	< .002 (.001)
5. Model 4 + Labor-Force Participation	15356.22 (11396)	.003 (.002)
6. Model 4 − Women * (Year')^2	15359.48 (11398)	—

^{a} Linearly constrained interaction effects are designated by '*', unconstrained interaction effects by 'x'; a '†' next to a logistic regression coefficient indicates significance at the .05 level (2-tailed test).
^{b} Dependent variable is coded '0' for the choice of the Republican and '1' for the choice of the Democratic presidential candidate.

Table 5.2 various subsets of our independent variables that may explain the gender gap. Our task is to test which variable(s) cause the statistically significant coefficient to shrink, thereby indicating causal influence.[67] Model 2 adds terms for the main effect of class-related factors, birth cohort, martial status, education, race, and region. While its improvement in fit is significant, the coefficient for the trend in the gender gap is not affected by the addition of model 2's variables (i.e. it is .005 [s.e. = .001] in both models 1 and 2). This means that the additional sociodemographic factors measured in model 2 do not explain the emergence of the gender gap. Model 3 adds two significant interaction effects, for gender-by-marital status, and gender-by-fifties generation. While this model improves over the fit of both models 1 and 2, the coefficient for the gender gap remains unchanged.[68]

In model 4, we test a different causal hypothesis, that it is women's greater entrance into the paid labor force that explains the gender gap. Model 4 differs from model 1 by considering also the interaction of gender and labor force status on vote choice. Not only does model 4 improve the fit of model 1, it results in the coefficient for the gender gap shrinking to statistical insignificance (< .002[s.e. = .001]), providing evidence that the changing rate of labor force participation among women explains the growth of the gender gap. In model 5, we test an additional feature of labor force participation by adding to model 4 an additional term for the main effect of labor force participation (i.e. the effect of LFP among men). Model 5 does not improve over the fit of model 4. Taken in tandem with the comparison of models 1 and 4, this result shows that labor force participation has an effect on vote choice *only* among women.

As a final test, we compare models 4 and 6. Model 6 is derived from model 4 by constraining the gender gap parameter to be equal to '0'. The comparison of their respective fits favors model 6, showing that the inclusion of the interaction between women and labor force participation is sufficient to explain away women's changing voting behavior over the entire 1952 to 1992 period. As a result, the inclusion of a trend parameter for the gender gap is now unnecessary in model 6. Taken in tandem with the steady growth of women in the paid labor force, this result provides evidence for the importance of work-related factors to the emergence of the gender gap.

The Mediating Role of Policy Attitudes

Having established that changing rates of labor force participation among women explain the emergence of the gender gap, we now examine the impact of attitudes towards gender roles and social services to evaluate whether these attitudes in turn mediate the effects of labor force participation on women's voting behavior. For these analyses, shown in Table 5.4, we take advantage of data from recent NES surveys that have asked questions about gender roles, social service spending, and feminist consciousness. While this data is only for the past three elections, our strategy is similar to the analyses of the 1952–1992 series: We compare models with explanatory factors (relating here to gender role attitudes and social service spending preferences), presenting for each model the coefficient representing the gender gap during the 1984–1992 period.[69] If this coefficient becomes statistically insignificant, it indicates that the independent variables for the model in question have explained away the gender gap in these three elections. (Note that labor force participation is not considered in Table 5.4's models, but analyzed separately in Table 5.5.).

In Table 5.4, model 2 readily improves the fit of model 1, corroborating our earlier result that women and men's vote choice have differed significantly during the 1984, 1988, and 1992 elections. The coefficient

TABLE 5.4. *Fit statistics and select coefficients for logistic regression models[a] of the gender gap in the 1984–1992 presidential elections[b]* (N = 2,581)

Models	Fit statistics −2LL (d.f.)	Coefficients $\beta_{women*(year')^2}$ (s.e.)
1. Election Year	3491.29 (2578)	—
2. Model 1 + Gender Main Effect	3482.15 (2577)	.243† (.080)
3. Model 2 + Gender Role Attitudes	3425.15 (2576)	.233† (.081)
4. Model 3 + Gender Role Attitudes * Women	3425.14 (2575)	.205 (.226)
5. Model 2 + Views of Social Service Spending	3094.13 (2576)	.041 (.087)
6. Model 5 − Gender Main Effect	3094.35 (2577)	—

[a] Linearly constrained interaction effects are designated by '*'; a '†' next to a logistic regression coefficient indicates significance at the .05 level (2-tailed test).
[b] Dependent variable is coded '0' for the choice of the Republican and '1' for the choice of the Democratic presidential candidate.

for gender indicates that women's vote choice differs from men by .243; this coefficient represents the phenomenon to be explained in subsequent models. Using model 3, we test the hypothesis that women and men's views of gender roles shape the gender gap. While the fit of model 3 is superior to model 2, the coefficient is largely unchanged (i.e. .243 vs. .233). We find no support for an interaction between gender role attitudes and gender (model 3 is preferred to model 4). Gender role attitudes, while an important source of voter preferences in their own right, do not appear to explain the gender gap in vote choice between men and women.[70]

The contrasting preferences for social services spending among men and women have a much larger impact. Model 5 adds to model 2 an additional term for the effect of social service spending. Not only does this model readily improve the fit of model 2, the coefficient has now shrunk to a non-significant .041[s.e. = .087]. Model 6's improvement over model 5 corroborates and extends our earlier finding that the effect of gender on vote choice disappears once male–female differences in spending preferences have been taken into account.

These analyses suggest that attitudes towards social service spending account for voting differences between men and women. But recall that our earlier analyses established that labor force participation predicts the gender gap. How can we reconcile these two findings? In Table 5.5, we address this seeming paradox by developing a more comprehensive portrait of the respective roles of our two explanatory factors: labor force participation and social services spending preferences. The most

TABLE 5.5. *OLS regression coefficients[a] (s.e. in parentheses) for analyzing the interrelationship between views of social service spending[b], gender, and labor force participation in the 1984–1992 presidential elections[c]* (N = 2,581)

	Models		
	Gender only	Labor force participation	Gender x LFP
β_0 (s.e.)	2.683† (.056)	2.761† (.074)	2.923† (.094)
β_{women} (s.e.)	.396† (.059)	.378† (.060)	.126 (.108)
$\beta_{labor\text{-}force\ participant}$ (s.e.)	—	−.101 (.064)	−.318 (.100)
$\beta_{women\ x\ labor\text{-}force\ participant}$ (s.e.)	—	—	.364† (.129)

[a] Significance at the .05 level (2-tailed test) is denoted by a '†'.
[b] Dependent variable is the 7-category Likert spending item (higher scores indicate a preference for increased service spending).
[c] All models also control for the main effects of election year (coefficients not presented in table).

plausible causal interpretation is that labor force participation shapes working women's (more favorable) views of social service spending, which in turn serves as the source of their voting differences with men. To consider the evidence for this interpretation, we now treat the spending item as our new dependent variable. By comparing the table's three models, we test whether the source of gender differences in views of social service spending is to be found in the distinctive preferences of working women.

Our results support the preceding interpretation. The first model's coefficient shows that women as a whole favor increased social service spending (relative to men's preferences). The second model adds to the first a term for the main effect of labor force participation. Corroborating our earlier results, the coefficient is not significant. The third column's model uses our earlier 'gendered' specification of the political effects of labor force participation by adding a term for the interaction of gender and labor force participation. The coefficient for this interaction is significant (.364[s.e. = .129]), and its presence in the model results in the coefficient for the main effect of gender shrinking to insignificance. In other words, rather than all women being more supportive of increased levels of spending on social programs, it is only working women who are especially likely to have this preference. These results thus provide evidence for the inference that gender differences in views of social service spending are a product of the specific preferences of working women.

Feminist Consciousness

Our final set of analyses examine the possible relevance of feminist attitudes to the gender gap. Given that the wording of the NES item measuring feminist consciousness has undergone significant changes (see Table 5.6), we treat these analyses separately from the earlier analyses of policy attitudes. Our strategy is identical to our earlier analyses. Note, however, that we treat each year separately in light of the question-wording changes in the NES item measuring affect towards the women's movement.

Our starting point is model 1's coefficient for the effect of gender on vote choice in each of the four years (see the second column). In the first three elections, however, adding the women's movement feeling

TABLE 5.6. *Fit statistics and select coefficients for logistic regression models[a] of the gender gap in the 1980* (N = 831), *1984* (N = 1,176), *1988* (N = 976), *and 1992* (N = 1,156) *presidential elections[b]*

Models	Fit statistics −2LL (d.f.)	Coefficients β_{women} (s.e.)
1980 Election		
1. Gender Main Effect	1128.47 (829)	.306† (.14)
2. Model 1 + Feelings Towards the Women's Liberation Movement	1060.03 (828)	.336† (.15)
1984 Election		
1. Gender Main Effect	1574.42 (1174)	.340† (.12)
2. Model 1 + Feelings Towards the Women's Liberation Movement	1442.90 (1173)	.322† (.13)
1988 Election		
1. Gender Main Effect	1340.79 (974)	.278† (.13)
2. Model 1 + Feelings Towards Feminists	1238.27 (973)	.276† (.14)
1992 Election		
1. Gender Main Effect	1565.43 (1154)	.270† (.12)
2. Model 1 + Feelings Towards the Women's Movement	1359.64 (1153)	.059 (.13)

[a] A '†' next to a logistic regression coefficient indicates significance at the .05 level (2-tailed test).
[b] Dependent variable is coded '0' for the choice of the Republican and '1' for the choice of the Democratic Presidential candidate.

thermometer item leaves the gender coefficient largely unaffected. The fit statistics favor model 2, showing that views of the women's movement do have a significant impact on vote choice.[71] However, the coefficients for the gender gap are largely unchanged, revealing that views of the women's movement do not explain the 1980, 1984, and 1988 gender gaps.

The results for the 1992 election differ, however. When the feeling thermometer item is added to the model, the gender gap coefficient becomes insignificant, indicating its congruence with women versus men's (contrasting) views of the women's movement. This result is worth elaborating. To express the point another way: it is only in 1992 that women and men's (contrasting) views of the women's movement result in gender-based differences at the ballot box. This result raises a question that is similar to the earlier one regarding the interrelationship of labor force participation, attitudes, and vote choice. Is it only working women who have disproportionately favorable views of the women's movement?

Using our earlier strategy, we examine in Table 5.7 the interrelationship of labor force participation, views of the women's movement, and vote choice. The results are very similar to the earlier analyses of spending preferences: male–female differences in views of the women's movement appear to be a product of the working women's distinctive attitudes. More specifically, the initial 6.126[s.e. = 1.35] coefficient for the main effect of gender is largely unchanged when the main effect of

TABLE 5.7. *OLS regression coefficients[a] (s.e. in parentheses) for analyzing the interrelationship between views of the women's movement[b], gender, and labor force participation in the 1992 presidential election* (N = 1,156)

	Models		
	Gender only	Labor-force participation	Gender x LFP
β_0 (s.e.)	58.682† (.991)	59.347† (1.38)	62.560† (1.86)
β_{women} (s.e.)	6.126† (1.35)	5.937† (1.38)	1.149 (2.27)
$\beta_{labor\ force\ participant}$ (s.e.)	—	−.930 (1.40)	−5.417† (2.19)
$\beta_{women\ x\ labor\text{-}force\ participant}$ (s.e.)	—	—	7.559† (2.85)

ᵃ Significance at the .05 level (2-tailed test) is denoted by a '†'.
ᵇ Dependent variable is the 100-point feeling thermometer (higher scores indicate more favorable views of the women's movement).

labor-force participation is entered in the model, but shrinks to a non-significant 1.149[s.e. = 2.27] when the interaction between gender and labor-force participation (7.559[s.e. = 2.85]) is added. The roughly 6° difference in men and women's feelings about the women's movement in 1992 is thus a product of the differences among working women versus men/non-working women. We thus infer that while feminist consciousness led to gender differences in 1992, it is the distinctive experiences of working women that ultimately explain this relationship in that election.

CONCLUSION

There have been many significant changes in the status of women in American society since World War II. Not surprisingly, these changes have important repercussions for political behavior. Our analysis of the origins and development of the gender gap provide evidence that it can be traced to the steady increase in the proportion of women in the paid labor force. The diagram presented in Figure 5.2 summarizes a simplified version the causal logic of the argument. The steadily increasing proportion of women in the workplace—an arena where women have been and continue to be disadvantaged relative to men—has resulted in a cumulative, net shift among women towards support for Democratic presidential candidates. The labor force/vote choice relationship among women is, however, mediated by their views of social provision and, more recently, by views of the women's movement. More women are dependent on an activist public sector for access to jobs, public social provision for help with childcare and other parental responsibilities, and (especially as actual or potential single mothers with lower paid employment prospects) income maintenance programs such as the Earned Income Tax Credit. As the party that has been more receptive

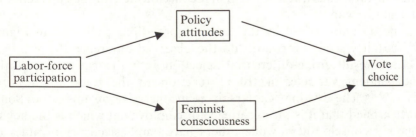

FIG. 5.2. Labor-force participation as a source of political attitudes and behavior

to building or maintaining such social programs, the Democrats have thus made relative gains among working women voters over the past four decades.

Our analyses show that the causal factors identified by the socialization and autonomy theses are largely irrelevant to the gender gap in presidential elections. We find that it is not socialization processes that all women experience, but later life experiences linked to work situation that is producing partisan effects. To be sure, the transformation of the traditional family is shaping voting preferences among both men and women, but for precisely that reason it cannot account for the growth of the gender gap.

The role of feminist consciousness in producing the gender gap is an interesting and complicated issue. Attitudes towards the women's movement do shape voting behavior, but because both men and women have come to view it in a more favorable light, their respective attitudes do not explain the emergence of the gender gap through 1988. In the 1990s, however, differences have emerged between men and women on their views towards the women's movement, and these differences have become important for explaining the gender gap. (We examine the 1996 election—and the much larger gender gap in that election—in more detail in Chapter 8.)

However, we cannot rule out another way in which rising feminist consciousness may be shaping the emergence of the gender gap. The scenario is illustrated in Figure 5.3. The top panel assumes that women are entering the labor force because of social and economic factors, such as family disruption, stagnating wages for male workers or increased economic opportunities. The bottom panel, by contrast, implies that rising feminist consciousness caused more women to enter the workforce in the first place. If the latter is a better representation of the underlying processes causing increasing number of women (especially with children) to enter the labor force, then we cannot rule out a more fundamental causal role for feminist consciousness in the emergence of the gender gap.

The question raised by the two interpretations suggested in Figure 5.3 is fairly straightforward: 'do the observed differences [in women's voting] result from differential selection into the categories of the independent variable, or from "reaction to the roles as they are lived"?'[72] The existing scholarship is inconclusive on this issue. Some have argued that it is the experience of employment which is the key to shaping consciousness, while others have emphasized prior values or beliefs about gender roles.[73] To adequately assess the role of cultural

Primacy of social and economic change

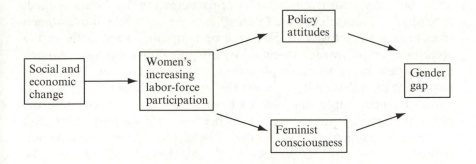

Primacy of attitudinal change

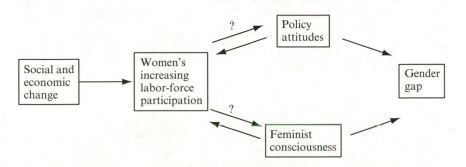

Fɪɢ. 5.3. Labor-force participation vs. attitudinal change as a source of political attitudes and behavior

self-selection versus employment socialization, we would need panel data which surveys women respondents before and after they make the decision to enter the workforce. No such data is available over the long time-period in which we are interested, and we have not attempted to generalize from the more historically limited panels that are available.[74]

With these caveats in mind, we infer that rising labor-force participation rates among women provide the best way of understanding the origins of the gender gap. Our measure of paid employment is, to be

sure, limited in important ways. It bears noting that our simple dichotomous labor force participation variable ignores relevant information
about both the quantity and quality of participation (i.e. hours worked,
type of job). This is undoubtedly significant. For example, more women
than men are employed in part-time or temporary jobs, without the
security of employment associated with regular full-time jobs. Women
are also less likely to be employed in higher wage occupations. It is
important to understand, however, that these qualitative and quantitative differences imply that our LFP variable may underestimate the
political effects of employment. In other words, if we had better data
on work situation over our entire time-series, the interrelationship
between gender, work experience, and vote choice might actually be
stronger that the results reported here would imply.

The increasing importance of work on gender-based political divisions has not been systematically understood by previous scholarly or
journalistic analysts. Even when political commentators have referred
to work-related factors among women, they have failed to grasp their
political significance. For instance, a *Time* cover story (14 October
1996), appearing during the final weeks of the 1996 campaign, suggested that 'Bob Dole and Bill Clinton will do anything to win the
hearts and votes of working moms, but many of them are too busy to
notice'. To the contrary, it appears that working women have noticed
and are choosing accordingly.

6

Race and the Social Bases
of Voter Alignments

In the postwar literature on social cleavages and political behavior, few ideas have been more central than the notion that in democratic polities no single cleavage is ever likely to become dominant. The underlying assumption is that individual voters have multiple, overlapping group memberships, producing 'cross-cutting' cleavages in the polity as whole. As a result, individuals are divided from one another not just by class, or race, or religion, or ethnicity, or gender; they are divided by *all* of these, and others as well. This is what makes the possibility of successful class-based revolutions appear virtually inconceivable in contemporary capitalist democracies, at least under normal conditions. It is also what prevents any one group from overpowering all others: the members of any powerful group are themselves divided along various lines.[1]

The continuing strength of these cross-cutting axes of division, however, is potentially undermined if a single cleavage becomes so powerful as to erode other cleavages. In the history of American political development race has unquestionably been the most important of the major social cleavages, influencing virtually all political processes in one way or another. The significance of the race cleavage in structuring electoral behavior has been so large since the early 1960s that many analysts have argued that it is displacing other cleavages, especially the class cleavage.

In this chapter we examine the consequences of the emergence of the race cleavage for other cleavages in presidential elections. The analyses we present have two objectives. First, we systematically compare the magnitude of each of the major social cleavages in American politics. Surprisingly, such a comparison has rarely been attempted in recent years. Moreover, the few existing comparisons suffer from some significant limitations, including problems with conceptualizations of the religion and class cleavages. Our analyses show, as expected, that the race cleavage is substantially larger than other social cleavages, but they also reveal important information about its comparative magnitude and the rank order of social cleavages.

Second, we explore the relationship between change in the political consequences of one social cleavage for other cleavages. For example, we ask whether the increasing importance of racial divisions tends to displace class divisions, and whether the increasing salience of the gender gap suppresses other types of political differences between social groups.

To answer both of these questions, we introduce and apply two new measures of social cleavages that allow us to gauge the interrelationships between these cleavages and vote choice.[2] These measures are related to the measures introduced in Chapters 3 through 5 in that they distinguish changes in the popularity of the Democratic or Republican candidates from changes in the political alignments of particular social groups. Additionally, in their multivariate form these measures can also be used to estimate the effects of individual social cleavages net of the influence of other variables.

RACE AND U.S. POLITICAL DEVELOPMENT[3]

The racial divide has been fundamental in U.S. history. Race was of decisive importance in each of the major turning points in political development.[4] Race shaped the structure of federalism during the drafting of the Constitution by virtue of the pressures extended by slave states to regulate conditions of labor at the subnational level. The Civil War was fought over slavery, and the furious conflicts over Reconstruction and its aftermath defined the fate of the new racial order in the South. By the turn of the twentieth century, blacks and poor whites were increasingly denied the right to vote, contributing to the establishment of a fragmented political system in which conservative Southern political interests had disproportionate influence over state-building processes during the Progressive Era and the New Deal.

After World War II, race became, once again, central to U.S. politics. The struggle for civil rights by African-Americans in the first two decades after World War II were central to the emergence of Johnson's Great Society. Since the mid-1960s, conflict over the *implementation* of the civil rights agenda contributed to the demise of the New Deal political order (and the traditional Democratic Party coalition).[5] Race continues to be a potent source of policy conflicts at the end of the millennium.

What is the Race Cleavage? Race as an Ideological vs. Social Cleavage

It is useful to distinguish between two separate race cleavages in American politics: a social cleavage and an ideological cleavage. Race as a social cleavage refers to the varying political orientations of whites and non-whites growing out of their different position in American society. To be sure, many important changes in the racial order have occurred: slavery and legal segregation backed by force are a thing of the past, and many forms of discrimination based on race or ethnicity are formally illegal. African-Americans have gained greater access to educational and employment opportunities that were once denied or severely circumscribed prior to the 1960s. A 'new' black middle class based on employment outside the African-American community has grown during this period.

Yet at the same time, many fundamental race-based inequalities remain largely unchanged. Housing segregation is actually greater today than in 1900. Public schools, four and a half decades after the landmark *Brown* v. *Board of Education* decision, remain heavily segregated by race and in some metropolitan areas segregation is increasing. The rapid expansion of the black middle class has stalled in recent years. While African-Americans have gained access to elected political office, this has tended to occur mostly in black majority districts, as many white voters remain reluctant to support black candidates. Blacks and whites continue to live in largely separate and unequal spheres of American society.[6]

In the context of U.S. electoral history, race has been an important and recurring source of direct political mobilization and partisan appeals.[7] Yet direct appeals along race lines, common between the 1940s and 1960s, are now increasingly rare. The race divide has instead become more subtle, manifesting itself in coded or symbolic forms, in recent decades. Many analysts have demonstrated the powerful effects of racial attitudes in structuring whites' political behavior. One main focus of the contemporary research literatures that study race as an ideological cleavage is the sources of white (and to a lesser extent, black[8]) racial attitudes. Although this literature spans several divergent theoretical perspectives, the most widely held view is that a 'new' or 'subtle racism' has emerged in recent decades. In contrast to earlier racial belief systems, this form of racism affirms individualistic principles of freedom and equal opportunity while simultaneously opposing the implementation of policies designed to achieve racial equality.[9]

The debate over the sources, structure, and consequences of race as an ideological cleavage is lively, important, and as yet unsettled.[10] It has potential relevance for understanding the operation of the racial cleavage at the level of normative conflict. However, systematic evaluation of race as an ideological cleavage is beyond the scope of this study.

Race and Electoral Politics

For those African-Americans who were able to vote prior to the 1930s, Republican partisanship was the norm. The legacies of the Civil War and the role of the Republican Party under Lincoln in bringing slavery to an end and in promoting (if later abandoning) Reconstruction in the South was decisive in securing this political allegiance. The limited empirical evidence available confirms that most African-Americans did support the Republican Party, even if the GOP did little after Reconstruction to maintain the alliance.[11] A more important factor was the role of the Democratic Party in the South in maintaining segregation, preventing blacks from voting, and encouraging the use of racist attitudes as a vehicle for mobilizing white voters. Democratic officials outside the South may have been unwilling participants in the creation of the Southern racial order, but they did little to challenge it until after World War II.

This was even true for the Roosevelt Administration during the 1930s. While Roosevelt is sometimes credited with taking some tentative steps towards integrating African-Americans into the New Deal political order, the Roosevelt Administration's direct initiatives on race were symbolic and ineffectual.[12] Indeed, some New Deal policies may have (intentionally or unintentionally) exacerbated racial inequalities.[13] None the less, it was during the 1930s that African-American voters realigned at the national level. The historian Nancy Weiss's estimates indicate that blacks still gave over 60% of their votes to Herbert Hoover in 1932. But by 1936, over 70% of African-American voters supported Roosevelt's re-election, the first time a majority had ever voted for the Democratic Party. Weiss and other analysts have concluded that this realignment appears to have been caused by black support for New Deal social and economic policies.[14]

Between 1936 and 1960, this new alignment of African-American voters with the Democratic Party was consolidated. During this period, African-Americans gave a substantial majority of their votes to Democratic candidates in each election, and the racial gap between whites and blacks during this period was typically in the range of 20%–35%.[15] With increased migration to the North during and after World War II, the African-American vote was becoming increasingly important for the Democratic Party in that region. In 1960, African-Americans gave over 70% of their votes to Democrat John Kennedy, producing a race gap of 23% in the NES data. The actual impact of the African-American vote during this period at the national level was modest, however, because of the continuing pattern of racial disfranchisement in the South. In 1960, for example, blacks provided just around 10% of the entire Kennedy vote.[16]

The electoral dimensions of the race cleavage underwent a second massive political shift in 1964.[17] The conservative Republican presidential bid of Barry Goldwater in that year employed powerful indirect appeals to white Southern voters through loaded phrases or 'codewords' understood by black and white voters alike as anti-black. As one journalist who accompanied Goldwater on a campaign swing through the deep South observed,

[Goldwater] did not, to be sure, make any direct racist appeals. He covered the South and never, in any public gatherings, mentioned 'race' or 'whites' or 'segregation' or 'civil rights.' But the fact that the words did not cross his lips does not mean that he ignored the realities they describe. He talked about them all the time in an underground, or Aesopian language — code that few in his audiences had any trouble deciphering. In the code, 'bullies and marauders' means 'Negroes.' 'Criminal defendants' means 'Negroes.' 'States' rights' means opposition to civil rights.[18]

At the same time that Goldwater was developing his Southern strategy, the Johnson Administration had pushed through the first major piece of Civil Rights legislation since Reconstruction, the Civil Rights Act of 1964. Virtually all African-American voters supported Lyndon Johnson in 1964,[19] and since that time, the NES data show that blacks have consistently given equal to or greter than 90% of their votes to Democratic presidential candidates (the sole exception being the unpopular 1972 Democratic nominee George McGovern, who none the less still received some 87% of the African-American vote).

In Figure 6.1 we present raw NES data that illustrate the strong alignment of African-Americans with the Democratic Party. In this figure, the solid line represents the proportion of black voters who chose the Democratic candidate in presidential election elections from 1952 through 1992; the dashed line represents the corresponding proportion of non-black voters who supported Democratic candidates during this time. (These calculations are for major party voters only, excluding non-voters and those supporting third party candidates.) Although African-American support for Democratic candidates was

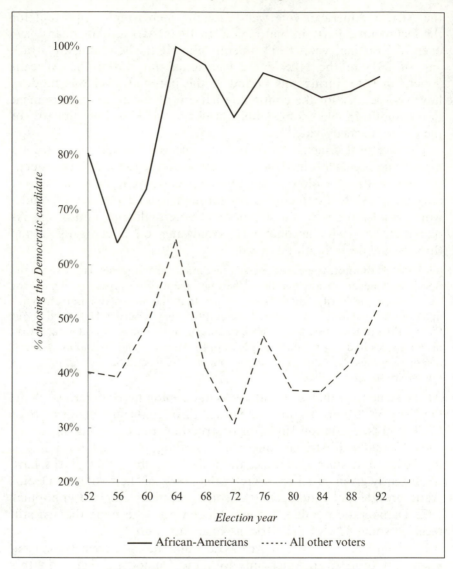

FIG. 6.1. Support for Democratic presidential candidates
among black vs. non-black voters, 1952–1992
Note: Data are from the National Election Surveys.

high prior to 1964, during and after this election black support
increased considerably, remaining at dramatically high levels. The
considerable distance between the levels of black and non-black support
for Democrats illustrates the subsequent race gap in presidential voting.

In doing so, it usefully demonstrates the strength of African-Americans' Democratic alignment in the face of factors that have sometimes been thought to attenuate black political loyalty.[20]

Race and the Decline of Class Voting?

A number of analysts have asserted that the growth of the race cleavage since the early 1960s has undermined the class bases of U.S. political parties.[21] This consensus includes analysts on both the left and the right.[22] Although there are variations, the core of this thesis is that as the Democratic Party has come to be identified with race-targeted social policies designed to improve the welfare of African-Americans, white working-class voters have increasingly turned away from that party. Robert Huckfeldt and Carol W. Kohfeld, for example, argue that 'the decline of class as an organizing principle in contemporary American electoral politics is directly related to the concurrent ascent of race'.[23] As more and more whites (especially working-class whites) become Republican voters in reaction to these perceptions, the class cleavage shrivels. The most systematic journalistic version of the thesis was developed by Thomas and Mary Edsall in their 1991 book *Chain Reaction*. The Edsalls argue that working-class white voters have become less supportive of the Democrats since the 1960s due to perceptions that Democratic politicians endorse policies in which tax dollars are spent on social programs targetted at African-Americans.[24]

Debates over this thesis have been heated, in part because it has important strategic implications. For instance, some commentators view the 'race displaces class' thesis as suggesting that the Democratic decline in presidential elections after 1964 is largely the result of the party's promotion of African-American interests. Even many liberal analysts have adopted versions of this position. For example, William Julius Wilson and Theda Skocpol have made explicit calls for 'race-neutral' social policies that would structure social programs in ways that do not appear to provide disproportionate benefits to African-Americans.[25] The 'universal' antipoverty programs they advocate would include measures such as job creation through public works programs, support for poor and low-income families (e.g. childcare subsidies, health insurance), and enhanced educational benefits. These types of programs, with their emphasis on enhancing work rather than welfare, are assumed to elicit greater support from working-class whites without invoking negative racial stereotypes.

The results of Chapter 3 cast doubt on some political lessons that have been drawn from the increasing race/declining class thesis. There is, for one thing, no evidence that class-based political alignments have experienced a net decline through 1992. In the specific case of non-skilled workers, further analyses (see Chapter 3) showed that it is not race but economic perceptions, and to a lesser extent welfare state attitudes, that have led to a decline in support for the Democratic Party since 1980. Skilled workers moved steadily away from the Democratic Party between 1952 and 1972, largely *before* the biggest impact of the racial cleavage is said to have occurred.

Still, other questions about the interaction between the race cleavage and other social cleavages remain. It is a reasonable surmise that in elections when the race cleavage is strongest, other cleavages should weaken.[26] By examining the four cleavages simultaneously, it is possible to assess the extent to which they vary independently of one another. That is the task of the empirical investigations in the next part of the chapter.

Our analyses test two distinct versions of the 'race displaces class' thesis. The strong version of the thesis asserts that as race emerges as a dominant social cleavage, it drives the class cleavage from the electoral landscape. The key assumption underlying the strong thesis is that white voters—through a process of political socialization—will come to view the Democratic Party as the agent of racial activism on behalf of African-American interests; even when race-related policy conflicts fade in salience, white voters (especially those in the working class) will continue to have such perceptions of Democratic candidates, thereby surpressing class voting. By contrast, the 'weak' version of the race-displaces-class thesis asserts that the class cleavage declines only when the race cleavage increases during a particular election. The main assumption underlying this version of the thesis is that white voters' perceptions of the Democratic Party's racial issue positions are malleable, and thus capable of revision providing the necessary cues are present during a particular election. In the analyses that follow, we consider the evidence for each version of the thesis.

MODELLING THE RELATIONSHIPS AMONG SOCIAL CLEAVAGES

Perhaps reflecting the assumption that social cleavages are declining in importance, there have been relatively few scholarly assessments of the overall magnitude of social group cleavages in American politics or their interrelationships with one another. In their periodic post-election surveys, Paul Abramson, John Aldrich, and David Rohde have regularly included a chapter on 'social forces and the vote', which presents bivariate measures of the size of different social cleavages in presidential voting.[27] Arthur Miller and Brad Lockerbie developed a multivariate investigation of the relative magnitudes of social factors in the 1952, 1968, and 1984 elections.[28] However, we have been unable to discover a study that develops an over-time, multivariate analysis of all four major social cleavages which includes an appropriate conceptualization of the class and religious cleavages.

Data and Measures

For the analyses in this chapter, the dependent variable is major party vote choice (coded '1' for the Democratic, and '0' for the Republican candidate). Because of significant limitations in the coding of the religious variable in the NES data prior to 1960 (described in Chapter 4 above), our analyses begin with the 1960 elections. We discussed the multi-category class and religion variables in Chapters 3 and 4. 'Gender' and 'race' are coded as dichotomies (women = 1, African-Americans = 1). In our multivariate analyses, we include measures of age (years), education (years), and region (coded '1' for non-Southern residence, and '0' for Southern residence) as controls.

Modelling Social Cleavages

The size of a social cleavage increases when the average difference in vote choice among the social groups comprising that cleavage grows, but decreases when these differences narrow. As before, to properly conceptualize the relationship among the four social cleavages it is necessary to develop measures to distinguish between changes that affect all categories of a cleavage variable from changes that have differential effects on one or more of its categories. In this chapter, we seek to determine not only whether the relationship between vote choice and a given social cleavage has changed over time, but whether these changes are related to trends in other social cleavages (e.g. the race/class relationship). The latter is a multivariate question which requires that we estimate the effect of change in a particular cleavage net of the corresponding changes affecting the other cleavages.

We employ logistic regression models to analyze our dichotomous dependent variable. Using the coefficients from our models, we derive two summary indices of social cleavages in presidential elections. Because of the standardization used in these indicies, they enable comparisons over time and between cleavages, even when the cleavage variables are polytomies (such as religion). For instance, an index score of .2 for the racial cleavage indicates that racial groups tend to differ from the overall mean by .2 (this could result from whites' predicted probability of voting for the Democratic candidate being .3, and African-Americans' corresponding probability being .7). A score of .1 on the religious cleavage (to continue our example), would indicate a smaller average deviation, enabling us to infer that the religious cleavage is half the magnitude of the racial cleavage.

Two Voting Cleavage Indices

Our first measure, which we term kappa (κ), is calculated as the standard deviation of the predicted probabilities of vote choice *m* (1 = Democratic candidate; 2 = Republican candidate) for a set of *j* cleavage categories at time *t*. Before calculating kappa, we first transform the logit coefficients from our model into predicted probabilities for each of the *j* categories of the variable representing a particular social cleavage. By virtue of the probability metric, kappa ranges between 0 and .5, with a κ of '0' indicating that the groups comprising a particular cleavage do not differ in their likelihood of choosing the Democratic over the Republican candidate. By contrast, a score of '.5' indicates maximal divergence in vote choice.[29]

$$\kappa_t = \sqrt{\frac{\sum_{j=1}^{J} (\hat{P}_{tjm} - \bar{P}_{tm})^2}{J}} \tag{6.1}$$

We use equation 6.1 to calculate two kappas for each of the four social cleavages in the analyses. The first of these indices is derived from a model including only the covariates for a specific cleavage; we thus term it *bivariate kappa*. In contrast to the first, our second set of voting cleavage indices are derived from a model predicting vote choice with covariates for all four cleavages. Accordingly, whereas the *bivariate* index measures trends in a specific cleavage without controlling for other social cleavages, the *multivariate* index measures trends in the presence of these controls.[30]

Both bivariate and multivariate kappas yield findings that help us to understand the interrelationship of social cleavages. By comparing the estimates for a particular cleavage according to each measure, we can determine whether the changes inferred using the bivariate measure are in fact the product of (more fundamental) changes stemming from change in *other* cleavages. For instance, if the bivariate kappa for the class cleavage is much larger than its multivariate counterpart, it implies that the class cleavage is in fact the product of other social cleavages (and thus shrinks when we take the other cleavages into account). Likewise, if the bivariate kappa for the class cleavage reveals a trend that disappears using the multivariate index, it implies that changes in some other cleavage explain the earlier trends in the class cleavage.

By comparing the differences between the bivariate and multivariate measures, we also can test the strong and weak versions of the 'race displaces class' thesis. If the strong version is true, we should observe a monotonic decline in the class cleavage once both race and class are measured in the same statistical model. By contrast, the weak version of the thesis implies that a (temporary) decline in the magnitude of the class cleavage will be accompanied by a corresponding increase in the race cleavage (without leading to a lasting decline in the class cleavage).

Equation 6.2 summarizes our second measure, which we term lambda (λ):

$$\lambda_{st} = \sqrt{\frac{\sum_{s=1}^{S} \sum_{j=1}^{J} (\hat{P}_{tsjm} - \bar{P}_{stm})^2}{SJ}} \tag{6.2}$$

λ_{st} is thus the mean of the four separate kappas and it measures the average size of the s social cleavages at time t. Lambda represents the *total* social cleavage (for the four cleavages) in a given election. Like kappa, it is measured in terms of probability, ranging between 0 and .5. If lambda declines over time, it shows that social cleavages as a whole have narrowed, as hypothesized by the declining cleavage thesis. Results using our bivariate and multivariate lambda indices enable us to test whether simultaneous changes in social cleavages have moved in complementary or divergent directions, thereby either producing change or overall stability in the total social cleavage.

RESULTS

To calculate kappa and lambda, we must first choose preferred models of trends in each of the four social cleavages. Our models build from the earlier analyses presented in Chapters 3 through 5. The first four rows of Table 6.1 present fit statistics for our preferred model of each cleavage. The fifth row presents fit statistics for our multivariate model measuring change in all four cleavages. The preferred models impose constraints on the year-by-cleavage parameters, thus implying that change in each cleavage follows substantively meaningful patterns. As a point of comparison, in the second column of Table 6.1 we present fit statistics for a 'full interaction model' that allows the cleavage and year variables to interact without any constraints.[31]

Our preferred model of change in the class cleavage reveals five class-specific trends, relating to professionals, managers, proprietors, skilled workers, and unskilled workers. Voting behavior among the remaining classes show no trends relative to the class-wide mean, but instead vary together, depending on the particular election. Since 1960, professionals have moved away from strong support for Republican presidential candidates. From 1960 through 1972, both managers and skilled workers' propensity to favor Republican candidates increased relative to the mean. In contrast to the linear trends relating to the preceding three classes, changes in proprietors' and nonnskilled workers' voting behavior are considerably more abrupt, with these two classes' support for Democratic candidates declining sharply after 1976 (and continuing through 1992). These one-step changes are captured by two parameters for the interaction of each class category by a time covariate (coded '1' for the 1980 through 1992 elections and '0' otherwise).

Our preferred model of the religious cleavage finds three category-specific changes in voting behavior. The first of these relates to liberal Protestants, who have moved from being the most Republican of religious groups to a point roughly equidistant between candidates of the two parties. The vote choice of Catholics, as we discussed in Chapter 4, has varied in tandem with the rest of the electorate but shows only a single category-by-year interaction relating to their disproportionate support for Democratic candidate Kennedy in 1960. Finally, we model change among conservative Protestants as an effect for the 1976 and 1980 elections, during which time born-again Democrat Jimmy Carter received relatively high levels of support among that segment of the electorate. Net of these three changes, the religious cleavage has been stable.

TABLE 6.1. *Fit statistics for logistic regression models of change in social cleavages and presidential vote choice, 1960–1992 (N = 9,905)*

Preferred models/change parameters[a]	Fit statistics for preferred models		Fit statistics for full interaction models	
	−2LL (d.f.)	BIC	−2LL (d.f.)	BIC
Class				
Professionals * Year$_{1964-92}$; Managers * Year$_{1960-\geq72}$; Self-Employed * Year$_{\geq1980}$ Skilled Workers * Year$_{1960-\geq72}$; Unskilled Workers * Year $_{four1980}$	13150.89 (9885)	−77,799	13088.70 (9842)	−77,466
Religion				
Liberal Protestants * Year$_{1960-1992}$; Catholics × Year$_{1960}$ Conservative Protestants × Year$_{1976/1980}$	12856.98 (9887)	−78,111	12796.22 (9842)	−77,758
Race				
Race × Election Year$_{\geq1964}$	12446.08 (9894)	−78,587	12436.27 (9887)	−78,532
Gender[b]				
Gender * (Year')^2	13340.43 (9894)	−77,691	13331.72 (9887)	−77,637
All[c] *social cleavages*				
Change parameters from four previous models; Women × Class$_{non-lfp}$	11636.08 (9868)	−79,157	11403.14 (9706)	−77,900

[a] Linearly constrained interaction effects designated by '*'; unconstrained interaction effects designated by '×' (note that all models fit main effects for election year and the social cleavage variable[s]).
[b] 'Year' is coded as follows: 1 = 1960; 2 = 1964. . . , 4 = 1972–1992.
[c] Includes additional parameters for main effects of age, years of education, and region (South = '1', '0' otherwise).

Our preferred model of change in the racial cleavage includes a single trend parameter relating to change in the relative support given to Democratic candidates among African-Americans during and after the 1964 election. As anticipated by the raw NES data (see Figure 6.1), this result implies that the pivotal 1964 Goldwater/Johnson contest had the result of shifting most of the remaining portion of African-American support to Democratic candidates for the duration of the 1964 to 1992 period. For gender, we find that a model positing an increasing gender gap is preferred.[32] As with race, the voting differences between women and men have their origins in the early 1960s, but (unlike race) the much smaller gender gap has been increasing steadily since this time (rather than remaining at a stable and very high level).

The final model in Table 6.1 includes covariates for all four cleavages, thereby providing a basis for answering questions about the inter-relationship between change in each cleavage. Our preferred model includes the main and interaction effect parameters from the four preferred models and a single, additional parameter for an interaction between gender and the 'non-full-time labor force' category of the class variable.[33] As analyzed in the next section, our preferred multivariate model's coefficients allow us to calculate kappa and lambda controlling for the presence of (and changes in) other cleavages. The bivariate trend indices, by contrast, are derived from the coefficients of the first four models (which do not control for the other social cleavages).

In Table 6.2, we present the coefficients for our preferred multivariate model of social cleavages and vote choice (from Table 6.1's last row). Given the preceding discussion (and the findings of our earlier chapters), our model's coefficients present few surprises. However, it is useful to note the significant ($-.33$ [s.e.$=.11$]) coefficient for the interaction between gender and labor force status, and also the non-significant ($.01$ [s.e.$=.02$]) coefficient for the interaction between gender and time. As discussed below, the comparison between bivariate and multivariate index results shows that the gender gap in presidential vote choice is produced by a class-related factor that affects women's political alignments.

Trends in Voting Cleavages

We present in Figure 6.2 the results for cleavage-specific trends, graphing the kappa estimates in the two panels of the figure. The left-hand panel displays trends in race, religion, class, and gender cleavages according to our bivariate kappas. By far the largest cleavage is for race,

TABLE 6.2. *Logistic regression coefficients[a] (s.e. in parentheses) for preferred model of all social cleavages and presidential vote choice[b] , 1960–1992* (N = 9,905)

Independent variables	Coefficient (s.e.)
Constant	1.01* (.25)
Election years (reference = 1960)	
1964	.95* (.11)
1968	−.05 (.12)
1972	−.53* (.12)
1976	.08 (.13)
1980	−.30* (.15)
1984	−.25 (.15)
1988	−.03 (.16)
1992	.43* (.17)
Race (reference = all else)	
African-Americans	1.20* (.38)
Race by time interactions[c]	
African Americans × Year$_{\geq 1964}$	1.87* (.38)
Religion (reference = other religion)	
Liberal Protestants	−.48* (.17)
Moderate Protestants	−.26 (.14)
Conservative Protestants	−.31* (.14)
Catholics	.56* (.14)
Jewish	1.92* (.20)
No religion	.93* (.16)
Religion by time interactions	
Catholics × Year$_{1960}$	1.10* (.21)
Conservative Protestants × Year$_{1976/1980}$	.48* (.13)
Liberal Protestants * Year$_{1960-1992}$	.10* (.02)
Class (reference = non-labor force participant)	
Professionals	−.20 (.17)
Managers	.16 (.46)
Routine white-collar employees	−.22* (.11)
Self-employed	−.26* (.13)
Skilled workers	1.18* (.41)
Non-skilled workers	.16 (.12)
Class by time interactions	
Professionals * Year$_{1964-\geq 1992}$	.03 (.03)
Managers * Year$_{1960-1972}$	−.17* (.08)
Self-employed × Year$_{\geq 1980}$	−.57* (.18)
Skilled Workers * Year$_{1960\geq 1972}$	−.27* (.09)
Non-skilled Workers × Year$_{\geq 1980}$	−.36* (.14)
Gender (reference = men)	
Women	.23* (.11)
Gender by time interactions	
Women * (Year)^2	.01 (.02)

TABLE 6.2. *Continued*

Independent variables	Coefficient (s.e.)
Additional interactions	
Women × non-labor force participant	−.33* (.11)
Region (reference = South)	
All other regions	−.04 (.06)
Years of education (continuous)	−.08* (.01)
Age (continuous)	−.01* (<.01)

[a] An asterisk indicates significance at the .05 level (2–tailed test).
[b] Dependent variable is coded '1' for the choice of the Democratic, and '0' for the choice of the Republican candidate.
[c] Unconstrained interaction effects designated by '×' (subscript denotes time period); linearly constrained interaction effects designated by '*' (subscript denotes time period).

which—as already implied by our model—increased dramatically after 1960. While average racial differences in presidential voting have fluctuated since that time, they show no sign of a net decline in magnitude. The multivariate kappas in the right-hand panel show that when the racial cleavage is estimated net of change in the other three cleavages (and the controls for age, education, and region), the picture of its evolution is very similar.

The second largest cleavage is for religion, with the results in Figure 6.2 showing that the average difference between each religious group and their overall mean is roughly *half* of the racial cleavage in the post-1964 period. The trend line for religious cleavages does reveal a net decline, although a sizable portion of this decline is attributable to the inflated religious differences of the 1960 election which were produced by Catholics' unusually high levels of support for Democratic (and Catholic) candidate John Kennedy. The multivariate index of the religious cleavage shows a similar picture of trends, though religious differences appear somewhat larger in the 1968 election when other cleavages and the controls are taken into account. As with the racial cleavage, the magnitude of the religious cleavage appears to be largely independent of the other three cleavages (which can be inferred by comparing the value of the bi versus multivariate kappas at each election). In fact, the comparison between trends under the bi versus multivariate measures shows that the religious cleavage is slightly suppressed by the other cleavages, given that the estimates for the multivariate kappas are larger in the 1980 through 1992 elections.

The class cleavage has not undergone a monotonic pattern of change,

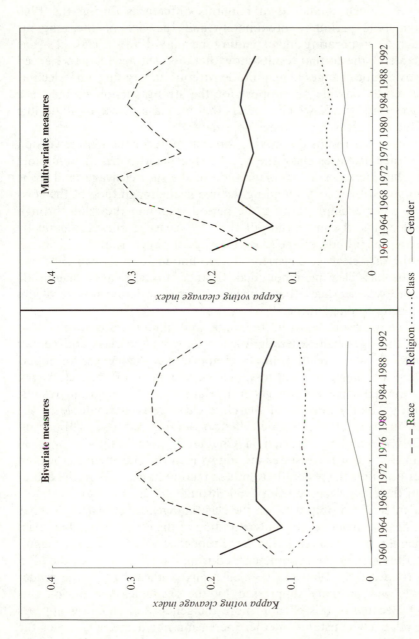

Fig. 6.2. Race, religion, class, and gender cleavages in presidential elections, 1960–1992

instead declining through 1972 and then rebounding. Class differences have been much smaller than religious differences during the 1960 through 1992 period, approximately half the size of the religious cleavage. Corroborating and extending the analysis of the class cleavage in Chapter 3, the current results show that this cleavage has experienced some over-time changes in magnitude without undergoing a net decline. These results provide no support for the strong version of the 'race displaces class' thesis, which predicts that the class cleavage will decline once the race cleavage becomes dominant.

However, our results do provide some support for the weaker version of the 'race displaces class' thesis. The right-hand panel in Figure 6.2 shows that increases in the magnitude of the race cleavage tend to be accompanied by a corresponding decline in the magnitude of the class cleavage. For example, during the period spanning the 1960 through 1972 elections, the magnitude of the race cleavage grew dramatically while the magnitude of the class cleavage declined slightly. Likewise, when the race cleavage experienced a decline in size between 1984 and 1992, the class cleavage rebounded. Changes in the relative magnitude of these two cleavages thus appear to have a significant, zero-sum relationship to one another.

The comparison between bivariate and multivariate results also reveals the significant interrelationship between the class and gender cleavages. This interrelationship has important consequences for understanding the magnitude and historical development of these cleavages. First, the class cleavage is generally larger in the bivariate results, illustrating that a portion of the class cleavage is attributable to the greater impact of class-related factors among women. This result parallels the finding reported in Chapter 5 concerning the political relevance of labor force status among women (but not men). However, it does not alter the generally trendless picture in changes in the evolution of the class cleavage from 1960 through 1992.

The interrelationship between the class and gender cleavages also has a significant impact on our understanding of the gender gap. Once class and gender are measured in the same model of vote choice, the magnitude of the gender cleavage increases during the earlier part of the NES series (between the 1960 and 1976 elections), indicating that the gender cleavage was partially suppressed by the class cleavage during this period. Because of this phenomenon, the gender cleavage now appears to be relatively constant—neither increasing nor decreasing—over the entire 1960 through 1992 series (see the right-hand panel of Figure 6.2). This phenomenon is itself a product of the growing proportion of women employed full-time in the labor force. More specifically, because this proportion is considerably smaller in early years in the NES series, it has a smaller impact on the overall political alignment of all women; however, as the proportion of working women grows, the political effects of this change on women's overall political alignment (and thus the gender gap) increases. It is thus only when we simultaneously control for the effects of class and gender that the (stable) political effects of labor force participation among women are visible throughout the entire NES series.

Trends in the Total Social Cleavage

Have the preceding patterns of change in specific social cleavages affected the total social cleavage in presidential elections? The results presented in Figure 6.3 provide us with a systematic means of exploring this issue, presenting lambda index scores for the total social cleavage using both bivariate and multivariate measures. The darker lines represent the average of the four cleavages. They show no net change in the magnitude of the total social cleavage during the 1960 through 1992 period.

To what extent is the growth of the racial cleavage responsible for preventing the total social cleavage from declining, as some analysts have suggested?[34] The lighter pair of trend lines in Figure 6.3 tests this hypothesis. We derive the scores comprising these trend lines by excluding race from the calculation of lambda. When the large race cleavage is deleted, the magnitude of the total social cleavage is predictably smaller. However, both bivariate and multivariate trend lines are now flat from 1964 through 1992, revealing no net trends (again noting that the 1960 inflation of the religious and total social cleavages is due to the exceptional support among Catholics for the Democratic candidate). Even had the politicization of the racial cleavage not occurred, there would be no decline in the total social cleavage.

Taken as a whole, these results show that the zero-sum interrelationship between the race and class cleavages has not produced an overall decline in the magnitude of the four social cleavages. Even if we completely ignore the race cleavage, the total social cleavage shows no change (much less decline) from the 1964 through 1992 elections. This phenomenon is attributable to the fact that the class cleavage has not experienced a net decline during this period. It also implies that even dramatic changes in the powerful race cleavage are unlikely to result in the displacement of all other social cleavages.

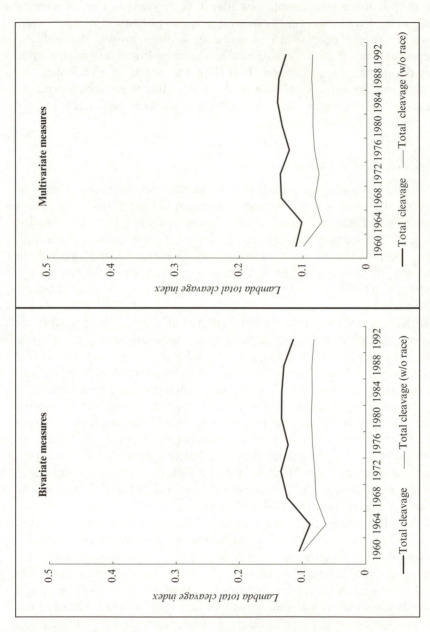

FIG. 6.3. The total social cleavage in presidential elections, 1960–1992

CONCLUSION

We find no support for the thesis that social cleavages as a whole have declined in magnitude in U.S. presidential elections since 1960. There have in fact been increases in two of the four major social cleavages we examine (race and gender), small decreases in one (religion), and no net change in the fourth (class). In terms of the rank order and relative magnitudes of each of the cleavages, we find, not surprisingly, that race has by far represented the largest cleavage during the period since 1964. African-American voters have overwhelmingly embraced the Democratic Party (in both relative and absolute terms), while white voters have moved away from that party. The next largest cleavage has been the religious cleavage, with the class and gender cleavages following (in order). Most interestingly, the ordinal ranking of the race, religion, class and gender cleavages has been stable since 1964 (although we will see in chapter 8 that this did not hold in 1996).

Because our analyses investigate the interrelationship between social cleavages, they help us to better understand some of the claims made in the literature about the impact of the rise of the race cleavages on other social cleavages. With respect to the race/class thesis, we find no support for the strong version of this thesis which asserts that the emergence of the race cleavage leads to a lasting dealignment of the class cleavage. However, we do find evidence supporting the weak version of the thesis, namely, that when the race cleavage grows during a particular election, the class cleavage experiences a corresponding shrinkage during that election. While some presidential elections have clearly been marked by the prominent use of campaign messages that activate the racial resentments of some whites, our results also imply that the zero-sum relationship between the race and class cleavages can be produced even in the absence of such explicit cues.[35] Nevertheless, despite the powerful impact of the race cleavage, our analyses also provide evidence that even large increases in this cleavage in future elections will be insufficient by themselves to displace the other three cleavages.

7

Party Coalitions

Most of the debates about the state of American political parties—and the nature of party decline and renewal—have centered on questions about the organizational capacities of the parties and their ability to carry out partisan policy goals once in government.[1] In this chapter, by contrast, we extend our analyses of social cleavages to consider how cleavages shape the two major parties electoral *coalitions*, and also where the votes that put parties (and their candidates) in office in the first place come from. A number of commentators have argued that the social bases of party coalitions have changed in ways that have significantly influenced their policy agendas. The growing gender gap, for example, has led to discussions of a possible 'feminization' of the Democratic Party. The widely used 'Reagan Democrat' label is based on the idea that since 1980 Republican presidential candidates are receiving a growing proportion of their votes from white, working-class voters. Others have asserted that the growing importance of educated middle-class voters has encouraged the Democrats to abandon their traditional focus on public policies aimed at the working and lower middle classes in favor of a policy agenda that addresses the interests of the educated middle class. The growing influence of the Christian Right agenda in the Republican Party is often attributed to their growing numbers at the ballot box. Virtually all commentators on race and politics have noted that the increasing importance of black votes to Democratic candidates makes Democratic politicians reluctant to abandon a strong civil rights platform.

All of these examples share the presupposition that social groups affect the formation of party coalitions and, ultimately, party strategies. In this sense, they stand in direct contrast to the 'declining significance of social cleavages' arguments considered in earlier chapters. The latter implies that the group foundations of the parties' electoral coalitions have become more similar over time. As the parties become detached from a distinct social foundation, the argument goes, other factors (organizational, elite-driven fundraising, etc.) become increasingly important. In Chapters 3 through 6, we have reconsidered and rejected claims about the declining significance of social factors with respect to group alignments through 1992. But these approaches may still be informative when it comes to examining the *impact* of social groups on the composition of party coalitions. Whereas group political alignments are affected solely by group-specific patterns of vote choice, party coalitions are also influenced by a group's size and turnout rate. We thus examine the possibility of declining social group impacts.

Our analyses in this chapter differ from most of the recent social science literature on social groups and political behavior. These literatures have focused on group differences in voting or partisanship independently of the actual impact of groups at the ballot box. The lack of attention to questions about group impacts is due to a nearly exclusive focus on the structural association of group membership and voting behavior. Structural questions ask about the relationship of group membership to voting behavior, and they can be answered using *margin-free* measures that do not take into account the relative size of a sub-group. Questions about the impact of group membership on party coalitions, by contrast, ask about their consequences for election outcomes, and they must be answered using *margin-dependent* measures (which do take into account sub-group size).[2] Since our ultimate concern is with political change, we cannot stop with margin-free measures (such as those employed in Chapters 3–6 above). Shifts in demographic proportions and levels of political participation are also of fundamental importance. The methodological approach we introduce in the chapter allows us to combine information about group-specific political alignments with appropriate adjustments for group size and turnout rates.

WHERE DO THE VOTES COME FROM?

How much more reliant are Democrats on the votes of women, blacks, and middle-class voters today than in the early 1960s? Do the Republicans really receive a significantly larger share of their total votes from conservative Protestants, the self-employed, or even the working class than previously? There have been a number of previous attempts to examine this issue. However, most of the existing research on the social bases of U.S. party coalitions has focused on the party identification of different groups of voters, rather than actual electoral coalitions.[3] John Petrocik, for example, sought to recast the classic debate over party realignment by examining group-based changes in party identification. Petrocik identified fifteen social groups (high, middle, and low status Northern Protestants, high/middle and low status Southerners, union members, Jews, Polish and Irish Catholics, other Catholics, etc.) and placed all respondents in one of those categories. Petrocik's analyses suggested that except for blacks and Jews, all groups exhibited a tendency to move away from Democratic Party identification and towards independent identification. The political transformation of the South (and social groups defined by their regional identities) was especially notable, showing movement from overwhelming Democratic support towards increasing similarity with the rest of the country.[4]

The most systematic examination of the changing social bases of partisanship has been developed in the work of the political scientists Harold Stanley and Richard Niemi. They go beyond Petrocik's use of exclusive group definitions to estimate a series of multivariate models of partisanship that control for overlapping group memberships. They report that a number of changes in patterns of group support have lessened the sociodemographic distinctiveness of the Democratic coalition, although they find fewer changes in the group bases of Republican identification during this period.[5]

While studies of the social bases of party identification—such as those of Petrocek and Niemi—are informative in their own right, ultimately it is voting which decides elections (and produces de facto electoral coalitions). The regular surveys by Robert Axelrod in the 1970s and 1980s have provided the most comprehensive portrait of the impact of social group voting patterns in presidential elections. Axelrod's approach defined the impact of social groups on party coalitions as a function of a group's voting behavior, turnout rate, and relative size within the electorate.[6] His analyses found declining contributions from Catholics, Southerners, and union households to the electoral coalitions of Democratic presidential candidates from the 1950s to the 1980s. While Axelrod's approach captures the main components of electoral coalitions, his measures are bivariate and thus do not permit him to assess the consequences of particular types of group memberships while simultaneously holding constant other factors. This is a matter of considerable importance in view of the multiple group memberships of all voters and the overlapping nature of many cleavages.

The only study of which we are aware that employs a multivariate approach to examining social group voting alignments over an extended historical period are those of Robert S. Erikson and his colleagues, although they do not consider group-specific turnout rates as a component of party coalitions.[7] Erikson et al. analyze social groups and presidential voting between 1952 and 1984. Their key innovation is to use a statistical model that distinguishes group-specific from electorate-wide shifts, similar to the approach employed in this study. They also control for the size of the different groups they examine, but only by using the NES sample proportions (an issue we discuss below). Their results suggest that with the exception of Southern whites, the decline in Democratic fortunes can best be understood not as the decay of an old coalition, but as a general decline in Democratic voting among all groups. In fact, they even find evidence of increasing class divisions in the profiles of the two parties. However, they employ fairly crude conceptualizations of the class and religious cleavages in their analyses: class is treated as a dichotomous income variable (family income in the bottom third versus all others), while the religious variables lump all Protestants together. As we have already seen, such measurement decisions may obscure underlying trends or even lead to the detection of spurious trends.

Reconceptualizing the Impact of Social Groups on Party Coalitions

The new approach to understanding the linkages between social groups and party developed here starts from four key assumptions. First, in line with the earlier studies by Axelrod and Erikson et al., we conceptualize party coalitions as pertaining to voting and election outcomes, rather than party identification. Second, we assume that an adequate understanding of group-specific contributions to party coalitions requires the use of a multivariate approach that distinguishes between electorate-wide and group-specific changes in turnout and vote choice. In keeping with previous studies of partisanship by Stanley and Niemi and previous studies of voters by Erikson et al., we thus employ multivariate models to calculate the group-specific probabilities of favoring the Democratic or Republican Party for a particular election.

Third, we take into account the size of the group in question. The importance of the size of particular groups is obvious: large groups have a bigger impact on party coalitions than small groups. Small groups such as Jews must have exceptionally strong and durable partisan loyalties to have much impact on the overall shape of the coalition. The changing size of groups is also of particular importance for our investigation. While a basic cleavage structure may remain in place, the size of key groups making up a cleavage may decline and thereby alter the structure of party coalitions.[8]

Finally, as shown originally by Axelrod, the rate of voter turnout within a group is a key component of a group's contribution. For instance, the impact of large groups can be limited by low turnout rates, or small groups can magnify their impact by high rates of participation. In general, this means that understanding the impact of group size requires that we conceptualize it as a proportion of *actual* voters within the electorate (rather than as a proportion of all eligible voters or the population as a whole). Successful electoral campaigns require the active participation of strongly aligned groups.

DATA AND MEASURES

As before, we examine NES data for presidential elections from 1960 through 1992. Our analyses proceed in two stages. First, we estimate group size, turnout rates, and voting alignment. While the voting alignment estimates follow directly from the analyses of the previous chapter, the size and turnout estimates are introduced here for the first time. In the second stage, we apply these estimates to analyze group contributions to party coalitions during the 1960–1992 period.

Dependent Variables

We use logistic regression models to analyze voter alignments (coded '1' for the Democratic and '0' for the Republican candidate, which we take from the previous chapter) and turnout rates (coded '1' a respondent reports voting and '0' otherwise). We then use the predicted probabilities for the main groups in our analyses to calculate their contribution to the major party coalitions.

Modelling the Impact of Social Groups on Party Coalitions

The measure of group impacts on party coalitions that we develop uses as its ingredients our estimates of group-specific alignments, size, and turnout rates. Equation 7.1 presents our initial formulation of the group impact index (γ_{lt}), where $l = 1$ for Democratic and 0 for Republican voters at election t. We refer to equation 7.1 as 'initial' because it ignores group-specific differences in turnout rates. Instead, the calculation of this index requires only that we know the predicted probability that the kth group will favor the l major party ($\hat{P}_{lkt}$), the size of the kth group at election t as a sample proportion ($\bar{X}_{kt}$), and the sample size (N) of the dataset for election t.[9]

$$\gamma_{lt} = \frac{\hat{P}_{lkt}\,\overline{X}_{kt}\,N_t}{\sum_{1}^{K}\hat{P}_{lkt}\,\overline{X}_{kt}\,N_t} \tag{7.1}$$

The index of social group impact in equation 7.1 is equivalent to the calculations described by Stanley and Niemi in their analyses of changes in the social group composition of party coalitions (albeit defined by party identification).[10] Predicted group-specific *voting alignments* can be obtained readily from a logistic regression model of vote choice, and the other quantities are unproblematic. This index has, however, two important limitations: it ignores group differences in turnout, and it takes as given the sample distribution for the social group variables in the NES.

We improve over these limitations using the 'corrected' index summarized by equation 7.2. The left-hand side of the equation is unchanged, as are group-specific alignments and sample size:

$$\gamma_{lt} = \frac{\hat{P}_{lkt}\,\hat{P}_{kmt}\,\mu_{kt}\,N_t}{\sum_{1}^{K}\hat{P}_{lkt}\,\hat{P}_{kmt}\,\mu_{kt}\,N_t} \tag{7.2}$$

However, in contrast to equation 7.1, equation 7.2 incorporates a correction for group size using Census data (μ_{kt}), and an additional parameter for group-specific turnout rates ($\hat{P}_{kmt}$), where $m = 1$ for voters and 0 otherwise (again for the kth social group at election t).[11] To calculate this index, we must also estimate the additional parameter for group-specific turnout rates. Once we have attained all the necessary estimates, we can then calculate the impact of the social groups in the analyses for a given election. These calculations represent the predicted proportion of a particular group amongst all Democratic or Republican voters (at a given election). By comparing a group's estimate with the corresponding figure for group size, we can thus gauge the over- or under-representation of that group in a party's coalition.

ANALYSES I: GROUP SIZE, TURNOUT, AND VOTE CHOICE

Group Size

The population distributions of the categories making up the class and religious cleavage have undergone substantial change since 1960. Most of these changes have been widely noted and require little comment here. Postindustrial economic development has altered the class structure, reducing the size of the manual working class and increasing the proportion of individuals in professional and managerial locations. How best to characterize and interpret these changes has been a matter of some controversy, of course, but the basic trends are not in dispute.

Similarly, analysts of religious demography have noted two basic trends: a significant decline in the mainline or liberal Protestant denominations (partially offset by increases in the more doctrinally conservative Protestant denominations, newer religious organizations including the non-denominational mega-churches, and other religious movements); and a rise in the proportion of individuals without religious affiliations.

To gauge the contributions of each of the groups we examine, it is necessary to include in the analyses appropriate adjustments for the (changing) size of these groups over time. We turn to Census Bureau data for information about the size of race, gender, and class categories to correct for the well-established overrepresentation of some groups of voters in the NES series (and the underrepresentation of others).[12] The use of Census data also addresses the problem of year-to-year sample variability in group size, a problem that can especially affect estimates for women and blacks (for which a couple of percentage point shifts in sampling distributions between elections can lead to an artificially large and misleading impact). For the religion variable, however, we rely on the NES sample proportions since the Census Bureau does not collect information on religion in view of the church/state separation doctrine.

Table 7.1 summarizes the size of the major social groups for the nine elections in the analysis. Not surprisingly, the univariate distribution of the race and gender variables change by no more than a couple of percentage points between 1960 and 1992. The distribution of the class variable, however, shows more extensive changes corresponding to the basic postindustrial trends found by other investigators.[13] The proportion of managers and professionals increases substantially relative to other classes in this period, with the proportion of routine white-collar workers are also increasing in size. The working-class categories, by contrast, are either stable (skilled workers) or declining (unskilled workers) in relative size. The residual non-full-time labor force category declines significantly during this period, mostly because of the entrance of women into the full-time labor force.

The most striking changes in the size of the key social groups we examine relate to the religious cleavage. Here we find that the proportion of liberal Protestants has declined by nearly half in a thirty-year period.

TABLE 7.1. *Sample/population distribution (% in columns) for groups in the analysis*

Social group	Source	1960	1964	1968	1972	1976	1980	1984	1988	1992
Race cleavage	*Statistical*									
All others	*Abstract of*	89.5	89.3	89.0	88.8	88.5	88.2	88.0	87.7	87.4
African American	*the US: 1995*	10.5	10.7	11.0	11.2	11.5	11.8	12.0	12.3	12.6
Religious cleavage	*1960–1992*									
Liberal Protestants	*National*	23.6	21.1	19.8	17.6	16.2	15.4	15.5	14.8	12.9
Moderate Protestants	*Election*	22.7	18.5	19.9	20.4	20.2	18.4	18.5	18.7	15.8
Conservative Protestants	*Studies*	26.0	28.7	29.9	28.4	26.9	26.7	26.6	30.2	28.5
Catholics		20.7	22.2	21.9	23.8	24.7	23.2	26.0	23.9	23.6
Jews		3.4	2.9	2.7	2.3	2.3	3.2	2.4	1.5	1.9
Other religions		2.3	3.0	2.7	3.3	4.0	4.2	2.8	2.2	3.7
No religion		1.3	3.6	3.2	4.3	5.8	9.0	8.2	8.7	13.6
Class cleavage	*1960, 1970,*									
Professionals	*1980, and*	5.9	6.7	7.5	8.0	8.3	8.6	9.1	9.6	10.0
Managers	*1990 Census*	3.1	3.5	4.0	4.7	5.8	6.9	7.8	8.7	9.7
Routine white-collar	*Public Use*	10.3	10.9	11.6	12.0	12.1	12.3	12.4	12.5	12.7
Self-employed (non-professionals)	*Microdata samples*	5.6	5.1	4.6	4.2	4.1	4.0	4.3	4.6	5.0
Skilled workers		7.1	7.3	7.4	7.4	7.3	7.2	7.2	7.3	7.3
Nonskilled workers		16.5	16.2	15.9	15.4	14.5	13.6	13.5	13.4	13.2
Non-full-time labor force		51.6	50.3	49.0	48.2	46.6	47.4	45.6	43.8	42.0
Gender cleavage	*Statistical*									
Men	*Abstract of*	49.4	49.2	49.0	48.8	48.7	48.6	48.7	48.7	48.8
Women	*the US: 1995*	50.6	50.8	51.0	51.2	51.3	51.4	51.3	51.3	51.2
NES Sample Size		874	1088	878	1565	1302	853	1353	727	1265

Moderate Protestant denominations have also declined, though not to the same degree as the liberal Protestant denominations. At the same time, the proportion of respondents without religion rises from a negligible number to around 9% by the 1980s. (We note that in 1992, the NES changed the wording of the religious identification question in such a way as to make it easier for respondents to report no religious affiliation; the proportion of respondents without religious affiliation become significantly higher than on other comparable surveys. We treat this figure with caution.) Both conservative Protestants and Catholics have increased slightly in size; the fact that the conservative Protestants grew slightly at the same time that liberal and moderate Protestant groups were declining magnifies the potential significance of these size changes.

Turnout

Overall turnout rates have fallen substantially since 1960, from 63% of adult citizens in 1960 (the postwar peak) to a shade under 50% in 1996. These falling turnout rates present an important paradox: participation has declined during a period in which many attributes long thought to encourage voting (such as educational levels) are rapidly rising in the general population, and legal and administrative barriers to participation (particularly registration) have fallen.[14] We will not attempt here to intervene in the general debate over declining turnout. However, an issue that is important for our investigation is the group-specific component of turnout change. Substantial literatures on the nature and causes of turnout changes among the groups comprising each of our four cleavage fields have been developed. There have been a number of theoretical efforts to pin down group-specific changes which are relevant for our investigation. The most important of these concern the religious and especially class cleavages (see Chapter 4's appendix for our discussion of religious turnout differences).

Race and Gender. Discussions of turnout changes among racial groups (African-American voters relative to whites) and gender (women relative to men) have been fairly straightforward. Previous analyses have documented the basic facts: turnout among African-American voters rose substantially in the early 1960s following the passage of the Voting Rights Act. At the national level it also appears to have been further stimulated by the Jesse Jackson presidential campaigns in 1984 and 1988, two years in which the black/white turnout gap is smallest.[15] But in 1992, the black/white turnout gap remained 8% in the NES data.

In the case of gender, the basic facts are also not in dispute. From the period of enfranchisement with the passage of the 19th Amendment in 1920 until the 1960s, men turned out to vote at higher rates than women. The gap steadily eroded over time, however, and by the 1970s men and women were voting at roughly comparable rates. (We should note that the NES series shows a weaker trend towards increased turn-out among women relative to men than the Census Bureau's Voter Supplement Surveys; in the latter series, turnout rates among women voters slightly surpass those of men in the 1980s and 1990s.)[16]

Class. In contrast to race and gender, there have been very significant debates over the nature of, and trends in, class turnout rates. The earliest studies of group differences in turnout establish clear evidence for a substantial turnout gap across the class structure. As Lester Milbrath put it in one early monograph on the subject, 'no matter how class is measured, studies consistently show that higher-class persons are more likely to participate in politics than lower-class persons.'[17] However, in multivariate analyses most of the effects of class location on the likelihood of voting are explained away by differences in educational achievement.[18] Aside from debates about the main effects of class on turnout (which are of less interest for our purposes here), a second key debate has developed over the role of class divisions in explaining the aggregate decline in turnout since 1960. Some authors have argued that the drop-off in turnout has been greatest among the working class and the poor.[19] Other analysts have rejected these claims, asserting that the fall-off has occurred more or less equally among all classes and that 'the voters remain the same.'[20] Either way, such trends would have implications for our group impact analyses. In particular, class-specific turnout trends involving working-class voters would affect the major party coalitions.

Turnout Analyses

The turnout analyses we present here are based on NES data. Respondents to the NES over-report voting by a very significant margin; for example, in 1996 just over 75% respondents to the NES claimed to have voted, while actual turnout was just under 50%. The reasons for this substantial over-estimation of turnout in the NES are well understood.[21] First, some respondents falsely claim to have voted, motivated, in part, by perceptions of social desirability stemming from citizenship duty. Second, the two-wave panel design of the NES, in

which respondents are initially interviewed before the election, stimu-
lates interest in the campaign and encourages people to vote who
otherwise might not. Finally, extremely low-income and low-education
voters who have the lowest turnout rates are underrepresented in the
NES sample. The turnout estimates provided in the Census Bureau's
voter supplement module, carried out in November of each election
year, provide significantly more accurate estimates of turnout. However,
the Census voter supplement studies only go back to 1964, and they do
not include information about respondents' religion. Since we are interested in trends in group-specific differences, our use of the NES data
should result in less measurement bias in comparison to electorate-wide
analyses. Indeed, virtually all past research on coalitions (with the sole
exception of Robert Axelrod's early studies) have assumed that social
groups have *identical* turnout rates which have not changed over time.
Our analyses, by contrast, systematically take into account group
differences in turnout, thereby capturing an important variable that
mediates group contributions to party coalitions.

Before presenting group-specific turnout rates, we must first gauge
the evidence for turnout trends among the specific social groups comprising each cleavage field. To this end, we compare a series of competing models of the relationship between social groups and voter turnout
for the 1960 through 1992 elections. Our strategy is thus the same as the
analysis in Chapter 6 of social groups and vote choice, with the difference being that we now examine voter turnout as our dependent
variable.

In Table 7.2, we present fit statistics with which to evaluate a series of
competing models of group-specific turnout. Model 1 includes the main
effects of election year, the four cleavage variables, and controls for
region, age, and education, thereby providing a baseline for comparing
subsequent models which include group-specific turnout trends. Model
2 readily improves over the fit of model 1, providing clear evidence for a
lasting change in voter turnout among African-Americans after 1960.
The lack of improvement in model 3's fit shows, however, that there is
no evidence for additional race-specific trends in turnout. Model 4 in
turn yields an improvement in fit over model 2, showing that the
candidacy of presidential candidate Jimmy Carter propelled conservative Protestants towards the ballot box (see Chapter 4 for further
information). The lack of improvement in model 5's fit provide no
evidence for additional religious group-specific trends in turnout.

Model 6 does not improve the fit of model 4, providing no evidence
for class-specific trends in voter turnout.[22] Similarly, model 7 does not

TABLE 7.2. *Fit statistics (degrees of freedom in parentheses) for logistic regression models of group-specific voter turnout in presidential elections[a] 1960–1992* (N = 14,068)

Models	Fit statistics	
	−2 log-likelihood (d.f.)	BIC
1. Election years, Race, Religion[b], Class, Gender, Region[b], Education (years), Age (years), and Women × Pre-franchise cohort (interaction effect[c])	13952.16 (14041)	−120,163
2. Model 1 + African Americans × Year$_{\geq 1964}$	13938.56 (14040)	−120,167
3. Model 1 + African Americans × Year (unconstrained)	13934.36 (14033)	−120,104
4. Model 2 + Conservative Protestants × Year$_{1976/80}$	13922.54 (14039)	−120,173
5. Model 4 + Religion × Year (unconstrained)	13859.30 (13992)	−119,787
6. Model 4 + Class × Year (unconstrained)	13868.52 (13992)	−119,778
7. Model 4 + Gender × Year (unconstrained)	13908.42 (14031)	−120,111
8. Model 4 + African Americans × Protestant	13912.51 (14038)	−120,174
9. Model 6 + All Two-Way Interactions: Race, Religion, Class, Gender	13832.64 (13979)	−119,690

[a] Data is from the National Election Studies. Dependent variable is coded '1' if a respondent reports voting, and '0' otherwise.
[b] Region is coded '1' for non-South, and '0' for residence in the South.
[c] −2 log-likelihood for model 1 without women × cohort interaction = 14022.11 (14042); BIC = -120,102.

improve the fit of model 4, providing no evidence of gender-specific trends in turnout. However, model 8 provides evidence for a significant race-by-religion interaction.[23] The comparison between models 8 and 9 favors model 8 according to the BIC index, but model 9 using the −2 log-likelihood statistic (the .04 *p*-value for the −2 log-likelihood statistic is just under the conventional .05 level of significance for the chi-square test). We were unable to find an 'intermediate' model including some of the interactions parameterized in model 9, and on grounds of parsimony, we thus side with the BIC result and choose model 8 as our preferred model of group-specific voter turnout.[24]

Table 7.3 presents the coefficients from our preferred model of group-specific turnout rates in presidential elections (Table 7.2's model 8).

TABLE 7.3. *Coefficients and predicted probabilities[a] for preferred model[b] of group-specific voter turnout in presidential elections, 1960–1992 (N = 14,068)*

Independent variables	Coefficient (s.e.)	$\hat{P}_{1960}$	$\hat{P}_{1964}$	$\hat{P}_{1968}$	$\hat{P}_{1972}$	$\hat{P}_{1976}$	$\hat{P}_{1980}$	$\hat{P}_{1984}$	$\hat{P}_{1988}$	$\hat{P}_{1992}$
Constant	-2.69* (.20)	—	—	—	—	—	—	—	—	—
Election years (reference = 1960)										
1964	-.47* (.12)	—	—	—	—	—	—	—	—	—
1968	-.76* (.12)	—	—	—	—	—	—	—	—	—
1972	-.97* (.11)	—	—	—	—	—	—	—	—	—
1976	-1.11* (.12)	—	—	—	—	—	—	—	—	—
1980	-1.26* (.12)	—	—	—	—	—	—	—	—	—
1984	-1.24* (.11)	—	—	—	—	—	—	—	—	—
1988	-1.12* (.13)	—	—	—	—	—	—	—	—	—
1992	-1.08* (.11)	—	—	—	—	—	—	—	—	—
Race (reference = all else)		.89	.84	.80	.76	.74	.71	.71	.73	.74
African-Americans	-1.32* (.32)	.69	.79	.74	.70	.67	.64	.64	.67	.68
Race by time interactions										
African-Americans × Year$_{\geq 1964}$	1.01* (.27)	—	—	—	—	—	—	—	—	—
Religion (reference = other religion)		.79	.70	.64	.59	.55	.52	.52	.55	.56
Liberal Protestants	.52* (.12)	.86	.80	.75	.71	.68	.64	.65	.68	.68
Moderate Protestants	.65* (.12)	.87	.82	.77	.73	.70	.67	.68	.70	.71
Conservative Protestants	.25* (.12)	.83	.75	.69	.65	.71	.68	.58	.61	.62
Catholics	.81* (.12)	.89	.84	.80	.76	.74	.71	.71	.73	.74
Jewish	.94* (.22)	.91	.86	.82	.78	.76	.73	.74	.76	.77
No religion	.01 (.13)	.79	.70	.64	.59	.56	.52	.52	.55	.56
Religion by time, race interactions										
Conservative Protestants × Year$_{1976/1980}$	.42* (.11)	—	—	—	—	—	—	—	—	—
African Americans × Protestants (homogeneous category)	.60* (.19)	—	—	—	—	—	—	—	—	—

	Coefficient									
Class (reference = non-labor force participant)	.89	.84	.80	.76	.74	.71	.71	.73	.74
Professionals	.73* (.09)	.95	.92	.89	.87	.85	.83	.84	.85	.86
Managers	.64* (.11)	.94	.91	.88	.86	.84	.82	.82	.84	.84
Routine white-collar employees	.55* (.07)	.94	.90	.87	.85	.83	.81	.81	.83	.83
Self-employed	.66* (.10)	.94	.91	.88	.86	.84	.82	.83	.84	.85
Skilled workers	.30* (.09)	.92	.88	.84	.81	.79	.76	.77	.79	.79
Nonskilled workers	.04 (.07)	.90	.85	.80	.77	.74	.71	.72	.74	.75
Gender (reference = men)	.89	.84	.80	.76	.74	.71	.71	.73	.74
Women	−.10* (.05)	.88	.83	.78	.74	.72	.68	.67	.71	.72
Gender by cohort interaction										
Women × Pre-franchisement generation[c]	−.95* (.11)	—	—	—	—	—	—	—	—	—
Region (reference = South)										
All other regions	−.44* (.05)	—	—	—	—	—	—	—	—	—
Years of education (continuous)	.22* (.01)	—	—	—	—	—	—	—	—	—
Age (continuous)	.04* (<.01)	—	—	—	—	—	—	—	—	—

[a] Asterisk next to a coefficient indicates significance at the .05 level (2-tailed test). Dependent variable is coded '1' if a respondent reports voting, '0' otherwise.

[b] Unconstrained interaction effects designated by '×' (subscript denotes time period); linearly constrained interaction effects designated by '*' (subscript denotes time period).

[c] Women born prior to 1901.

These coefficients reveal dramatic differences in voter turnout amongst social groups. For example, nonskilled workers are the least likely class to vote, while conservative Protestants and those with 'no religion' have the lowest participation rates amongst religious groups. As before, our primary interest lies with using the model's coefficients to calculate group-specific turnout rates. The nine columns of the table following the coefficients present the predicted probabilities we use in our later analyses.

Group Alignments

Our estimates of group-based alignments are the estimates developed in the previous chapter. In the chapter appendix, we formally present these results (in Table 7A.1). Like the estimates from Table 7.3, we use the predicted probabilities for each specific social group in a particular election as a component of our analysis of the impact of social cleavages on party coalitions.

ANALYSES II: CHANGES IN THE SOCIAL BASES OF U.S. PARTY COALITIONS

We now have sufficient information about group size, turnout, and voting alignments to develop an analysis of how and to what extent the national party coalitions have changed since 1960. Our 'impact' estimates for the Democratic Party's coalition are presented in Table 7.4. In the first nine columns we present estimates for the social group bases of the Democratic coalition for each election from 1960 through 1992. The estimates in each of these columns are the predicted proportion of group-specific voters amongst all Democratic voters; the net change in this proportion between the 1960 and 1992 presidential elections is summarized in the final column. The corresponding estimates for the Republican coalition are presented in Table 7.5. (In the case of the religious cleavage, however, we note the net change from 1964 to 1988, in view of the unique Kennedy 1960 effect, and the changed wording of religiosity question in 1992 which inflated the proportion of respondents with no religious identification.)

   The results for racial groups present a portrait of divergent changes in the two major party coalitions. Over time, African-American voters have increased their presence in the Democratic coalition. Not surprisingly, when the Democratic candidate loses, the exceptional loyalty of

TABLE 7.4. *The impact[a] of social groups on the Democratic coalition, 1960–1992*

Social group	1960	1964	1968	1972	1976	1980	1984	1988	1992	Δ_{Net}
Race cleavage										
All others	90	87	88	79	83	80	80	81	83	−7
African-Americans	10	13	12	21	17	20	20	19	17	+7
Religious cleavage[b]										
Liberal Protestants	16	19	17	15	13	13	15	16	13	−3
Moderate Protestants	16	18	17	16	15	13	14	15	17	−3
Conservative Protestants	19	24	22	19	27	26	17	20	20	−4
Catholics	38	28	32	35	31	29	36	32	29	+4
Jews	7	5	6	6	4	7	6	5	3	0
Other religions	2	3	2	3	3	3	2	2	3	−1
No religion	2	4	4	6	6	10	10	10	14	+6
Class cleavage										
Professionals	6	7	8	9	9	10	11	11	12	+6
Managers	3	3	3	3	5	5	6	7	8	+5
Routine white-collar	10	11	11	11	12	13	13	13	13	+3
Self-employed (non-professionals)	5	5	4	4	4	3	3	3	4	−1
Skilled Workers	8	8	8	7	7	7	7	7	7	−1
Nonskilled workers	17	17	17	17	16	13	13	13	13	−4
Non-full-time labor force	51	49	49	48	48	49	47	45	43	−8
Gender cleavage										
Men	50	51	51	51	51	51	51	52	51	+1
Women	50	49	49	49	49	49	49	48	49	−1

[a] Numbers in columns are the predicted proportion of a row-specific group among all Democratic voters in a specific election year. Numbers in the last column are the predicted change in these proportions (for a given group) between 1960 and 1992. Predicted proportions do not all sum to 100 due to rounding error.

[b] Changes in the net impact of religious groups on the Democratic coalition are calculated for 1964 vs. 1988 (due to the unusually high degree of Catholic support given to Democratic candidate John Kennedy in 1960 and the introduction of a new NES measure of respondents with no religion in 1992).

black voters results in their considerable overrepresentation in the Democratic coalition (e.g. 20% in 1984 and 19% in 1988). The predicted net increase between 1960 and 1992 in the proportion of African-American Democratic voters is a more modest 7%, owing to Democrat Bill Clinton's improved performance among major party white voters in the 1992 election. (Because we measure racial group membership as a dichotomy, the non-black results are simply the mirror image.) The main finding for the racial basis of the Republican coalition is that black voters declined to little more than a token presence after 1960.

The religious group bases of party coalitions have experienced even more dramatic changes over time. The shrinking numbers of liberal Protestant voters has had an impact, and combined with their decreasing Republican alignment resulted in a massive 12% decline in their

TABLE 7.5. *The impact[a] of social groups on the Republican coalition, 1960–1992*

Social group	1960	1964	1968	1972	1976	1980	1984	1988	1992	Δ_{Net}
Race cleavage										
All others	97	100	99	99	99	99	99	99	99	+2
African-Americans	3	0	1	1	1	1	1	1	1	−2
Religious cleavage[b]										
Liberal Protestants	30	26	22	19	18	16	16	14	12	−12
Moderate Protestants	27	21	23	24	25	22	23	23	21	2
Conservative Protestants	31	33	31	30	28	29	28	34	34	+1
Catholics	9	15	18	22	22	22	25	21	21	+6
Jews	1	1	1	0	1	1	16	1	1	0
Other religions	2	3	2	3	3	4	2	2	3	−1
No religion	1	2	2	2	3	5	5	5	7	+3
Class cleavage										
Professionals	7	8	9	9	9	9	9	10	10	+3
Managers	4	5	5	6	8	9	10	12	14	+10
Routine white-collar	13	13	13	14	14	14	14	14	14	+1
Self-employed (non-professionals)	7	7	6	6	6	6	6	7	7	0
Skilled Workers	4	5	7	8	8	7	7	7	7	+3
Nonskilled workers	14	14	14	14	12	13	13	13	13	−1
Non-full-time labor force	51	48	46	45	43	42	40	38	35	−16
Gender cleavage										
Men	48	47	48	48	47	49	50	48	47	−1
Women	52	53	52	52	53	51	50	52	53	+1

[a] Numbers in columns are the predicted proportion of a row-specific group among all Republican voters in a specific election year. Numbers in the last column are the predicted change in these proportions (for a given group) between 1960 and 1992. Predicted proportions do not all sum to 100 due to rounding error.

[b] Changes in the net impact of religious groups on the Republican coalition are calculated for 1964 vs. 1988 (due to the unusually high degree of Catholic support given to Democratic candidate John Kennedy in 1960 and the introduction of a new NES measure of respondents with no religion in 1992).

contributions to the Republican coalition between 1964 and 1988.[25] Conservative Protestants have increased their presence in the Republican coalition, but the increase is a modest 1% if we compare 1964 with 1988. Consistent with our findings about the stability in their political alignment and turnout (with the exception of the 1976 and 1980 elections), the impact of conservative Protestant group membership has not led to either a dramatic change or a clear tilt towards the Republican coalition. Finally, while the presence of Catholics in the Democratic coalition has not changed much since 1964, they show a steady and large increase in the Republican coalition during this period (+6). This is the result of their increased size, and, more importantly, the fall-off in votes from liberal Protestants in the overall composition of the Republican coalition.

Both parties have seen a large increase in the proportion of voters without religious affiliation over this period. Among Democratic voters, one out of ten voters in 1988 had no religious affiliation, up from just 4% in 1964 (and 2% in 1960). (The figure rises to 14% in 1992, but that figure is not strictly comparable because of the change in question wording.) Although secular people are commonly thought of as liberals, the proportion of voters without religious affiliation has also increased in the Republican coalition, from 2% in 1964 to 5% in 1988 (7% in 1992 with the new question wording).[26]

The class bases of the two parties have undergone significant revisions. (In evaluating these results, it is important to keep in mind that the magnitude of the shifts among the working population is reduced by the large residual non-full-time labor force category.) Although professionals have grown as a proportion of the labor force, their +3% growth in the Republican coalition is slightly less than their +4% growth in the general population during this same period (see Table 7.1). However, professionals' increasing tendency to favor Democratic presidential candidates has made them a larger presence in the Democratic coalition (showing a net predicted increase of 6% between 1960 and 1992). The reverse pattern is observed for managers, who have experienced a 10 percentage point increase in the Republican coalition, but a smaller (5%) increase in the Democratic coalition. Both parties have become more oriented towards the educated middle classes, but Democratic gains have come disproportionately from professionals while Republican gains have come mostly from managers.

Other classes show generally smaller over-time change in their impact. Our results for the self-employed show little change in either coalition. The self-employed have experienced a large shift in alignment towards the Republicans (see Chapter 3). However, their small (and slightly declining) size has largely offset the impact of this change. Skilled and nonskilled workers remain a small presence in the Republican coalition, although skilled workers have grown in the Republican coalition (+3%) over this period. However, both skilled and nonskilled workers have experienced drops in their contribution to the Democratic coalition. While the two working-class categories combined have slightly increased their presence in the Republican coalition (+2%), they have declined in their contributions to the Democratic coalition (−5%).

Our residual non-full time labor force category shows very sharp declines in both coalitions, with a much larger drop (−16%) for the Republican coalition. While this result is by itself difficult to interpret

given the heterogeneous nature of this group, it helps to underscore the
changing class character of the Republican coalition. The importance
of managers has increased dramatically (+10%), while support from
housewives and other individuals outside the paid labor force has
declined. Both parties receive more votes from employed persons in
all classes than in 1960, but the impact of this shift is twice as great for
the Republicans.

The results for gender appear at first glance paradoxical. We find only
fairly minute changes in the contribution of women voters to both
parties' coalitions in Tables 7.4 and 7.5. Indeed, the analysis actually
suggests a slight *drop* in the contribution of women to the Democratic
coalition). This result flies in the face of evidence of a rising gender gap
in voter alignment (see Chapter 5). The answer, however, lies in our
earlier findings about the source of the gender gap in voting. Because it
is largely a product of class-related factors (the entrance of increasing
numbers of women into the full-time labor force), once we control for
the effects of labor force participation the gap disappears. This means
that the gendering of the two parties' coalitions is apparent only when
we ignore simultaneous, class-related changes affecting the coalitions.
The raw figures from the NES bear this out: in 1960, women voters were
49% of all Democratic voters, but were 60% in 1980 and 58% in 1992. It
is this latter result which has excited commentators about a possible
'feminization' of the Democratic Party. But because the raw figures are
not derived from a multivariate model that includes controls for labor
force status, they suggest a potentially misleading story that exaggerates
the importance of gender *per se* on the composition of the Democratic
(and Republican) Party coalition.

The Party of Non-Voters

Finally, in Table 7.6, we present the results for the composition of the
'party of non-voters.' Because the size of this group is much larger than
in comparable capitalist democracies—indeed, it is the most distinctive
feature of the contemporary U.S. polity—it is worth taking note of its
social composition. With regard to the race cleavage, African-American
voters' presence among all non-voters declined substantially from 25%
in 1960 to a stable 14% through 1988 (15% in 1992). Given that our
analyses find very little religious group-specific changes in turnout rates,
changes in the likelihood that the seven religious groups in our analyses
will be non-voters are driven primarily by changes in their respective
sizes. As a result, liberal Protestants have shrunk considerably in the

TABLE 7.6. *The impact[a] of social groups on the nonvoting public, 1960–1992*

Social group	1960	1964	1968	1972	1976	1980	1984	1988	1992	Δ_{Net}
Race cleavage										
All others	75	86	86	86	86	86	86	85	85	+10
African-Americans	25	14	14	14	14	14	14	14	15	−10
Religious cleavage[b]										
Liberal Protestants	24	20	19	17	17	16	15	14	12	−6
Moderate Protestants	21	16	18	18	20	18	16	19	14	3
Conservative Protestants	32	35	36	33	26	25	31	35	32	0
Catholics	16	17	17	19	21	20	21	19	18	+2
Jews	2	2	2	2	2	3	2	1	1	−1
Other religions	3	4	4	5	6	6	4	3	5	−1
No religion	2	5	4	6	8	13	11	12	18	+7
Class cleavage										
Professionals	3	4	5	5	6	6	6	6	6	+3
Managers	2	2	3	3	4	5	6	6	7	+5
Routine white-collar	7	8	8	8	9	9	10	9	10	+3
Self-employed (non-professionals)	4	3	3	3	3	3	3	3	3	−1
Skilled Workers	6	6	7	7	7	7	7	7	7	+1
Nonskilled workers	18	18	18	17	17	16	15	15	15	−3
Non-full-time labor force	61	59	56	56	54	55	54	53	51	−10
Gender cleavage										
Men	47	48	47	47	47	46	45	47	47	0
Women	53	52	53	53	53	54	55	53	53	0

[a] Numbers in columns are the predicted proportion of a row-specific group among all nonvoters in a specific election year. Numbers in the last column are the predicted change in these proportions (for a given group) between 1960 and 1992. Predicted proportions do not all sum to 100 due to rounding error.

[b] Changes in the net impact of religious groups on the nonvoters are calculated for 1964 vs. 1988 (due to the unusually high degree of Catholic support given to Democratic candidate John Kennedy in 1960 and the introduction of a new NES measure of respondents with no religion in 1992).

non-voting public, while respondents with no religion have increased substantially (showing a net 7% increase between 1964 and 1988, and a larger 13% increase using the new 1992 NES measure).

The results for the class cleavage are also largely a product of changes in the size of specific classes. For instance, although professionals and managers enjoy unusually high (and stable) turnout rates, their presence among the non-voting public has increased simply because of their growing proportion within the postindustrial workforce. Similarly, non-skilled workers have the lowest likelihood of turning out to vote of any class, but represent a smaller share of non-voters by virtue of their declining numbers during this period covered by the NES series. Finally, the results for the impact of our non-labor force participant category and the gender cleavage attest to the growing presence of women in both the labor force and in the electorate.

CONCLUSION

This chapter has examined changes in the impact of major social groups on U.S. party coalitions between the 1960s and the 1990s. Some of our key findings have been anticipated by other scholars: for example, the growing importance of African-Americans and the declining contribution of working-class voters to the Democratic coalition. The current analyses provide a useful corroboration, however, given our use of multivariate models that take into account group-specific turnout rates and adjusted group size. They also underscore a critical dynamic of the contemporary racial bases of the two parties: elections in which Democratic presidential candidates do well reduce the overrepresentation of black voters in the party's coalition.

Another finding that confirms and extends the conventional wisdom concerns the shrinking impact of liberal Protestants on both parties. Declining numbers of liberal Protestants in the electorate has meant that both parties receive fewer votes from this group than before. The impact is magnified within the Republican coalition, however, due to the erosion of liberal Protestants' once strong alignment with that party. Indeed, it may not be an exaggeration to say that the increased prominence of the Christian Right in the Republican Party is due not so much to a rapid increase in votes from conservative Protestants, but instead from the loss of the moderating influence of liberal (and moderate) Protestant voters.

Our analyses also deliver some new, counterintuitive findings about the social group basis of major party coalitions. For the Democrats, the most significant development is the striking growth of professional voters in their electoral coalition. Professionals were twice as numerous among all Democratic voters in 1992 as they were in 1960. Nonskilled workers—who were *three times* as large a presence as professionals in the 1960 coalition—provided only a handful more votes than professionals by 1992. The ratio of working class to professional/managerial votes in the party has gone from 2.8:1 in 1960 to an astounding 1.1:1 by 1992. The claim that the social bases of the 'new' Democratic Party have made that party increasingly receptive to the demands of more affluent voters—a point widely asserted on the political left—is clearly borne out by these figures.

The Declining Social Bases of Party Coalitions?

We opened the chapter by noting that defenders of the declining social cleavage thesis may have been incorrect with respect to the political alignments of key social groups, they could none the less be right with respect to the composition of the two party's coalitions. This is because changes in group size and turnout rates may alter the actual impact of social cleavages in elections. Inspection of Tables 7.4 and 7.5 lend some support to the declining cleavage thesis. In the case of the class cleavage, the profiles of the two parties are clearly more similar in 1992 than they were in 1960. By 1992, both parties were getting 20% of their votes from working-class voters, and while the Republicans got 24% of their votes from managers and professionals, the Democrats received fully 20% of their votes from these two elite classes.

Similarly, in the case of the religious cleavage, the sharp erosion of contributions from liberal Protestants to the Republican coalition has altered and narrowed the diffferences between the parties. In 1964, liberal Protestants provided 26% of Republican votes and 19% of Democratic votes. By 1988 and 1992, they actually made slightly larger contributions to the Democratic coalition. Both parties have seen an increase in non-religious voters (although the increase has been greater on the Democratic side).

It is often said in American politics that the two major parties are mirror images of one another. In the common scholarly formulation of this thesis, the parties were once far apart in their social composition but are now becoming increasingly similar. One of the central concerns in this book was to examine the declining social cleavage thesis from the standpoint of political alignments of different social groups in the electorate. In Chapters 3 through 6, we presented results about group alignments that were largely inconsistent with the claim that social groups were becoming similar in their electoral alignments. However, when we take into account the effects of turnout rates and (especially) demographic shifts in the size of social groups, a stronger case can be made for the convergence thesis. Race and gender differences between the parties have grown. But in the case of religion and especially class, arguments about the declining role of social divisions have greater relevance to understanding the sources of compositional similarity between the Democratic and Republican coalitions. We discuss these implications in the conclusion.

APPENDIX: CHANGES IN
GROUP POLITICAL ALIGNMENTS

The estimates of group-based voting behavior used in this chapter are similar to the results from the previous chapter. We present them in this appendix for the benefit of those readers who wish to follow the modelling procedures more closely. In the first two columns of Table 7.A1, we present the coefficients and standard errors for our preferred model of group-specific political alignments in presidential elections from 1960 through 1992. We take the preferred model from the previous chapter as our point of departure, and adopt Stanley and Niemi's procedure for calculating these predicted probabilities.[27] That is, we calculate the expected probability for each individual respondent in the pooled NES dataset; the predicted group-specific probability for a given election is then the average of the predicted probabilities of all (individual) group members in that year. Note also that the first step of these calculations takes into account not only the main effects of year and group membership, but also their interaction (if these are present in the model) representing changes in that groups' political alignment. In the remaining columns of Table 7.A1, we thus present the predicted probabilities of favoring the Democratic candidate for each election.

Our interest in this chapter lies in using the predicted probabilities to calculate the (margin-dependant) impact of social groups on party coalitions, and we use the nine columns of predicted probabilities for the subsequent calculations presented in the text of the chapter itself.

APPENDIX TABLE 7.A1. *Coefficients and predicted probabilities[a] for preferred model[b] of group-specific alignments in presidential voting, 1960–1992 (N = 9,905)*

Independent variables	Coefficient (s.e.)	$\hat{P}_{1960}$	$\hat{P}_{1964}$	$\hat{P}_{1968}$	$\hat{P}_{1972}$	$\hat{P}_{1976}$	$\hat{P}_{1980}$	$\hat{P}_{1984}$	$\hat{P}_{1988}$	$\hat{P}_{1992}$
Constant	.99* (.24)	—	—	—	—	—	—	—	—	—
Election years (reference = 1960)										
1964	.95* (.11)	—	—	—	—	—	—	—	—	—
1968	−.05 (.12)	—	—	—	—	—	—	—	—	—
1972	−.55* (.12)	—	—	—	—	—	—	—	—	—
1976	.05 (.13)	—	—	—	—	—	—	—	—	—
1980	−.34* (.16)	—	—	—	—	—	—	—	—	—
1984	−.28 (.15)	—	—	—	—	—	—	—	—	—
1988	−.05 (.16)	—	—	—	—	—	—	—	—	—
1992	−.42* (.16)	—	—	—	—	—	—	—	—	—
Race (reference = all else)		.78	.76	.53	.41	.56	.46	.47	.53	.65
African Americans	1.20* (.38)	.92	.99	.96	.94	.96	.95	.95	.96	.98
Race by time interactions										
African Americans × Year$_{\geq 1964}$	1.87* (.40)	—	—	—	—	—	—	—	—	—
Religion (reference = other religion)		.41	.64	.39	.28	.42	.33	.34	.39	.51
Liberal Protestants	−.48* (.17)	.30	.55	.33	.25	.40	.33	.37	.45	.59
Moderate Protestants	−.26 (.14)	.34	.58	.33	.23	.36	.27	.28	.33	.44
Conservative Protestants	−.31* (.14)	.33	.56	.32	.22	.46	.37	.27	.32	.43
Catholics	.56* (.14)	.78	.76	.53	.41	.56	.46	.47	.53	.65
Jewish	1.92* (.20)	.82	.92	.82	.73	.83	.77	.78	.82	.88
No religion	.93* (.16)	.63	.82	.62	.50	.65	.55	.57	.62	.72
Religion by time interactions										
Catholics × Year$_{1960}$	1.10* (.21)	—	—	—	—	—	—	—	—	—
Conservative Protestants × Year$_{1976/1980}$	.48 (.13)	—	—	—	—	—	—	—	—	—
Liberal Protestants * Year$_{1960-1992}$	.10* (.02)	—	—	—	—	—	—	—	—	—

Variable	Coefficient (SE)									
Class (reference = non-labor force participant)		.78	.76	.53	.41	.56	.46	.47	.53	.65
Professionals	−.21 (.17)	.74	.72	.49	.38	.53	.44	.47	.53	.65
Managers	.12 (.46)	.75	.68	.40	.26	.44	.30	.31	.37	.48
Routine white-collar employees	−.23* (.11)	.74	.71	.47	.35	.50	.40	.42	.47	.59
Self-employed	−.27* (.13)	.73	.70	.46	.34	.49	.27	.28	.33	.44
Skilled workers	1.14* (.41)	.87	.82	.56	.37	.52	.42	.43	.49	.61
Nonskilled workers	.16 (.12)	.81	.78	.57	.45	.60	.41	.43	.48	.60
Class by time interactions										
Professionals * Year$_{1964 \geq 1992}$	.03 (.03)	—	—	—	—	—	—	—	—	—
Managers * Year$_{1960-1972}$	−.16* (.10)	—	—	—	—	—	—	—	—	—
Self-employed × Year$_{\geq 1980}$	−.56* (.18)	—	—	—	—	—	—	—	—	—
Skilled workers * Year$_{1960 \geq 1972}$	−.26* (.09)	—	—	—	—	—	—	—	—	—
Nonskilled × Year$_{\geq 1980}$	−.35* (.15)	—	—	—	—	—	—	—	—	—
Gender (reference = men)		.78	.76	.53	.41	.56	.46	.47	.53	.65
Women	.20 (.12)	.76	.73	.50	.38	.52	.43	.44	.50	.61
Gender by time interaction										
Women * Year$_{(1960-\geq 1980)}^{2}$	<.01 (<.01)	—	—	—	—	—	—	—	—	—
Additional interactions										
Women × non-labor force participant	−.33* (.11)	—	—	—	—	—	—	—	—	—
Region (reference = South)										
All other regions	.04 (.06)	—	—	—	—	—	—	—	—	—
Years of education (continuous)	−.08* (.01)	—	—	—	—	—	—	—	—	—
Age (continuous)	−.01* (<.01)	—	—	—	—	—	—	—	—	—

[a] Asterisk next to a coefficient indicates significance at the .05 level (2-tailed test). Dependent variable is coded '1' for the Democratic, '0' for the Republican candidate.

[b] Unconstrained interaction effects designated by '×' (subscript denotes time period); linearly constrained interaction effects designated by '*' (subscript denotes time period).

8

Social Cleavages in the 1996 Election

In 1996, Democratic incumbent Bill Clinton won a second term in office, becoming the first two-term Democratic president since Franklin Roosevelt and also the first two-term president since Woodrow Wilson never to win a majority of the popular vote. Clinton's first term in office was marked by a remarkable series of policy and political twists and turns. Elected in 1992 with an increased Democratic majority in both houses of Congress, Clinton initially pursued a reform-oriented agenda. In the spring of 1993 he proposed a variety of expansionary fiscal measures aimed at increasing employment and easing the country out of recession. In the fall of 1993, Clinton dramatically unveiled a sweeping proposal for national health insurance. He also introduced welfare reform measures designed to move recipients into the paid labor force, albeit with the intention of first winning passage of the health reform. The Administration's health reform proposals failed in Congress, and going into the 1994 midterm elections Clinton's personal popularity had declined, and the Administration could point to few policy victories.

In the 1994 midterm elections, Republicans picked up a large number of new seats in both the House and the Senate, enough to give them control of both houses for the first time since the early 1950s. Upon taking office, new Republican House speaker Newt Gingrich led a showdown over governmental finances and future government deficits, producing a protracted and unprecedented shutdown of the federal government in 1995. In the face of the shutdown and other unpopular initiatives of the Republican congressional leadership, and benefiting from strong economic growth, Clinton's popularity began to rise in the second half of his term. Clinton seemed to find an effective public voice as the centrist bulwark against the Republican congressional majority and their increasingly unpopular public policy agenda. At the same time, Clinton adopted or promoted conservative policy positions in a number of substantive policy arenas (e.g. crime, welfare reform, national defense).

In 1996, policy conflicts between Clinton and the Republicans seemed destined to play a major role in the campaign. But the Republican nominee for president—Kansas Senator and Senate Majority Leader Bob Dole—proved ineffectual in convincing voters that they should abandon a divided government. Clinton also bene-fited from a strong economy, with unemployment levels dropping to their lowest levels in many years by the summer of 1996. Strong economic growth also made it possible for the Administration to proclaim future balanced budgets, as increased tax receipts made possible sharp deficit reduction without the deep programmatic cuts that Republicans (and third party candidate Ross Perot) had insisted were necessary. Clinton maintained a steady lead in the polls through-out most of 1996, and by election day the result was largely a fore-gone conclusion.

The 1996 presidential campaign was nevertheless significant for a number of reasons. It was the first presidential election in a generation where the existence of a Republican congressional majority made it possible that Republicans would control both the legislative and executive branches of the national government. 1996 also saw the first significant campaign (and vote) for a third party candidate over two consecutive elections in the twentieth century.[1] It saw the continued expansion of the gender gap, as the candidates made repeated appeals to women voters. (One of the new voter stereotypes fostered by the media during this election was that of the 'soccer mom'.) In an unprecedented campaign, AFL-CIO unions poured millions of dollars into advertising campaigns designed to increase support for both Clinton and specific Democratic congressional candidates among working-class voters.

In this chapter, we extend our analyses to consider the 1996 elec-tion. We ask whether, and in what ways, the impact of social cleavages increased, decreased, or remained constant in the face of the tumul-tuous four years between 1992 and the end of the unusual 1996 presidential campaign. Have the changing alignments of key social groups discovered in previous chapters remained constant during this time? Have trends observed in earlier years continued through 1996? And what bearing do the causal factors identified by researchers as explaining elections in the 1990's—economic voting and the import-ance of 'new' policy conflicts relating to gender and family—have on cleavage voting? We first consider the main theoretical interpretations that have been developed to explain recent patterns of political change in presidential elections. We then present our analyses of social cleavages in the 1996 presidential election, developing a comparison between these results and our earlier analysis of the 1960 through 1992 elections.

In similar fashion to the scholarly debates we addressed in Chapter 6, our theoretical concern is with the *relative* political alignments of major social groups. As a result, our focus is on whether the four main cleavages in U.S. politics—and the social groups comprising these cleavages—have experienced any additional changes during the 1990s. While some of the interpretations discussed below imply the existence of such changes, it is necessary to use the broader, historical perspective of the entire post-1960 period to properly gauge the evidence for recent trends.

THEORETICAL INTERPRETATIONS OF THE 1992 AND 1996 ELECTIONS

Economic Explanations

Virtually all scholarly analysis and commentary on presidential elections in the 1990s have emphasized the crucial roles played by economic factors in explaining Bill Clinton's electoral success. In 1992, Clinton was the beneficiary of widespread perceptions of personal and national economic malaise.[2] He was also the beneficiary of improved voter perceptions of economic prosperity in 1996.[3] However, there were clearly limited political benefits for the Democratic Party as a whole from economic factors: during this same period, the Party lost control of Congress for the first time in a generation.[4]

Given our concern with patterns of stability and change in group-specific political alignments, we do not directly address the role of economic factors in explaining the outcome of the 1996 election. There are, however, two potential points of relevance to our analysis. First, the causal importance of economic factors—given that they represent a cross-cutting set of political cleavages—may have reduced the salience of social group memberships, and thus the magnitude of social cleavages. Economic factors may also have played a significant role in relation to social cleavages because of variable perceptions of economic welfare on the part of different social groups. In the analyses developed below, we consider this phenomenon in analyzing one of the more dramatic examples of group-specific change in 1996: the political dealignment of nonskilled workers.

Political Change and New Cleavages

A second theoretical focus of interpretations of recent presidential elections is on the political importance of new cleavages relating to non-economic issues, especially those linked to ongoing policy conflicts over women's rights, family, and gay and lesbian civil rights.[5] One particularly notable cleavage in the 1990s relates to struggles over the meaning and implementation of 'family values'. While clear-cut differences in the parties' policy platforms on such issues are a relatively recent development,[6] there is evidence that the 1992 election marked a turning point in the importance of such issues as a source of the vote.[7] Divergent images of gender personified by Barbara Bush and Hillary Clinton, the conflict surrounding the nomination of Clarence Thomas to the U.S. Supreme Court and the accompanying issue of sexual harassment all represent related developments.[8]

In similar fashion to economic factors, emerging cleavages relating to gender, family, and civil rights issues may affect social cleavages if specific groups have experienced disproportionate shifts in attitudes toward such issues or if the political effects of these attitudes differ for specific groups. As analyzed in Chapter 3, both these scenarios are relevant to understanding the changing alignments of specific classes; in particular, professionals' disproportionately liberal attitudes toward civil rights issues may continue to fuel their realignment with the Democratic Party.

The Decline or Partial Restoration of the New Deal Coalition?

Debates over recent trends in party coalitions have the most direct relevance to understanding the role of social cleavages and social groups in the 1996 election. As discussed in Chapter 7, most of the scholarly literature on party coalitions has emphasized the changing composition of these coalitions, focusing especially on declining rates of Democratic support amongst several of that party's traditional constituencies. For example, in the most recent update of their research on changing party coalitions, Harold Stanley and Richard Niemi report further declines in rates of Democratic Party identification among Southern whites and self-identified members of the working class through 1992.[9] After noting the growing presence of fundamentalist Protestants in the Republican coalition, and also that Catholic voters' level of Democratic identification was lower in 1992 than in the period before 1980, they conclude that 'it is time to declare the New Deal coalition dead'.[10] If true, this interpretation implies that members of the working class, Catholic voters, and residents of the South continue to experience a disproportionate reduction in their support for Democratic candidates.

However, a number of prominent analysts have viewed the Clinton elections as partially restoring some elements of the New Deal coalition, especially in 1996. Ruy Teixeira argues that Clinton's re-election in 1996 (and his rebound after the Republican takeover of Congress in 1994) were the result of renewed party support among traditionally Democratic groups.[11] Citing a variety of exit poll surveys, Teixeira hypothesizes that Clinton's strategic emphasis on 'old Democrat programs' (he lists Medicare, Medicaid, education, and the environment) prompted higher levels of support and political interest among working women and also male voters with no more than a high school education. Teixeira assumes that underlying this hypothesized shift toward greater Democratic support is a class-related causal factor: the disproportionate risk and exposure of these voters—and the working class in general—to postindustrial economic uncertainties.[12]

Similarly, former Clinton pollster Stanley Greenberg argues that the Clinton presidential campaigns

won back the Reagan Democrats. The 1996 Clinton campaign may have aspired to win upscale suburban voters and lay the basis for a conservative, 'new Democrat' politics. But that is not what happened at the polls. . . . The new Clinton voters of 1996—the bloc that raised Clinton's support from 43 to 49 percent of the vote—were overwhelmingly downscale. They were from lower- and middle-income families . . . [and] were non-college-educated voters: over three-quarters had not earned a four-year college degree.

In Greenberg's account, Clinton's electoral success hinges on the demise of the 'Reagan Democrats', those 'working class voters supporting the party of business'.[13] This turnaround is traceable in large part to Clinton's support for social policies designed to benefit working families that have been cut or threatened by the Republican congressional majority.

If the accounts of these analysts are true, a partial renewal of the Democratic coalition is in the process of emerging. It implies that support among traditionally Democratic social groups (especially workers) should have increased in comparison to preceding elections. We consider this possibility.

DATA AND MEASURES

For the analysis developed in this chapter, we use data from the National Election Studies pre- and post-election survey of the 1996 presidential election. Following our analyses of the race, religion, class, and gender cleavages, we consider the magnitude of, and interrelationship between these cleavages in the 1996 election. As before, our analysis of social cleavages draws a distinction between the individual (race, religion, class, and gender) cleavage and the total social cleavage (the average difference in voter alignments produced simultaneously by all four major cleavages). Although the 1996 election represents the passage of only an additional four-year period, it is possible that the total social cleavage has remained stable despite underlying changes in the four major cleavages. Likewise, it is also possible that changes in the total social cleavage are produced by changes affecting only a single cleavage; our analyses addresses these and other possible patterns of change.

We again make use of the two sets of cleavage indices introduced in Chapter 6: the kappa index of specific cleavages; and the lambda total cleavage index. As a necessary prelude to calculating these two sets of indices, we first estimate a multivariate model of vote choice whose coefficients measure the respective effects of the four main cleavages and the control variables discussed below.

Variables in the Analysis

Our dependent variable is major party vote choice in 1996 (coded '1' for Bill Clinton, and '0' for Bob Dole). Our measurement of social cleavages is identical to that used in earlier chapters: race is a dichotomy (coded '1' for African-Americans, and '0' otherwise); religion is a seven-category variable (analyzed as six dummy variables for liberal Protestants, moderate Protestants, conservative Protestants, Catholics, Jews, respondents with no religion, and respondents in 'other religions' serving as the reference in the regression); class is a seven-category variable (analyzed as six dummy variables for professionals, managers, routine white-collar employees, self-employed non-professionals, skilled workers, nonskilled workers, with non-labor-force participants serving as the reference in the regression); and gender is a dichotomy (coded '1' for female, and '0' for male voters).

Following our findings about the interdependence of the class and gender cleavages in Chapter 5, we also consider the interaction effect between women and non-labor force participation in the analysis. The three control variables in the analysis are region (coded '1' for regions outside the South, and '0' for Southern residence); years of education (measured as a continuous variable); and age (also measured as a continuous variable).

RESULTS

Group-Specific Voter Alignments in 1996

Our first set of analyses investigate the relative voter alignments of the social groups comprising our four major cleavages in 1996. These analyses are presented below in Table 8.1. The estimates in this table are the coefficients of our multivariate model (with standard errors presented in parentheses) predicting major party vote choice.

In keeping with the results from Chapter 6, the coefficient for the effect of race on vote choice has by far the largest impact of any variable, as indicated by the massive, 4.72 coefficient. Even in an election in which the Democratic candidate received a majority of non-African-American support (among major party voters), black voters remain disproportionately Democratic in their preferences.[14]

Results for the effect of religious group membership on vote choice are also similar to our earlier findings in Chapter 4. Jewish voters remain by far the most likely to support the Democratic candidate, followed by respondents with no religion, Catholics, and the 'other religion' category. Although the three Protestant groups had the lowest levels of Democratic candidate support in 1996, their relative ranking corresponds well to our earlier findings for these groups, with liberal Protestants being significantly less Republican in their preferences than moderate or conservative Protestants.

Results for the class cleavage reveal that professionals' dramatic realignment with the Democratic Party has continued through the 1996 election. In this election, in fact, professionals were the *most* Democratic of any of the seven classes in this election. Their level of Democratic support far exceeds that of either skilled or nonskilled workers. The respective coefficients for these three classes are .41, −.05, and .08. If there was a class basis to the Democratic coalition in 1996, it was to be found among professionals.

The very low levels of Democratic support among the two working-class categories are striking. Even managers were more Democratic in

TABLE 8.1. *Logistic regression coefficients[a] (s.e. in parentheses) for preferred model of social cleavages and presidential vote choice[b], 1996* (N = 1,025)

Independent variables	Coefficient (s.e.)
Constant	2.35* (.72)
Race (reference = all else)	
African Americans	4.72* (1.0)
Religion (reference = other religion)	
Liberal Protestants	−.32 (.41)
Moderate Protestants	−.63 (.41)
Conservative Protestants	−.82* (.40)
Catholics	.02 (.39)
Jewish	2.94* (1.1)
No religion	.58 (.44)
Class (reference = non-labor-force participant)	
Professionals	.41 (.29)
Managers	.19 (.33)
Routine white-collar employees	.12 (.35)
Self-employed	−.12 (.36)
Skilled workers	−.05 (.38)
Nonskilled workers	.08 (.35)
Gender (reference = men)	
Women	.70* (.19)
Interactions	
Women x Non-labor force participant	−.46 (.30)
Region (reference = South)	
All other regions	.08 (.16)
Years of education (continuous)	−.18* (.04)
Age (continuous)	.01 (<.01)

[a] An asterisk indicates significance at the .05 level (2-tailed test).
[b] Dependent variable is coded '1' for the choice of the Democratic, and '0' for the choice of the Republican candidate.

their voting preferences in 1996 than either skilled or nonskilled workers! These results thus reveal a significantly different set of class-based
alignments in 1996 than in earlier elections in the NES series. As
discussed below, this represents not only a dramatic extension of earlier,
class-specific trends (i.e. declining levels of Democratic Party support
among workers) but also provices a significant overall contraction of
the class cleavage in 1996. When measured by occupation, there is little
support for theories asserting that the Clinton presidency has partially
revived the old class alignments of the New Deal order.[15]

The results for the effects of gender are nearly the reverse of that
found for class. The .70 coefficient for gender indicates that the odds

that working women supported Clinton over Dole were over two times larger than the corresponding level of support given by men.[16] The magnitude of the gender cleavage was thus considerably larger in 1996 than in earlier elections, a result we discuss in greater detail below. Whereas the kappa index score for the gender gap in 1992 was .04 (translating into a predicted .08 difference in the probability of Democratic vote choice among women versus men), the corresponding index score in 1996 is .07 (amounting to a predicted .14 difference in probability). Because the modest rise in women's labor force participation rates during this time cannot explain the 75% increase in the size of the gender gap, other causal factors are clearly at work.[17] However, the most important finding in the face of a growing, multiple issue-driven gender gap is the persistence of the class-related gender cleavage analyzed in Chapter 5. Our analyses show that while non-working women decisively favored Clinton over Dole, the margin of support given to Clinton by working women was an *additional* 11%. We can thus safely conclude that the emergence of multiple gender 'gaps' in U.S. politics is consistent with the longstanding divide produced by the contrasting locations and divergent policy preferences of working versus non-working women.

Figure 8.1 presents a set of summary measures of the political alignments of the social groups comprising the four cleavages. These measures are the predicted probability that a particular group supported the Democratic candidate in the 1996 election, and they are derived from the logistic regression model from Table 8.1.[18] In the figure, we rank order the groups comprising a particular cleavage according to the strength of their Democratic alignment, with the least Democratic groups appearing at the extreme left-hand side of each figure and each subsequent group having a greater or equal degree of Democratic support as the preceding group.

The steep slope of the line connecting the two racial groups shows the magnitude of the race cleavage in 1996. The next largest cleavage is that of religion, and as discussed earlier conservative Protestants are the least Democratic religious group, followed by moderate Protestants, liberal Protestants, and the other four groups in the analysis. As anticipated by the regression coefficients, the class cleavage in 1996 is distinguished by the underlying similarity of most of the class categories.

By virtue of the interaction between labor force participation and gender, the class and gender cleavages intersect with one another, and the residual, non-labor force participation category is comprised of two separate categories (depending upon whether this group is male or female). Notably, non-working women—while considerably less

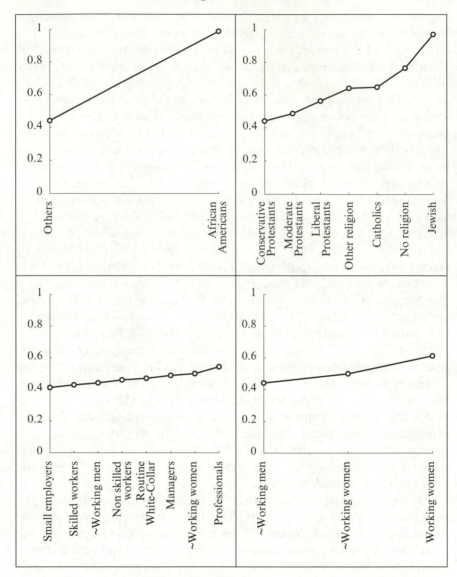

Fig. 8.1. Political alignments of major social groups in 1996
Note: Scores on the charts' y-axes are the predicted probability of
Democratic vote choice.

Democratic than working women—are nevertheless the second most Democratic category in the figure for the class cleavage. With respect to the gender cleavage, the political alignments of men, working women, and non-working women all differ significantly. This reflects not only the importance of gender in the 1996 election, but also the importance of labor-force participation as a factor that shapes women's political alignments.

Trends in Specific Social Cleavages

We now examine whether the race, religion, class, and gender cleavages have experienced any changes in the 1990s. Extending our earlier analysis from Chapter 6, we present kappa index scores for all ten elections in the 1960 through 1996 series. As discussed earlier, our calculation of these scores enables direct comparison between the results for 1996 and those found for earlier elections.

The race cleavage remains by far the largest social cleavage, with its magnitude being approximately twice as large as the next largest cleavage (the religion cleavage). The race and religion cleavages both experienced similar, modest increases in magnitude between 1992 and 1996: the race cleavage increased in size from .25 to .27, and the religion cleavage increased from .15 to .17. When viewed from the perspective of the entire NES series, the race cleavage shows considerable election-to-election fluctuation with a net increase in magnitude since its initial, dramatic expansion in the 1964 election. By contrast, the religion cleavage has experienced far less over-time variability once we put the unusual 1960 election in its proper historical context (see Chapter 4).

By virtue of their interdependence as well as several dramatic trends in the 1990s, the class and gender cleavages have experienced a more extensive pattern of change. From 1960 through 1992, the class cleavage was significantly larger than the gender cleavage, and neither cleavage displayed any clear signs of contraction or expansion. However, two dramatic events reversed the rank ordering of these cleavages in 1996. First, the class cleavage declined sharply in magnitude, equaling its smallest index value from 1972. Second, the gender cleavage experienced an equally large increase in magnitude, nearly doubling its 1992 index score.

Sources of the Decline of the Class Cleavage

What accounts for the sharp decline in the class cleavage between 1992 and 1996? The first part of the explanation lies with the surprisingly low

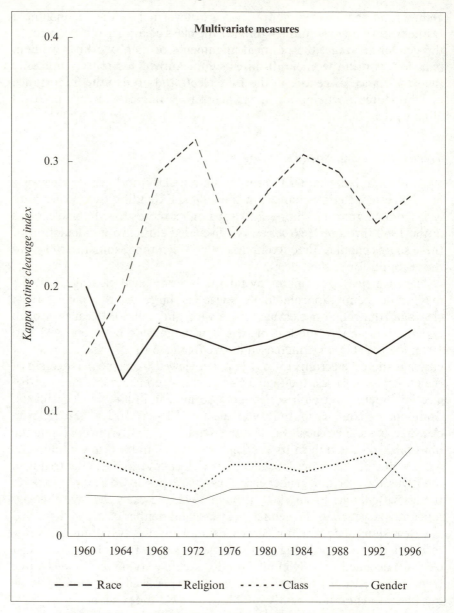

FIG. 8.2. Social cleavages in presidential elections, 1960–1996
Note: Index scores for each cleavage control for the political effects of
other social cleavages and also age, education, and region.

levels of Democratic support given by nonskilled workers. Whereas the relative alignments of other classes are quite consistent with their corresponding positions in earlier elections, nonskilled workers moved from being the *most* Democratic class in all earlier elections to only the *fourth* most Democratic class in 1996. Professionals, routine white-collar employees, and managers were all significantly more supportive of Clinton in comparison to nonskilled workers. As a result, nonskilled workers abrupt movement towards the political center resulted in the contraction of the class cleavage in 1996.

The preceding inference can be appreciated by considering the following counterfactual scenario. Had nonskilled workers been merely as Democratic in their alignment as professionals in 1996, the subsequent .05 index score for the magnitude of the class cleavage would be comparable to the corresponding index score for 1988 (.06), and indistinguishable from the corresponding index score for 1984 (.05). As a result, the sharp decline between 1992 and 1996 would have flattened out considerably, revealing instead only a slight *increase* in the class cleavage in the 1992 election.

What causal factors might account for the shift in nonskilled workers' political alignment in 1996?. Following our earlier analyses from Chapter 3, we consider the two main factors that resulted in lower levels of Democratic Party support among nonskilled workers during (and after) the 1980 election: evaluations of personal economic satisfaction and attitudes toward the welfare state. If nonskilled workers were disproportionately negative in their economic evaluations in 1996, such perceptions help to explain their disproportionately low levels of support for Democratic candidate Clinton. Likewise, further erosion of support for the welfare state—itself associated with Democratic support—can also help contribute to a suitable explanation.

These expectations are supported by the 1996 data. With the single exception of routine white-collar employees, nonskilled workers report the highest level of economic dissatisfaction in 1996. Over 27% of nonskilled workers evaluated their personal economic situation as 'worse than' a year ago; by contrast, the corresponding figures for the two most Republican classes were 18% (among the self-employed) and 10% (among managers). Unskilled workers thus reported unusually high levels of economic dissatisfaction under a Democratic presidential administration, and these levels were considerably higher than the corresponding levels experienced by classes that have traditionally been aligned with the Republican Party.

We also consider the role played by attitudes toward the welfare state.

Between 1992 and 1996, nonskilled workers' level of support for social welfare declined slightly. While the magnitude of this change is itself quite small (.10 on the seven-point NES welfare state item), it nevertheless reveals that nonskilled workers' experiences under a Democratic administration did nothing to stem their small but significant long-term decline in support for the welfare state. The complementary political effects of these changes suggest that nonskilled workers' shift away from an historically strong alignment with the Democratic Party is more than a temporary fluctuation.

Trends in the Total Social Cleavage

How have changes in the race, religion, class, and gender cleavages affected the total social cleavage? We examine this question in Figure 8.3, which displays the lambda index scores for each of the ten elections. We also recalculate the index by ignoring race, allowing us to examine whether we obtain a different picture of trends in the absence of ongoing changes affecting the powerful racial cleavage.

The darker line shows the over-time development of the total social cleavage since 1960. The magnitude of the total social cleavage increased slightly between 1992 and 1996 (from .13 to .14). Given the 1960 index score of .11, the total social cleavage has grown in magnitude during this 36-year period. When we ignore the race cleavage, our estimates (plotted by the lighter line) reveal far less change between 1964 and 1996, but no evidence of a decline in magnitude. Because these estimates ignore race, the disproportionately large religious cleavage in 1960 has a considerably greater impact on the magnitude of the overall social cleavage, thereby leading to an inflated index score for that year. However, as discussed in Chapter 4, these features were unique to this particular election. Taken together, these results provide clear evidence for the ongoing—and even increasing significance—of social cleavages.

CONCLUSION

The analyses developed in this chapter provide a useful vantage point from which to understand long-term patterns of change in social cleavages as well as some recent developments. With regard to group-specific patterns of change, African-Americans and Jewish voters remain disproportionately Democratic in their political alignments, whereas conservative Protestants and non-professional employers

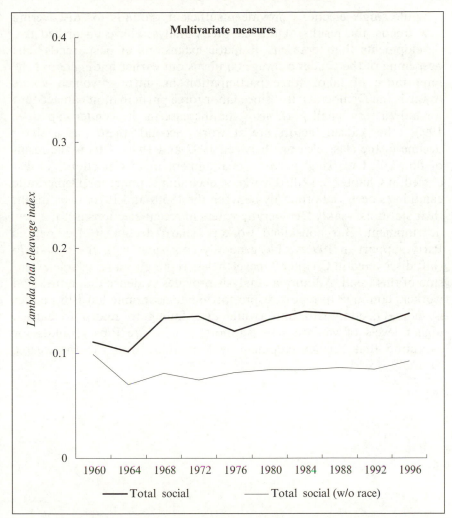

FIG. 8.3. The total social cleavage in presidential elections, 1960–1996
Note: Index scores control for the political effects of age, education, and region.

remain firmly aligned with the Republican Party. Extending their earlier trends, liberal Protestants are considerably less Republican than other Protestant voters, while professionals continue to grow in both their relative and absolute levels of support for Democratic candidates. We also find that Catholic voters remain in a Democratic alignment, being significantly more likely to support the Democratic over the Republican candidate than members of the three main Protestant groups.

While single elections provide insufficient grounds for discovering new trends, the results of this chapter's analyses have unearthed two developments that represent dramatic extensions of past trends. The deepening of the gender cleavage confirms our earlier finding about the importance of labor force participation in shifting women voters towards the Democrats. But since labor force participation can account for only a very small portion of the increase in the gender gap since 1992, other causal factors are at work. Second, there was a sharp decline in the class cleavage between 1992 and 1996. This is the result of nonskilled workers' partisan dealignment in this election. As discussed in Chapter 3, skilled workers' declining support for Democratic candidates occurred primarily between the 1950s and 1970s; as a result, their status as weakly Democratic voters in recent elections is not a new development. But nonskilled workers' sharp decline in Democratic Party support in 1996, while generally consistent with the post-1976 shift discovered in Chapter 3, nevertheless represents a very large extension of this trend. Additional analysis provides evidence that nonskilled workers continue to report disproportionate economic hardship under Democratic administrations (while also failing to return to earlier, higher levels of welfare state support). There are thus grounds for expecting that this development will continue into the foreseeable future.[19]

9

Third Party Candidates

The institutional characteristics of the U.S. party system place enormous obstacles to the emergence of successful third party or independent candidates. As a result, our primary focus in this study has been on support for major party presidential candidates. However, and in spite of their extremely low probability of success, third party candidacies are a periodic feature of U.S. presidential elections. The two most recent presidential elections (1992 and 1996) have seen H. Ross Perot receive a significant share (19% and 9%, respectively) of the popular vote. It is thus likely that significant third party candidates will appear in some future elections.

In this chapter, then, we consider the interrelationship between social cleavages and support for third party candidates. More specifically, we examine the candidacies of George Wallace (1968) and Ross Perot (1992 and 1996). These represent the three most successful third party efforts in the postwar era. (The only other independent campaign of note in this period was the 1980 bid of John Anderson, but Anderson received just 6.5% of the popular vote.) The 1992 and 1996 elections also provide us with a unique opportunity to observe changes in the social bases of support for an independent candidate (Perot) over two different elections. Since 1840, virtually all third party candidates or minor parties before Perot won significant votes in only one election given that they were unable to mobilize significant support a second time[1].

THIRD PARTY PRESIDENTIAL CAMPAIGNS: THEORY AND HISTORY

The institutional barriers faced by third party presidential candidates are well-known and require only brief explication. Indeed, the more interesting question is why third party candidates[2] sometimes perform as well as they do in the face of these obstacles. The 'wasted vote' problem plagues all such campaigns, especially campaigns that start off with modest poll numbers that suggest the candidate can at best achieve the status of spoiler. With the exception of the 1992 Perot campaign, every third party candidate (at least since the advent of survey research) has seen their support erode in the final weeks of the campaign, when voters come to realize the possibility of success is remote.[3] Third party candidates also tend to face great difficulty in competing for funds with major party candidates.[4] The disparity in campaign resources is magnified by the difficulty in gaining access to the ballot, which requires a time-consuming and costly state-by-state effort, which major party candidates are spared. Third party candidates rarely receive comparable news media coverage, and such coverage often focuses on their uphill battle than on issues they are seeking to promote.[5]

Despite these obstacles, third party candidates run in every election, and in 10 of the 25 elections in the twentieth century their combined vote has exceeded 5% (see Figure 9.1).

The historical presence of significant third party campaigns show that the recent campaigns of Wallace, Anderson, and Perot are not unequivocal indicators of recent party decline. Although there have

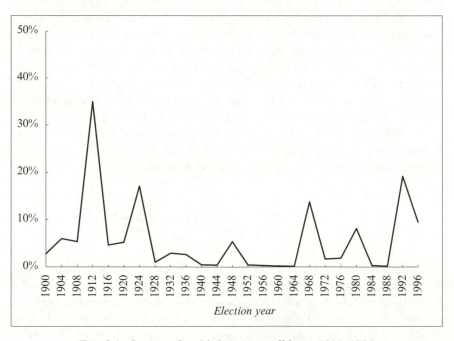

FIG. 9.1. Support for third party candidates, 1900–1996

been many studies of individual third party campaigns, there has been relatively little systematic scholarly work comparing two or more different campaigns. The most notable work on third party presidential campaigns is that of Steven Rosenstone and his colleagues. They attempt to model the factors that predict higher levels of third party support in some elections. Their evidence suggests that three factors are crucial. One factor is issue unresponsiveness on the part of major parties. When the two parties cannot (or will not) accommodate public opinion on one or more issues, a space emerges within which third party candidates may attempt to fill. Good examples of such 'wedge' issues would be the refusal of the major parties to endorse the views of Southern segregationists (giving impetus to the 1948 Strom Thurmond campaign and the 1968 George Wallace campaign), or the inability of the major parties to develop convincing plans to balance the federal budget (a key issue for John Anderson in 1980 and the dominant theme of the 1992 Perot campaign).

Second, Rosenstone et al. show that 'nationally prestigious' third party candidates (such as current or former presidents or vice-presidents, or current or former members of Congress or governors who have run previous national campaigns on a major party ticket or in major party primaries) do better than candidates lacking one or more of these attributes. All of the major third party candidates of the twentieth century fit this profile, except for H. Ross Perot. Prestigious candidates have some degree of previous name recognition, are more likely to be taken seriously by the news media, and are better positioned to raise campaign funds.[6] Prestigious candidates also typically do better when they run against two unpopular major party candidates, although the unpopularity of the major party candidates may in part reflect the viability of the third party candidate.

Finally, Rosenstone et al. argue that third party campaigns benefit from the influx of new voters with weak partisanship, or holdover voters of previous third party campaigns. These voters are more likely to support third party candidates in comparison to partisan voters. The high proportion of nominally independent partisans in the present electoral era thus offers some opportunities for third party entrepreneurs.[7]

Social Bases of Third Party Campaigns

There have been few attempts to develop systematic comparative analyses of the social bases of different third party candidates.[8] Some of the most significant third party campaigns have built upon a clear social base. The populist People's Party of 1892, for example, drew support overwhelmingly from small farmers in the South and Midwest. Socialist Party presidential candidate Eugene Debs drew votes from urban workers, Jews, and Eastern and Southern European immigrants in the early part of the twentieth century. Strom Thurmond's 1948 campaign was almost entirely a regional phenomenon, eliciting strong support in Southern states but receiving very few votes outside that region. George Wallace similarly drew votes from Southern segregationists in his third party bid in 1968, but the exact nature of the Wallace vote has remained a matter of some controversy in the aftermath of that campaign.

The social bases of other third party campaigns have received little attention. In particular, this is true for Ross Perot's two recent presidential campaigns, despite their significant vote totals. Our investigations in this chapter attempt to fill that void by analyzing the three most important third party campaigns of the postwar period (George Wallace and the two Ross Perot bids). We ask whether these campaigns had significant identifiable constituencies, or, alternatively, whether they drew voters from among all groups.

ANALYSES

Our analyses focus on three elections (1968, 1992, and 1996). The dependent variable is coded '1' if a respondent supports the leading independent candidate (Wallace, Perot, and Perot, respectively) and '0' if (s)he supports either major party candidate. The independent variables in the models are also coded as before. Race is a dichotomy (coded '1' for African-Americans, and '0' otherwise); religion is a seven–category variable (analyzed as six dummy variables for liberal Protestants, moderate Protestants, conservative Protestants, Catholics, Jews, respondents with no religion, and respondents in 'other religions' serving as the reference in the regression); class is a seven–category variable (analyzed as six dummy variables for professionals, managers, routine white-coller employees, self-employed non-professionals, skilled workers, nonskilled workers, with non-labor-force participants serving as the reference in the regression); and gender is a dichotomy (coded '1' for female and '0' for male). Three control variables in the analyses are region (coded '1' for regions outside the South and '0' for Southern residence); years of education (measured as a continuous variable); and age (also measured as a continuous variable).

The 'Politics of Rage': The 1968 Wallace Campaign[9]

In 1968, former governor of Alabama and champion of racial segregation, George Wallace, campaigned for president, receiving just under 14% of the popular vote. Wallace was the most articulate and nationally prominent defender of the Southern racial regime in the middle 1960s. Upon taking office as governor of Alabama in 1963, Wallace delivered a fiery speech, written for him by a close advisor and Ku Klux Klan organizer, in which he declared that 'In the name of the greatest people that have ever trod the earth, I draw the line in the dust and toss the gauntlet before the feet of tyranny . . . and I say . . . segregation now . . . segregation tomorrow . . . segregation forever.'[10] Wallace gained national notoriety later that year when he defiantly and dramatically refused to integrate the University of Alabama in a showdown with federal Department of Justice officials.

Wallace's career was built inside the Democratic Party; except for his 1968 campaign, Wallace was a southern Democratic politician. He sought the Democratic nomination for president three times (1964, 1972, and 1976) and spent most of the last three decades of his public career as a Democrat in the governor's office in Alabama. There are three very clear (and somewhat distinct) themes running through Wallace's presidential bids: race, anti-Communism, and anti-elitist populism.[11] In his early presidential campaigns especially, Wallace openly sought the support of white voters opposed to civil rights legislation. Although using less direct language when speaking to Northern audiences, Wallace deployed aggressive red-baiting rhetoric in characterizing civil rights advocates and movement leaders. His use of populist themes was most apparent in his aggressive attacks on what he called the 'pointy heads', government bureaucrats and liberal intellectuals.

Coming in the wake of the recent successes of the civil rights movement and the landmark 1965 Voting Rights Act, the particular appeals of the Wallace campaign have led many analysts to expect that some social groups (Southerners, of course, but also white working-class voters) disproportionately supported his presidential bid. Did social group memberships have a significant impact on voting for Wallace? Table 9.1 shows the results of our analysis. With respect to the racial cleavage, not one African-American respondent in the 1968 NES reported voting for Wallace. However, because of black voters' strong alignment with the Democratic Party had already matured by 1968, the very large coefficient for race in Table 9.1 is perhaps best understood as reflecting the overwhelming support of African-Americans for

Third Party Candidates

TABLE 9.1. *Social cleavages and third party vote choice,*[a]
1968—analyzing the Wallace vote (N = 970)

Independent variables	Coefficient (s.e.)
Constant	2.87* (1.1)
Race (reference = all else)	
African Americans	−8.39 (.10)
Religion (reference = other religion)	
Liberal Protestants	−.39 (.73)
Moderate Protestants	−.34 (.72)
Conservative Protestants	.33 (.70)
Catholics	−.51 (.72)
Jewish	.19 (.93)
No religion	−.20 (.96)
Class (reference = non-labor-force participant)	
Professionals	−1.10* (.54)
Managers	.17 (.48)
Routine white-collar employees	.42 (.43)
Self-employed	−.42 (.45)
Skilled workers	−.41 (.44)
Non-skilled workers	.49 (.32)
Gender (reference = men)	
Women	−.74* (.27)
Region (reference = South)	
All other regions	−1.30* (.25)
Years of education (continuous)	−.16* (.04)
Age (continuous)	−.03* (.01)

[a] Dependent variable is coded '1' for the choice of George Wallace, and '0' for the choice of a major party candidate.
An asterisk indicates significance at the .05 level (2-tailed test).

Democratic candidate Hubert Humphrey. Indeed, the raw NES data show that less than 4% of black voters supported Republican candidate Richard Nixon. With respect to white voters, recent research has established the role of contextual effects (in particular, the proportion of African-Americans in a particular regional area) in explaining white support for explicitly racist political campaigns such as those of Wallace and the later state-level campaigns of David Duke in Louisiana. These arguments generally assert that whites feel more threatened, and hence more likely to support, racially conservative campaigns in areas where black density is high.[12] We cannot, however, directly test this claim with the 1968 NES data.[13]

A number of early analysts of the Wallace vote claimed to find a distinct religious basis to his support. Some analysts claimed that fundamentalist Protestants were disproportionately Wallace supporters, while others claimed that Catholics were more likely to support him.[14] Our results reveal that religious group memberships had *no* significant impact on voting for Wallace in 1968.[15] Bivariate analyses show that conservative Protestants were disproportionately likely to support Wallace (20%).[16] But in multivariate analyses including controls for the effects of education and region, the apparent relationship between membership in doctrinally conservative Protestant denominations and support for Wallace is shown to be largely spurious. To express the point another way, conservative Protestants were disproportionately supportive of Wallace not because of their religion, but instead because of their low educational levels and tendency to live in the South. These results also show that Catholics were no more likely to be attracted to Wallace than members of other religious groups, as some earlier analysts have postulated.[17]

In the aftermath of the 1968 campaign, a number of analysts argued that class divisions were important in locating Wallace's appeal. Most of these analysts have argued that Wallace did best among those occupational groups most threatened by civil rights and African-American progress.[18] Turning to the class cleavage, the -1.10 coefficient for professionals is significant, indicating that professionals were far less likely than non-labor force participants (the reference category) to support Wallace over a major party candidate. In keeping with research on the occupational sources of racial tolerance and civil rights, being a professional in 1968 provided this segment of the electorate with reason to oppose the champion of racial segregation.[19] (Wallace's frequent attacks on the 'psuedo-intellectual elite' may have also contributed to eroding his support among this group.) Surprisingly, however, the remaining five classes are indistinguishable from the reference category (deleting the variables for these classes from the model results in a non-significant 7.60 increase in-$2LL$). Class differences thus provide little insight into the sources of the Wallace vote. Widespread assertions that Wallace found significant support among white workers (as opposed to white voters) are simply not supported.[20] Other than professionals' opposition, a distinct class basis to the Wallace vote is simply not identifiable.

Writing before clear evidence of a gender gap had emerged, few analysts paid much attention to gender differences in the Wallace vote. Yet these differences were significant. The coefficient for gender represents a sizable difference in female versus male support for

Wallace, with men being far more likely to support Wallace than women.[21] In fact, the gender gap in third party support in 1968 is considerably larger than the corresponding difference between women and men's willingness to support Democratic over Republican candidates in 1968.[22]

Finally, region, education, and age all have significant effects. As is well known, Southern residents were substantially more likely to support the former governor of Alabama; the −1.30 coefficient in Table 9.1 indicates that the odds of Southern respondents supporting Wallace was over three and a half times larger than the corresponding level for non-Southern respondents. Better-educated voters were significantly less supportive of Wallace, with the coefficient showing that each additional year of education is predicted as lowering the log-odds of Wallace support by .16.[23] Age also has a negative effect, with older voters being less supportive of Wallace (once their social group memberships and sociodemographic characteristics are taken into account).

The most striking overall finding of Table 9.1, however, is the relative weakness of social factors in explaining where Wallace gained his votes. In contrast to many of the early interpretations of the Wallace vote, we find that neither the class nor religious cleavages were significant factors. On the other hand, one cleavage that has been ignored by commentators (gender) turns out to be significant.

The 1992 Perot Campaign

The billionaire Texas businessman H. Ross Perot mounted significant independent presidential bids in 1992 and 1996. Perot's campaigns were unusual in two different respects. First, he ran as a complete outsider to the political system, never having held political office. Perot was a billionaire business owner, the founder of Electronic Data Systems, a Dallas-based computer services firm which became enormously successful when he won contracts to administer the Medicare program in the 1960s.[24] Perot gained early notoriety for his rabid activism on behalf of Vietnam POWs, frequently criticizing the government for its failure to take action to find those missing in action. He gained further public attention when, after selling his company to General Motors and gaining a seat on the GM board, he became a vocal critic of the company (and eventually had his stock bought out by GM for a wildly inflated $742 million in exchange for his silence). Perot entered public life openly embracing the outsider label. Although there have been other third party candidates who never held office, Perot was the only candidate in the twentieth century to win significant numbers of votes.

Perot's campaigns were unusual in that he sought to position himself ideologically somewhere between the major party candidates, offering a policy menu of strict fiscal discipline combined with no support for the social issue agenda of the Christian Right. Perot's major issues centered around the need to 'overhaul the political system,' particularly with regard to eliminating the federal budget deficit.[25] His calls for reform had some appeal to voters on both the right and the left. For the former, criticisms of 'big government' were central; for the latter, his calls to end the domination of politics by monied interests resonated with issues raised in the 1992 primaries by former California Governor Jerry Brown.[26] Most independent or third party campaigns in twentieth century U.S. political history have either had a clear left- or right-wing ideological bent, or were focused around a single key issue. Perot's centrism is unusual in this respect, following in many respects the model of the less successful 1980 John Anderson campaign.

The 1992 Perot campaign astounded many seasoned observers of American politics by garnering nearly 19% of the popular vote, the highest total for an independent campaign since Teddy Roosevelt's Bull Moose campaign in 1912. The final vote total was surprising for a number of reasons. Perot was the first third party candidate who gained votes in the final weeks of the campaign; the normal pattern has been for slippage generated by voters becoming convinced that the candidate has no chance of success. Further, although some commentators have emphasized high levels of disaffection in the electorate, Rosenstone and his colleagues have convincingly demonstrated that there was in fact no difference between 1992 and 1980 (when independent John Anderson won just 6.6% of the vote).[27] The electorate was also no more alienated from the parties in 1992 than in 1980, and the extent of national economic problems were in fact substantially less than in 1980. Rosenstone et al. hypothesize that such factors alone cannot account directly for more than a third of the Perot vote, Perot's financial resources (and lavish expenditures), however, were of such a magnitude as to enable him to take advantage of disaffection in a way that previous candidates could not.

By 1996, Perot and his supporters had stiched together a new political organization, called the Reform Party, under whose banner Perot again sought the presidency. However, between 1992 and 1996 Perot's public support had waned, and the Reform Party lost many of Perot's 1992 activists who objected to his rigid, centralized control over the state-level party organizations. The Reform Party's controversial presidential primary, in which former Colorado Governor Richard Lamm ran against Perot but complained that many of his supporters never received ballots, did little to build confidence in the party. Spending far less on his campaign (relying mostly on the public financing for which he was eligible as a result of his 1992 showing), and shut out of the presidential debates, Perot's vote total slumped to 8.5%. None the less, in historical context the 1996 Perot vote is highly significant: it is the fourth highest third party total in the twentieth century, and the relative successes of the Perot campaigns are likely to inspire future efforts by outsider aspirants to the presidency.[28]

1992: The First Perot Campaign

To what extent do the major social cleavages in American society help us understand the patterning of support received by Perot? Table 9.2 reports our analyses for the 1992 campaign. The racial cleavage parallels the earlier results for the 1968 election: African-American voters were disproportionately unsupportive of Perot, but this tendency is a product of their very strong preference for Democratic candidates over *any* other alternative.[29] Results for the religion and class cleavages show even less relevance to Perot's support: deleting the variables measuring these cleavages from the model reduces its fit by a non-significant 15.00 (12 d.f.), providing clear evidence that neither religious groups nor classes varied significantly in their willingness to support Perot relative to a major party candidate.

Results for the gender cleavage show greater relevance: women were significantly less supportive of Perot in comparison to men. The −.42 logit coefficient for the impact of gender represents a large effect.[30] However, levels of support for Perot among working versus nonworking women are largely indistinguishable.[31] In other words, the effect of gender on the choice of Perot in 1992 appears to represent an entirely different phenomenon from the gender cleavage investigated in Chapter 5. All women, not just working women, were less likely to vote for the Texas billionaire.

With respect to other social factors, Perot received greater support outside his native South. Younger voters were more supportive of his candidacy in comparison to older voters. Finally, level of education had no significant impact on the likelihood of favoring Perot over the major party presidential candidates.

Overall, the 19% of the national vote received by Perot had few clear

TABLE 9.2. *Social cleavages and third party vote choice,*[a]
1992—analyzing the Perot vote (N = 1,447)

Independent variables	Coefficient (s.e.)
Constant	−.13 (.69)
Race (reference = all else)	
African Americans	−1.98* (.52)
Religion (reference = other religion)	
Liberal Protestants	.22 (.41)
Moderate Protestants	.02 (.40)
Conservative Protestants	−.31 (.40)
Catholics	.08 (.39)
Jewish	−.17 (.62)
No religion	.13 (.41)
Class (reference = non-labor-force participant	
Professionals	−.28 (.25)
Managers	.08 (.28)
Routine white-collar employees	−.06 (.26)
Self-employed	.56* (.26)
Skilled workers	.16 (.31)
Nonskilled workers	−.08 (.25)
Gender (reference = men)	
Women	−.42* (.16)
Region (reference = South)	
All other regions	.49* (.19)
Years of education (continuous)	−.04 (.04)
Age (continuous)	−.02* (.01)

[a] Dependent variable is coded '1' for the choice of H. Ross Perot, and '0' for the choice of a major party candidate.
An astrisk indicates significance at the .05 level (2-tailed test).

social bases. Our analyses generally confirm those reported by some earlier analysts.[32] Perot did somewhat better among whites and men, but there were little significant differences among class and religious groups. His appeal in 1992 cut across the normal social divides in American politics. Explanations of his support cannot usefully start from an analysis of social group alignments.

Perot Voters in 1996

Between 1992 and 1996, the major issue championed by Perot in 1992 (the unbalanced federal budget) had been addressed by the two major parties. It might be expected that, lacking a clear wedge issue, the social bases of support for Perot's second presidential bid would sharpen as his vote total reflected only core supporters. However, Perot's voters were in fact even more idiosyncratic in 1996 than in 1992. African-American voters again gave little support to Perot, and religious groups and classes were statistically indistinguishable in their corresponding levels of support.[33] Women are predicted as being less supportive of Perot, but the coefficient for gender is small and not close to achieving statistical significance. Of the remaining variables, only age has a statistically significant effect, with older voters again being less supportive of Perot in comparison to younger voters. Coupled with his declining vote total, Perot's increasingly idiosyncratic sources of support appear to reflect the loss of focus by the Reform Party after 1992.

TABLE 9.3. *Social cleavages and third party vote choice,[a] 1996—analyzing the Perot vote* (N = 1,022)

Independent variables	Coefficient (s.e.)
Constant	−1.24 (1.3)
Race (reference = all else)	
African Americans	−1.69* (.74)
Religion (reference = other religion)	
Liberal Protestants	.28 (.81)
Moderate Protestants	.27 (.80)
Conservative Protestants	.65 (.78)
Catholics	.13 (.78)
Jewish	−.27 (1.3)
No religion	1.10 (.78)
Class (reference = non-labor-force participant)	
Professionals	−.48 (.39)
Managers	−.22 (.47)
Routine white-collar employees	−.11 (.42)
Self-employed	.07 (.51)
Skilled workers	.20 (.48)
Nonskilled workers	.36 (.39)
Gender (reference = men)	
Women	−.18 (.25)
Region (reference = South)	
All other regions	.35 (.28)
Years of education (continuous)	−.01 (.06)
Age (continuous)	−.03* (.01)

[a] Dependent variable is coded '1' for the choice of H. Ross Perot, and '0' for the choice of a major party candidate.
An asterisk indicates significance at the .05 level (2-tailed test).

CONCLUSION

The analyses of third party candidates developed in this chapter provide a useful perspective on the development and ongoing evolution of social cleavages in U.S. politics. If our analyses had found evidence for consistently large effects of cleavages on third party vote choice, this might lend support to the contention that the political relevance of social cleavages is increasingly to be found outside the electoral space defined by the major parties. However, we find no evidence for this scenario.

Instead, social cleavages, where they are relevant to third party candidacies, appear to reflect an underlying opposition to Republican candidates among key groups (in the case of the race cleavage) or an emerging but not fully mature cleavage (in the case of gender in 1968). The significant effect of gender in 1992 is of an altogether different character than the gender gap among major party voters (and the emerging alignment of working women with Democratic presidential candidates). All women, not just working women, were less likely to vote for Perot. Not only do the religion and class cleavages have virtually no impact on third party candidates in 1968, 1992, and 1996, the combined effects of social cleavages outside the arena of major parties is considerably smaller than the corresponding effects on Democratic versus Republican vote choice discussed in Chapter 6. Taken together, these considerations imply that even a large increase in overall levels of support for such candidates in the future will likely have little impact (and will not by themselves displace) social cleavages among major party voters.

The limited relevance of social cleavages to third party candidates also illustrates an important difficulty faced by political actors who operate outside of the organizational framework provided by the Democratic and Republican parties. As shown in Chapter 6, the major parties have enjoyed distinctive sociodemographic profiles during the past four decades, relying on the political mobilization and longstanding alignments of key social groups. These bases of support provide major party candidates with a 'starting point' from which to begin their drive for office. However, even the most successful independent presidential campaigns in recent decades have been unable to mobilize longstanding religion and class cleavages.

In comparison to the two major parties, then, third party candidates face greater obstacles in securing the durable constituencies necessary to create lasting political organizations and remain competitive in national elections. Moreover, as Perot's second bid for presidential office demonstrates, there is a tendency for single issue-oriented presidential campaigns to founder once a key wedge issue is incorporated into the respective policy stances of the major parties. The durability of social cleavages is a sign of a well-established set of conflicts involving not only voters' material interests and political preferences, but also a set of political organizations able to mobilize and elicit the loyalty of specific social groups.

10

Conclusion

Having reached the end of our investigations, we can now consider in greater detail the political and theoretical relevance of our results. Understanding the social bases of the two major political parties in the United States cannot, by itself, explain which party is likely to win the next election. There are many other causal factors than social cleavages that affect election outcomes. Moreover, a central assumption of our approach is that the political consequences of social cleavages for electoral outcomes are mediated by other, more proximate factors (which in turn have multiple causes). None the less our findings have implications for the future trajectories of the Democratic and Republican parties in light of postindustrial social and economic developments and cultural changes in American society. We identify the most important of these changes and their likely impacts on the social bases of party coalitions below.

In terms of theoretical issues, our work suggests some ways of thinking about the utility, as well as the limits, of what we have called the 'sociological approach' to studying political behavior. A growing chorus of scholars have argued that social cleavages have declined in political importance throughout the mature democracies. Although based on limited empirical evidence, this conclusion has been widely accepted and interpreted as both an indicator and cause of contemporary patterns of political change. We find little evidence for this sweeping conclusion in the U.S. context. The total social cleavage—the average of the race, religion, class, and gender cleavages—has actually increased in size during the twelve elections between 1952 and 1996. While a significant portion of this increase is attributable to the growth and durability of the race cleavage, our conclusions about the overall stability of the total social cleavage would not be affected by ignoring the racial cleavage.

In this chapter, we examine in more detail these political and theoretical conclusions. We begin with a discussion of the political consequences of changing social group alignments for the Democratic and Republican coalitions. We then summarize the relevance of our study for the debates over the sociological approach to political behavior.

THE NEW DEAL COALITION: DEAD OR ALIVE?

There can be little question that, at the end of the century, the Democratic Party no longer looks the same as it did at mid-century. By 1992, professionals and managers were as numerous in the Democratic coalition as skilled and nonskilled workers. Approximately six out of every ten Democratic votes in recent elections come from women, and three out of ten are coming from racial and ethnic minorities. These startling changes have occurred in the course of forty years, reflecting far-reaching changes in both political alignments and group size.

Professionals and Social Issue Liberalism

The most striking change affecting class politics in the U.S. is the political realignment of professionals with the Democratic Party. Not only has this fundamental shift in political alignment resulted in the growing dependence of Democratic candidates on professionals (and, to a lesser extent, managers), it also signals the maturation of several important ideological changes affecting the relationship of public opinion and political institutions. The first of these relates to the increasingly liberal views on social issues—especially those relating to civil rights for women and African-Americans—among the U.S. public in general. Professionals are not the only segment of the electorate whose voting behavior is affected by social issues. Indeed, our analyses suggest the increasing political relevance of such attitudes in providing voters with a basis for evaluating and choosing between the presidential candidates of the two major parties. As the policy positions of the Democratic and Republican parties on these issues have diverged substantially over time, it has made it easier for voters to begin to make attributions about such differences. Taken together, these changes constitute an important institutional transformation: in contrast to the political environment of U.S. parties prior to the civil rights era of the middle 1960s, the contemporary party system is one in which conflicts over civil rights and civil liberties form an essential divide. Increasingly, this divide separates the two parties and their respective supporters.

Changes in group size are magnifying the importance of these trends.

The proportion of voters employed in the professional and managerial occupations are growing rapidly relative to the working class. As a result, their political importance has increased. If professionals and managers were in the same political alignment in the 1990s as in the 1960s, the competitiveness of the Democratic Party in national politics would have declined substantially. The growing importance of social issues, and the increasing proportion of members of these classes with liberal attitudes on these issues has enabled the Democrats to win an increasing numbers of professional and managerial votes.

Decline of Working-Class Support

The dealignment of nonskilled (white) workers from the Democratic Party is one of the most striking results of the 1996 election. It also appears to reflect a further evolution of nonskilled workers' post-1976 trend. When coupled with the earlier dealignment of skilled workers, nonskilled workers' more recent dealignment provides further evidence for the transformation of the New Deal coalition. Nonskilled workers have not perceived as much economic gain in the Clinton years in comparison with other classes; and hence their support for Clinton did not increase as much as other classes between 1992 and 1996. Similarly, in the late 1970s they experienced higher levels of economic distress under Democrat Jimmy Carter, reducing their support considerably.[1] Whether the trend among nonskilled workers can be reversed is unclear. What is clear is that Clinton's rhetorical support of programs aimed at working families did little to stem the disproportionate decline in nonskilled workers' political loyalty.

A second, important consequence of the increasing representation of professionals and managers in the Democratic coalition is a corresponding willingness by party leaders to either take for granted or effectively ignore the concerns of working-class voters. The declining presence of both skilled and nonskilled workers within the Democratic coalition—a product of both shifts in alignment, and, to a lesser extent, changes in size—has effectively decreased the relevance of their votes. Likewise, the stable but disproportionately low rates of political participation among these classes appear to provide Democratic strategists with little incentive to adopt appeals that would lead to greater working-class mobilization. In fact, by the 1980s the combined presence of both skilled and nonskilled workers within the Republican coalition is virtually identical to their presence within the Democratic coalition.

The growing ability of Republican candidates to induce working-class

defections from the Democrats while supporting regressive fiscal policies (e.g. massive tax transfers to affluent citizens) is one of the more
remarkable features of the recent political past. A number of analysts
have hypothesized that this is due to the persistence of racism among
the white working class. The results of Chapter 6 are not inconsistent
with this thesis (showing, for example, that when the race cleavage is
highest the class cleavage tends to decline). However, our analyses of
the sources of nonskilled workers' dealignment beginning in 1980 show
that they are not primarily driven by race but rather economic perceptions and, to a lesser extent, declining support for the welfare state.
While the latter has been plausibly connected to racial attitudes in some
of recent research, the more important economic factor has no such
connection.

Gender

In conjunction with the growth of professionals and managers in the
Democratic Party coalition, the decline of working-class support
appears likely to push that party away from its historic commitments
to government-funded social programs and the welfare state. However,
the rising gender cleavage (which reaches an all-time high in 1996) along
with the growing importance of racial and ethnic minority voters in the
Democratic coalition potentially provides an alternative social foundation for the New Deal/Great Society policy agenda.

We find clear evidence that long-term shifts in the political alignment
of working women account for the gender cleavage in presidential
voting through the 1980s. In 1992 and 1996, however, the rising partisan
importance of other gender-related issues has led to multiple gender
cleavages, in turn increasing the overall gap between women and men
voters. The gender cleavage is also notable in light of its status as an
emerging source of voter alignments in the contemporary U.S. The case
of gender illustrates that social inequalities can eventually produce a
full-blown social cleavage when coupled with high levels of group conflict and an opportunity for voters to make attributions about party
differences. Our interpretation is also consistent with the inference that
social movement organizations—the women's liberation movement and
its organizational opponents—have helped to translate latent conflicts
over gender into partisan issues that propelled the Democratic and
Republican parties in divergent directions. Unlike cleavages that origin-
ate primarily in the political-entrepreneurial activities of party leaders,
contemporary differences involving the specific alignments of working

women appear to pre-date the growing polarization of the parties on policy issues relating to family and gender roles.

However, we also infer that the New Deal cleavage surrounding the Democratic party's greater willingness to support government provision of basic social services clearly provided the initial opportunity for working women's shift in political alignment. Had there not already been some political-institutional basis with which voters could differentiate the parties in terms of their likelihood of supporting public social spending, it is unlikely that the growing number of employed female voters would have had reason to support Democratic candidates in the first place. In this sense, the legacy of the New Deal and Great Society were of critical significance in contributing to new voter alignments

Race and Ethnic Cleavages

African-Americans have provided extremely consistent support for Democratic candidates at the national level. Our estimates show that although African-Americans make up 12% of the population (and despite lower turnout rates than whites), they have provided approximately two out of every ten Democratic votes in recent elections. Increased economic opportunities and the growth of the black middle class since the early 1960s has not led to increased support for the Republican Party. On some policy issues, racial polarization may even be increasing, most notably in the case of affirmative action. Although projecting into the future is difficult, nothing in American political life at present appears likely to pull significant numbers of African-American voters away from the Democratic Party presidential candidates.

The importance of the racial and ethnic divide in American politics is magnified by the rapid growth in the size and political alignment of the Hispanic population.[2] Because of the very low numbers of Hispanics in the NES sample before the 1980s, it proved impractical to include them as a separate category in our historical analyses. Still, there can be little doubt of their growing electoral importance given their increasing size since the 1960s. Hispanics doubled their proportion in the entire U.S. population between 1970 and 1990 (going from 4.5% of the population to 9.0%), and future projections by the Census Bureau indicate that they will increase to more than 22% by 2050.

The political alignment of Hispanic voters is often thought to be contested, and there have been cases of Republican candidates who have successfully appealed to Hispanic voters.[3] However, although not as consistently Democratic as African-Americans, Hispanic voters (other than Cuban-Americans) have been strong Democratic partisans.[4] In his recent overview of Latino politics, Louis DeSipio collected a variety of exit poll data with large enough samples to reliably estimate the Hispanic vote. The average of these surveys show Hispanic voters giving 56% of their votes to the Democrat (Jimmy Carter) in 1980, 63% to Walter Mondale in 1984, 68% to Michael Dukakis in 1988, and 58% to Bill Clinton in the three-way 1992 race (67% of major party voters).[5] The combination of growing size and Democratic alignment has alarmed some conservative analysts. The lead article in the 16 June, 1997 issue of the conservative journal *National Review*, for example, declares that 'demography is destiny' and that when it comes to the growing minority populations in the United States, 'the trend is not our friend.' The authors, Peter Brimelow and Ed Rubinstein, present a series of projections which combine an assumption of constant levels of partisan alignment and turnout with Census population projections (putting Hispanics at 23% of the electorate by the 2052 election). They conclude that unless the Republican Party moves soon to shut down immigration from Central America, they will find it increasingly more difficult to win national elections in the twenty-first century.[6]

The potential impact of the Hispanic vote at present, however, is currently diluted by their very low turnout rates. The Current Population Survey's Voter Supplement surveys show that eligible Hispanic voters report voting at a rate approximately half that of white voters.[7] Moreover, many Hispanics are not citizens, and hence disfranchised in federal elections. Over time, the proportion of Hispanics who become eligible to vote will increase, and turnout levels may also begin to increase with rising educational and income levels. Because Hispanics are concentrated heavily in large population states (California, Texas, Florida, and New York), their current electoral impact is reduced in the short run. Nevertheless, as they become an increasingly large segment of the electorate they will have disproportionate influence in presidential elections because of the institutional design of the electoral college, which rewards success in larger states.

Democratic Dilemmas

The increasing importance of working women and minority voters within the Democratic coalition presents a number of strategic opportunities as well as conflicts. If both African-American and Hispanic voters maintain approximately their current level of support for the Democratic Party, and the group size and turnout rates of Hispanic voters continue to increase, the Democrats stand to gain in future elections.[8] A similar pattern can be expected if the proportion of women in the labor force continues to grow. However, the new professional/ managerial voters (as well as the need to raise increasingly large sums from affluent individuals and Political Action Committees) encourage party leaders and candidates to resist further increases in social spending or taxes. In general, these changes help to explain support among leaders of both major parties for public policies that disproportionately benefit upper-income voters. But in the Democratic coalition, the growing importance of minority and women voters will exert counterweight pressures on Democratic politicians to support programs that address problems faced by these groups.

One likely scenario is for Democratic strategists to simply resist the dilemma by taking advantage of voters' lack of alternatives. In an environment in which political institutions make viable third party organizations virtually impossible, minority voters have few political alternatives to the Democratic Party at the national level. Moreover, there is little chance at present that the issues that have driven their political alignments since the New Deal will be embraced by the Republican Party. As long as the Democrats remain slightly more supportive of these programs (as well as containing to support civil rights measures), they can be expected to hold the allegiance of African-American voters.[9] In the case of Hispanic voters, Democratic opposition to anti-immigration measures (including California's Proposition 187[10]) may help to further solidify the alignment of Hispanics with the Democratic Party.

An alternative political scenario, promoted by many on the Democratic Party's left-wing, calls for the party to reach out aggressively to non-voters (disproportionately located in the working class) as a way of building a new progressive majority. The assumption is that left populist political campaigns could address the broader concerns of minorities, workers, and poor people who are currently indifferent to what they perceive as the limited range of political options. This would lead to increased turnout and a shake-up of the structure of the Democratic coalition. But there are grounds for questioning the assumptions underlying this scenario. First, research on voter turnout consistently has found that factors relating to 'social connectedness', not issue-driven dissatisfaction, are a central cause of turnout decline during the past thirty years.[11] Second, mobilization efforts may have the effect of propelling not only Democratic partisans but also Republican and independent voters, thereby muting the partisan advantage of higher turnout rates.[12]

Probably the strongest impetus for restoring or reformulating the New Deal coalition rests with the emergence of reform-oriented social movements from below. If it were possible to link them effectively to mainstream Democratic electoral campaigns, such movements might be effective in mobilizing nonvoters and latent party loyalists, while also producing attitude change among the remainder of the electorate. These scenarios underlay the eras of the 1930s and the 1960s, and they may have future applicability as well.[13]

RELIGION AND THE NEW REPUBLICAN COALITION

At the heart of our social cleavage analysis of changes in the Republican coalition is an investigation of the role of religion. While much ink has been spilled on the growing influence of the Christian Right in the Republican Party, our analyses show that a key social factor behind their right turn is the political dealignment and shrinking size of liberal Protestants. When juxtaposed with the relatively stable and very strong presence of doctrinally conservative Protestants within the Republican coalition, our results help to explain the alignment and partisan consequences of conservative Christian voters in the U.S. In contrast to the popular but misleading interpretation discussed in Chapter 4, this segment of the electorate has not experienced a relative shift (much less a realignment) when considered in relation to electorate-wide changes during the past three decades. However, the declining numbers of doctrinally (and politically) more liberal Protestants have given conservative Protestants a greater presence within the Republican Party coalition. The moderating influence of liberal Protestants has eroded significantly. The correspondingly greater influence of conservative Protestants produces a clearer image of religious/political polarization. These developments reveal how both public and journalistic perceptions of party polarization can be fueled by changes in party coalitions.

Republican Dilemmas

When viewed from the standpoint of social group contributions to major party coalitions, the major dilemma facing the Republican Party in coming elections is the party's adoption of conservative social issue stances and their partial (and at times substantial) embrace of the Christian Right platform. These positions are driving some key groups of supporters—e.g. professionals, managers, liberal Protestants—into centrist or even Democratic alignment. As these are some of the fastest growing segments of the electorate, the Republicans might have reasonably expected to be in a position to dominate national politics in the twenty-first century if the old alignments had held. The fact they have not in large part reflects the role of social issue divisions and their impact on particular social groups.

A related Republican dilemma centers on women voters. Republican support for 'traditional' family values and opposition to social programs aimed at supporting working families have not been popular with working women. In the 1950s and 1960s, their differences with the Democrats on these issues were both less well-defined and of smaller political consequence, due to the more limited number of women in the labor force. But as the proportion of women in the labor force has steadily risen, the negative electoral consequences of Republican domestic policy stances are beginning to emerge. Republican strategists increasingly face multiple challenges in appealing to women voters, with the growth of additional gender cleavages that stem from issue conflicts which are independent of the rising labor force participation of women.

RETHINKING THE SOCIOLOGICAL APPROACH

The sociological approach to political behavior that we have described in this book identifies the potential sources of social cleavages in voters' patterns of support for particular parties. Our theoretical interpretation emphasizes that the mere existence of social or economic inequalities, whatever their quality or quantity, are insufficient to produce full-blown cleavages. Even extensive patterns of group conflict and identification are not, in themselves, sufficient to produce social cleavages in the political system. Instead, political-organizational and institutional factors are also necessary.

When coupled with our empirical results, these general theoretical considerations help us to better understand the utility as well as the limitations of the sociological approach. The over-time development of the class and gender cleavages are particularly instructive in this context. The recent contraction in this cleavage does not by itself represent evidence against the sociological approach; indeed, a relative strength of this approach is the perspective it provides on cleavages that experience contractions over time.

However, developing a suitable explanation for the recent decline in the class cleavage does illustrate a key limitation of the sociological approach. More specifically, our interpretation of cleavages suggests three potential sources of this decline (and especially the dealignment of nonskilled and skilled workers). One possible explanation, a reduction in the level of social structural inequality involving class, is clearly inadequate; if anything, such inequalities have *increased* over the past 25 years. A decline in the patterns of group conflict involving classes (and workers, in particular) could potentially explain class dealignment. But the recent period appears not to involve less class struggle but rather an increasing willingness on the part of employers to supress unions and a vigorous renewal of the labor movement in recent years.

Finally, the recent decline in the class cleavage may be linked to political-organizational/institutional factors. The major parties have arguably become increasingly similar in their patterns of class-specific electoral appeals, targeting middle class or economically median voters and increasingly employing political rhetoric that defines the majority of the electorate as having similar economic interests.

However, we find clear evidence that the declining presence of workers within the Democratic coalition is due to their changing partisan preferences. More specifically, nonskilled workers' political dealignment is a function of a small but genuine change in policy preferences coupled with a larger tendency to experience personal, economic dissatisfaction during Democratic presidencies (and a corresponding tendency to experience *higher* rates of economic satisfaction under the administrations of Republican presidents). A suitable explanation would of necessity require moving beyond the framework of the sociological approach developed in this study.

By contrast, the case of gender provides a telling example of the explanatory power of the model. Like the class cleavage, the gender cleavage is characterized by extensive patterns of social-structural inequality. The rising proportion of women in the workforce has meant that these sources of inequality have been felt by growing numbers of women. The rise of the women's movement and the spread of feminist consciousness has sharpened the sense of group conflict over the past three decades. The political consequences of gender have become consolidated into a mature cleavage as the Democratic and Republican Parties have increasingly taken distinct positions on policies and issues relating to the interests and situation of working women.

Even in a relatively clear case such as that of gender, however, the sociological approach can tell only part of the story. The recent emergence of multiple gender 'gaps' in the presidential elections of the 1990s nicely illustrates this point. Contemporary political differences involving gender include not only the cleavage between working women versus other voters but also between issues and forms of group consciousness that unify all women versus men voters. This emerging ideological dimension of the gender gap operates in complementary relationship with sources of division arising from socioeconomic inequalities.

In conclusion, then, we offer two theoretical generalizations. First, the sociological approach is of greatest explanatory relevance when over-time developments in social cleavages involve changes stemming from trends in social structure, group conflict, or political-organizational factors. By contrast, when specific groups within a cleavage field experience a change in their alignment stemming from other causal factors, the sociological approach will be insufficient to account for such change. The important cases of nonskilled workers and liberal Protestants best exemplify this latter scenario.

Second, by virtue of its focus on fundamental patterns of social-structural inequality, the sociological approach not only identifies the causal origins of mature social cleavages, but also the potential sources of future cleavages. The gender cleavage again illustrates the emergence of a mature cleavage from inequalities that were once of very limited relevance to electoral politics. In doing so, it also illustrates the intellectual relevance of examining questions about social structural inequalities that have not yet produced social cleavages. Consider, for instance, the case of nonskilled workers. Whereas the 'decline of class' interpretations discussed in this study would compel scholars to abandon the subject, our sociological approach implies a more fruitful direction for research is to address specific questions about the precise causal factors behind such class-specific changes in political alignments. To express the matter another way, the relevant issue is not simply that nonskilled workers have become less firmly aligned with the Democratic Party, but why unskilled workers' relatively disadvantageous class position has *not* propelled them into a stronger alignment with the Democratic Party.

We emphasize that the sociological approach differs sharply from the subset of 'decline' interpretations which assume that recent patterns of social change have produced increasing group similarities and thus convergent group interests. While this pattern applies selectively to

some U.S. religious groups, there are also many instances of fundamental and increasing, patterns of group-based inequalities in
contemporary American society. The existence of these inequalities
underlie both the actual and the potential development of social cleavages in the United States. Only the dissolution of these inequalities will
render a sociological approach wholly irrelevant to the study of
American politics.

NOTES

NOTES TO THE INTRODUCTION

1. In referring to the 'sociological approach', we caution that it is hardly the only distinctive contribution of sociologists to the study of politics. In the area of political behavior, research on the impact of social networks has been an important contribution. The attention sociologists have also given to rigorously analyzing other political phenomena—such as the rise and development of welfare states, social movements and other forms of non-institutional politics, the politics of families and workplaces, and the influence of the capitalist world-system on nation states—indicate some of those contributions.

2. Russell Dalton and Martin Wattenberg, 'The Not So Simple Act of Voting', in *Political Science: The State of the Discipline II*, ed. Ada Finifter (Washington, DC: American Political Science Association, 1993), quotes at pp. 199–200; see also Dalton, 'Comparative Politics: Micro-Behavioral Perspectives', in *A New Handbook of Political Science*, ed. Robert E. Goodin and Hans-Dieter Klingemann (New York: Oxford University Press, 1996). We cite and discuss other examples of the recent critique of the sociological approach in Chapter 1 below.

3. Although there is a considerable recent journal literature (which we cite and discuss in the chapters that follow), the last book-length treatment of these topics in the U.S. is David Knoke's 1976 work, *The Social Bases of Political Parties* (Baltimore: Johns Hopkins University Press, 1976).

NOTES TO CHAPTER 1

1. Friedrich Engels, 'The Tactics of Social Democracy', in *The Marx/Engels Reader*, ed. Robert W. Tucker (New York: Norton, 1978), p. 571. The most systematic analysis of class voting and the historical development of the social democratic movement in Europe can be found in Adam Przeworski, *Capitalism and Social Democracy* (New York: Cambridge University Press, 1985), chap. 1; and Adam Przeworski and John Sprague, *Paper Stones: A History of Electoral Socialism* (Chicago: University of Chicago Press, 1986). There were, to be sure, heated debates within the Marxist tradition over the viability of electoral socialism; from leaders of the SPD and many other Marxists affiliated with the 2nd International through to the 'Eurocommunist' movement after World War II have debated the possibility of bringing about socialism through electoral means. Marxist critics of the 2nd International tradition, most famously Lenin and Luxemburg, asserted that no bourgeois democracy would ever permit such an

outcome. For an overview of the range of opinions within the Marxist tradition about the viability of an electoral road to socialism, see the discussion in Ralph Miliband, *Marxism and Politics* (New York: Oxford University Press, 1977), pp. 154–90.

2. Lowe, quoted in Robert McKenzie and Allan Silver, *Angels in Marble: Working Class Conservatives in Urban England* (Chicago: University of Chicago Press, 1968), pp. 4–5.

3. Werner Sombart, *Why is There No Socialism in the United States?* (White Plains, NY: M. E. Sharpe, 1976 [1906]); Selig Perlman, *A Theory of the Labor Movement* (New York: Augustus M. Kelley, 1970 [1928]). Seymour Martin Lipset's various writings about the origins of American exceptionalism have generally adopted a similar position. See most recently his *American Exceptionalism: A Double Edged Sword* (New York: Norton, 1996). For the debate about the historical dimensions of American 'exceptionalism' (i.e. the absence of a strong socialist movement or political party), see e.g. Kim Voss, *The Making of American Exceptionalism: The Knights of Labor in the Nineteenth Century* (Ithaca, NY: Cornell University Press, 1994); Jerome Karabel, 'The Failure of American Socialism Reconsidered', *Socialist Register*, 18 (1979): 204–27; and the essays in Byron Shafer (ed.), *Is America Different?* (Oxford: Clarendon Press, 1991).

4. We discuss the history of the scholarly debates over nineteenth-century ethno-religious cleavages in American politics in more detail in Chapter 4 below. A concise general survey can be found in Robert P. Swierenga, 'Ethnoreligious Political Behavior in the Mid-Nineteenth Century', in *Religion and American Politics*, ed. Mark A. Noll (New York: Oxford University Press, 1990).

5. For discussion and examples of such arguments, see e.g. Sara Alpern and Dale Baum, 'Female Ballots: The Impact of the Nineteenth Amendment', *Journal of Interdisciplinary History*, 26 (1985): 43–67; Sandra Baxter and Marjorie Lansing, *Women and Politics: The Visible Majority* (Ann Arbor: University of Michigan Press, 1983), pp. 17–22; Ethel Klein, *Gender Politics* (Cambridge, Mass.: Harvard University Press, 1984), pp. 13–21, 142–43; J. Stanley Lemons, *The Woman Citizen: Social Feminism in the 1920s*, 2nd edn. (Chicago: University of Chicago Press, 1977), pp. 157–58; Theda Skocpol, *Protecting Soldiers and Mothers* (Cambridge, Mass.: Harvard University Press, 1992), pp. 505–06.

6. See e.g. Stuart A. Rice, *Quantitative Methods in Politics* (New York: Russell and Russell 1969 [1928]), esp. chaps. 12–13; and Herbert Tingsten, *Political Behavior: Studies in Election Statistics* (Totowa, NJ: Bedminster Press 1963 [1937]). The influential sociologist W. F. Ogburn published a number of early voting studies using ecological techniques, including William F. Ogburn and Delvin Peterson, 'Political Thought of Social Classes', *Political Science Quarterly*, 31 (1916): 300–17; Ogburn and Lolagene C. Coombs, 'The Economic Factor in the Roosevelt Elections,' *American Political Science Review*, 34 (1940): 719–27.

7. This point has been made by Dalton and Wattenberg, 'The Not So Simple Act of Voting', p. 196.

8. The landmark criticism of early ecological voting studies appeared in 1950: William S. Robinson, 'Ecological Correlation and the Behavior of Individuals', *American Sociological Review*, 15 (1950): 351–57; see also the recent work of

Gary King on ecological inference, *A Solution to the Ecological Inference Problem* (Princeton: Princeton University Press, 1997). There were, to be sure, early election surveys conducted in the 1930s and early 1940s. Gallup began polling voters in presidential elections in 1936, and included a rudimentary battery of items on respondents' occupation. For a creative recent attempt to make use of this dataset, see David Weakliem and Anthony Heath, 'The Secret Life of Class Voting', in *The End of Class Politics?*, ed. Geoff Evans (New York: Oxford University Press, forthcoming). For a useful overview of the history of these early survey efforts, see Jean Converse, *Survey Research in the United States* (Berkeley: University of California Press, 1986), pp. 267–378.

9. The term 'electoral sociology' as a label for the Columbia School is used by Dalton and Wattenberg, 'The Not So Simple Act of Voting', p. 196. For a concise recent commentary situating the revolutionary contributions of the Columbia School, see Edward Carmines and Robert Huckfeldt, 'Political Behavior: An Overview', in *The New Handbook of Political Science*, ed. Robert E. Goodin and Hans-Dieter Klingemann (New York: Oxford University Press, 1996). On the organizational history of the Bureau of Applied Social Research, see Converse, *Survey Research in the United States*, pp. 267–304.

10. Paul F. Lazarsfeld, Bernard R. Berelson, and Hazel Gaudet, *The People's Choice* (New York: Columbia University Press, 1948). A very useful overview of this and other early voting studies, which also contains valuable background information about the context of these studies, can be found in Peter Rossi, 'Four Landmarks in Voting Research', in *American Voting Behavior*, ed. Eugene Burdick and Arthur J. Brodbeck (Glencoe, Ill.: Free Press, 1959). Rossi notes that Lazarsfeld was interested in how the mass media influences consumer preferences and had hoped originally to conduct a panel study of advertising and changes in consumer preferences due to exposure to media advertising. Unable to get funding for that project, Lazarsfeld switched to something with a less commercial focus: presidential elections. Following this, funding was readily secured from the Rockefeller Foundation. See Rossi, 'Four Landmarks', pp. 15–16.

11. Lazarsfeld and his colleagues reported evidence suggesting that the vote switchers were among the least informed and involved in the panel, drawing the conclusion that their switches reflected lack of information rather than careful evaluation of the candidates.

12. See Lazarsfeld et al., *The People's Choice*, p. 26.

13. For discussions of the political homogeneity of primary reference groups, see Lazarsfeld et al., *The People's Choice*, pp. 137–49; see also the second major Columbia study, Bernard R. Berelson, Paul F. Lazarsfeld, and William N. McPhee, *Voting: A Study of Opinion Formation in a Presidential Campaign* (Chicago: University of Chicago Press, 1954), pp. 88–109. For discussions of selective perception and projection in voters' evaluations of information received about the candidates during the political campaign, see *The People's Choice*, pp. 80–82, 151–52; *Voting*, pp. 215–33.

14. For some representative examples of these criticisms, see V. O. Key and Frank Munger, 'Social Determinism and Electoral Decision: The Case of Indiana', in

American Voting Behavior, ed. Eugene Burdick and Arthur J. Brodbeck (Glencoe, Ill.: The Free Press, 1959); and, more generally, Angus Campbell, Philip E. Converse, Warren Miller, and Donald Stokes, *The American Voter* (New York: Wiley), 1960, esp. pp. 347–48.

15. There has been a profusion of recent work on the impact of social networks on political behavior; see esp. the work of Robert Huckfeldt and John Sprague, *Citizens, Politics and Social Communication* (New York: Cambridge University Press, 1995). For other arguments for the revival of the Columbia School approach, see David Weakliem and Anthony Heath, 'Rational Choice and Class Voting', *Rationality and Society*, 6 (1994): 243–70.

16. Lipset received his Ph.D. at Columbia in 1948, although his primary mentor was Robert Merton, not Lazarsfeld. But Lipset was involved with early efforts to carry on the Columbia research in the 1950s (see e.g. Berelson et al., *Voting*, p. 303, n. 30), he co-authored papers on voting with Lazarsfeld (see e.g. Lipset, Lazarsfeld, Allan H. Barton, and Juan Linz, 'The Psychology of Voting: An Analysis of Political Behavior', in *Handbook of Social Psychology*, ed. Gardiner Lindzey (Cambridge, Mass.: Addison-Wesley, 1954). His general orientation to comparative-historical research on voting behavior and especially socialist and right-wing movements tended to emphasize social attributes and group processes broadly consistent with the original Columbia School model. As the head of the Behavioral Sciences Division of the Ford Foundation in the late 1950s, Bernard Berelson approved funding for Lipset's research on social cleavages and democracy, some of which would form a core part of his 1960 book *Political Man*. For Lipset's own recollections of his ties to Columbia, see his 'Steady Work: An Academic Memoir', *Annual Review of Sociology*, 22 (1996): 1–27; and also William Buxton, *Talcott Parsons and the Capitalist Nation-State* (Toronto: University of Toronto Press, 1985), chap. 11 (on 'Seymour Martin Lipset and the Sociology of Politics').

17. Lipset, *Political Man*, p. 303 (quote). Lipset's student Robert Alford extended the Lipset model in his widely cited and discussed study of the social bases of party coalitions in the Anglo-American capitalist democracies. Alford's approach focused primarily on class differences between voters, defined in terms of blue- versus white-collar voters. He found that class voting was highest in Britain and Australia, countries where the labor movement had close ties to the dominant left-wing party. See Alford, *Party and Society* (Chicago: Rand-McNally, 1963). The debate over Alford's methodological innovations for studying class voting are the subject of further discussion in the next chapter.

18. See esp. *Political Man*, pp. 230–78.

19. Seymour Martin Lipset and Stein Rokkan, 'Cleavage Structures, Party Systems, and Voter Alignments: An Introduction', in *Party Systems and Voter Alignments*, ed. S. M. Lipset and Stein Rokkan (New York: Free Press, 1967).

20. The mediation of social cleavages by political institutions, the nature and timing of the development of the party system, and, more generally, the structure of a nation's economic and social order are key themes in Lipset and Rokkan's comparative-historical work, and ones that have been widely discussed by other authors as well. See e.g. Lipset, *Revolution and Counter-*

revolution (New York: Anchor Press, 1970) and *Political Man*; Przeworski and Sprague, *Paper Stones*; and Stefano Bartolini and Peter Mair, *Identity, Competition and Electoral Availability* (New York: Cambridge University Press, 1990). E. E. Schattschneider's concept of the 'mobilization of bias' in his *The Semi-Sovereign People* (New York: Holt, Rinehart, 1960) also has clear parallels with this position; see Mark Franklin et al., 'Introduction', in *Electoral Change*, ed. Mark Franklin, Thomas Mackie, and Henry Valen (New York: Cambridge University Press, 1992), pp. 5–6.

21. Lipset and Rokkan, 'Cleavage Structures, Party Systems, and Voter Alignments: An Introduction', p. 50. The Lipset/Rokkan synthesis generally reflected the consensus view that the established cleavage patterns were likely to persist well into the future. See e.g. the multicountry analyses contained in Richard Rose (ed.), *Electoral Behavior: A Comparative Handbook* (New York: Free Press, 1974). This famous conclusion was buttressed by Lipset's more general theoretical assumption about the routinization of social cleavages in modern democratic polities. In contrast to the functionalist theories of mid-century American sociology, Lipset viewed social conflicts arising out of unequal relationships and class inequalities as becoming institutionalized by opportunities present in competitive party systems. So long as loyal support for a party provided a group of voters the possibility of bringing about desired policies, participation offered voters a stake in the outcome. This, in turn, legitimated the operation of democratic institutions, channeling otherwise disruptive conflicts through a more orderly political process.

22. The major scholarly works of the early Michigan School were Angus Campbell, Gerald Gurin, and Warren E. Miller, *The Voter Decides* (Evanston, Ill.: Row, Peterson, 1954); Campbell et al., *The American Voter*; Philip E. Converse, 'The Nature of Belief Systems in Mass Publics,' in *Ideology and Discontent*, ed. David Apter (New York: Free Press, 1964); Angus Campbell, Philip E. Converse, Warren E. Miller, and Donald Stokes (eds.), *Elections and the Political Order* (New York: Wiley, 1966).

23. As Jack Dennis has cleverly put it, 'part of what gives the Michigan team's research its plausibility is that groupism was only demoted, not retired. The Michigan School never threatened to kill off groupism in electoral studies, but merely to hold it as a permanent hostage.' Dennis, 'Groups and Political Behavior', *Political Behavior*, 9 (1987): 323–72, quote at p. 324.

24. Campbell et al., *The American Voter*. The discussion of the funnel metaphor is developed at pp. 24–32. The lack of political sophistication is a theme developed through *TAV*, but see esp. pp. 248–50. The most influential statement of political sophistication is developed in Converse's widely discussed 1964 essay, 'The Nature of Belief Systems in Mass Publics'. Debates over other claims about political sophistication have raged since the appearance of *TAV*; the most important contributions can be found in Norman Nie, Sidney Verba, and John Petrocik, *The Changing American Voter*, 2nd edn. (Cambridge, Mass.: Harvard University Press, 1981); and Eric R. A. N. Smith, *The Unchanging American Voter* (Berkeley: University of California Press, 1989). The comparison between the Michigan School's 'psychological' approach and the Columbia School's

'sociological' model is standard in political behavior textbooks; but for a more recent statement arguing for their complementarity, see Carmines and Huckfeldt, 'Political Behavior: An Overview.'

25. Indeed, it probably would not be stretching matters too much to suggest that as a research program, cleavage-oriented models of electoral behavior were running up against the limits of the questions they posed. Rather than continually expanding the range of new questions that could be addressed or solved, cleavage theorists had to continually account for the failure of voters to behave as their social group memberships would predict. The political instability of the Western democracies since the 1960s raised serious questions about the Lipset/Rokkan model of stable cleavage structures, and the capacity of that model to account for contemporary political change. The broader and causally pluralistic Michigan model, by contrast, more easily succeeded in posing productive questions about the interaction between group interests, political psychological processes, and vote outcomes.

26. Warren E. Miller and J. Merrill Shanks, *The New American Voter* (Cambridge, Mass.: Harvard University Press, 1996).

27. There is a considerable body of research assessing the economic consequences of different kinds of political regimes. Since World War II, inflation has generally been higher and unemployment lower when Democrats hold the White House and vice-versa when Republicans are in office. These findings appear to be fairly robust and have held up in studies employing different methodologies. See e.g. Douglas Hibbs, *The American Political Economy* (Cambridge, Mass.: Harvard University Press, 1987).

28. Anthony Downs, *An Economic Theory of Democracy* (New York: Harpers, 1957), p. 36 (quote).

29. Lipset et al., 'The Psychology of Voting: An Analysis of Political Behavior,' p. 1136 (quote).

30. The idea of 'sociotropic' voting was popularized by Donald Kinder and D. Roderick Kiewiet, 'Sociotropic Politics: The American Case', *British Journal of Political Science*, 11 (1981): 129–61. For an overview of these approaches, see D. Roderick Kiewiet, *Macroeconomics and Micropolitics* (Chicago: University of Chicago Press, 1983), esp. chap. 1; and Susan Welch and John Hibbing, 'Financial Conditions, Gender, and Voting in American National Elections,' *Journal of Politics*, 54 (1992): 197–213.

31. This blurring of the distinction between self-interest and altruism in the concept of sociotropic politics tends to undermine the core insights of the economic model. It becomes nothing more than a subset of 'goal-oriented' political behavior. See Carmines and Huckfeldt, 'Political Behavior: An Overview'.

32. For a general overview of the differences between the retrospective and prospective approaches, see e.g. Morris Fiorina, *Retrospective Voting in American National Elections* (New Haven: Yale University Press, 1981); and Kiewiet, *Macroeconomics and Micropolitics*. Retrospective models of presidential elections have been used to predict, with somewhat uneven results, the expected outcomes of presidential elections. The most widely discussed of

these predictive models include Ray C. Fair, 'The Effect of Economic Events on Votes for President,' *Political Behavior* 18 (1996): 119–39; and Michael Lewis-Beck and Tom W. Rice, *Forecasting Elections* (Washington, DC: Congressional Quarterly Press, 1992).

33. The blurriness of the distinction suggests that such concepts can readily be used by other theoretical approaches in analyzing voting behavior.

34. Unemployment increases the slackness of the labor market, particularly at the bottom end, holding down wage growth and increasing the number of poor households without full-time employment (or threatening same). For evidence of the effects of unemployment on different occupational and income groups; Hibbs, *The American Political Economy*, pp. 43–62; Christopher Jencks, *Rethinking Social Policy* (Cambridge, Mass.: Harvard University Press, 1992), pp. 152–70. Inflation, by contrast, hurts affluent households because a much greater share of their total income comes from property (which is taxed more highly as a result of inflation), because inflation negatively impacts the bond and stock markets, and finally because the price of luxury items rises faster than more basic items. For these arguments, see e.g. Hibbs, *The American Political Economy*, pp. 63–124.

35. See esp. Hibbs, *The American Political Economy*, 127–41; see also Hibbs, 'The Dynamics of Political Support for American Presidents among Occupational and Partisan Groups', *American Journal of Political Science*, 26 (1982): 313–32.

36. For an excellent overview of the intellectual history of the concept of the 'reference group', see Eleanor Singer, 'Reference Groups and Social Evaluations', in *Social Psychology: Sociological Perspectives*, ed. Morris Rosenberg and Ralph H. Turner (New York: Basic Books). For applications of reference group theory to voting, see Arthur H. Miller, Christopher Wlezien, and Anne Hildreth, 'A Reference Group Theory of Partisan Coalitions', *Journal of Politics*, 53 (1991): 1134–49; and Jeffrey W. Koch, *Social Reference Groups and Political Life* (Lanham, Md: University Press of America, 1995).

37. Samuel Stouffer et al., *The American Soldier* (Princeton: Princeton University Press, 1949); Robert K. Merton, *Social Theory and Social Structure* (New York: Free Press, 1957), pp. 225–386.

38. For brief overviews of these distinctions, see Pamela J. Conover, 'The Role of Social Groups in Political Thinking', *British Journal of Political Science*, 18 (1988): 51–76, at pp. 52–53; and Arthur Miller et al., 'Group Consciousness and Political Participation,' *American Journal of Political Science*, 25 (1981): 494–511, at pp. 496–97.

39. The most influential research and theorizing about the group identification, or the 'social identification model', can be found in Henri Tajfel, *Human Groups and Social Categories* (New York: Cambridge University Press, 1981); see also John C. Turner, *Rediscovering the Social Group* (Oxford: blackwell, 1987). The earliest experimental work on voting can be found in Leon Festinger's 1947 paper, 'The Role of Group Belongingness in a Voting Situation', *Human Relations*, 1 (1947): 154–80. For more recent applications to empirical voting patterns in the United States, see esp. the work of Arthur H. Miller, Patricia

Gurin, and their colleagues: Miller et al., 'Group Consciousness and Political Participation', and Patricia Gurin, Arthur H. Miller, and Gerald Gurin, 'Stratum Identification and Consciousness', *Social Psychology Quarterly*, 43 (1980): 30–47.

40. See esp. Jack Dennis, 'Groups and Political Behavior: Legitimation, Deprivation, and Competing Values'.

41. This point has been raised in the literature on the role of feminist consciousness in shaping the political behavior of women. See e.g. Klein, *Gender Politics*; Patricia Gurin, 'Women's Gender Consciousness', *Political Opinion Quarterly*, 49 (1985): 143–63; Elizabeth A. Cook, 'Feminist Consciousness and Candidate Preference among American Women, 1972–88', *Political Behavior*, 15 (1993): 228–46. We discuss these literatures in more detail (with full references) in Chapter 5.

42. The most influential work in this vein is that of Paul Sniderman, Richard A. Brody, and Philip Tetlock, *Reasoning and Choice* (New York: Cambridge University Press, 1991), chap. 6; see also Koch, *Social Reference Groups and Political Life*, chap. 6.

43. Dennis, 'Groups and Political Behavior', p. 325 (quote). Dennis goes on to note that group consciousness is not, however, a sufficient condition for group influence.

44. For examples of such arguments, see Conover, 'The Role of Social Groups in Political Thinking'; and Dennis, 'Groups and Political Behavior'. It should be noted, however, that the value-added explanatory power of subjective consciousness is often modest or nonexistent, depending on the particular phenomena under investigation. For discussion, see Jeffrey W. Koch, 'Is Group Membership a Prerequisite for Group Identification?', *Political Behavior*, 15 (1993): 49–60.

45. Our general analytical strategy, discussed in Chapters 3–5 below, will be to make use of group identification measures where possible as controls. We discuss this strategy in the next chapter.

46. For an overview of these shifts and their possible link to the decline of traditional political cleavages, see Michael Rempel and Terry N. Clark, 'Post-industrial Politics: A Framework for Interpreting Citizen Politics since the 1960s,' in *Citizen Politics in Post-Industrial Societies*, ed. Terry N. Clark and Michael Rempel (Boulder, Colo.: Westview Press, 1997).

47. Lipset, 'Party Coalitions and the 1980 Election', in *Party Coalitions in the 1980s*, ed. Seymour Martin Lipset (San Francisco: Institute for Contemporary Studies, 1981), pp. 23–24 (quote).

48. Mark Franklin, 'The Decline of Cleavage Politics', in *Electoral Change*, ed. Mark Franklin, Thomas Mackie, and Henry Valen (New York: Cambridge University Press, 1992), p. 388 (quote).

49. These quotations or phrases are offered, in order, from Terry N. Clark, Seymour Martin Lipset, and Michael Rempel, 'The Declining Political Significance of Social Class', *International Sociology*, 8 (1993); David Butler and Dennis Kavanaugh, *The British General Election of 1983* (New York: St Martin's Press, 1984), p. 8 (quote); Richard Rose and Ian McAllister, *Voters Begin to Choose*

(Newbury Park, Calif.: Sage Publications, 1986), e.g. pp. 7, 162; Ronald Inglehart, *Culture Shift in Advanced Industrial Society* (Princeton: Princeton University Press, 1990), passim; Franklin, 'The Decline of Cleavage Politics', p. 404 (quote).

50. Cees van der Eijk et al., 'Cleavages, Conflict Resolution and Democracy', in *Electoral Change*, ed. Mark Franklin, Thomas Mackie, and Henry Valen (New York: Cambridge University Press, 1992), p. 430 (quote). See also Russell J. Dalton, *Citizen Politics in Western Democracies* (Chatham, NJ: Chatham House Publishers, 1988).

51. For an analysis of this confounding of the traditional lines of class division in conjunction with social movements for tax relief, see Clarence Lo, *Small Property Versus Big Government* (Berkeley: University of California Press, 1990) (analyzing the origins of the 1978 campaign for passage of Proposition 13, mandating a sharp cut in property taxes, in California).

52. For the U.S. data, see Steven Brint, *In an Age of Experts* (Princeton: Princeton University Press, 1994); for the cross-national data, see Gosta Esping-Andersen (ed.), *Changing Classes* (Newbury Park, Calif.: Sage Publications, 1993). We discuss this evidence in more detail in Chapter 7 below.

53. See e.g. Claude Fischer et al., *Inequality by Design* (Princeton: Princeton University Press, 1996); Sheldon Danziger and Peter Gottschalk, *Unequal America* (Cambridge, Mass.: Harvard University Press, 1995); Sheldon Danziger and Peter Gottschalk (eds.), *Uneven Tides: Rising Inequality in America* (New York: Russell Sage, 1993); Robert H. Frank and Philip J. Cook, *The Winner-Take-All Society* (New York: Free Press, 1995); Frank Levy, *The New Dollars and Dreams* (New York: Russell Sage, 1998).

54. William Julius Wilson, *The Declining Significance of Race* (Chicago: University of Chicago Press, 1978).

55. For evidence that the relative material improvement of African-Americans came to a halt in the 1970s, see e.g. National Research Council, *blacks and American Society* (Washington DC: National Academy of Sciences Press, 1989); National Urban League, *The State of black America 1996* (Washington, DC: National Urban League, 1997); Reynolds Farley and Walter R. Allen, *The Color Line and the Quality of Life in America* (New York: Russell Sage, 1987). For evidence that white racial antagonism towards African-Americans persists and may even be strengthening, see Donald R. Kinder and Lynn Sanders, *Divided by Color* (Chicago: University of Chicago Press, 1996).

56. We discuss this evidence and related changes in the economic, social, and political participation of women in more detail in Chapter 5.

57. From the mid-1950s through 1980, the average pay of female and male full-time, year-round employees was 59% of that of men; by 1990 it had risen to 72% (declining sharply to 71% by 1992); but among prime working age persons, women's wages were 79% of those of men by 1992. See Ruth Milkman and Eleanor Townsley, 'Gender and the Economy', In *The Handbook of Economic Sociology*, ed. Neil Smelser and Richard Swedberg (Princeton: Princeton University Press), p. 604; and Daphne Spain and Suzanne Bianchi, *Balancing Act* (New York: Russell Sage, 1996), pp. 111–13. These economic gains relative

to men have not, however, necessarily benefited all women. Rather, they appear to reflect (1) declining or stagnating men's wages and (2) dramatic wage gains made by women in elite professional and managerial occupations. See esp. Annette Bernhardt, Martina Morris, and Mark Handcock, 'Women's Gains, Men's Losses? The Shrinking Gender Gap in Earnings', *American Journal of Sociology*, 101 (1995): 302–28.

58. On the household division of labor and its social consequences, see esp. Arlie Hochschild, *The Second Shift* (New York: Avon, 1989). For a slightly more optimistic view of trends in the distribution of household labor, see Beth A. Shelton, *Women, Men and Time: Gender Differences in Paid Work, Housework, and Leisure Time* (Westport, Conn. Greenwood Press, 1992). On the economic consequences of rising divorce rates, see e.g. Annemette Sorenson, 'Estimating the Economic Consequences of Separation and Divorce: A Cautionary Tale from the United States', in *Economic Consequences of Divorce*, ed. Lenore Weitzman & Mavis Maclean (New York: Oxford University Press, 1992), pp. 263–282.

59. Robert Wuthnow, *The Restructuring of American Religion: Society and Faith since World War II* (Princeton: Princeton University Press, 1988), esp. chap. 5; and *Christianity in the Twenty-First Century* (New York: Oxford University Press, 1993), pp. 156–57. Evidence about declining religious marital homogamy is presented in Matthijs Kalmijn, 'Shifting Boundaries: Trends in Religious and Educational Homogamy', *American Sociological Review* 56 (1991): 786–800.

60. For discussions and evidence of change in the economic status of the major religious groups, see e.g. Andrew Greeley, *Religious Change in America* (Cambridge, Mass.: Harvard University Press, 1989).

61. For evidence about the growth of strict churches, see esp. Roger Finke and Rodney Stark, *The Churching of America* (New Brunswick, NJ: Rutgers University Press, 1992).

62. Some of the leading examples of this approach can be found in: Nie, Verba, and Petrocik, *The Changing American Voter*; Rose and McAllister, *Voters Begin to Choose*; Mark Franklin, *The Decline of Class Voting in Britain* (New York: Oxford University Press, 1985); Inglehart, *Culture Shift in Advanced Indsutrial Societies*, esp. chap. 10.

63. John C. Pierce, Kathleen M. Beatty, and Paul R. Hagner, *The Dynamics of Public Opinion* (Glenview, Ill.: Scott Foresman, 1982.)

64. However, we should note that there is little evidence for a general increase in ideological sophistication or consistency. Despite the potentially richer information environment, voters' actual levels of political knowledge appears to have changed little since the 1950s. The paradox of rising educational levels and stagnant knowledge suggests that other causal factors are offsetting the educational effect. For discussion, see Michael Delli Carpini and Scott Keeter, *What Americans Know About Politics and Why It Matters* (New Haven: Yale University Press, 1996).

65. The most systematic early attempts to show that the changing political environment of the late 1960s had transformed the ideological and informational capacities of voters was Nie, Verba, and Petrocik, *The Changing American Voter*. Since then, political psychologists have developed broader theories

that seek to understand how voters are capable of reasoning even in the absence of information. See especially Sniderman, Brody, and Tetlock, *Reasoning and Choice*; Samuel Popkin, *The Reasoning Voter* (Chicago: University of Chicago Press, 1991); and John R. Zaller, *The Nature and Origins of Mass Opinion* (New York: Cambridge University Press, 1992).

66. For the distinction between class voters and independent voters, see especially Rose and McAllister, *Voters Begin to Choose*; Franklin, *The Decline of Class Voting in Britain*; see also the overview and critique of this distinction in David Weakliem, 'Two Models of Class Voting', *British Journal of Political Science*, 25 (1995): 254–70.

67. Smith, *The Unchanging American Voter*. Evidence for a general post-1960s increase in ideological consistency appears to have been an artifact of the methodology in *The Changing American Voter*. See George F. Bishop, Robert W. Oldendick, and Alfred J. Tuchfarber, 'Change in the Structure of American Political Attitudes: The Nagging Question of Question Wording'.

68. See Ben Wattenberg, *Values Matter Most* (New York: Free Press, 1995), esp. pp. 97–136. Wattenberg's earlier work with Richard Scammon (*The Real Majority* (New York: Coward, McCann, and Geoghegan, Inc., 1970)) was one of the earliest articulations of the claim that a crisis of 'family values' is transforming political cleavages by creating new, cross-cutting loyalties. For other recent arguments to this effect, see James D. Hunter, *Culture Wars* (New York: Basic Books, 1991).

69. Lipset, *American Exceptionalism*.

70. Everett C. Ladd, 'Liberalism Turned Upside Down', *Political Science Quarterly*, 91 (1976–77): 577–600. For other discussions of these trends in the United States, see the essays in B. Bruce-Biggs (ed.), *The New Class?* (San Diego: Harcourt, Brace, 1979); Thomas Edsall, *The New Politics of Inequality* (New York: Norton, 1984), esp. chap. 4; Kevin Phillips, *Post-Conservative America* (New York: Random House, 1982); and Robert Kuttner, *The Life of the Party* (New York: Penguin, 1987). For the international and comparative literatures on the transformations of left parties towards a more middle-class electorate (and the subsequent decline of their class-centered appeals), see Lipset, *Political Man*, esp. pp. 503–23; Inglehart, *Modernization and Post-Modernization*, esp. chap. 8.

71. Inglehart's major books include, in order, *The Silent Revolution* (Princeton: Princeton University Press, 1977); *Culture Shift in Advanced Industrial Society* (1990); Paul Abramson and Inglehart, *Value Change in Global Perspective* (Ann Arbor: University of Michigan Press, 1995), and Inglehart, *Modernization and Post-Modernization* (Princeton: Princeton University Press, 1997); Wattenberg, *Values Matter Most*; Lipset, *American Exceptionalism*. A notable recent analysis of the claim about the rising importance of values in American politics can be found in R. Michael Alvarez and John Brehm, 'American Ambivalence Towards Abortion Policy', *American Journal of Political Science*, 30 (1995): 1–25. For other versions of the 'two lefts' hypothesis, see Claus Offe, 'New Social Movements: Challenging the Boundaries of Institutional Politics', *Social Research*, 52 (1985): 817–68; Dalton, *Citizen Politics in Western Democracies*; and Anthony Giddens, *The Next Left* (Stanford, Calif.: Stanford University Press, 1994).

72. We cite much of the voluminous postmaterialist literature in Clem Brooks and Jeff Manza, 'Do Changing Values Explain the New Politics?', *The Sociological Quarterly*, 35 (1994): 541–70. Some evidence of the influence of Inglehart's thesis can be seen in the extraordinary number of countries (43 at last count) where his 'postmaterialist' survey has been fielded. The battery has been included in the National Election Study in the United States since 1972, and it has now been incorporated into the International Social Survey Program.

73. Inglehart, *Silent Revolution*, p. 3 (quote).

74. The major contributions to the debate over the social origins of McCarthyism can be found in Daniel Bell (ed.), *The Radical Right* (New York: Doubleday, 1963); see also the brilliant dissection of those essays by Michael P. Rogin, *The Intellectuals and McCarthy* (Cambridge, Mass.: MIT Press, 1967). For a useful overview of the history of the social science debates, see William B. Hixon, *Search for the American Right Wing* (Princeton: Princeton University Press, 1992), pp. 9–48.

75. We discuss the Christian Right in much more detail in Chapter 4, and we take up the race thesis in Chapter 6 below.

76. Here again, a large literature could be cited. For some key texts, which vary in their interpretation but essentially endorse versions of the postindustrial politics thesis, see e.g. Scott Lash and John Urry, *The End of Organized Capitalism* (Madison: University of Wisconsin Press, 1987); Claus Offe, *Disorganized Capitalism* (Cambridge, Mass.: MIT Press, 1987); David Harvey, *The Condition of Postmodernity* (Oxford: blackwell, 1989); Anthony Giddens, *The Future of the Left*.

77. This theme of the disruption of stable class-based alignments by postindustrial economic trends and the globalization of production and exchange is present in many of the essays in Frances Fox Piven (ed.), *Labor Parties in Postindustrial Capitalism* (New York: Oxford University Press, 1992).

78. This argument is part of the postmodern theoretical arsenal; it has also been put forcefully by Giddens, *The Future of the Left*; and Lash and Urry, *The End of Organized Capitalism*.

79. Przeworski and Sprague, *Paper Stones*. In a provocative critical essay on the Przeworski/Sprague model, Diane Sainsbury argues that the mathematical models and the limits of the official aggregate data sources they rely upon lead Przeworski and Sprague to severely overestimate the vote trade-off faced by social democratic parties. See her 'Party Strategies and Electoral Trade-Off of Class-Based Parties', *European Journal of Political Research*, 18 (1990): 29–50.

80. The proposition that class voting and nonvoting may be linked is developed by Sidney Verba, Norman Nie, and Jae-On Kim, *Participation and Political Equality* (New York: Cambridge University Press, 1978); see also Michael Hout, Clem Brooks, and Jeff Manza, 'The Democratic Class Struggle in the United States, 1948–1992', *American Sociological Review*, 60 (1995): 805–28; and Walter Dean Burnham, *The Current Crisis in American Politics* (New York: Oxford University Press, 1982), esp. 25–57 and 121–65 (noting that 'the 'real'

class struggle, the point at which class polarization is most salient, is not found in the contests between Democrats and Republicans but between the active electorate and the non-voting half of the adult population'); and Lipset, *Political Man*, pp. 194–95 (arguing that 'Although American workers are overwhelmingly Democratic, the party's low emphasis on ideology and class organization does not encourage political interest among the workers as do those European 'workers' parties which have been to some degree parties of integration'). In their work on the origins of high rates of nonvoting in the United States, Frances Fox Piven and Richard Cloward argue that institutional factors such as complex state-level registration laws were adopted to restrict the franchise among both minorities and workers, and have had the consequence of deepening the class skew in participation. See Piven and Cloward, *Why Americans Don't Vote* (New York: Pantheon, 1988). Left- and right-wing political activists frequently appeal to party elites to concentrate on mobilizing core groups and thereby increase participation, but there is little evidence to date that either party has made significant gains from such a strategy. For general analyses of class-based differences in political participation, see Sidney Verba, Kay Lehman Schlozman, and Henry E. Brady, *Voice and Equality* (Cambridge, Mass.: Harvard University Press, 1997), chap. 7.

81. Useful overviews of the transformation of the Democratic Party can be found in the historical essays in Steven Fraser and Gary Gerstle (eds.), *The Rise and Fall of the New Deal Order* (Princeton: Princeton University Press, 1989).

82. For a useful general overview of the growing importance of money in politics, see Edsall, *The New Politics of Inequality*. On the functioning of the PAC system in Congress, see esp. Dan Clawson, Alan Neustadtl, and Denise Scott, *Money Talks: Corporate PACs and Political Influence* (New York: Basic Books, 1992). For the effects of corporate money on the Democratic Party, see G. William Domhoff, *The Power Elite and the State* (New York: Aldine de Gruyter, 1990), esp. pp. 225–82; Thomas Ferguson and Joel Rogers, *Right Turn: The Decline of the Democrats and the Future of American Politics* (New York: Hill and Wang, 1986).

83. Following earlier analysis of these data by Martin Wattenberg, *The Decline of American Political Parties, 1952–1994* (Cambridge, Mass.: Harvard University Press, 1996), we code 'don't know' responses with the 'no difference' category. This is necessary to make results comparable over time, given that in 1964 and 1968 the 'don't know' response was not on the NES questionnaire (thus artificially inflating the proportion of respondents in the 'no difference' category). Note that if we were to ignore the 'don't know' responses throughout the NES series, estimates of the increasing trend toward party differences would be even larger.

84. The 1968–76 decline also coincides with the period that has been identified by cognitive mobilization and value conflict theories as the time during which their hypothesized developments originated. However, the data presented in Figure 1.1 imply that any causal forces that reduced voters' perceptions were subsequently integrated into longstanding perceptions of party differences, in turn serving to enhance such perceptions. In Chapter 6, we investigate in greater

detail a related causal scenario, that the rising importance of political cleavages based on issue-driven conflicts have emerged alongside existing cleavages based on social group memberships.

85. An important discussion of the evolution of race as an issue can be found in Edward Carmines and James Stimson, *Issue Evolution* (Princeton: Princeton University Press, 1989).

86. For empirical evidence of increased polarization in Congress, see Keith T. Poole and Howard Rosenthal, *Congress: A Political-Economic History of Roll-Call Voting* (New York: Oxford University Press, 1997).

NOTES TO CHAPTER 2

1. Weber's most important statement is in the famous essay 'Class, Status and Party', in *Economy and Society* (Berkeley: University of California Press, 1978 [1922]), pp. 926–39.

2. Some other attempts to define the concept of cleavage employ a similar type of logic. Writing in 1966, for example, the political scientist Harry Eckstein defined a 'segmental cleavage' as existing 'where political divisions follow very closely, and especially concern lines of objective social differentiation, especially those particularly salient in a society'. He distinguishes 'segmental cleavages' from two other types of political conflicts, 'cultural divergence' and 'specific disagreements', the latter pair referring to controversial policies or issues not arising out of social-structural divisions. Harry Eckstein, *Division and Cohesion in Democracy* (Princeton: Princeton University Press, 1966), p. 34.

3. Robert Dahl, 'The American Oppositions', pp. 48–53, and 'Some Explanations', esp. pp. 367–86, in Dahl (ed.), *Political Oppositions in Western Democracies* (New Haven: Yale University Press, 1966); Erik Allardt and Pertti Pesonen, 'Cleavages in Finnish Politics', in *Party Systems and Voter Alignments*, ed. Seymour Martin Lipset and Stein Rokkan (New York: Free Press, 1967), esp. pp. 325–26; Douglas W. Rae and Michael Taylor, *The Analysis of Political Cleavages* (New Haven: Yale University Press, 1970). An excellent overview of the alternative uses of the 'cleavage' concept in the intellectual history of the field can be found in Bartolini and Mair, *Identity, Competition, and Electoral Availability*, pp. 212–25.

4. Franklin, Mackie, and Valen, 'Introduction: Social Cleavages and Political Alignments', pp. 4–5 (quote).

5. Alan Zuckerman, 'Political Cleavage: A Conceptual and Theoretical Analysis', *British Journal of Political Science*, 5 (1975): 231–48, quote at p. 237. Bartolini and Mair offer a concise general definition of the cleavage that implies the same basic point: 'Cleavages may be conceived of as forces which both shape and condition electoral behavior, their relative strength or hold being indicated by the extent to which they afford a degree of elasticity of electoral choice.' *Identity, Competition, and Electoral Availability*, p. 212.

6. Bartolini and Mair, *Identity, Competition and Electoral Availability*, esp. chap. 9 ('Cleavage Systems').

7. Ibid., p. 214 (quotes).

8. '[I]t is not differences in occupation *qua* occupation, or differences in language *qua* language, which may produce the respective cleavage, but rather the nature and intensity of the emotions and reactions which may accompany membership in these occupational or linguistic groups, and the kind of social and political bonds which organizationally unite the individuals who belong to them. In short, cleavages cannot be reduced to the outgrowths of social stratification; rather, social distinctions become cleavages when they are organized as such.' Ibid., p. 216. For a recent cross-national analysis of the magnitude of the class cleavage across multiple national contexts, suggesting its widely varying impact in different political systems, see Paul Nieuwbeerta, *The Democratic Class Struggle in Twenty Countries, 1945–90*, Ph.D. thesis (University of Nijmegen, 1995).

9. This is one of the key arguments advanced by Edward Carmines and James Stimson in their analysis of the rise of the race cleavage in American politics after the 1950s. Before the 1950s, there were significant blocs of racial liberals and racial conservatives in both the Republican and Democratic Parties; beginning with the 1964 election (the Johnson/Goldwater campaign), racial divisions became increasingly aligned with the parties. See Carmines and Stimson, *Issue Evolution*.

10. The historian Byron Shafer, for example, argues that: 'Two key aspects of political structure seem particularly likely to generate elements of political structure which in turn shape electoral politicking and its outcomes. The first of these are the inherent divisions of group identification within that social base, four of which have received particular attention across American history. In the American context, race and ethnicity, religion and culture, social class, and region have been treated as central social divisions at various points.' Shafer, 'The Notion of an Electoral Order,' in *Is America Different?*, ed. Bryan Shafer (Oxford: Clarendon Press, 1991), p. 41.

11. For example, Philip Converse's overview of the sources of political divisions in twelve industrial capitalist democracies concluded that four broad types of divisions were of paramount importance: social status/class, religion, urban/rural residence, and region. See Converse, 'Some Priority Variables in Comparative Electoral Research', p. 729.

12. There is also a practical reason for focusing on objective membership: it was not until 1972 that the NES began to include a regular battery of group consciousness measures. Hence, it would be impossible to use these items for the entire time period covered by our investigations.

13. V. O. Key, 'A Theory of Critical Elections', *Journal of Politics*, 17 (1955): 3–18, and 'Secular Realignments and the Party System', *Journal of Politics*, 21 (1959): 198–210. For the history of the realignment debates and a full bibliography through 1987, see e.g. Harold F. Bass, 'Background to the Debate: A Reader's Guide and Bibliography', in *The End of Realignment?*, ed. Bryan Shafer (Madison: University of Wisconsin Press, 1991).

14. Theorists of dealignment point to such political trends as decreasing partisanship among the electorate as a whole (esp. as signified by the increasing

proportion of independent voters), increased ticket-splitting, the rise of candidate-centered politics, and more generally the breakup of the New Deal coalition without its replacement by a similarly durable political majority. For a general theoretical overview of dealignment, see Edward Carmines, 'Unrealized Partisanship: A Theory of Dealignment', *Journal of Politics*, 49 (1987): 376–400.

15. For discussion, see L. Robert, S. Erikson, Thomas D. Lancaster, and David W. Romero, 'Group Components of the Presidential vote, 1952–1984, *Journal of Politics*, 51 (1989): 337–46.

16. The cross-cutting cleavage idea can be traced to Georg Simmel, pluralists such as David Truman (in *The Governmental Process* (New York: Alfred A. Kopf, 1951)), and, in the context of voting behavior, Lipset's *Political Man*. The reinforcing idea has been a staple of recent theorizing about the intersection of 'class, race and gender'. For discussions of these issues, see Przeworski, *Capitalism and Social Democracy*, pp. 92–97; and Mary Jackman, *The Velvet Glove* (Berkeley: University of California Press, 1994), pp. 122–24.

17. The other major, repeated cross-sectional survey, the General Social Survey, also contains items measuring social group memberships and vote choice in presidential elections. However, the GSS also has significant limitations for our research. First, it surveys respondents some five months after the election; second, the GSS lacks the economic items we use to measure aspects of class-related interests; third, it has employed a split-ballot design that sharply restricts the sample size in multivariate analysis; and most importantly, the GSS does not cover the critical period of time prior to 1968. Private polling organizations such as Gallup, Harris, CBS/New York Times, and others have conducted ongoing surveys of voters and exit polls which could also be drawn upon in this study. The Gallup poll in particular goes back to the 1930s. But these surveys do not have the full battery of sociodemographic items required to measure social group memberships.

18. For an overview of the history of the NES in the institutional context of Michigan survey research, see Converse, *Survey Research in the United States*, pp. 340–78.

19. Items measuring Latino or Asian-American identity are not available until very late in the NES series. Moreover, once missing values on the voting and social group variables are taking into account, the number of respondents in these groups sharply declines. For example, in 1980, the number of Latino voters sampled in the NES is under 15, and adding missing values on the additional variables we analyze reduces the number to virtually nil.

20. Wright's major works are *Classes* (London: Verso, 1985), and *Class Counts* (New York: Cambridge University Press, 1996).

21. Whatever anomalies introduced by our reliance on an occupation-based class scheme, they may, in practice, be no greater than that of alternative schemes which probe more deeply into the concrete employment situation of survey respondents. See e.g. Gordon Marshall, David Rose, Howard Newby, and Carolyn Vogler, *Social Class in Modern Britain* (London: Unwin Hyman, 1988).

NOTES TO CHAPTER 3

1 Outside of elections, of course, the political influence of corporate and upper-class groups in the United States is unquestionably significant, but goes beyond the scope of this chapter. For further discussion of these issues, see e.g. Domhoff, *The Power Elite and the State.*

2. There have been relatively few investigations of class bias in turnout across different countries. For a handful of exceptions, see e.g. Verba, Nie, and Kim, *Participation and Political Equality*; Burnham, *The Current Crisis in American Politics*, esp. pp. 121–65; and, more recently, Weakliem and Heath, 'The Secret Life of Class Voting'. For further discussion of the nonvoting literature, see Chapter 7 below.

3. Lipset, *Political Man*, pp. 230, 303 (quotes).

4. See e.g. Douglas Rae, *The Political Consequences of Electoral Laws*, rev. edn. (New Haven: Yale University Press, 1971); Rein Taagepera and Matthew S. Shugart, *Seats and Votes: The Effects and Determination of Electoral Systems* (New Haven: Yale University Press, 1989). More recently, the debate over electoral laws has centered around discussions of how best to organize minority voting districts. See Lani Guinier, *Tyranny of the Majority* (New York: Free Press, 1994).

5. There are many historical accounts of the failure of socialist and communist parties in the United States. For a sampling of different views, see e.g. Paul Buhle, *Marxism in the United States* (London: Verso, 1987); James Weinstein, *Ambiguous Legacy: The Left in American Politics* (New York: New View-points, 1975); Daniel Bell, *Marxian Socialism in the United States* (Ithaca, NY: Cornell University Press, 1997 [1967]); John Patrick Diggins, *The Rise and Fall of the American Left* (New York: Norton, 1992). Probably the most notable class-based political formation from below was that of the populists, who succeeded in establishing a political presence in a number of Southern states in the 1880s and early 1890s, and saw their 1892 presidential candidate James Weaver win 8.5% of the vote (while carrying four states). But as a political movement, populism was destroyed by a combination of ballot restrictions in Southern states and the ability of the Democratic Party to absorb populist leaders and co-opt populist issues (notably the free coinage of silver) into its broad tent. The standard historical treatment of the populist movement is Lawrence Goodwyn, *Democratic Promise: The Populist Moment in America* (New York: Oxford University Press, 1976); for the explicit difficulties of constructing the 'People's Party', see Steven J. Rosenstone, Roy L. Behr, and Edward H. Lazarus, *Third Parties in America*, 2nd edn. (Princeton: Princeton University Press, 1996), pp. 67–75; for contemporary residues, see Michael Kazin, *The Populist Persuasion* (New York: Basic Books, 1995).

6. For recent treatments of these issues, see e.g. Jill Quadagno, 'From Old Age Assistance to Supplemental Security Income: The Political Economy of Relief in the South', in *The Politics of Social Policy in the United States*, ed. Margaret Weir, Ann S. Orloff, and Theda Skocpol (Princeton: Princeton University Press,

1988) and *The Color of Welfare* (New York: Oxford University Press, 1994); Domhoff, *The Power Elite and the State*; and Edwin Amenta, *Bold Relief: Institutional Politics and the Origins of Modern American Social Policy* (Princeton: Princeton University Press, 1998), esp. pp. 20–22.

7. The sole exception to this was the 1934–38 period when an overwhelming Democratic majority in the North made Southern votes less crucial. This is the argument of Amenta, *Bold Relief.* But even here, Southern members of Congress were able to win important changes to these measures which drastically limited their applicability to the Southern economy. For example, agricultural and domestic workers were exempted from coverage in the case of both the National Labor Relations Act and (initially) the Social Security Act.

8. For additional discussion, see e.g. Douglas Ashford, *The Emergence of the Welfare States* (Oxford: blackwell, 1987); Dietrich Rueschemeyer, Evelyne Stephens, and John Stephens, *Capitalist Development and Democracy* (Chicago: University of Chicago Press, 1992); and John Markoff, *Waves of Democracy* (Thousand Oaks, Calif.: Pine Forge Press, 1996).

9. For superb analytical treatments of the ways these institutional and political developments undermined the American labor movement in comparison to similar movements in Europe, see Victoria C. Hattam, *Labor Visions and State Power* (Princeton: Princeton University Press, 1993); and Voss, *The Making of American Exceptionalism.* On the intervention of the courts, see esp. William Forbath, *Law and the Shaping of the American Labor Movement* (Cambridge, Mass.: Harvard University Press, 1991).

10. Voss, *The Making of American Exceptionalism*, pp. 231–49.

11. This is a central argument of James Sundquist, *Dynamics of the Party System*, rev. edn. (Washington, DC: Brookings Institute, 1983).

12. This point is made forcefully by Amenta, *Bold Relief*, esp. pp. 4–6. His data shows that in 1938, the U.S. devoted 29.4% of all government spending to social programs, and fully 6.31% of GNP was consumed by these programs. Conversely, among the next most generous countries, the United Kingdom was devoting 17.5% of all government spending and 5% of GNP, Sweden just 17.8% and 3.15%, and the Netherlands just 10.2% and 1.98%, respectively.

13. W. F. Ogburn and Estelle Hill, 'Income Classes and the Roosevelt Vote in 1932', *Political Science Quarterly*, 50 (1935): 186–93; and Ogburn and Coombs, 'The Economic Factor in the Roosevelt Elections'.

14. Dewey Anderson and Percy Davidson, *Ballots and the Democratic Class Struggle* (Stanford, Calif.: Stanford University Press, 1943), esp. 82–163.

15. For one example of these difficulties, see the debate over the issue of whether Roosevelt's electoral successes were the result of the mobilization of new voters or the realignment of existing voters. Cf. Kristi Andersen, *The Creation of a Democratic Majority, 1928–1936* (Chicago: University of Chicago Press, 1979); and Robert S. Erikson and Kent Tedin, 'The 1928–1936 Partisan Realignment: The Case for the Conversion Hypothesis', *American Political Science Review*, 75 (1981): 951–65.

16. Versions of these arguments can be found in the following sources: Sundquist,

Dynamics of the Party System, esp. pp. 198–239; Paul Abramson, *Generational Change in American Politics* (Lexington, Mass.: Lexington Books, 1975), pp. 7–8; Everett C. Ladd with Charles Hadley, *Transformations of the American Party System* (New York: Norton, 1975), pp. 69 ff.; David Lawrence, *The Collapse of the Democratic Majority* (Boulder, Colo.: Westview Press, 1997), pp. 34–35. Lawrence has provided a useful overview of some of the debates discussed in this paragraph.

17. See e.g. Paul R. Abramson, John H. Aldrich, and David W. Rohde, *Change and Continuity in the 1992 Elections* (Washington, DC: Congressional Quarterly Press, 1994), pp. 152–55; Gerald Pomper, *Voter's Choices: Varieties of American Electoral Behavior* (New York: Dodd, Mead, 1975), p. 57; Ladd with Hadley, *Transformations of the American Party System*, p. 73. For journalistic arguments to this effect, see Kevin Phillips, *The Emerging Republican Majority* (Garden City, NY: Anchor Books, 1970); Edsall, *The New Politics of Inequality* and (with Mary Edsall) *Chain Reaction: The Impact of Race, Rights, and Taxes on American Politics* (New York: Norton, 1991).

18. For a list of the many different uses of this single image of the class/vote relationship, see Jeff Manza, Michael Hout, and Clem Brooks, 'Class Voting in Capitalist Democracies since World War II: Dealignment, Realignment, or Trendless Fluctuation?', *Annual Review of Sociology*, 21 (1995): 137–63, pp. 141–42.

19. See David Weakliem, 'Race Versus Class? Racial Composition and Class Voting, 1936–1992.' *Soical Forces*, 75 (1997): 939–56; and Weakliem and Heath, 'The Secret Life of Class Voting.' From a comparative perspective, see Paul Nieuwbeerta, 'The Democratic Class Struggle in Postwar Societes: Class Voting in Twenty Countries, 1945–1990,' *Acta Sociologica*, 39 (1996): 345–84.

20. Lawrence, *The Collapse of the Democratic Majority*, p. 36 (quote).

21. Richard Hamilton, *Class and Politics in the United States* (New York: Wiley, 1972), esp. pp. 537–41; Knoke, *Continuity in American Politics*, p. 68 (quote).

22. William Form, *Divided We Stand: Working Class Stratification in America* (Urbana: University of Illinois Press, 1985) and *Segmented Labor, Fractured Politics* (New York: Plenum, 1995). Sociologists David Halle and Frank Romo, in an investigation of the political behavior of blue-collar workers since the early 1950s, argue that American workers have not shifted significantly toward the Republican Party. See their 'The Blue Collar Working Class: Continuity and Change', in *America at Century's End*, ed. Alan Wolfe (Berkeley: University of California Press, 1991).

23. Miller and Shanks, *The New American Voter*, esp. chap. 9.

24. In E. P. Thompson's famous formulation in the preface to *The Making of the English Working Class* (New York: Vintage, 1963), 'class is a relationship, and not a thing' (p. 11). For further discussion of these issues, see John R. Hall, 'The Reworking of Class Analysis', in *Reworking Class* (Ithaca, NY: Cornell University Press, 1997); David Grusky and Jesper Sorensen, 'Can Class Analysis Be Salvaged?', *American Journal of Sociology*, 103 (1998): 1187–1234; and Rick Fantasia, *Cultures of Solidarity* (Berkeley: University of California Press, 1988), chap. 1.

25. Kurt J. Mayer, *Class and Society* (New York: Random House, 1962), pp. 41–42; this passage is quoted by Hamilton, *Class and Politics*, p. 64, n.11. The view that the blue-collar/white-collar divide is fundamental has a long history in sociology. It can be traced, as Daniel Bell has shown, to the problems arising out of the rapid growth of white-collar employment for the logic of Marxian revolutionary theory, and the debates this generated within German Marxism. See his *The Coming of Post-Industrial Society* (New York: Basic Books, 1973), pp. 49–119. Later attempts to defend the distinction as fundamental can be found in Alford, *Party and Society*, pp. 73–79.

26. For a useful overview of this trajectory, see Gosta Esping-Andersen, 'Post-industrial Cleavage Structures: A Comparison of Evolving Patterns of Social Stratification in Germany, Sweden and the United States', in *Labor Parties in Postindustrial Societies*, ed. Frances Fox Piven (New York: Oxford University Press, 1992); and Gøsta Andersen (ed.), *Changing Classes* (Newbury Park, CA: Sage Publications, 1993).

27. The distinction between 'relational' and 'gradational' conceptions of class was popularized by Erik Olin Wright; see e.g. his *Class Structure and Income Determination*, pp. 3–18.

28. These prestige rankings were generated by variations on the influential Index of Socio-Economic Status designed by Otis Dudley Duncan in the early 1960s. In the tradition that built upon Duncan's initial formulation, all occupations are assigned scores based on estimates of the social prestige drawn from survey data. For an overview of these debates, see the classical and contemporary readings collected in David Grusky (ed.), *Social Stratification* (Boulder, Colo.: Westview Press, 1994), pp. 204–41.

29. These distinctions loosely synthesize the insights of the two dominant theoretical approaches to class analysis in the social sciences today, that of Robert Erikson and John Goldthorpe, on the one hand, and Erik Olin Wright, on the other. There has been a passionate debate about the relative merits of the two approaches; see e.g. Marshall et al., *Social Class in Modern Britain*.

30. For further discussions of the market power of professionals arising out of their credential assets, see Eliot Friedson, *Professional Powers* (Chicago: University of Chicago Press, 1986); Randall Collins, *The Credential Society* (New York: Academic Press, 1979), esp. chap. 6; Magali Sarfetti Larson, *The Rise of Professionalism* (Berkeley: University of California Press, 1977); and Charles Derber, William Schwartz, and Yale Magrass, *Power in the Highest Degree* (New York: Oxford University Press, 1990).

31. John Goldthorpe, *Class Structure and Social Mobility in Britain* (New York: Oxford University Press, 1987); and Robert Erikson and John H. Goldthorpe, *The Constant Flux* (Oxford: Clarendon Press, 1993); Anthony Heath, Roger Jowell, and John Curtice, *How Britain Votes* (London: Pergamon, 1985) and Heath et al., *Understanding Political Change* (London: Pergamon, 1991); Barbara and John Ehrenreich, 'The Professional-Managerial Class', in *Between Labor and Capital*, ed. Pat Walker (Boston: South End Press, 1979). For recent state-of-the-art discussions of this issue, see esp. the essays by Colin Mills, Mike Savage and Anthony Heath, and John Goldthorpe in Tim Butler and Mike Savage (eds.), *Social Change and the Middle Classes* (London: UCL Press, 1995).

32. See Michael Hout and Robert Hauser, 'Hierarchy and Symmetry in Social Mobility', *European Sociological Review*, 8 (1992): 239–66.

33. Clem Brooks and Jeff Manza, 'The Social and Ideological Bases of Middle Class Political Realignments in the United States, 1972–1992', *American Sociological Review*, 62 (1997): 191–208.

34. We note that this conceptualization of working-class categories captures one crucial distinction (the level of market power and economic security maintained by each group) but neglects other economically relevant distinctions. For example, one might want to distinguish among workers in different branches of industry (esp. service sector vs. manufacturing), public sector vs. private sector, and so forth. See e.g. Form, *Divided We Stand*, pp. 1–52 for a more sophisticated treatment.

35. In addition to the statistical power gained by not discarding a sizable portion of the data, including the non-full labor-force participants is also necessary to conduct comparisons between the class cleavage and other politically relevant cleavages, which we take up in Chapters 6 and 7.

36. As a result of this coding decision, we note that the composition of the residual class category has changed considerably: the proportion of non-working housewives has declined over time as increasing numbers of women have entered the labor force (see Chapter 5), and the proportion of retirees has grown with increased average longevity. The category is thus made up of a different group of individuals in the 1990s than in the 1950s.

37 We are indebted to Szonja Szelenyi's elegant overview of these theoretical debates in her essay 'Women and the Class Structure', in *Social Stratification*, ed. David B. Grusky (Boulder, Colo.: Westview Press, 1994).

38. The conventional view has historically been associated with structural-functionalist analyses of stratification. See e.g. Talcott-Parsons, *Essays in Sociological Theory* (New York: Free Press, 1954). But it has been given a vigorous restatement by John Goldthorpe in 'Women and Class Analysis: In Defence of the Conventional View', *Sociology*, 17 (1983): 465–88. See also the special issue of *Sociology*, vol. 18 (1984) containing discussions of the Goldthorpe argument, and Goldthorpe's reply, 'Women and Class Analysis: A Reply to the Replies', *Sociology*, 18 (1984): 491–99.

39. See e.g. Michael Hout, 'More Universalism, Less Structural Mobility: The American Occupational Structure in the 1980s', *American Journal of Sociology*, 93 (1988): 1358–1400. The 'joint classification' label for placing contemporary families in the class structure on the bases of the occupations of women as well as men was introduced by Nicky Britten and Anthony Heath in their 'Women, Men, and Social Class', in *Gender, Class, and Work*, ed. Eva Garmarnikow et al. (London: Heinemann, 1983).

40. In an earlier study, co-authored with Michael Hout, we employed a retrospective question about the respondents' vote in the 1948 election, available on the 1952 NES. See Hout, Brooks, and Manza, 'The Democratic Class Struggle in the United States, 1948–1992', paper presented at the World Congress of the International Sociology Association, Bielefeld, Germany, 18–24 July, 1994. In that study, we were concerned specifically with questions about

the role of the 1948 election in skewing debates over class voting trends, though we were wary about the problem of errors stemming from respondents' recall of an event occurring four years previously. In the analyses presented in this chapter, however, we do not make use of the retrospective question.

41. While these constraints are cumbersome to express in formal notation, their reference to specific periods and the implied structure of the trends are not difficult to understand, and they result in a parsimonious model that restricts class-specific trends to particular classes and specific elections (or blocks of elections). For the full details of the model specification, see Clem Brooks and Jeff Manza, 'Class Politics and Political Change in the United States, 1952–1992', *Social Forces*, 79: 379–409.

42. These trends are parameterized by using a covariate for time coded '0' for 1952–1960, '1' for 1964, '2' for 1968, . . ., and '8' for 1992. This coding enables professionals' vote choice to experience a linear pattern of change over and beyond any electorate-wide effects that influence all voters.

43. This constraint is consistent with our concept of a 'critical realignment', but we must first gauge the magnitude of these two changes to determine whether they qualify as realignments.

44. Voting trends for these two classes are measured using a time covariate coded '1' for 1956, '2' for 1960, . . ., and '5' for 1972 (and all years thereafter).

45. See Hout, Brooks, and Manza, 'The Democratic Class Struggle in the United States', 805–28; and Manza et al., 'Class Voting in Capitalist Democracies since World War II' for additional discussion of this approach—and its advantages over previous approaches—to measuring the class cleavage in political behavior.

46. As discussed in Chapter 6, class-specific voting can be measured using either the logit coefficient for a specific class category, or alternatively, a predicted probability for that category. To give an example of each, consider a simple, two-class (and two-party) polity with the subsequent logistic regression co-efficients of -1.0 and 1.0. Taking the standard deviation of these two numbers yields an index of 1.0, indicating that the average deviation between these classes and the electorate-wide mean is one logit. Alternatively, if the predicted probability of favoring one party (in the same two-party polity) is .5 for one class and 0 for the other, the index score representing the magnitude of the class cleavage is now .25 (using the probability scale). Both sets of calculations are generally consistent, and in this chapter we use the logistic regression co-efficient for each class (and thus the logit metric) in calculating index scores.

47. As discussed in detail by Adrian Raftery ('Bayesian Model Selection in Sociology', *Sociological Methodology*, 25 (1995): 111–63), approximate Bayes factors that range between 5 and 10 can be construed as providing 'strong' evidence for the inference in question. By contrast, a factor of 11 or larger is indicative of 'decisive' evidence.

48. The voting patterns of routine white-collar workers have moved them towards the Democratic Party (relative to the mean), but given that our model does not include a trend parameter pertaining specifically to this class. For this reason, some caution should be used when interpreting this apparent trend.

49. For some classical statements, see e.g. Talcott Parsons, 'The Professions and the Social Structure', in *Essays in Sociological Theory* (New York: Free Press, 1954); Lipset, *Political Man*, esp. chap. 2.

50. For discussion of this, see e.g. J. Craig Jenkins and Kevin Leicht, 'Class Analysis and Social Movements: A Critique and Reformulation', in *Reworking Class*, ed. John R. Hall (Ithaca, NY: Cornell University Press, 1997) pp. 369–97.

51. Simultaneously however, the resurgence of conservative political and economic trends in the Anglo-American democracies during the 1980s has led to partial revival of the classical view. See e.g. Goldthorpe, 'On the Service Class, Its Formation and Future', in *The New Working Class*, ed. Richard Hyman and Robert Price (London: MacMillan, 1982), and Goldthorpe, 'The Service Class Revisited', in *Social Change and the Middle Class*, ed. Tim Butler and Mike Savage (London: UCL Press, 1995); Derber, Schwartz, and Magrass, *Power in the Highest Degree*; Robert Reich, *The Work of Nations* (New York: Alfred A. Knopf, 1991); and Brint, *In an Age of Experts*. Brint's work adopts a middle ground, emphasizing the ways in which the professions are a 'divided stratum'.

52. See Brooks and Manza, 'The Social and Ideological Bases of Middle Class Political Realignment'.

53. 'New class' theory has a long history. It can be traced as far back as the enthusiasms for a rational, scientific order run by engineers and scientists in the writings of Saint-Simon. Anarchist theorists such as Bakunin and Machajski coined the term 'new class' to criticize the scientistic assumptions and dominance of intellectuals in the social democratic and Marxist parties affiliated with the Second International. In the United States, theories of 'managerial' capitalism in which highly trained corps of managers and engineers were replacing capitalist owners in making key planning and investment decisions have had a long history, including famous contributions by Veblen, Berle and Means, Burnham, and Galbraith. Some early and influential theories of postindustrial society emphasized the rising importance of expert knowledge as a source of political and economic power in postwar social structures; see esp. Bell, *The Coming of Post-Industrial Society*. The Great Society project of the 1960s spawned a number of analyses of the apparently growing radicalism among important segments of the American intelligentsia that could be plausibly described as a 'new class'. These interpretations would include, most notably, the neoconservative contributions in Bruce-Briggs (ed.), *The New Class?*. Finally, a number of interpretations claimed to find a broader trend toward political liberalism, even radicalism, among the educated middle classes which has important implications for future political change. The leading versions of this argument can be found in Ehrenreich and Ehrenreich, 'The Professional-Managerial Class'; and Alvin Gouldner, *The Future of Intellectuals and the Rise of the New Class* (New York: Continuum, 1979). For excellent overviews of the history of the new class thesis, see Gouldner, *The Future of Intellectuals*, pp. 94–100; and Ivan Szelenyi and Bill Martin, 'The Three Waves of New Class Theories', *Theory and Society*, 17 (1988): 645–67.

54. This is argued, for example, by many of the contributors to Bruce-Biggs (ed.),

The New Class?; see also Michele Lamont, 'Cultural Capital and the Liberal Political Attitudes of Professionals', *American Journal of Sociology*, 92 (1987): 1501–06.

55. See e.g. Steven Brint, '"New Class" and Cumulative Trend Explanations of the Liberal Political Attitudes of Professionals', *American Journal of Sociology*, 90 (1984): 30–71.

56. The latter argument is broadly consistent with Gouldner's argument in *The Future of Intellectuals*. Gouldner emphasizes the anti-bourgeois elements of New Class ideology, and in particular the attraction of some segments to varieties of state socialism in which the state assumes significant political control over the market.

57. The evolution of Inglehart's arguments and empirical evidence in support of the postmaterialist thesis can be traced in his three major books, *The Silent Revolution* (1977), *Value Shift in Industrial Society* (1990), and most recently *Modernization and Post-Modernization* (1997).

58. The 'two lefts' thesis with reference to the U.S. context is developed in Lipset, *Political Man*, pp. 503–23; Ladd, 'Liberalism Upside Down'; Edsall, *The New Politics of Inequality*, pp. 49–64; and John Zipp, 'Social Class and Social Liberalism', *Sociological Forum*, 1 (1986): 301–29. For an analysis of the two lefts thesis in the West European context, see David Weakliem, 'The Two Lefts? Occupation and Party Choice in France, Italy, and the Netherlands', *American Journal of Sociology* 96 (1991): 1327–61.

59. The most famous argument to this effect was made by Lipset, *Political Man*, chap. 5.

60. See e.g. Bell (ed.), *The Radical Right*; Seymour Martin Lipset and Earl Raab, *The Politics of Unreason: Right-Wing Extremism in America, 1790–1970* (Chicago: University of Chicago Press, 1978).

61. See e.g. Domhoff, *The Power Elite and the State*.

62. Clarence Lo, *Small Property Versus Big Government* (Berkeley: University of California Press, 1990).

63. C. Wright Mills, *White Collar* (New York: Oxford University Press, 1951), pp. 52–53 (quote).

64. Richard Hamilton, *Restraining Myths* (New York: Wiley, 1975). In his discussion of working-class segmentation in the United States, William Form also noted the unique composition of the ranks of the self-employed, containing many people with working-class occupations who have found market niches for self-employment. See his *Divided We Stand*, chap. 4. Form's discussion of these working-class proprietors has shaped our own discussion in this section.

65. See esp. the debate between George Steinmetz and Erik Olin Wright ('The Fall and Rise of the Petty Bourgeoisie', *American Journal of Sociology*, 94 (1989): 973–1018), on the one hand, and Marc Linder and John Houghton ('Self-Employment and the Petty Bourgeoisie: Comment on Steinmetz and Wright', *American Journal of Sociology* 96 (1990): 727–34), on the other. Steinmetz and Wright argue that the ranks of the self-employed have swelled since the 1960s, reflecting a general trend in advanced capitalist societies in which more space for entrepreneurial activity has opened. Linder and

Houghton's counter-argument asserts that the increasing proportion of the self-employed in the economically active population is drawn largely from the ranks of the marginalized working class. See also Linder's *Farewell to the Self-Employed* (Westport, Conn.: Greenwood Press, 1994). Support for the Steinmetz and Wright position can be found in some of the recent work on the New Class thesis, which has emphasized the increasing capacity of professionals to translate knowledge capital into economic capital. See esp. Hansfried Kellner and Frank Heuberger (eds.), *The Hidden Technocrats* (New Brunswick, NJ: Transaction Publishers, 1992).

66. See Chapter 1 for further discussion. For a good general recent overview of sociological work on the U.S. working class, see Form, *Divided We Stand*, chap. 1.

67. See the recent state-of-the-art review of research on trends towards rising inequality by Martina Morris and Bruce Western, 'Inequality in Earnings at the Close of the 20th Century', *Annual Review of Sociology*, 25 (1999): in press. For a recent review of the empirical evidence, see Lawrence Mishel (comp.), *The State of Working America 1998* (Ithaca, NY: Cornell University Press, 1999).

68. Some analysts would point to the support given by white working-class voters to the Jesse Jackson and Pat Buchanan presidential campaigns of the 1980s and 1990s as one piece of evidence. However, this support was limited and inconsistent, and not significant enough to propel either Jackson or Buchanan into serious contention for their respective party's presidential nomination. Others have claimed that falling turnout among working-class voters reflects indifference with the political choices they are offered. However, there is little evidence that turnout rates have fallen faster among working-class voters in comparison to other voters (see Chapter 7 below).

69. We will also consider a version of the working-class segmentation thesis that is most closely associated with William Form. We explore these issues through examining whether and to what extent sociodemographic cleavages within the nonskilled working class are associated with the changes in their voting behavior. See esp. Form, *Divided We Stand* and *Segmented Labor, Fractured Politics*.

70. Lipset, *Political Man*, pp. 87–126.

71. See e.g. the classical study of Samuel Stouffer, *Communism, Conformity, and Civil Liberties* (Garden City, NY: Doubleday, 1955); see also Clyde Z. Nunn, Harry J. Crockett, Jr., and J. Allen Williams, Jr., *Tolerance for Nonconformity* (San Francisco: Jossey-Bass, 1978); and Herbert Hyman and Charles Wright, *Education's Lasting Influence on Values* (Chicago: University of Chicago Press, 1979). Melvin Kohn's work on the consequences of occupational self-direction provides a middle ground, arguing that while education is decisive for determining parental values and capacity for independent thought or conformity, the work setting reinforces these tendencies one way or the other. Those in jobs which allow for creativity and self-expression become more independent and tolerant, while those in heavily routinized jobs do not. See e.g. Kohn, *Class and Conformity* (Homewood, Ill.: Dorsey Press, 1969).

72. We consider this thesis—and the relevant literatures—in more detail in Chapter

6 below. Probably the work which most typifies this stance is that of Edsall and Edsall, *Chain Reaction.*

73. This thesis is most closely associated with the work of Walter Dean Burnham. See *The Crisis in American Politics* (New York: Oxford University Press, 1982). See also David Halle, *America's Working Man* (Chicago: University of Chicago Press, 1984), esp. pp. 189–249.

74. For overviews of these literatures, see the sources cited above in Chapter 1.

75. The NES question asks: 'Some people feel the government in Washington should see to it that every person has a job and a good standard of living. Others think the government should just let each person get ahead on their own. Where would you place yourself on this scale, or haven't you thought much about this?'

76. For analyses of the basic trends, see Michael Goldfield, *The Decline of Organized Labor in the United States* (Chicago: University of Chicago Press, 1989); for details on union decline in the U.S. over this period in comparative perspective, see e.g. Bruce Western, *Between Class and Market: Postwar Unionization in the Capitalist Democracies* (Princeton: Princeton University Press, 1997).

77. See e.g. Fiorina, *Retrospective Voting in American National Elections*; Kiewiet, *Macroeconomics and Micropolitics*; Abramson, Aldrich, and Rohde, *Change and Continuity in the 1992 Elections*; R. Michael Alvarez and Jonathan Nagler, 'Economics, Issues, and the Perot Candidacy: Voter Choice in the 1992 Presidential Election', *American Journal of Political Science*, 39 (1995): 714–744; and Brooks and Manza, 'Class Politics and Political Change'.

78. As displayed near the bottom of the table, we allow the economic evaluation item to have a different political effect in the 1980 election, thereby capturing the single case during the 1972–1992 series in which economic dissatisfaction with the incumbent was directed against a Democratic president (Jimmy Carter).

79. We have discussed this phenomenon in greater detail in our earlier study. See Brooks and Manza, 'The Social and Ideological Bases of Middle Class Political Realignment'.

80. We note that these two estimates have different signs because while class-related factors would have led to a slight Republican voting trend among professionals, a small decrease in political alienation helps to explain their Democratic voting trend.

81. Brint, *In an Age of Experts*; Mary R. Jackman, 'General and Applied Tolerance: Does Education Increase Commitment to Racial Integration?' *American Journal of Political Science*, 22 (1978): 302–24.

82. Kuttner, *The Life of the Party*, p. 112 (quote).

83. To state this point another way, if the magnitude of the class cleavage had declined substantially when social issue attitudes were included in the model, we would expect that the dotted trend lines representing these estimates would approach the x-axis, indicating a class cleavage approaching zero.

84. The results for the 1952–1992 series also reveal the slight upward trend that characterized the class cleavage (not controlling for the social issue cleavage) between 1972 and 1992. Most importantly, the twin class cleavage scores are

virtually indistinguishable, showing that the estimates for the class cleavage obtained from the 1972–1992 series are nearly identical to those obtained using the entire series. As a result, limiting the analyses of the class and social issue cleavages to the six 1972–1992 election studies do not introduce any bias into estimates of the trend and magnitude of the class cleavage during this period.

NOTES TO CHAPTER 4

1. This incident is reported in Rossi, 'Four Landmarks in Voting Research', p. 18, n. 18 ('Dr. Lazarsfeld related that George Gallup expressed disbelief when he told him of his finding that this factor was independently related to voting behavior'); and noted in Seymour Martin Lipset, 'Religion and Politics in the American Past and Present', in *Revolution and Counterrevolution* (New York: Anchor Press, 1970), p. 306. Gallup, it should be noted, soon began including questions about religious group memberships on his election surveys, developing a rich data archive scholars have made use of ever since. However, even the finest social science research on religion and politics in this early period tended to assume that religious differences were ultimately explicable in terms of class and/or ethnic differences. For example, in the preface to the revised (1963) edition of his pathbreaking 1961 book *The Religious Factor* (New York: Doubleday, 1963), the sociologist Gerhard Lenski claims that it did not prove necessary to consider denominational differences among Protestants because 'those which can be shown to be statistically significant almost without exception vanish with controls for class or region of birth' (p. xi). Summing up much of the conventional literature, N. J. Demerath and Rhys Williams have noted that 'While students of voting do cite religious affiliation as a significant variable, they often tend to interpret its effects less in terms of theology and ecclesiastical influence than in terms of ethnic, class, and regional factors lurking beneath the symbolic surface.' See their 'Religion and Power in the American Experience', in *In Gods We Trust*, ed. Thomas Robbins and Dick Anthony (New Brunswick, NJ: Transaction Publishers, 1991), p. 434.

2. The relative lack of attention to religious influences on politics is surprising in that comparative empirical research usually finds that the religious cleavage is a more important factor than class in explaining voter alignments. See e.g. Richard Rose and Derek Unwin, 'Social Cohesion, Political Parties, and Strains in Regimes', *Comparative Political Studies*, 2 (1969): 7–67; Rose, *The Problem of Party Government* (London: MacMillan, 1974); Converse, 'Some Priority Variables in Comparative Electoral Research', pp. 727–45; Arend Lijphart, 'Religious vs. Linguistic vs. Class Voting', *American Political Science Review*, 73 (1979): 442–58; Robert Dahl, *Dilemmas of Pluralist Democracy* (New Haven: Yale University Press, 1982), chap. 4; G. Bingham Powell, *Contemporary Democracies: Participation, Stability and Violence* (Cambridge, Mass.: Harvard University Press, 1982); Michael Mann, 'Sources of Variation in Working Class Movements in Twentieth-Century Europe', *New Left Review*, 212 (1995): 14–54.

3. There is, unfortunately, no systematic overview of the now burgeoning religion and political behavior literature. A useful place to begin would be Kenneth D. Wald, *Religion and Politics in the United States*, 3rd edn. (Washington, DC: Congressional Quarterly Press, 1996), chap. 6; see also David Leege, 'Religion and Politics in Theoretical Perspective', in *Rediscovering the Religious Factor in American Politics*, ed. David Leege and Lyman Kellstedt (Armonk, NY: M. E. Sharpe, 1993).

4. For a general overview of American 'religious exceptionalism', see Andrew Greeley, 'American Exceptionalism: The Religious Phenomenon', in *Is America Different?*, ed. Byron E. Shafer (New York: Oxford University Press, 1991); and Edward Tiryakian, 'American Religious Exceptionalism: A Reconsideration', *Annals of the American Academy of Political and Social Science*, 527 (1993): 40–54.

5. Talleyrand cited in Tom Smith, 'Classifying Protestant Denominations', *Review of Religious Research*, 31 (1990): 225. To get a sense of the bewildering array of denominations, sects, and unaffiliated churches in the United States see, the extraordinary *Encyclopedia of America Religions*, compiled by J. Gordon Melton (5th edn, Detroit: Gale Research, 1996). It identifies the existence of some 1,730 separate religious bodies. It is thus seems likely that the sauce/ religion *ratio* has not improved much since Tallyrand.

6. Tocqueville's famous conclusion ('There is no country in the world where the Christian religion retains a greater influence over the souls of men than in America') is often cited. For an overview, see Tiryakian, 'American Religious Exceptionalism', pp. 41–42. For Weber's views, see 'The Protestant Sects and the Spirit of Capitalism', in *From Max Weber*, ed. H. H. Gerth and C. Wright Mills (New York: Oxford University Press, 1958 [1906]), pp. 302–03.

7. The journalist William Safire has put the point nicely, commenting specifically on the 1992 national party conventions but in terms that are widely applicable: 'the name of the Lord is being used as a symbol for the other side's immorality, much as the American flag was used in previous campaigns as a symbol for the other side's lack of patriotism.' William Safire, 'God Bless Us', *New York Times*, 27 August 1992, p. A23, quoted in Stephen Carter, *The Culture of Disbelief* (New York: Basic, 1993), p. 47.

8. Survey data has consistently shown that Americans spend a lot more time praying than they do having sex, among other things. See Greeley, *Religious Change in America*, p. 58. Greeley reports NORC survey data showing that only 2% of Americans never pray, and that even a third of those who do not believe God exists pray at least once a week, and 16% of non-believers pray everyday.

9. See e.g. Wald, *Religion and Politics in the United States*, chap. 1; Robert S. Erikson, Norman R. Luttbeg, and Kent L. Tedin, *American Public Opinion: Its Origins, Content and Impact* (New York: MacMillan, 1988); Paul Lopatto, *Religion and the Presidential Election* (New York: Praeger, 1985), chap. 2; George Gallop, Jr., 'Religion in American 50 Years: 1935–1985', Gallup Report No. 236 (Princeton: Gallup, 1985); Walter Dean Burnham, 'The 1980 Earthquake', in *The Hidden Election*, ed. Thomas Ferguson and Joel Rogers (New York: Pantheon, 1981), pp. 132–140.

10. George Gallup, Jr. and Jim Castelli, *The People's Religion* (New York: Mac-Millan, 1989), p. 4.
11. Lipset, *American Exceptionalism*, pp. 61–62 (quote, citations omitted). Other scholars report similar findings. See e.g. Robert Booth Fowler and Allen Hertzke, *Religion and Politics in America* (Boulder, Colo.: Westview Press, 1995), p. 28.
12. In several northeastern states, the Congregationalist church was the established church, holding an official monopoly in New Hampshire (until 1817), Connecticut (until 1818), and Massachusetts (until 1833).
13. See Robert C. Liebman, John R. Sutton, and Robert Wuthnow, 'Exploring the Social Sources of Denominationalism: Schisms in American Protestant Denominations, 1890–1980', *American Sociological Review*, 53 (1988): 343–52.
14. In comparing U.S. religious development with that of other societies, it is important to maintain proper perspective. In a recent comparative study of contemporary religious political mobilizations around the world, the sociologist Jose Casanova has made the important observation that 'what truly demands explanation [is] the striking European pattern of secularization, that is, the dramatic decline of religion there'. Casanova, *Public Religions in the Modern World* (Chicago: University of Chicago Press, 1994), p. 28.
15. Lee Benson, *The Concept of Jacksonian Democracy: New York as a Test Case* (Princeton: Princeton University Press, 1961); Samuel P. Hays, *American Political History as Social Analysis* (Knoxville: University of Tennessee Press, 1980), esp. pp. 51–132; Richard P. McCormick, *The Second American Party System* (Chapel Hill: University of North Carolina Press, 1966); Paul Kleppner, *The Cross of Culture: A Social Analysis of Midwestern Politics, 1850–1900* (New York: Free Press, 1970), and *The Third Electoral System: 1853–1892* (Chapel Hill: University of North Carolina Press, 1979); Richard Jensen, *The Winning of the Midwest: Social and Political Conflict, 1888–1896* (Chicago: University of Chicago Press, 1971); and Ronald Formisano, *The Birth of Mass Political Parties: Michigan, 1827–1891* (Princeton: Princeton University Press, 1971) and *The Transformation of Political Culture: Massachusetts Parties, 1790s–1840s* (New York: Oxford University Press, 1983).
16. For contemporary examples, see Joseph Blau (ed.), *Social Theories of Jacksonian Democracy: Representative Writings of the Period, 1825–50* (Indianapolis: Bobbs-Merrill, 1954); John R. Bordo, *The Protestant Clergy and Public Issues, 1812–1848* (Princeton: Princeton University Press, 1954).
17. See e.g. Daniel Dreisbach, 'Introduction: A Debate on Religion and Politics in the Early Republic', in *Religion and Politics in the Early Republic: Jasper Adams and the Church/State Debate*, ed. Daniel Dreisbach (Lexington: University of Kentucky Press, 1997); John M. Murrin, 'Religion and Politics in America from the First Settlements to the Civil War', in *Religion and American Politics*, ed. Mark Noll (New York: Oxford University Press, 1990); and Lipset, 'Religion and Politics', pp. 308–13.
18. This position is developed in Kleppner, *The Cross of Culture*, pp. 71–72, and *The Third Electoral System*, pp. 185–89; Jensen, *The Winning of the Midwest*, pp. 62–73; and Robert P. Swierenga, 'Ethnoreligious Political Behavior in the Mid-Nineteenth

Century', in *Religion and American Politics*, ed. Mark A. Noll (New York: Oxford University Press, 1990), pp. 151–55.

19. For a concise summary of the main findings from the literature on partisan alignments of religious voters in the nineteenth century, see Swierenga, 'Ethnoreligious Political Behavior', p. 157.

20. For a broad overview of the alignments of this period, see Walter Dean Burnham, 'The System of 1896', in *The Evolution of American Electoral Systems*, ed. Paul Kleppner (Westport, Conn.: Greenwood Press, 1981).

21. The major challenge to Democratic hegemony in the South—the populist movement of the 1880s and 1890s—explicitly sought to create a transethnic, class-based movement, but electoral analyses of the populist vote suggest that it drew much more extensively from pietist than nonpietist religious traditions. See Kleppner, *The Third Electoral System*, pp. 287–88; Kazin, *The Populist Persuasion*, pp. 39–40.

22. The major exception was Jewish voters, who realigned sharply during the 1920s and 1930s with the Democratic Party. See e.g. Gerald Gamm, *The Making of the New Deal Democrats* (Chicago: University of Chicago Press, 1986), pp. 45–74.

23. See e.g. Samuel Lubell, *The Future of American Politics*, 3rd edn (New York: Harper & Row, 1965); Sundquist, *Dynamics of the Party System*; A. James Reichley, *Religion in American Public Life* (Washington, DC: Brookings Institute, 1985), pp. 225–29.

24. A good general summary of the changes within the major religious traditions during the 1960s and beyond can be found in Wade C. Roof and William McKinney, *American Mainline Religion* (New Brunswick, NJ: Rutgers University Press, 1987), pp. 11–39.

25. For analyses of the growth of social issue liberalism within the Protestant mainline, and the tensions it generated, see e.g. Harold Quinley, *The Prophetic Clergy: Social Activism among Protestant Ministers* (New York: Wiley, 1974); Jeffrey Hadden, *The Gathering Storm in the Churches* (Garden City, NY: Anchor, 1969); Richard Neuhaus, *The Naked Public Square* (Grand Rapids, Mich.: Eerdmans, 1984), esp. chap. 3. For analyses of the consequences of mainline liberalism for the patterning of church growth, see Finke and Stark, *The Churching of America*, esp. pp. 237–74.

26. For useful overviews of the CR mobilization, see e.g. Steve Bruce, *The Rise and Fall of the New Christian Right* (New York: Oxford University Press, 1988); Sara Diamond, *Roads to Dominion* (New York: Guilford Press, 1995), pp. 161–77; Jerome Himmelstein, *To the Right: The Transformation of American Conservatism* (Berkeley: University of California Press, 1990), pp. 97–128.

27. A valuable survey of these changes, and their impact on the Catholic laity, is developed in Andrew Greeley, *American Catholics since the Council* (Chicago: Thomas More, 1985). Greeley has emphasized that the fall-off in attendance among Catholics between 1968 and 1975 was likely precipitated by a conservative 1968 encyclical on birth control rather than Vatican II. See *Amerian Catholics since the Council*, pp. 55 ff.

28. Among the most useful analyses of the new religious movements is that of

Robert Wuthnow. See esp. his *The Restructuring of American Religion* (Princeton: Princeton University Press, 1988). For other treatments, see Bryan Wilson (ed.), *The Social Impact of New Religious Movements* (New York: Rose of Sharon Press, 1981); Mary Douglas and Steven Tipton (eds.), *Religion and America: Spirituality in a Secular Age* (Boston: Beacon Press, 1982).

29. See e.g. Wald, *Religion and Politics in the United States*, p. 21; and Anthony Heath, Bridget Taylor, and Gabor Toka, 'Religion, Morality and Politics', in *International Social Attitudes: The Tenth BSA Report*, ed. Roger Jowell, Lindsay Brook, and Lizanne Dowds (Aldershot, England: Dartmouth, 1993), pp. 49–80.

30. Conservative theories of the 'new class', are probably the main exponents of this view of the political importance of a rising secular humanistic intelligentsia. For a sampling of the relevant writings along these lines, see B. Bruce-Biggs (ed.), *The New Class?* (San Diego: Harcourt Brace, 1979); for a useful criticism, noting that plenty of educated 'new class' members can be found among evangelical religious denominations as well, see James D. Hunter, 'The New Class and the Young Evangelicals', *Review of Religious Research*, 22 (1980): 155–69.

31. John Green and James Guth, 'The Bible and the Ballot Box: The Shape of Things to Come', in *The Bible and the Ballot Box*, ed. James Guth and John Green (Boulder, Colo.: Westview Press, 1991), p. 207. For a similar formulation, see Lyman Kellstedt, John Green, James Guth, and Corwin Smidt, 'Religious voting Blocs in the 1992 Election', *Sociology of Religion*, 55 (1994): 307–26, esp. 322–24.

32. Useful overviews of the history of tensions between religious traditionalists and modernizers in the U.S. context would include Garry Wills, *Under God: Religion and Politics in America* (New York: Simon and Shuster, 1990); and James D. Hunter, *American Evangelicalism* (New Brunswick, NJ: Rutgers University Press, 1983).

33. A superb explication of the historical origins and contemporary manifestations of these differences can be found in Wills, *Under God*.

34. James D. Hunter's argument about growing 'culture wars' is relevant in this context. Hunter argues that American political life is increasingly divided into two warring camps of ideological liberals and conservatives which cut across denominational divides (thus uniting conservative Catholics and Jews with conservative Protestants). Hunter popularized the 'culture wars' thesis in his 1991 book *Culture Wars* (New York: Basic Books, 1991). The thesis has generated consider critical discussion; for some recent criticisms, see e.g. Rhys Williams (ed.), *Culture Wars in American Politics* (New York: Aldine de Gruyter, 1997).

35. In treating religiosity as a mediating factor which strengthens the political importance of religious group membership for political behavior, we follow the lead of previous scholars. See Geoffrey Layman, 'Religion and Political Behavior in the United States', *Public Opinion Quarterly*, 61 (1997): 288–316, at p. 290.

36. Studies of 'contextual effects' of individual churches also demonstrates the potential political relevance of church attendance in combination with denomination membership for political behavior. See e.g. Kenneth D. Wald, Dennis

Owen, and Samuel Hill, 'Churches as Political Communities', *American Political Science Review*, 82 (1988): 531–48; Christopher Gilbert, *The Impact of Churches on Political Behavior* (Westport, Conn.: Greenwood Publishers, 1993).

37. Similarly, it may turn out that religious attendance is more likely to change attitudes on some issues but not others. This is a central finding of Michael Welch and David Leege's study of conservative Catholic churches, 'Dual Reference Groups and Political Orientations: An Examination of Evangelically Oriented Catholics', *American Journal of Political Science*, 35 (1991): 28–56. Such findings may have general applicability, although to the best of our knowledge no one has pursued this intriguing line of research beyond Welch and Leege's investigation of Catholics.

38. Layman provides the clearest evidence about the growing importance of religious beliefs in the structuring of the religious political cleavage. See his 'Religion and Political Behavior in the United States'.

39. It is worth noting that treating denomination-based divisions as a religious cleavage has some intriguing parallels to the class cleavage. Like class location, an individual member of a religious tradition may have varying degrees of attachment to the religious beliefs and practices of their denomination. In similar fashion to the variety of class origins and destinations, levels of religiosity and individual biographies create many different types of links between religious group membership and subjective attachments.

40. Rodney Stark, 'Modernization, Secularization, and Mormon Success', in *In Gods We Trust*, ed. Thomas Robbins and Dick Anthony (New Brunswick, NJ: Transaction Publishers, 1991), p. 201 (quote). Daniel Bell plausibly asserts that 'From the end of the nineteenth to the middle of the twentieth century, almost every sociological thinker—I exempt Scheler and a few others expected—religion to disappear by the onset of the twenty-first century'. Bell, 'The Return of the Sacred? The Argument on the Future of Religion', *British Journal of Sociology*, 28 (1977): 419–49, at pp. 421–22.

41. For overviews of the secularization model, see esp. David Yamane, 'Secularization on Trial: In Defense of a Neosecularization Paradigm', *Journal for the Scientific Study of Religion*, 36 (1997): 109–22; and Casanova, *Public Religions in the Modern World*, chap. 1. Our threefold distinction in this paragraph follows Casanova's unpacking of the secularization thesis. The most plausible contemporary defenses of the model would include Yamane, 'Secularization on Trial'; and Roy Wallis and Steve Bruce, 'Secularization: The Orthodox Model', in *Religion and Modernization*, ed. Steve Bruce (New York: Oxford University Press, 1992), pp. 8–30. Wallis and Bruce reinterpret secularization theory in terms of the claim that religious organizations have declined in their ability to influence the state and control political life. This 'weak' version of the secularization thesis is more reasonable, but of less theoretical significance, than the broader theory. Casanova, *Public Religion*, offers a more nuanced approach, arguing that secularization can be found in some realms but not others.

42. Finke and Stark, *The Churching of America, 1776–1980*, esp. pp. 15–16 (presenting evidence that 'religious adherence' rates grew nearly linearly from a mere 17% of all Americans in 1776 to 62% in 1980).

43. C. Kirk Hadaway, Penny L. Marler, and Mark Chaves, 'What the Polls Don't Show: A Closer Look at U.S. Church Attendance', *American Sociological Review*, 58 (1993): 741–52. These authors argue that actual attendance rates in American churches are about one-half of the rates reported by respondents to social surveys. They base these conclusion on a comparison of a telephone survey in one county in Ohio with actual head counts (estimated primarily from church sources) from all churches in the county. For criticisms of the Hadaway et al. analysis, see Michael Hout and Andrew Greeley, 'What Church Officials' Reports Don't Show', *American Sociological Review*, 64 (1998): 113–19. Hadaway et al. reply in 'Over-reporting Church Attendance in America: Evidence That Demands the Same Verdict', *American Sociological Review*, 64 (1998): 122–30, presenting some further evidence from other studies that suggest some growth in the amount of over-reporting of religious attendance has increased over time.

44. Wuthnow has developed arguments for the declining significance of denominations thesis in many publications. See esp. his *The Restructuring of American Religion*; *The Struggle for America's Soul* (Grand Rapids, Mich.: William B. Eerdmans Publishing Company, 1989); and *The Future of Christianity* (New York: Oxford University Press, 1993). A recent empirical defense of the thesis can be found in Layman, 'Religion and Political Behavior in the United States'.

45. See e.g. Rodney Stark and Charles Y. Glock, *American Piety: The Nature of Religious Commitment* (Berkeley: University of California Press, 1968), esp. chap. 11; Roof and McKinney, *American Mainline Religion*, esp. pp. 244–51. Robert Bellah's widely discussed notion of 'civil religion' suggests a similar set of conclusions, which Wuthnow has made more explicit than Bellah himself by distinguishing between 'liberal' and 'conservative' civil religions. See *The Restructuring of American Religion*, chaps. 10–11.

46. Lenski, *The Religious Factor*, emphasized the deep divisions between the three dominant religious groupings, so much so that he speculated at the end of the book about the possible rise of a 'compartmentalized' society in which growing tensions among religious groups would eventually emerge. See *The Religious Factor*, pp. 362–66. See also Will Herberg's mid-century treatment, *Protestant, Catholic, Jew: An Essay in American Religious Sociology* (Garden City, NY: Doubleday, 1960), esp. pp. 140–42, 244–45.

47. The survey data, however, do not show evidence of a statistically significant increase in 'warm' feelings among Protestants towards Catholics or Jews, and vice-versa, over the period from the early 1960s to the mid-1980s. See Greeley, *Religious Change in America*, pp. 62–65.

48. Wuthnow, *The Restructuring of American Religion*, pp. 88 ff. It should be noted that other surveys have shown somewhat more limited evidence of increased denominational switching, and that it appears to be primarily true only for Protestants, esp. mainline Protestants. See e.g. Greeley, *Religious Change in America*, pp. 60–62.

49. Matthijs Kalmijn, 'Shifting Boundaries: Trends in Religious and Educational Homogamy', *American Sociological Review*, 56 (1991): 786–800.

50. Wuthnow relies heavily on the assumption that ecumenicism is growing in

importance. For an important empirical critique of this idea, see Finke and Stark, *The Churching of America*, pp. 199–236.

51. Wuthnow, *The Struggle for America's Soul*, p. 78 (quote).
52. Wuthnow has primarily been concerned with analyzing religious conflict and public opinion, not voting behavior *per se*. The voting context is obviously different, but because of limitations in the NES items prior to 1980, we cannot directly test his thesis over the entire time period. The one study which has used voting behavior to investigate the Wuthnow thesis is Layman's 'Religion and Political Behavior in the United States'. Using NES data, Layman finds evidence of (1) increasing salience of orthodox religious beliefs for voting behavior; and (2) declining strength of traditional cleavages between conservative and liberal denominations. His results show, however, only a very modest increase in the effects of religious beliefs on voting behavior, most likely because of the inadequate NES measures of religious beliefs before 1980 limits his analysis to the period since then.
53. Abramson, Aldrich, and Rohde, *Change and Continuity in the 1992 Elections*, p. 156; for other similar conclusions based on similar measures, see Arthur H. Miller and Martin P. Wattenberg, 'Politics from the Pulpit: Religiosity and the 1980 Elections', *Public Opinion Quarterly*, 48 (1984): 301–17; Steven Brint and Susan Kelley, 'The Social Bases of Political Beliefs in the United States: Interests, Cultures, and Normative Pressures in Comparative-Historical Perspective', *Research in Political Sociology*, 6 (1993): 277–317, at p. 307.
54. Edward G. Carmines and Harold W. Stanley, 'The Transformation of the New Deal Party System: Social Groups, Political Ideology, and Changing Partisanship among Northern Whites, 1972–1988', *Political Behavior*, 14 (1992): 213–237, at p. 224.
55. Lopatto, *Religion and the Presidential Election*, chap. 3.
56. For an overview and critique of some common general media stereotypes of evangelical voters, see J. David Woodard, 'Evangelicals and the Media', in *Contemporary Evangelical Political Involvement*, ed. Corwin Smidt (Lanham, Md.: University Presses of America, 1989), pp. 119–31.
57. For some of the representative studies (among the many published in the 1980s coming to essentially the same conclusion), see e.g. Emmett H. Buell, Jr. and Lee Sigelman, 'An Army that Meets Every Sunday? Popular Support for the Moral Majority in 1980', *Social Science Quarterly*, 66 (1985): 426–34; Jerry Perkins, 'The Moral Majority as a Political Reference in the 1980 and 1984 Elections', in *Religion and Political Behavior in the United States*, ed. Ted G. Jelen (New York: Praeger, 1989), pp. 157–68.
58. For representative arguments about the decline of the CR in the late 1980s, see e.g. Bruce, *The Rise and Fall of the Christian Right*, esp. chap. 5, and 'The Inevitable Failure of the New Christian Right', *Sociology of Religion*, 55 (1994): 229–42; Michael D'Antonio, *Fall from Grace: The Failed Crusade of the Christian Right* (New Brunswick, NJ: Rutgers University Press, 1992); Clyde Wilcox, 'Premillennialists at the Millennium: Some Reflections on the Christian Right', *Sociology of Religion*, 55 (1994): 243–62.

59. One survey of activists, consultants, journalists, university professors, and other informed persons in the summer of 1994 showed that of the 50 state Republican Party organizations, fully 18 were estimated by the respondents to have a majority of leaders connected to CR organizations (including such large states as California, Texas, and Florida), while 13 had between 25% and 50% of the party leadership connected to the CR. See John F. Persinos, 'Has the Christian Right Taken Over the Republican Party?', *Campaigns and Elections*, 15 (September 1994): 21–24. For more elaborate scholarly analyses of CR political activism and its consequences, see Mark Rozell and Clyde Wilcox (eds.), *God at the Grass Roots: The Christian Right in the 1994 Elections* (Lanham, Md: Rowman and Littlefield, 1995). The authors in the Rozell and Wilcox volume come to very different conclusions about the impact of CR groups in different states, but in general there appears little evidence that openly identified CR candidates win votes that non-CR conservatives would not also win (and in many contexts CR candidates probably lose votes that a non-CR conservative would receive).

60. Mark Regnerus, David Sikkink, and Christian Smith, 'Voting with the Christian Right: Contextual and Individual Patterns of Electoral Influence', *Social Forces*, 81 (1999): in press.

61. For overviews emphasizing the political power of the CR, see esp. Himmelstein, *To The Right*; Diamond, *Roads to Dominion*, esp. chaps. 7 and 10. For studies reporting evidence of an electoral shift of evangelical Christians toward the Republican Party, see Green and Guth, 'The Bible and the Ballot Box: The Shape of Things to Come', p. 217; Lyman A. Kellstedt and John C. Green, 'Knowing God's Many People: Denominational Preference and Political Behavior', in *Rediscovering the Religious Factor in American Politics*, ed. David Leege and Lyman Kellstedt (Armonk, NY: M. E. Sharpe, 1993), p. 56; and Kellstedt, Green, Guth, and Schmidt, 'Religious Voting Blocs in the 1992 Election: Year of the Evangelical?', p. 308. The most nuanced assessment is that of Regnerus et al., 'Voting With the Christian Right'.

62. See e.g. Ted Jelen, 'The Effects of Religious Separatism on White Protestants in the 1984 Presidential Elections', *Sociological Analysis*, 48 (1987): 30–45; Clyde Wilcox, 'The New Christian Right and the Mobilization of the Evangelicals', in *Religion and Political Behavior in the United States*, ed. Ted Jelen (New York: Praeger, 1989), p. 143.

63. See e.g. Bruce, *The Rise and Fall of the New Christian Right*, pp. 101–02; Corwin Smidt, 'Contemporary Evangelical Political Involvement: An Overview', in *Contemporary Evangelical Political Involvement*, ed. Corwin Smidt (Lanham, Md: University Presses of America, 1989), p. 2; Wilcox, 'The New Christian Right and the Mobilization of the Evangelicals'; Kevin Phillips, *Post-Conservative America* (New York: Random House, 1982), pp. 49–50; and Miller and Wattenberg, 'Politics from the Pulpit: Religiosity and the 1980 Elections'.

64. Among the analysts who have reached this conclusion, see Lopatto, *Religion and the Presidential Election*; John Petrocik, *Party Coalitions: Realignments and the Decline of the New Deal Party System* (Chicago: University of Chicago Press, 1981); Henry Kenski and William Lockwood, 'Catholic Voting Behavior

in 1988: A Critical Swing Vote', in *The Bible and the Ballot Box*, ed. James L. Guth and John C. Green (Boulder, Colo.: Westview Press, 1991), pp. 173–88; Richard Scammon and Ben Wattenberg, *The Real Majority* (New York: Coward, McCann and Geoghegan, 1970), pp. 64–65; E. J. Dionne, 'Catholics and the Democrats: Estrangement But Not Desertion', in *Party Coalitions in the 1980s*, ed. Seymour Martin Lipset (San Francisco: Institute for Contemporary Studies, 1981), pp. 307–25; Green and Guth, 'The Bible and the Ballot Box: The Shape of Things to Come'; Lyman Kellstedt and Mark Noll, 'Religion, Voting for President, and Party Identification, 1948–1984', in *Religion and American Politics: From the Colonial Period to the 1980s*, ed. Mark A. Noll (New York: Oxford University Press, 1990), pp. 355-79 and Kellstedt and Green, 'Knowing God's Many People: Denominational Preference and Political Behavior'; Reichley, *Religion in American Public Life*, pp. 224–25, 299–301. Standing virtually alone against the scholarly consensus that Catholics have realigned is the work of Andrew Greeley. See e.g. his *Religious Change in America*, pp. 76–86, and *American Catholics since the Council*, chap. 3.

65. Abramson, Aldrich, and Rohde, *Change and Continuity in the 1992 Elections*, p. 156 (quote).

66. Dionne, 'Catholics and the Democrats: Estrangement But Not Desertion', p. 308. For examples of some of the long-held stereotypes of Catholic voters as slaves to urban political machines such as those of Tammany Hall in New York, see the literature and discussion in David Leege, 'Catholics and the Civic Order: Parish Participation, Politics, and Civic Participation', *Review of Politics*, 50 (1988): 704–37, at p. 704. Debunking anti-Catholic stereotypes with systematic empirical evidence has long been a central focus of Andrew Greeley's work; see for example his *The American Catholic* (New York: Basic Books, 1977) and, more recently, *The Catholic Myth* (New York: Scribner's, 1990).

67. On the economic 'swing voter' interpretation, see e.g. Henry Kenski and William Lockwood, 'Catholic Voting Behavior in 1988: A Critical Swing Vote', in *The Bible and the Ballot Box*, ed. James L. Guth and John C. Green (Boulder, Colo.: Westview Press, 1991), pp. 173–87, at p. 173; Kellstedt et al., 'Religious Voting Blocs in the 1992 Election', pp. 323–24. For arguments about the increasing importance of candidate-centered appeals among Catholic voters, see e.g. Fowler and Hertzke, *Religion and Politics in America*, p. 96.

68. See Green and Guth, 'The Bible and the Ballot Box', p. 215 (quote). For similar interpretations, see e.g. Lyman A. Kellstedt, 'Evangelicals and Political Realignment', in *Contemporary Evangelical Political Evolvement*, ed. Corwin Schmidt (Lanham, Md: University Presses of America, 1989), p. 99; Kellstedt and Mark A. Noll, 'Religion, Voting for President, and Party Identification', pp. 359–61; Kenski and Lockwood, 'Catholic Voting Behavior', p. 174.

69. See esp. Greeley, *Religious Change in America*, chap. 7; on access to elite positions, see James D. Davidson, Ralph E. Pyle, and David V. Reyes, 'Persistence and Change in the Protestant Establishment, 1930–1992', *Social Forces*, 74 (1995): 157–75. An earlier analysis by Davidson, charting trends through the mid-1970s, showed Catholics still significantly underrepresented in most fields.

Davidson, 'Religion among America's Elite: Persistence and Change in the Protestant Establishment', *Sociology of Religion*, 55 (1994): 419–40, esp. p. 434.

70. Examples of this argument by conservatives, which was very popular in the late 1960s and 1970s, but less so more recently, would include Phillips, *The Emerging Republican Majority*, pp. 140–75, 461–74; and William Gavin, *Street Corner Conservative* (New Rochelle, NY: Arlington House, 1975); and William Rusher, *The Making of a New Majority Party* (New York: Sheed and Ward, 1975).

71. On the overrepresentation of members of mainline Protestants in the American elite, the classical treatments are those of C. Wright Mills, *The Power Elite* (New York: Oxford University Press, 1956), e.g. pp. 60, 106, 127–28; and E. Digby Baltzell, *The Protestant Establishment* (New York: Random House, 1964). For evidence of historical change in the power and influence of the Protestant mainline, see Davidson, Pyle, and Reyes, 'Persistence and Change in the Protestant Establishment, 1930–1992'; and Roof and McKinney, *American Mainline Religion*.

72. For declarations that mainline Protestants have become less Republican, see e.g. Lopatto, *Religion and the Presidential Election*, p. 53; for claims that they remain overwhelmingly Republican, see Kellstedt and Noll, 'Religion, Voting for President, and Party Identification,' pp. 369–70.

73. Perhaps related to this are arguments about political consequences of the sharp fall-off in regular church attendance among mainline Protestants, esp. among younger people, who are less exposed to traditional religious messages as a consequence. See e.g. David Leege, 'The Decomposition of the Religious Vote: A Comparison of White, Non-Hispanic Catholics with Other Ethnoreligious Groups, 1960–1992', paper presented at the Annual Meetings of the American Political Science Association, Washington, DC, 2–5 September 1993.

74. This interpretation is broadly consistent with Finke and Stark's argument about the inevitable erosion of strictness within denominations. See their *The Churching of America*, esp. chap. 5 on the case of the Methodists.

75. A 1990 review identified some 34 different approaches to operationalizing Protestant denominations. Smith, 'Classifying Protestant Denominations', pp. 226–234.

76. Charles Y. Glock and Rodney Stark, *Religion and Society in Tension* (Chicago: Random House, 1965); Stark and Glock, *American Piety*, chap. 11; see also Lopatto, *Religion and the Presidential Election*; James R. Wood, 'Authority and Controversial Policy: The Churches and Civil Rights', *American Sociological Review*, 35 (1970): 1057–69. For a related, but more fine-grained scheme, see Smith, 'Classifying Protestant Denominations'.

77. In the early years of the NES series, broad denominational families such as 'Methodist,' 'Presbyterian', and 'Reformed' are not further subdivided. It is thus necessary to make a single coding decision about the families (and to maintain it over the course of the entire time-series). The most unusual feature of this particular scheme is that it places Methodists in the 'liberal' Protestant category, while 'Presbyterians' (including members of the liberal Presbyterian Church (U.S.A), and the smaller evangelical Presbyterian churches, notably the

Presbyterian Church in America and the Orthodox Presbyterian Church) are placed in the 'moderate' category. In many ways this violates the longstanding alignment of denominations, in which the upstart Methodists were historically outside the elite Protestant denominations whereas the Presbyterians were at the center. Some analysts have indeed reversed the coding we have adopted, putting Presbyterians in the 'liberal' Protestant category and Methodists in the 'moderate' category. See esp. Roof and McKinney, *American Mainline Religion*, pp. 78–99. However, we think the Stark/Glock coding approach is appropriate. There is evidence that, on average, Methodist churches and members are at least as liberal as Presbyterian churches on doctrinal matters, and that these doctrinal differences go back to the 1960s. See e.g. Stark and Glock's survey data from the period in *American Piety*, passim. This survey data showed that Methodist respondents were more likely to have doubts about the existence of God or that Jesus is the son of God, less likely to believe in miracles or heaven. It is important to note, however, that GSS data does not confirm all of the early Stark/Glock findings. See Roof and McKinney, *American Mainline Religion*, pp. 186–228. There also appear to be differences in the nature of the Churches themselves. A panel of religious experts surveyed by Dean Hoge in the late 1970s rated the United Methodist Church as significantly more liberal on theological matters than the Presbyterian churches. Hoge, 'A Test of Theories of Denominational Growth and Decline', in *Understanding Church Growth and Decline, 1950–1978*, ed. Dean Hoge and David A. Roozen (New York: Pilgrim Press, 1979), pp. 183–86. There are also important divisions among Presbyterians, some of which can be traced to before the Civil War, in which smaller churches are firmly evangelical in their orientation. Because these smaller groups cannot be separated from the rest of the (liberal) Presbyterians, we follow Stark and Glock in placing the Presbyterians in the moderate Protestant category.

78. In his more recent writings, Stark has explicitly acknowledged the limitations of these types of coding schemes; see e.g. Rodney Stark and William Bainbridge, *The Future of Religion* (Berkeley: University of California Press, 1985), pp. 42–48.

79. This scheme is developed in Kellstedt and Green, 'Knowing God's Many People'.

80. It is important to qualify this by noting that due to very rapid growth in recent years, Mormons have now surpassed Jews in size.

81. This is because the number of Greek Rite Catholics is miniscule in most years of the NES (in fact, in some years there are none in the sample). Stark and Bainbridge (*The Future of Religion*, p. 46) point out that there are, in addition to the Greek Rite Catholics, over 30 separate Catholic denominations. The divisions among Roman Catholics are not, we would argue, comparable to the divisions among the major Protestant denominational families.

82. For the most recent and thorough analysis of the politics of the Jewish community, see Seymour Martin Lipset and Earl Raab, *Jews and the New American Scene* (Cambridge, Mass.: Harvard University Press, 1995), esp. chap. 6.

83. For an overview of the growth of the 'no religion' category, see Norval Glenn,

'The Trend in "No Religion" Respondents to U.S. National Surveys, Late 1950s to Early 1980s', *Public Opinion Quarterly*, 51 (1987): 293–314.

84. Greeley, *Religious Change in America*, p. 33. Stark and Bainbridge, *The Future of Religion*, chaps. 15, 17 present evidence that the 'nones' are the most likely of the denominational groups to believe in the mystical and the supernatural, and 'these people are the group most taken with several occult beliefs and are, perhaps, the most easily available for conversion to a cult movement' (p. 47).

85. This distinction is developed by John Condron and Joseph Tamney, 'Religious "Nones": 1957 to 1982', *Sociological Analysis*, 46 (1985): 415–23; and is endorsed by Roof and McKinney, *American Mainline Religion*, p. 99.

86. For an overview of these differences between the pre- and post-1989 NES pilot, see Leege, 'Religiosity Measures on the National Election Studies'.

87. A related problem with the religious attendance variable on the NES is that the response categories were substantially modified starting in 1972. Prior to 1972, respondents could choose 'regularly', 'often', 'seldom', or 'never'; beginning in 1972, the NES moved towards a more clearly specified set of categories: 'every week', 'almost every week', '1–2 times a month', 'few times a year', or 'never'. Changing the response categories may have improved the reliability and validity of the attendance measure, but at the cost of risking over-time comparability in the NES time-series. Our approach has been to treat the pre-1972 'regularly' and the post-1972 'every week' and 'almost every week' as the same. In 1968, 39% of respondents reported 'regularly' attending, while in 1972 27% reported attending 'every week' and 12% reported attending 'almost every week'. However, the convergence in these two categories is not a completely accurate representation of reality, as this period (1968–72) was one in which there was a significant fall-off in regular church attendance. See Michael Hout and Andrew Greeley, 'The Center Doesn't Hold', *American Sociological Review*, 52 (1987): 325–45. However, it constitutes our best attempt to reconcile this problem in the NES time-series, and the burden of proof is on an alternative specification to show improved results.

88. This is the approach, for example, of Kellstedt and Green, 'Knowing God's Many People'; and Leege, 'Religiosity Measures on the National Election Studies'.

89. Lopatto, *Religion and the Presidential Election*, places all Baptists in his moderate category, but after 1972 places Southern Baptists in the conservative category. This approach suffers from a severe pre-/post-1972 disjuncture which is problematic, even if it takes advantage of the additional information available on the NES after 1972. The convention of making use of region to identify 'Southern' Baptists prior to 1972 was common many years ago, but is now viewed as problematic in that the SBC has numerous churches outside the South, and non-SBC Baptist churches are found throughout the South as well.

90. As in previous chapters, our dependent variable is partisan vote choice (coded '1' for the Democratic candidate). We use a logistic specification to analyze this dichotomous dependent variable, as with our turnout analyses (coded '1' if respondent reports voting).

91. More formally, our preferred model is

$$\Phi_{ij} = \alpha_j + \sum_{K=1}^{K} \beta_{kj}^{T} C_{ik} + \sum_{l=1}^{L} \beta_{lj}^{R} D_{il} + \beta_{2j}^{RT} D_{i2} Y_{i0} + \beta_{4j}^{RT} D_{i4} Z_{i0}$$
$$+ \beta_{5j}^{RT} D_{i5} C_{i0}$$

(4.1)

where the βs superscripted by RT to indicate a religion-by-time interaction represent hypotheses about voting trends for three specific religious groups: liberal Protestants ($l = 2$), conservative Protestants ($l = 4$), and Catholics ($l = 5$). For liberal Protestants, the β_{2j} interaction for liberal Protestant interaction is constrained by Y_{i0}, a fixed score for person i, which is coded 0 to 8 for the election years (i.e. '0' for 1960, '1' for 1964, . . . , '8' for 1992). Given this linear constraint, the inclusion of this new parameter in the model represents the hypothesis that liberal Protestants' likelihood of choosing the Democratic candidate has increased at a constant rate (in logits) for each election since 1960. The β_{4j} and β_{5j} represent more limited patterns of change among conservative Protestants and Catholics. Z_{i0} is coded '1' for the 1976 and 1980 elections (when born-again presidential candidate Jimmy Carter was running for office), and '0' otherwise, and it constrains the conservative Protestant-by-year interaction to capture their tendency to favor the Democratic candidate during these two elections. C_{i0} is coded '1' for the 1960 election, and '0' otherwise, and it constrains the Catholic-by-year interaction to measure Catholic voters' disproportionate support for John Kennedy.

92. To identify all p coefficients for a given year, we constraint the coefficients to sum to zero.

93. Adding an additional parameter to model 2 for a linear voting trend pertaining to Catholics fails to improve model fit according to $-2LL$ ($-2LL = 10890.80$), and results in a worse fit according to BIC ($-66,545$).

94. We note that adding additional interactions between church attendance and (all) election years does not improve the fit of the model ($-2LL = 10494.58$ @ 7d.f.; BIC $= -66,742$). Model 6's single attendance-by-year $_{= 1992}$ interaction effect is thus sufficient to capture the interaction between church attendance and time.

95. Indeed, much of the outpouring of journalistic analyses of an ostensibly surging New Right came in the wake of the 1980 and 1984 elections, in which conservative Protestants were moving away from the higher levels of support they accorded Carter in 1976 (and also 1980). This shift, however, becomes illusory when viewed from the standpoint of the longer NES series.

96. For further discussion of this latter point, see Lipset and Raab, *Jews and the New American Scene*, chap. 6; Lee Sigelman, 'Jews and the 1988 Election: More of the Same?' in *The Bible and the Ballot Box*, ed. James L. Guth and John C. Green (Boulder, CO: Westview Press, 1991), pp. 188–203; and Abramson, Aldrich and Rohde, *Change and Continuity in the 1992 Elections*, p. 156.

97. Given that the moderate category is a diverse group including both unclassified and nondenominational Protestants, some caution should, however, be taken in interpreting these results.

98. Model 4's similar lack of improvement in fit over model 2 provides evidence

that the two additional group-specific interactions with time we found for presidential vote choice (relating to Catholics and liberal Protestants) are irrelevant in the case of turnout.

99. Note that because they are calculated relative to the overall mean, the group-specific estimates of turnout rates in figure 3 do not reveal the well-known *electorate-wide* decline in turnout since 1960. This decline can, however, be observed from the election year (main effect) coefficients presented in Table 4.

100. Note also that in Table 4.6, we restrict our analyses of the NES data to Protestants and Catholics, given that it is sufficient to know whether Catholics were—relative to Protestant voters—as supportive of Democratic candidates in the 1950s as in 1960.

101. We also tested an alternative measure of this hypothesis, modifying model 3 so that Catholics' vote choice in the 1956, 1956, and 1960 elections were constrained to be equal; this alternative model decisively worsened the fit of model 2.

102. We reiterate that our analysis examines only white voters. The rapidly growing proportion of nonwhite Catholics in the U.S., esp. among Latinos and also African-Americans, is increasing Catholic support for Democrat candidates.

103. Because the items measuring potentially relevant causal factors are available only after the 1972 survey, we limit our explanatory analyses of liberal Protestants' trend to the 1972 to 1992 period. Since the trend continues vigorously (and linearly) during the entire period, this limitation should be of little consequence, since the mechanisms explaining the shift after 1972 can be expected to also be operating prior to 1972.

104. For an overview of Carter's 1976 campaign and presidency and its appeals to evangelical Protestants, see Leo Ribuffo, 'God and Jimmy Carter', in *Transforming Faith*, ed. M. L. Bradbury and James B. Gilbert (Westport, Conn.: Greenwood Press, 1989), pp. 141–60.

105. This is an argument that has also been made by Clyde Wilcox, 'Fundamentalists and Politics: An Analysis of the Effects of Different Operational Definitions', *Journal of Politics* 48 (1986): 1041–51; and James D. Hunter, 'Operationalizing Evangelicalism: A Review, Critique, and Proposal', *Sociological Analysis*, 42 (1982): 363–72, at pp. 363–64.

NOTES TO CHAPTER 5

1. For analyses of gender and political behavior in Western Europe, see e.g. Pippa Norris, 'The Gender Gap in Britain and America', *Parliamentary Affairs*, 38 (1985): 192–201, and 'The Gender Gap: A Cross-National Trend?', in *The Politics of the Gender Gap*, ed. Carol M. Mueller (Newbury Park, Calif.: Sage Publications, 1988), pp. 217–34; Nancy J. Walker, 'What We Know about Women Voters in Britain, France and West Germany', in *Different Roles, Different Voices*, ed. Marianne Githens, Pippa Norris, and Joni Lovenduski (New York: HarperCollins, 1994), pp. 61–70.

2. Turnout rates of men and women voters in recent presidential elections, as

estimated by the Census Bureau's special voter supplement analysis—generally considered the most reliable of the available surveys—show that men had a 5% higher turnout rate than women in 1964, but by 1992 women had a 2% higher turnout rate than men. See U.S. Bureau of the Census, *Voting and Registration in the Election of November 1992*, p. v.

3. Alison Mitchell, 'Clinton Campaign Puts an Emphasis on Female Voters', 28 October 1996, p. A-1 [National Edition].

4. 'Gender Gap Wider Yet, GOP Session is Told', 27 November 1996, p. A-22 [National Edition].

5. The Democrats have been more aggressive in courting women voters, for instance by setting aside one-half of delegate slots at all party conventions and national party organizations for women, and in making major efforts to recruit women candidates to run for Congress. See Carol Mueller, 'The Gender Gap and Women's Political Influence', *Annals of the American Academy of Political and Social Sciences*, 515 (1991): 23–37.

6. '[U]ntil the gender gap made front-page headlines in 1980, a women's vote was not taken seriously by mainstream politicians. A majority of journalists, however, did not immediately recognize the voting differences or understand their importance. Nor were reporters eager to write about the gender gap until the issue became fashionable.' Kathy Bonk, 'The Selling of the "Gender Gap"', in *The Politics of the Gender Gap*, ed. Carol M. Mueller (Newbury Park, Calif.: Sage Publications, 1988), pp. 82–83; see also Jane Mansbridge, 'Myth and Reality: The ERA and the Gender Gap in the 1980 Election', *Public Opinion Quarterly*, 49 (1985): 164–78, at p. 166. In the aftermath of the 1980 and 1982 elections, for example, former NOW president Eleanor Smeal asserted that 'There is no doubt. The gender gap is the new wild card in political sweepstakes. Women will elect the next president of the United States. We've already put governors in power in New York, Texas, and Michigan, and sent a dozen senators and Congress people to Washington.' Eleanor Smeal, *Why and How Women Will Elect the Next President* (New York: Harper and Row, 1984), p. 1 (quote). For other examples, see Rhodes Cook, 'Democratic Clout is Growing as the Gender Gap Widens', *Congressional Quarterly Weekly Report*, 50 (1992): 3265–68; Mueller, 'The Gender Gap and Women's Political Influence'. Some early feminist academic analysts of the gender gap have also made predictions of this sort. For example, the political scientist Ethel Klein declared after the 1984 election that 'the gender gap helped keep [Ronald] Reagan's coattails short' and that 'The Republicans do have a problem with women, one that they need to defuse in order to become the majority party'. Klein, 'The Gender Gap', *Brookings Review*, (Winter 1985): 33–37, quote at p. 33.

7. For examples of these appeals—and their apparent successes—see Mansbridge, 'Myth and Reality'. However, Mansbridge also demonstrates that feminist leaders exaggerated the evidence about the gender gap in order to promote passage of the ERA. Her analyses show that differences in support for the ERA (or the salience of that support) did little to explain voting differences between men and women in the 1980 elections.

8. M. Kent Jennings, 'Preface', in *The Politics of the Gender Gap*, ed. Carol

M. Mueller (Newbury Park, Calif.: Sage Publications, 1988), p. 12 (quote); see also Julio Bourquez, Edie N. Goldenberg, and Kim F. Kahn, 'Press Portrayals of the Gender Gap', in *The Politics of the Gender Gap*, ed. Carol M. Mueller (Newbury Park, Calif.: Sage Publications, 1988).

9. There is also evidence that men and women differ in their evaluation of political officeholders. See e.g. Martin Gilens, 'Gender and Support for Reagan: A Comprehensive Model of Presidential Approval', *American Journal of Political Science*, 32 (1988): 19–49.

10. See e.g. Tom Smith, 'The Polls: Gender and Attitudes Towards Violence', *Public Opinion Quarterly*, 48 (1984): 384–96; Sara Ruddick, *Maternal Thinking* (Boston: Beacon Press, 1989); Bella Abzug, *The Gender Gap* (Boston: Houghton Mifflin, 1984), pp. 116–31.

11. Kathleen Frankovic, 'Sex and Politics: New Alignments, Old Issues', *PS* 15 (1982): 439–48; Mansbridge, 'Myth and Reality'; David O. Sears and Leonie Huddy, 'On the Origins of Political Disunity among Women', in *Women, Politics and Change*, ed. Louise Tilly and Patricia Gurin (New York: Russell Sage, 1990); Smith, 'The Polls: Gender and Attitudes Toward Violence'; and Ruddick, *Maternal Thinking*; see also Gilens 'Gender and Support for Reagan: A Comprehensive Model of Presidential Approval', for the role of the same issues in presidential evaluations.

12. See e.g. Frances Fox Piven, 'Women and the State: Ideology, Power and the Welfare State', in *Gender and the Life Course*, ed. Alice Rossi (New York: Aldine de Gruyter, 1985); Cynthia Deitch, 'Sex Differences in Support for Government Spending', in *The Politics of the Gender Gap*, ed. Carol M. Mueller (Newbury Park, Calif.: Sage Publications, 1988), pp. 192–216; Stephen Erie and Martin Rein, 'Women and the Welfare State', in *The Politics of the Gender Gap*, ed. Carol M. Mueller (Newbury Park, Calif.: Sage Publications, 1988), pp. 173–91. In their comprehensive survey of public opinion polls, Robert Shapiro and Harpreet Mahajan find that women on average give 3% more support to government programs to create jobs, redistribute income, or for other programs to support the poor. See Shapiro and Mahajan, 'Gender Differences in Policy Preferences', *Public Opinion Quarterly*, 50 (1986): 42–61, at p. 51.

13. Some analysts have suggested a third major area of attitudinal differences between men and women, on issues such as gender equality (including support for the ERA) and reproductive rights (see e.g. Ethel Klein, *Gender Politics* (Cambridge, Mass.: Harvard University Press, 1984), pp. 157–64; Smeal, *Why and How Women Will Elect the Next President*, esp. pp. 19–21). More recent research, however, has not found much evidence of gender differences on these issues (see e.g. the exhaustive survey of public opinion polls reported in Shapiro and Mahajan, 'Gender Differences in Policy Preferences', pp. 53–54). Furthermore, men (as well as women) have become more liberal over time, and the gap between the genders remains unchanged. For critical discussions of the women's issues thesis, see esp. Mansbridge, 'Myth and Reality: The ERA and the Gender Gap in the 1980 Election'; and Patricia Gurin, 'Women's Gender Consciousness', *Political Opinion Quarterly*, 49 (1985): 143–63. It is important to note that there are also some issues (e.g. drugs, pornography, sex education,

birth control, and prayer in the public schools) in which women have been found to be more consistently more conservative than men. See e.g. Virginia Sapiro, *The Political Integration of Women* (Urbana: University of Illinois Press, 1983), p. 150.

14. In the 1996 elections, for example, the Voter News Service data report gender gaps in Senate elections as large as 21% (in the Max Cleland/Guy Millner race in Georgia, narrowly won by Democrat Cleland).

15. See e.g. Sara Alpern and Dale Baum, 'Female Ballots: The Impact of the Nineteenth Amendment', *Journal of Interdisciplinary History*, 26 (1985): 43–67; J. Stanley Lemons, *The Woman Citizen* (Chicago: University of Chicago Press, 1977), esp. pp. 157–58; Klein, *Gender Politics*, pp. 17–22.

16. For full references and documentation, see Jeff Manza and Clem Brooks, 'The Gender Gap in U.S. Presidential Elections: When? Why? Implications?', *American Journal of Sociology*, 103 (1998): 1237, n. 3.

17. For an insider's account of the Republican Party's abandonment of issues of interest to women since the early 1970s, see Tanya Melich, *The Republican War Against Women* (New York: Bantam, 1996). A liberal Republican, Melich's overview of the gradual decline of the moderate wing of the Republican Party shows some of the ways that the GOP has adopted an increasingly conservative issue agenda in recent years.

18. We should note that not all previous analysts have accepted this dating or the logic of this analysis. For example, Sandra Baxter and Marjorie Lansing, *Women and Politics* (Ann Arbor: University of Michigan Press, 1983), p. 179; Alice Rossi, 'Beyond the Gender Gap: Women's Bid for Political Power', *Social Science Quarterly*, 64 (1983): 718–33, at p. 718.

19. The estimates shown in the right panel are based on the result of our empirical analyses, presented in detail later in the chapter. These estimates are preferable to the left-hand panel because they show that election-to-election fluctuation is a product of changes effecting all voters, as opposed to changes in the underlying gender cleavage.

20. For studies reporting such findings, see e.g. Maurice Duverger, *The Political Role of Women* (Paris: UNESCO, 1955); Gabriel Almond and Sidney Verba, *The Civic Culture* (Boston: Little Brown, 1965), p. 325; Mattei Dogan, 'Political Cleavage and Social Stratification in France and Italy', in *Party Systems and Voter Alignments*, ed. Seymour Martin Lipset and Stein Rokkan (New York: Free Press, 1967), p. 167; Inglehart, *The Silent Revolution*, chap. 7; Rose, *The Problem of Party Government*, pp. 37–38; for other citations and discussion of this literature, see Norris, 'The Gender Gap: A Cross-National Trend?', pp. 217–221.

21. Malcolm M. Willey and Stuart A. Rice, 'A Sex Cleavage in the Presidential Election of 1920', *Journal of the American Statistical Association*, 19 (1924): 519–20.

22. Bernard Berelson and Paul Lazarsfeld, 'Women: A Major Problem for the P.A.C.', *Public Opinion Quarterly*, 9 (1945): 79–82; Louis Harris, *Is There a Republican Majority?* (New York: Harper & Row, 1954), pp. 104–17. The forward to the Harris volume, written by Lazarsfeld and Samuel Stouffer, explicitly endorses Harris's conclusions regarding women voters (p. xi).

23. Lipset, *Political Man*, p. 217 (quote). In his influential treatment of civil liberties attitudes, Samuel Stouffer asserts that women's lack of engagement with politics leads them to be less politically tolerant than men. See his *Communism, Conformity, and Civil Liberties* (Garden City, NY: Doubleday, 1955), pp. 131–49.

24. Almond and Verba, *The Civic Culture*, p. 325 (quote).

25. It is important to note that there is often some overlap between models which identify more than one factor in explaining the gender gap. They should be viewed as ideal types rather than verbatim summaries of the views of all of the scholars who have written on the gender gap.

26. The most influential statements of this position can be found in Nancy Chodorow, *The Reproduction of Mothering* (Berkeley: University of California Press, 1978); see also Carol Gilligan, *In A Different Voice: Psychological Theory and Women's Development* (Cambridge, Mass.: Harvard University Press, 1982), p. 100. For applications to politics, see Paula Feltner and Leneen Goldie, 'The Impact of Socialization and Personality on the Female Voter', *Western Political Quarterly*, 27 (1974): 680–92; Robert D. Hess and Judith V. Tourney, *The Development of Political Attitudes in Children* (Chicago: Aldine, 1967); and Rita Mae Kelly and Mary Boutilier, *The Making of Political Woman: A Study of Socialization and Role Conflict* (Chicago: Nelson-Hall, 1974).

27. Nancy Chodorow's influential work on the psychodynamics of the mother–child relationship, *The Reproduction of Mothering*, offers another view of the process through which gender socialization occurs in childhood. Chodorow argues that the existence of family structures in which women do most of the child-raising have important long-term effects on boys/men and girls/women. Little girls develop a sense of connectedness to others because of the continuities between themselves and their mothers, while boys develop a masculine identity which (growing out of their need to distinguish themselves from their mothers) generally precludes development of the same types of nurturing instincts.

28. See Susan Welch and John Hibbing, 'Financial Conditions, Gender, and Voting in American National Elections', *Journal of Politics*, 54 (1992): 197–213; Arthur H. Miller, 'Gender and the Vote: 1984', pp. 268–72; Baxter and Lansing, *Women and Politics*, p. 188.

29. Adult socialization models emphasize the limited and partial character of childhood socialization for actual adult roles such as 'mother', 'father', 'wife', and 'husband'. See e.g. Jesse Bernard's influential *The Future of Marriage* 2nd edn (New Haven, CT: Yale University Press, 1982). Studies of career expectations, marriage, and families find evidence of the mediating role of adult situation on the long-term consequences of childhood socialization. See e.g. Anne Machung, 'Talking Career, Thinking Job', *Feminist Studies*, 15 (1989): 35–58.

30. For an overview of the contemporary division of labor in contemporary middle-class families, see esp. Arlie Hochschild, *The Second Shift* (New York: Avon, 1989).

31. Ruddick, *Maternal Thinking*. Ruddick's major application of the concept of 'maternal thinking' is an attempt to understand the significantly lower levels of

support expressed by women for militarism and an aggressive foreign policy, but her ideas clearly could be extended into a general explanation of the gender gap in political behavior.

32. This point is well made in the 'symbolic politics' model. For an application to the case of gender politics, see Sears and Huddy, 'On the Origins of Political Disunity among Women'.

33. See e.g Frankovic, 'Sex and Politics: New Alignments, Old Issues'; Keith Poole and Harmon Ziegler, *Women, Public Opinion and Politics* (New York: Longman, 1985), pp. 65–68; Sears and Huddie, 'On the Origins of Disunity among Women'.

34. See esp. Shapiro and Mahajan, 'Gender Differences in Policy Preferences: A Summary of Trends From the 1960s to the 1980s'.

35. In some elections—mmost notably 1964 (Goldwater vs. Johnson), 1972 (Nixon vs. McGovern), and in the elections of the 1980s (Reagan vs. Carter, Reagan vs. Mondale, and Bush vs. Dukakis)—there have been clear and unmistakable differences between the Democratic and Republican presidential candidates on force issues. But in many other elections—such as in the 1950s, 1968, 1976, and 1992—those differences were considerably more muted.

36. Jean Bethke Elshtain, 'Reclaiming the Socialist-Feminist Citizen', *Socialist Review*, 74 (1984): 23–30, quote at p. 24.

37. Sears and Huddy, 'On the Origins of Political Disunity among Women', pp. 274–75 (quote).

38. Susan Carroll, 'Women's Autonomy and the Gender Gap: 1980 and 1982', in *The Politics of the Gender Gap*, ed. Carol Mueller (Newbury Park, Calif.: Sage Publications, 1988), p. 257 (quote).

39. See e.g. Heidi Hartmann, 'The Family as the Locus of Gender, Class, and Political Struggle', *Signs*, 6 (1981): 366–94; Christine Delphy, *Close to Home: A Materialist Analysis of Women's Oppression* (Amherst: University of Massachusetts Press, 1984).

40. Carroll, 'Women's Autonomy and the Gender Gap', p. 241.

41. These general types of arguments about the linkages between men's and women's interests within families have been controversial. Most notably, debates over where to place working women in the class structure have been vigorously contested, beginning with Joan Acker's 1973 critique of mainstream stratification research for 'intellectual sexism' in its treatment of women, and John Goldthorpe's equally emphatic 1983 defense of what he calls 'the conventional view' of deriving the family's class solely from the labor market position of the husband/father. See Joan Acker, 'Women and Social Stratification: A Case of Intellectual Sexism', *American Journal of Sociology*, 78 (1973): 936–45; Goldthorpe, 'Women and Class Analysis: In Defence of the Conventional View', and 'Women and Class Analysis: A Reply to the Replies'.

42. The most recent and accessible overview of these trends can be found in Spain and Bianchi, *Balancing Act*. For an insightful general discussion of the political importance of these issues, see Rossi, 'Beyond the Gender Gap: Women's Bid for Political Power'.

43. Spain and Bianchi, *Balancing Act*, p. 26.

44. Andrew Cherlin, *Marriage, Divorce, Remarriage* (Cambridge, Mass.: Harvard University Press, 1992), pp. 24–25 (on likelihood of divorce); Sara McLanahan and Lynne Casper, 'Growing Diversity and Inequality in the American Family', in *The State of the Union*, ed. Reynolds Farley. New York: Russell Sage, 1995), p. 9 (on ratios of divorced to married persons); Spain and Bianchi, *Balancing Act*, p. vii.

45. The negative financial consequences of divorce for women are well known; see e.g. Karen C. Holden and Pamela J. Smock, 'The Economic Costs of Marital Dissolution', *Annual Review of Sociology*, 17 (1991): 51–78.

46. Frankovic, 'Sex and Politics: New Alignments, Old Issues', p. 444 (quote); Carroll, 'Women's Autonomy and the Gender Gap: 1980 and 1982', Arguments emphasizing the autonomy of women as an explanation for the gender gap have also been advanced by Rossi, 'Beyond the Gender Gap'; and Kathleen Gerson, 'Emerging Social Divisions among Women: Implications for Welfare State Politics', *Politics and Society*, 15 (1987): 213–21. Carroll's concept of autonomy encompasses two aspects, marital status and income (the latter an attempt to measure the capacity of female respondents to live independently of men).

47. For analyses of the marriage gap in presidential voting, see esp. Paul W. Kingston and Steven E. Finkel, 'Is There a Marriage Gap in Politics?' *Journal of Marriage and the Family*, 49 (1987): 57–64; Herbert F. Weisberg, 'The Demographics of a New Voting Gap', *Public Opinion Quarterly*, 51 (1987): 335–43; and Eric Plutzer and Michael McBurnett, 'Family Life and American Politics: The "Marriage Gap" Reconsidered', *Public Opinion Quarterly*, 55 (1991): 113–27.

48. Explanations for the marriage gap have included demographic differences between married and unmarried persons (Weisberg, 'Demographics') and the claim that 'married people are more likely to own property and to worry about protecting it' or 'to have, or to expect, children and, if so, to take a benign view of authority and a dim view of social disorder'. Martin Plissner, 'The Marriage Gap', *Public Opinion* (February–March 1983): 53.

49. Pamela J. Conover, 'Feminists and the Gender Gap', *Journal of Politics*, 50 (1988): 985–1010; Cook, 'Feminist Consciousness and Candidate Preference among American Women'. Other studies emphasizing the importance of feminist identities in shaping women's political views and/or behavior would include Gurin, 'Women's Gender Consciousness'; Elizabeth A. Cook, 'Measuring Feminist Consciousness', *Women and Politics*, 9 (1989): 71–88; Arthur Miller, Anne Hildreth, and Grace Simmons, 'The Mobilization of Gender Group Consciousness', in *The Political Interests of Gender*, ed. Kathleen B. Jones and Anna G. Jonasdottir (Newbury Park, Calif.: Sage Publications, 1988); for a comparison of the role of 'feminist' identities among men and women voters, see Elizabeth A. Cook and Clyde Wilcox, 'Feminism and the Gender Gap: A Second Look', *Journal of Politics*, 53 (1991): 1111–22.

50. See e.g. Mansbridge, 'Myth and Reality: The ERA and the Gender Gap in the 1980 Election'.

51. Spain and Bianchi, *Balancing Act*, p. 82; Milkman and Townsley, 'Gender and the Economy', p. 603.

52. For recent analyses of the patterning of economic inequality by gender in the contemporary United States, see esp. Bernhardt, Morris, and Handcock, 'Women's Gains or Men's Losses?'. Working women in 1992 earned, on average, 71 cents for every dollar earned by working men, up from 59 cents as recently as 1980; for a summary, see Spain and Bianchi, *Balancing Act*, pp. 108–12. However, as Bernhardt et al., 'Women's Gains or Men's Losses?' have shown, much of this increase is driven by educated professional and managerial women who have inflated the average income of all women. There has been relatively little change in the income gap for women in routine white collar or service sector jobs.

53. See e.g. Trond Petersen and Laurie, A. Morgan, 'Separate and Unequal: Occupation-Establishment Sex Segregation and the Gender Wage Gap' *American Journal of Sociology*, 101 (1995): 329–65.

54. As discussed earlier, this was one of the standard explanations offered by many of the postwar political behavior classics for the lower turnout rates among women.

55 Because of their lower average wages and the increase in the number of female-headed households, a growing percentage of women are either directly or indirectly dependent on the full range of social programs that subsidize wages or children. The latter includes childcare subsidies and marital leave legislation, programs that disproportionately benefit working women. Working women have also benefited from affirmative action programs that seek to reduce inequalities in access to jobs and educational opportunities.

56. This argument has been made most elegantly by Kristin Luker in her study of reproductive rights and anti-abortion activists, *Abortion and the Politics of Motherhood* (Berkeley: University of California Press, 1984), esp. chap. 5. Similar arguments have been made by Rossi, 'Beyond the Gender Gap'; Klein, *Gender Politics*; Kathleen Gerson, *Hard Choices: How Women Decide about Work, Career, and Motherhood* (Berkeley: University of California Press, 1985), and 'Emerging Social Divisions among Women: Implications for Welfare State Policies'; and Myra Marx Ferree, 'Working Class Feminism: A Consideration of the Consequences of Employment', *Sociological Quarterly*, 21 (1980): 173–84.

57. See e.g. Gertrude Bancroft, *The American Labor Force: Its Growth and Changing Composition* (New York: John Wiley, 1958), p. 38.

58. For an overview of the demographic evidence, see esp. Spain and Bianchi, *Balancing Act*, esp. pp. 79–90.

59. See e.g. Daniel Wirls, 'Reinterpreting the Gender Gap', *Public Opinion Quarterly*, 50 (1986): 316–30.

60. For application of a generational approach to gender differences, see Beth Schneider, 'Political Generations and the Contemporary Women's Movement'. *Sociological Inquiry*, 58 (1988); 4–21.

61. The wording of this item has changed during the four surveys we analyze. In the 1980 and 1984 surveys, the referent of this item is the 'women's liberation movement'; in 1988, the referent is 'feminists'; and in 1992, the referent is the 'women's movement'. Given this change in question wording, we analyze each of these four surveys separately (rather than analyze them jointly, using election year as a covariate in our models).

62. More formally, our measure of the gender gap is calculated as the standard deviation of the probability of Democratic vote choice among women and men. This measure can be calculated using either the raw NES data (see Figure 5.1's first panel), or using the predicted probabilities according to a given statistical model (see Figure 5.1's second panel). Either way, this index measures the average difference in voting behavior among men and women at a given year (t = '1' for 1952, '2' for 1956, . . . , '11' for 1992), and by comparing index scores we can thus infer the strength and direction of change in the gender gap over time.

63. Our preferred model of change in the gender gap has a single additional coefficient (β_{gj}) for the (changing) effect of being female (g = 1) during the 1952 through 1992 elections. In equation 5.1 (below), D_{i1} is a dummy variable for gender. The final term, $(Z_0)^2$, is a constant with fixed scores for year (0 = 1952, 1 = 1956, . . . 6 = 1976, and 7 for years $\geq$ 1980). The '2' superscript indicates that the constant is squared, and the constraint on time produced by this exponential function results in the distinctive trend line observed in the graphed estimates of Figure 5.1's right-hand panel. In the course of our analyses, we compare this model to competing specifications of change in the gender gap.

$$\hat{y}_{ij} = \beta_j + \sum_{t=1}^{T}\beta_{tj}\,C_{it} + \sum_{g=1}^{1}\beta_{gj}\,D_{ig}\,Z_0^{\,2} \qquad (5.1)$$

64. Model 3 consumes the same degrees of freedom as model 2, but yields a considerably smaller $-2LL$ statistic, indicating its superiority to model 2.

65. Note that model 6's specification of the gender gap exploits a modification of the year-squared term in model 5. In this model, the year variable is coded the same except for the past four elections (which receive the same score of '7'). This constraint in the year scores has the effect of flattening out the voting trend among women in recent (i.e. the 1980 through 1992) elections, while still allowing for a curvilinear increase in their likelihood of Democratic vote choice from 1952 through 1976. Model 6 results in a smaller $-2LL$ statistic than either model 4 (by 1.91) or model 3 (by 3.91); the BIC test thus provides positive evidence favoring model 6 over both these models. We evaluated the fit of a model that adds to model 6 an additional term for the main effect of gender. The resultant (3.36) reduction in -2 log-likelihood (for 1 degrees of freedom) favors model 6. Model 6's BIC of $-106,223$ is also superior to the BIC for model 3 ($-106,219$). We consider the gender gap in the recent 1996 election in Chapter 9.

66. The comparison between models 6 and 7 examines the evidence for any residual change in the gender gap (as captured by the unconstrained interaction of gender-by-time). The $-2LL$ test (as well as BIC) easily favors model 6, making it our preferred model.

67. The sample size for these analyses is somewhat smaller than in Table 5.2, reflecting the presence of missing values for the independent variables in Table 5.3's models.

68. These two-way interactions represent an interesting result in their own right. The .208 (s.e. = .099) coefficient for the gender-by-cohort interaction indicates

that being a female member of the 1950s generation increases one's likelihood of Democratic vote choice. By contrast, the −.234 (s.e. = .095) coefficient for gender-by-marital status indicates that unmarried women are actually less likely than their male counterparts to vote Democratic. This result is contrary to the expectations of the women's autonomy thesis, but it is largely irrelevant to explaining our main phenomenon of interest: the emergence of the gender gap in vote choice.

69. Given the stability of the gender gap since 1980 according to our preferred model (see Figure 5.1), it is sufficient to measure the gender gap during the 1984–1992 period as the main effect of gender, rather than a gender-by-time interaction, as would be appropriate when elections prior to 1980 are analyzed.

70. The explanation for this is that men and women's gender role attitudes are, on average, quite similar. Their respective means on the gender role item during the three elections in question are 4.44 and 4.49, showing that ideological differences in views of gender roles are cross-cutting in relation to gender. Between-gender differences are—to express this point another way—far less important than within-gender differences in gender role attitudes.

71. We also tested for an interaction between gender and views of the women's movement, finding no evidence for this interaction effect in all four elections.

72. Andersen and Cook, 'Women, Work, and Political Attitudes', *American Journal of Political Science*, 29 (1985): 606–25, quote at p. 609.

73. For the argument about the role of work socialization in shaping women's consciousness, see esp. Gerson, *Hard Choices*; Virginia Sapiro, 'Feminism: A Generation Later', *Annals of the American Academy of Political and Social Sciences*, 515 (1991): 10–22; and Ferree, 'Working Class Feminism'; for a more equivocal set of findings, see Andersen and Cook, 'Women, Work and Political Values'. This question returns us to the issues raised by advocates of the 'postmaterialism' thesis we discussed in Chapters 1 and 3.

74. The NES series does, however, contain several short-term panel studies, one running from 1956–60, another from 1972–76, and a more recent one from 1992–94.

NOTES TO CHAPTER 6

1. Pluralist classics include David Truman, *The Governmental Process* (New York: Alfred A. Knopf, 1951); and Robert Dahl, *Who Governs?* (New Haven: Yale University Press, 1961).

2. We formally introduced these measures in Clem Brooks and Jeff Manza, 'Social Cleavages and Political Alignments: U.S. Presidential Elections, 1960–1992', *American Sociological Review* 62 (1997): 937–46

3. We reiterate that because of limitations in the NES data, our discussion and analysis of racial and ethnic divisions is limited to the black/white cleavage. We also note that our usage of the term 'race' reflects our assumption that race is not a biological fact but instead a cultural construct. Our analysis of the black/non-black racial cleavage should thus be understood as investigating some of

the political-behavioral consequences of racial labeling, inequality, and group interactions during a specific historical era.

4. There are, of course, an enormous number of contributions to the historiography of race in American political development. One recent contribution which we have found helpful as an overview of the entire process is Michael Goldfield, *The Color of Politics* (New York: New Press, 1997).

5. For an analysis of the process through which race became a focal point of political conflict between the Democratic and Republican parties, see Carmines and Stimson, *Issue Evolution*.

6. For evidence on the points made in this paragraph, see esp. Reynolds Farley, *blacks and Whites: Narrowing the Gap?* (Cambridge, Mass.: Harvard University Press, 1984); and Farley and Allen, *The Color Line and the Quality of Life in America*; Douglas Massey and Nancy Denton, *American Apartheid* (Cambridge, Mass.: Harvard University Press, 1993); and Gary Orfield, *The Growth of Segregation in American Schools* (Alexandria, Va: NSBA Council of Urban Boards of Education, 1993); and Andrew Hacker, *Two Nations* (New York: Scribner's, 1992); and Keith Reeves, *Voting Hopes or Fears?* (New York: Oxford University Press, 1997).

7. The disfranchisement of African-Americans was esp. important in this regard. After the brief interlude of Reconstruction, most Southern blacks were barred from voting through a variety of measures established by Southern states from the 1880s onward. These included such devices as poll taxes, literacy tests, the white primary, multiple ballot boxes, and 'grandfather' clauses. The effectiveness of these measures is apparent from the raw turnout figures: while 76% of voting age adult citizens in the South participated in 1876, by 1920 Southern turnout had fallen to just 19%. See Piven and Cloward, *Why Americans Don't Vote*, pp. 30, 54. For an overview of these devices, see Jack M. Bloom, *Class, Race and the Civil Rights Movement* (Bloomington: Indiana University Press, 1987); Piven and Cloward, *Why Americans Don't Vote*, chaps. 2–3; and William Winders, 'The Roller Coaster of Class Conflict: Class Segments, Mass Mobilization, and Voter Turnout in the United States, 1840–1996', *Social Forces* (1999).

8. Once neglected, the study of black racial attitudes has increasingly emerged as a important source of insight into public opinion on race. See e.g. Lee Sigelman and Stephen Tuch, 'Metastereotypes: blacks' Perceptions of Whites Stereotypes of blacks', *Public Opinion Quarterly*, 61 (1997): 87–101; Katherine Tate, *From Protest to Politics* (Cambridge, Mass.: Harvard University Press, 1993); Kinder and Sanders, *Divided by Color*.

9. The 'principle/implementation gap' is coined by Howard Schuman and his colleagues. See Schuman, Charlotte Steeh, Lawrence Bobo, and Maria Krysan, *Racial Attitudes in America: Trends and Interpretations*, revised edn (Cambridge, Mass.: Harvard University Press, 1997). The 'new racism' is a generic label to apply to a family of concepts. Some of the leading contributions are as follows. 'Symbolic racism': David Sears and Donald Kinder, 'Prejudice and Politics: Symbolic Racism Versus Racial Threats to the Good Life', *Journal of Personality and Social Psychology*, 40 (1981): 414–31; and David Sears, 'Symbolic Racism', in *Eliminating Racism: Profiles in Controversy*, ed. Phyllis A. Katz and Dalmas

A. Taylor (New York: Plenum, 1988), pp. 53–84; 'subtle racism': Thomas Pettigrew and Roel W. Meetens, 'Subtle and Blatent Prejudice in Western Europe', *European Journal of Social Psychology* 25 (1995): 57–75; 'racial resentment': Kinder and Sanders, *Divided by Color*. We should note that there is a conservative counterargument touting the 'end of racism' which points esp. to changes in white attitudes on basic principles. See e.g. Stephen Thernstrom and Abigail Thernstrom, *America in black and White: One Nation, Indivisible* (New York: Simon and Shustr, 1997); Dinesh D'Souza, *The End of Racism* (New York: Free Press, 1995); and Byron M. Roth, *Prescription for Failure: Race Relations in the Age of Social Science* (New Brunswick, NJ: Transaction Publishers, 1994). Paul Sniderman's work stands in the center, acknowledging the persistence of racial prejudice but arguing that it is general political values, not race attitudes, which shape whites' positions on race or other social policy issues. See e.g. Sniderman and Thomas Piazza, *The Scar of Race* (Berkeley: University of California Press, 1993).

10. For a recent collection of papers demonstrating the ongoing nature of the race politics debate, see *Public Opinion Quarterly*'s 'Special Issue on Race', vol. 61, no.1 (1997).

11. See Richard B. Sherman, *The Republican Party and black America: From McKinley to Roosevelt* (Charlottesville: University of Virginia Press, 1973).

12. For an overview, see Nancy Weiss, *Farewell to the Party of Lincoln* (Princeton: Princeton University Press, 1983). The ineffectiveness and irrelevance of New Deal measures to attack racial injustice are demonstrated in the famous 1944 study by Gunnar Myrdal, *An American Dilemma: The Negro Problem and Modern Democracy* (New York: Harper, 1944).

13. For an excellent recent overview of these issues, see Robert C. Lieberman, *Shifting the Color Line* (Cambridge, Mass.: Harvard University Press, 1998). Nowhere were the destructive consequences of the New Deal agenda felt more sharply than in the area of housing policy. See especially Massey and Denton, *American Apartheid*.

14. See Weiss, *Farewell to the Party of Lincoln*, esp. pp. 180–235.

15. See e.g. Abramson et al., *Change and Continuity in the 1992 Elections*, p. 146.

16. See Harold Stanley and Richard Niemi, 'Partisanship and Group Support Over Time', in *Controversies in Voting Behavior*, ed. Richard Niemi (Washington, DC: Congressional Quarterly Press, 1993). We discuss and report our own estimates of the changes in African-American contributions to the Democratic coalition in Chapter 7.

17. For discussions of the importance of the Goldwater campaign, see Carmines and Stimson, *Issue Evolution*, chap. 5; and Robert Huckfeldt and Carol W. Kohfeld, *Race and the Decline of Class in American Politics* (Urbana: University of Illinois Press, 1989), chap. 1.

18. Richard Rovere, *The Goldwater Caper* (New York: Harcourt, 1965), p. 143 (quote). This passage is also cited in Kinder and Sanders, *Divided by Color*, p. 225.

19. In fact, in the NES presidential election year survey for 1964, every African-American respondent in the survey who reported voting supported Johnson.

20. A number of scholars and analysts have speculated that growing class divisions within the African-American community will create different perceptions of self-interest and, ultimately, in voting behavior. This thesis is associated most closely with William Julius Wilson's *The Declining Significance of Race* (Chicago: University of Chicago Press, 1978), which launched a furious set of debates. Many general theories of black political behavior have assumed that economic diversity will eventually lead to political diversity. For examples, see the review by Michael Dawson and Ernest J. Wilson, 'Paradigms and Paradoxes: Political Science and African-American Politics', in *Political Science: Looking to the Future*, vol. 1, ed. William P. Crotty (Evanston, Ill.: Northwestern University Press, 1991), pp. 189–234. By contrast, however, Dawson has argued persuasively that economic class divisions among African-Americans have not eroded group solidarity at the ballot box because of the power of group affect and perceptions of racial group interests among blacks. See Dawson, *Behind the Mule*, esp. chaps. 5–6.

21. Phillips, *Post-Conservative America*; Edsall and Edsall, *Chain Reaction*; Huckfeldt and Kohfeld, *Race and the Decline of Class in American Politics*; Weakliem, 'Race Versus Class? Racial Composition and Class Voting, 1936–1992'; Jim Sleeper, *The Closest of Strangers: Liberalism and the Politics of Race in New York* (New York: Norton, 1990); Jonathan Reider, 'The Rise of the Silent Majority', in *The Rise and Fall of the New Deal Order* ed. Steven Fraser and Gary Gerstle (Princeton: Princeton University Press, 1989); Michael Tomsky, *Left for Dead* (New York: Free Press, 1996).

22. On the right, see Ronald Radosh, *Divided They Fell: The Demise of the Democratic Party 1964–1996* (New York: Free Press, 1996); on the center-left, see William Julius Wilson, *The Truly Disadvantaged* (Chicago: University of Chicago Press, 1987); and on the left, Frances Fox Piven and Richard Cloward, *The Breaking of the American Social Compact* (New York: New Press, 1998), pp. 101, 439. Piven and Cloward's argument is historically nuanced, attending to the larger structural and political roots of this process.

23. Huckfeldt and Kohfeld, *Race and the Decline of Class in American Politics*, pp. 1–2 (quote).

24. Edsall and Edsall, *Chain Reaction*, passim. We might note that there are important parallels between many of the arguments attributing the electoral consequences of racial resentment among the working class and the working-class authoritarianism thesis we examined in Chapter 3.

25. See Wilson, *The Truly Disadvantaged*, esp. pp. 149–59; Theda Skocpol, *Social Policy in the United States* (Princeton: Princeton University Press, 1995), pp. 250–74.

26. See e.g. Huckfeldt and Kohfield, *Race and the Decline of Class in American Politics*, p. 23.

27. See e.g. Abramson, Aldrich, and Rohde, *Change and Continuity in the 1992 Elections*, chap. 5.

28. Arthur Miller and Brad Lockerbie, 'The United States of America', in *Electoral Change*, ed. Mark Franklin, Thomas Mackie, and Henry Valen (New York: Cambridge University Press, 1992). Miller and Lockerbie's conclusion are, like

Abramson et al., suspect in that they use a very limited conceptualization of the class and religious cleavages. We discuss these issues and related literatures in the next chapter.

29. Using our earlier example of race, κ = .5 would be obtained if whites' predicted probability of Democratic voting was 0.0 while African-Americans' corresponding probability was 1.0 (thus the standard deviation of these two probabilities would be .5).

30. The multivariate indices must be calculated for specific values of the independent variables. For these measures, we calculate the probability of choosing the Democratic candidate using as a baseline Southern, white, male, conservative Protestant who is out of the labor force and who is at the sample means for age (46.69 years) and education (12.42 years).

31. With the exception of the class cleavage, none of the full interaction models of change in individual cleavages are close to improving the fit of the preferred models presented in the first column. For the class cleavage, the difference in −2 log-likelihood for the two models is significant at the .05 level, but BIC rejects the full interaction model. Given the BIC results as well as our earlier findings for the class cleavage in Chapter 3, we select the more parsimonious model (in column one).

32. As discussed in Chapter 5, this pattern of change represents a significant deviation from linearity, with women's relative tendency to support Democratic candidates growing exponentially through 1976 but flattening out over the next four elections.

33. While the −2 log-likelihood test chooses the full interaction model, we found no evidence for any other significant inter-cleavage interactions using a more detailed series of comparisons (thus corroborating BIC's choice of our preferred model).

34. This point is made, for example, by Miller and Lockerbie, 'The United States of America'.

35. This point can be better appreciated when considering instances such as the 1984 election in which racial frames and messages were far less in evidence than in the 1988 election (and George Bush's use of inflammatory racial imagery in the infamous Willie Horton ads). Nevertheless, as presented in Figure 6.2, the race cleavage was very large and the class cleavage disproportionately small during this election. Understanding whether such results are the product of an unrelated, third process or instead the result of communicative processes mobilizing latent racial attitudes would significantly advance scholarly knowledge about the causal sources of the interrelationship between the race and class cleavages.

NOTES TO CHAPTER 7

1. In the classical 'tripod' model advanced originally by V. O. Key, American political parties were simultaneously 'party-in-the-electorate', 'party-in-government', and 'party-as-organization'. V. O. Key, *Politics, Parties & Pressure*

Groups, 5th edn (New York: Crowell, 1964), p. 371; for some recent work on parties which build from the Key framework, cf. John H. Aldrich, *Why Parties? The Origins and Transformation of Political Parties in America* (Chicago: University of Chicago Press, 1995); Daniel M. Shea and John C. Green (eds.), *The State of the Parties* (Lanham, Md.: Rowman & Littlefield, 1994); and John Coleman, *Party Decline in America* (Princeton: Princeton University Press, 1996).

2. The distinction between 'margin-free' and 'margin-dependent' measures is elegantly spelled out in a study of cross-national gender segregation by Maria Charles and David Grusky, 'Models for Describing the Underlying Structure of Sex Segregation,' *American Journal of Sociology*, 100 (1995): 688–732.

3. See e.g. Knoke, *Change and Continuity in American Politics*; John R. Petrocik, *Party Coalitions* (Chicago: University of Chicago Press, 1981) and 'Realignment: New Party Coalitions and the Nationalization of the South', *Journal of Politics*, 49 (1987): 347–75; Stanley and Niemi, 'Partisanship and Group Support Over Time'; Carmines and Stanley, 'The Transformation of the New Deal Party System'; William Flanigan and Nancy Zingale, *Political Behavior of the American Electorate*, 5th edn (Washington, DC: Congressional Quarterly Press, 1994), chap. 5.

4. See Petrocik, *Party Coalitions* and 'Realignment'.

5. The main innovation of these authors is to use coefficients from multivariate models of social groups and party identification to derive estimates of (changes in) the impact of group membership on Democratic, Republican, and Independent identification. As discussed in detail below, we adopt a similar multivariate approach here (albeit using vote choice as our dependent variable), also taking into account (corrected) group size and turnout rates in our calculations.

6. See e.g. Robert Axelrod, 'Where the Votes Come From: An Analysis of Electoral Coalitions', *American Political Science Review*, 66 (1972): 11–20, and 'Presidential Election Coalitions in 1984', *American Political Science Review*, 80 (1986): 281–84.

7. Robert S. Erikson, Thomas D. Lancaster, and David W. Romero, 'Group Components of the Presidential Vote, 1952–84', *Journal of Politics*, 51 (1989): 337–46.

8. This is what James Sundquist argued happened in the case of the New Deal class coalition after World War II: the basic social and ideological cleavages remained in place in the 1950s, but there were fewer voters on the Democratic Party side of the class divide. See Sundquist, *The Dynamics of the Party System*.

9. The k sample proportions in the analysis sum to 1.0 (i.e. for jth social cleavage); thus, we can calculate in turn the impact of the sub-groups comprising each of the j cleavages.

10. Stanley and Niemi, 'Partisanship and Group Support'.

11. Strictly speaking, the Census figures for group size are themselves sample estimates (derived from the Public Use Microdata Data samples), but we use the familiar μ notation for the population parameter to distinguish them from the NES sample proportions.

12. We discuss this issue in more detail in a 1994 conference paper co-authored

with Michael Hout entitled 'The Democratic Class Struggle in the United States, 1948–1992'. The same paper was later published in abbreviated form, without the discussion of occupation in the NES, under the same title in 1995 in the *American Sociological Review.*

13. It is important to keep in mind that these figures are for the entire population, not just the working population, and thus would appear more dramatic if we examined only the working population. The change in the distribution among the working population only from 1960 to 1990—and using the coding scheme we introduced in Chapter 3—looks like this: professionals .12/.17; managers .06/.17; routine white-coller .21/.22; self-employed .12/.09; skilled workers .15/ .13; and nonskilled workers .34/.23.

14. The most important of these legal barriers were the variety of restrictions found in Southern states aimed at preventing African-Americans from voting. Most of these were outlawed by the Voting Rights Act of 1965. Many states have further loosened voter registration requirements in recent years, and in 1993 the 'motor voter' legislation required each state to make registration materials available at the time at departments of motor vehicles, among other provisions.

15. This argument is developed by Tate, *From Protest to Politics.*

16. For the Census reports, see e.g. U.S. Census Bureau, *Voting and Registration in the Election of November 1992*, Current Population Report P20–466 (Washington, DC: Government Printing Office, 1993).

17. Lester Milbrath and M. L. Goel, *Political Participation*, 2nd edn (Washington, DC: University Presses of America, 1982), p. 116 (quote).

18. This was a central point of Raymond Wolfinger and Stephen Rosenstone's influential assessment, in *Who Votes?* (New Haven: Yale University Press, 1980). For a more recent assessment, see Jan E. Leighley and Jonathan Nagler, 'Individual and Systemic Influences on Turnout: Who Votes? 1984', *Journal of Politics*, 54 (1992): 718–40.

19. See e.g. Burnham, *The Current Crisis in American Politics* and 'The Turnout Problem', in *Elections American Style*, ed. A. J. Reichley, (Washington, DC: Brookings Institute, 1987); Weakliem and Heath, 'The Secret Life of Class Voting'.

20. For the increasing class skew argument, see esp. Burnham, *The Current Crisis in American Politics*; for the latter position, see esp. Jan Leighley and Jonathan Nagler, 'Socioeconomic Class Bias in Turnout: The Voters Remain the Same', *American Political Science Review*, 86 (1992): 725–36.

21. For a useful overview of these issues, see esp. Brian D. Silver, Barbara Anderson, and Paul Abramson, 'Who Overreports Voting?', *American Political Science Review*, 80 (1986): 613–24.

22. We thus tentatively conclude that arguments attributing class skew to the turnout decline since 1960 are probably not supportable. Workers have been no more turned off by political developments than professionals, managers, routine white-collar workers, or the self-employed. See also Hout, Brooks, and Manza, 'The Democratic Class Struggle', for a similar conclusion based on earlier analyses.

23. More specifically, the −2 log-likelihood statistic selects model 8 over model 4,

with the BIC index score of 1 also indicating positive evidence favoring model 8. Note that the interaction effect in question is constrained to apply equally to all three Protestant groups (i.e. these three groups are treated as a single, homogenous category). As shown in Table 7.3, the coefficient for this interaction is large and positive (.60[s.e. = .19]), indicating that membership in any of the three Protestant groups substantially raises black voter turnout.

24. We note that the potential risk of over-estimating group-specific differences in turnout is far greater with model 9, given that it includes an additional 59 coefficients in comparison to model 8.

25. As noted in Tables 7.3 and 7.4 (and also in Appendix Table 7.A1), we summarize the net change in each religious group's representation in the major party coalitions (and in the composition of non-voters) using the years 1964 and 1988 as our end-points. The reason is that the 1960 election involved the unusual overrepresentation of Catholic voters in the Democratic coalition, while the NES introduced a new measure that yielded considerably larger numbers of respondents with no religion starting in 1992. We note that using 1960 and 1992 as the end-points for the calculations of net changes generally leads to *larger* estimates of the actual magnitude of religious group-specific changes.

26. This finding would tend to support the survey evidence, discussed in Chapter 4, that the category of respondents without religious affiliation are divided between those who are truly seculars and those who believe in God but have no current religious identification.

27. See Stanley and Niemi, 'Partisanship and Group Support' and their 1995 update, 'The Demise of the New Deal Coalition,' in *Democracy's Feast: Elections in America*, ed. Herbert Weisberg (Chatham, NJ: Chatham House Publishers, 1995).

NOTES TO CHAPTER 8

1. No previous third party candidate had received as much as 5% in two consecutive elections prior to Perot's bids. We discuss issues surrounding third party candidacies in the next chapter.

2. See Abramson, Aldrich, and Rohde, *Change and Continuity in the 1992 Elections*, chap. 7; Miller and Shanks, *The New American Voter*, pp. 490–492. Michael Alvarez and Johnson Nagler ('Economics, Issues and the Perot Candidacy: Voter Choice in the 1992 Presidential Election') show that while economic considerations were the most important factor affecting 1992 vote choice, perceptions of economic dissatisfaction benefited Democratic challenger Clinton but not independent candidate Perot in their campaigns against Republican presidential incumbent Bush.

3. See Michael Alvarez and Jonathan Nagler, 'Economics, Entitlements, and Social Issues: Voter Choice in the 1996 Presidential Election', *American Journal of Political Science*, 42 (1998): 1349–63, for an analysis that compares the respective effects of economic perceptions and policy attitudes on presidential vote choice.

4. Walter Dean Burnham, 'Bill Clinton: Riding the Tiger', in *The Election of 1996: Reports and Interpretations*. ed. Gerald Pomper et al. (Chatham, NJ: Chatham House Publishers, 1997), pp. 14–15.
5. In their analysis of the 1992 presidential election, Miller and Shanks (*The New American Voter*, pp. 302–306) present evidence that attitudes toward family, sexuality, and 'traditional' morality had both direct and indirect effects on vote choice. Morris Fiorina has offered a more general interpretation which proposes that attitudes toward issues of this sort represent one of four separate dimensions along which voters are currently arranged. Fiorina, 'The Electorate at the Polls in the 1990's', in *The Parties Respond: Changes in American Parties and Campaigns*, 2nd edn, ed. Sandy Maisel (Boulder, Colo.: Westview Press, 1994).
6. See Jo Freeman, 'Feminism and Family Values: Women at the 1992 Democratic and Republican Conventions', P*S: Political Science & Politics*, 26 (1993): 21–28.
7. See Herbert Weisberg and David Kimball, 'Attitudinal Correlates of the 1992 Presidential Vote: Party Identification and Beyond', in *Democracy's Feast: Elections in America*, ed. Herbert Weisberg (Chatham, NJ: Chatham House Publishers, 1995).
8. See Elizabeth Cook and Clyde Wilcox, 'Women Voters in the "Year of the Woman"', in *Democracy's Feast: Elections in America*, ed. Herbert Weisberg (Chatham, NJ: Chatham House, 1995).
9. Stanley and Niemi, 'The Demise of the New Deal Coalition'.
10. See ibid., p. 237.
11. Ruy Teixeira, 'Finding the Real Center', *Dissent*, 44 (1997): 51–59.
12. See ibid., p. 53.
13. Stanley Greenberg, 'Popularizing Progressive Politics, in *The New Majority*, ed. Stanley Greenberg and Theda Skocpol (New Haven: Yale University Press, 1997), pp. 279–98 (quotes at p. 284). This collection is an attempt by a group of left-of-center social scientists to reorient Democratic Party political strategies towards rhetorical and policy initiatives designed to appeal to working families.
14. The raw NES data for 1996 reveal that among major party voters, 53% of non-black voters supported Clinton, whereas the corresponding figure for African-American voters was 99%.
15. These results imply that the convergence of the major party coalitions we noted in the last chapter deepened in 1996 with the further dealingment of working-class voters.
16. Assuming a baseline probability of men being likely to favor the Democratic (.50) and Republican (.50) candidates, the .70 coefficient translates into an expected .67 probability of supporting Bill Clinton among working women.
17. The important work of Carol Chaney, R. Michael Alvarez, and Jonathan Nagler finds that the gender gap in recent presidential elections has multiple sources in women and men's contrasting attitudes and policy preferences. Whereas women are more supportive of government involvement in the provision of childcare and jobs, men are significantly more supportive of the use of force and also more likely to identify themselves as 'conservatives'. While political behavior researchers have long analyzed such differences in preference,

Chaney et al. demonstrate that the latter account for the majority of the gender gap in recent presidential elections. Our analysis complements this research, providing evidence that women's labor-force status creates contrasting policy preferences among working and non-working women. See their 'Explaining the Gender Gap in U.S. Presidential Elections, 1980–1992', *Political Research Quarterly*, 51 (1998): 311–40; and 'Explaining the Gender Gap in the 1992 U.S. Presidential Election', unpublished manuscript, Department of Political Science, University of California, Riverside.

18. These estimates must be calculated for specific values of the independent variables. The baseline values we employ are for the probability of choosing the Democratic candidate among non-full-time working, southern, White, male, conservative Protestants who are at the sample means for age (46.69 years) and education (12.42 years). Note that these baseline values are the same as those employed in Chapter 6; this allows us to make direct comparisons between the 1996 results and the earlier results from the analysis of the 1960–1992 series.

19. We would not, of course, rule out the possibility that a different kind of Democratic Presidential candidate than Clinton might attract higher levels of relative working-class support.

NOTES TO CHAPTER 9

1. If we arbitrarily define 'significant' as 5% of the national vote, Perot is in fact the only repeater. The next closest cases are the Free Soil candidacies of Martin Van Buren (1848, 10%) and John P. Hale (1852, 4.9%), or the Socialist presidential campaigns of the 1910s, Eugene Debs (1912, 6%), Allan Benson (1916, 3%), and Debs again (1920, 3.5%).

2. Throughout this chapter, we will follow conventional usage and use 'third party' to refer to all presidential candidates not running under a major party label, although in many cases (including Wallace in 1968) the 'party' involved is really a vehicle created for the primary purpose of supporting the candidate at the top of the ticket. Perot's 1992 bid, in fact, was truly an independent candidacy, although the creation of the Reform Party in conjunction with his 1996 candidacy may lead to the creation of a more durable organization.

3. On this point, see Rosenstone, Behr, and Lazarus, *Third Parties in America*, p. 41. This work has shaped our thinking about many of the historical and theoretical issues raised by third party candidacies discussed in this chapter.

4. Again, Perot's 1992 campaign was unusual in this respect. By spending $73 million dollars, his campaign actually outspent the major party candidates in direct expenditures, although Bush and Clinton both benefited from millions of dollars in funds raised and spent by their respective party organizations (including so-called 'soft money' expenditures). It is also worth noting that the 1968 George Wallace campaign managed to raise nine million dollars, an amount significantly lower than that of Republican Richard Nixon but not much lower than Democrat Hubert Humphrey.

5. On this point, see Rosenstone, Behr, and Lazarus, *Third Parties in America*, pp. 33 ff.

6. The outlier here is again Perot. Rosenstone, Behr, and Lazarus argue that by pouring such a large amount of his personal fortune into his campaign, Perot was able to acquire an instant organizational framework, pay for ballot access drives, and most importantly gain media legitimacy as a viable candidate. He was also able to make use of extensive media buys in the last month of his campaign to bring his message directly to potential voters in long 'infomercials'.

7. For similar views about third party campaigns in light of the 1968 Wallace vote, see Lipset and Raab, *The Politics of Unreason*, chaps. 10–11.

8. While there have been some studies of the social bases of particular candidates, we have found virtually no studies comparing more than one such candidate.

9. Our section heading is taken from the title of Dan Carter's biography of George Wallace by that title (New York: Simon and Shuster, 1995).

10. Quoted in Carter, *The Politics of Rage*, p. 11.

11. Of the two recent biographies of Wallace, Stephen Lesher (in *George Wallace: American Populist* (Reading, Mass: Addison-Wesley, 1994)) emphasizes Wallace's populism, while Carter, *The Politics of Rage*, insists on the centrality of Wallace's racial views in defining his political appeal in the 1960s.

12. The classical statement of the contextual effects thesis was originally developed in V. O. Key, *Southern Politics* (New York: Knopf, 1949); for more recent arguments about the role of contextual effects on whites' political attitudes and behavior, see Weakliem, 'Race Versus Class?'; James M. Glaser, 'Back to the black Belt: Racial Environment and White Racial Attitudes', *Journal of Politics*, 56 (1994): 21–41; and Michael Giles and Kaenen Hertz, 'Racial Threat and Partisan Identification', *American Political Science Review*, 88 (1994): 316–26.

13. It is possible to use state-level racial composition to estimate some of these effects, although state-level information provides a very crude indicator of racial composition in particular communities.

14. On Protestant fundamentalists, see Anthony Orum, 'Religion and the Rise of the Radical White: The Case of Southern Wallace Support in 1968', *Social Science Quarterly*, 51 (1970): 674–88. On Catholics, see e.g. Lipset and Raab, *The Politics of Unreason*, chap. 10.

15. Corroborating this point, if we delete the variables measuring religious group membership from the model, the increase in $-2LL$ is a non-significant 9.25 with 6 degrees of freedom.

16. Support for Wallace was more extensive among conservative Protestants (20%) than any other religious group; both liberal Protestants (8%) and moderate Protestants (9%) were considerably less supportive of Wallace.

17. Lipset and Raab, *The Politics of Unreason*.

18. See e.g. ibid., chap. 10; Philip Converse, Warren Miller, Jerrold G. Rush, and Arthur C. Wolfe, 'Continuity and Change in American Politics: Parties and Issues in the 1968 Elections', *American Political Science Review*, 63 (1969): 1083–1105; Irving Crespi, 'Structural Sources of the George Wallace Constituency'. *Social Science Quarterly*, 52 (1971): 115–32. Other analysts report that

the Wallace vote was found among 'hardhat' working-class voters. The major exception to these claims was that of Hamilton, *Class and Politics in the United States*, pp. 460–67, who argued that there was no difference between manual and nonmanual workers in support for Wallace once the effects of region were taken into account.

19. See esp. Herbert McClosky and Alida Brill, *Dimensions of Tolerance: What Americans Believe about Civil Liberties* (New York: Russell Sage Foundation, 1983), chap. 8.

20. These findings lend support to Hamilton's 1972 findings critical of the widespread assertion that there is a working-class foundation to the Wallace vote.

21. For instance, assuming that the probability of men supporting Wallace over the major party candidates is .15, the corresponding expected probability of women preferring Wallace is approximately .08.

22. The raw NES data show that the gender gap in major party vote choice in 1968 was only 1%. However, the gender gap between working versus non-working women in 1968 was a very substantial 8%. As discussed in detail in Chapter 5, this reflects the long-term institutional sources of the gender gap in presidential elections; however, because there were far fewer women working full-time during this period, the overall gender gap in male versus female Democratic support is considerably smaller than in later years in the NES series.

23. The negative relationship between education and support for Wallace can be understood in light of the very large relationship between education and racial tolerance. See e.g. McCloskey and Brill, *Dimensions of Tolerance*; Sniderman, Brody, and Tetlock, *Reasoning and Choice*. Because education tends to promote racial tolerance, the highly educated are disposed, all else being equal, to oppose racially intolerant political candidates.

24. Perot's reliance on contracts from the federal government (and his aggressive pursuit of them) leads his biographer Gerald Posner to refer to him as a 'welfare billionaire'. See Posner, *Citizen Perot: His Life & Times* (New York: Random House, 1996), chap. 4.

25. Ross Perot, *United We Stand: How We Can Take Back Our Country* (New York: Hyperion Books, 1992), p. 23.

26. To be sure, Perot was much more explicit about the former (detailing where he would cut, and advocating institutional reforms such as the line-item veto that would make it easier for future presidents to resist excessive government spending), than he was about reforming the political process to reduce the power of money and make it more accessible to citizens. Given the decisive role of Perot's personal resources in making his campaign possible, this should hardly be surprising.

27. See Rosenstone, Behr, and Lazarus, *Third Parties in America*, chap. 9.

28. We would note that other examples of ideologically centrist outsider campaigns for the presidency have been seriously mounted. Steve Forbes, an heir to the Forbes publishing empire, made a bid for the Republican nomination in 1996 which attracted some initial support. At this writing, Forbes is planning a second presidential bid in 2000, albeit running as an ideological conservative championing much of the policy agenda of the Christian Right. Running under

the banner of Perot's Reform Party in Minnesota, former professional wrestler Jesse Ventura was elected governor in 1998.

29. The raw NES data for 1992 reveal that whereas 92% of black voters supported Clinton, only 2% supported Perot, and 6% supported Bush.

30. Assuming for expository purposes a baseline value of 0 logits (representing a .5 probability of choosing Perot over a major party candidate), this coefficient translates into a .10 *decrease* in the probability of choosing Perot.

31. While the raw NES data indicate that 15% of working women and 13% of non-working women supported Perot, the subsequent t-value for comparing these two proportions is .33, well below the usual .05 level of significance for a 1-tailed test ($t_{\alpha=.05} = 1.65$). This result provides strong evidence against the assumption that working and non-working women had different levels of support for Perot.

32. See e.g. Herb Asher, 'The Perot Campaign,' in *Democracy's Feast*, ed. Herbert F. Weisberg (Chatham, NJ: Chatham House Publishers, 1995), pp. 153–75.

33. Deleting the 12 variables measuring the religion and class cleavages yields a non-significant 14.26 increase in $-2LL$ for the model in Table 9.3.

NOTES TO CHAPTER 10

1. The fact that Democratic candidates were blamed for economic disappointment while during the Republican Administrations of the 1980s nonskilled workers perceived economic improvement (relative to other classes) is striking. Objective economic indicators (contrasting the 1980s and early 1990s with the first Clinton term, for example) cannot account for these different trends. Rather, they suggested a more substantial pattern of disappointment with the Democratic Party that affects not only the economic evaluations but other (unmeasured) beliefs.

2. We use the term 'Hispanic' in this chapter to include a highly diverse group of individuals with ethnic origins in the Americas. A more fine-grained analysis would seek to distinguish on the basis of national and/or ethnic origins more carefully than our more inclusive term implies. We thus caution that our use of the term should not preclude such an analysis.

3. Probably the most notable recent example is Texas Republican Governor George W. Bush, Jr., who according to exit polls won a solid majority of the Hispanic vote in his 1998 re-election bid for Governor.

4. Most of the Cuban-American population in the United States came to this country after the 1959 revolution, and they have been overwhelmingly Republican voters. See Louis DeSipio, *Counting on the Latino Vote* (Charlottesville: University of Virginia Press, 1996), pp. 38–39. Whether this pattern will hold in the future is an open question. As DeSipio notes, aside from anti-Castro, anti-Communist sentiment, the Cuban-American community none the less has been considerably more progressive and pro-union on domestic policy issues than the Republican Party in recent years.

5. DeSipio, *Counting on the Latino Vote*, p. 31.

6. Brimelow and Rubinstein, 'Electing a New People', *The National Review*, 16 June 1997. Recalling earlier anti-immigrant diatribes, they argue that the Republican coalition 'is being drowned—as a direct result of the 1965 Immigration Act . . . Nine-tenths of the immigrant influx is from groups with significant—sometimes overwhelming—Democratic propensities. After thirty years, their numbers are reaching critical mass. And there is no end in sight.'

7. See U.S. Census Bureau, *Voting and Registration in the Election of November 1992*, p. v (showing white/Hispanic self-reported turnout differences of 61%/30% in 1980, 61%/33% in 1984, 59%/29% in 1988, and 64%/29% in 1992). The *National Review* article, however, assumes a much lower turnout gap of just 10% between white and Hispanic voters.

8. That African-American and Hispanic voters will continue to maintain their recent levels of Democratic support in future elections is, of course, impossible to know. However, the institutional barriers faced by any third party movement make it exceedingly unlikely that black and Hispanic voters will have a viable alternative to the major parties.

9. One danger for the Democrats that is often discussed is the possibility that minorities and workers will react to Democratic Party's abandonment of the New Deal/Great Society social agenda by taking the 'exit' option of nonvoting. Some analysts, notably Walter Dean Burnham, have argued that this has in fact happened since 1964 among working-class voters. We doubt this scenario. There is little evidence that turnout decline has been disproportionately concentrated among the working class, as we reported in Chapter 7. Furthermore, rising education levels among more recent cohorts of minorities and workers will tend to increase their participation rates, even if other factors drive it down.

10. Proposition 187 was an initiative on the California ballot in November 1994 that outlawed the provision of all state-funded social services to illegal immigrants (who are disproportionately Hispanic).

11. Ruy Teixeira, *The Disappearing American Voter* (Washington, DC: Brookings Institute, 1992); Steven Rosenstone and John M. Hansen, *Mobilization, Participation, and Democracy in America* (New York: MacMillan, 1993).

12. See Dean Lacy and Barry C. Burden, 'The Vote-Stealing and Turnout Effects of Ross Perot in the 1992 U.S. Presidential Election', *American Journal of Political Science*, 43 (1999): 233–55.

13. We note that the relative desirability of this scenario is a key issue separating much of the Democratic Party's mainstream from its left-wing. While both these groups increasingly acknowledge the institutional constraints on viable national coalitions, it is the left that welcomes the possibility of a rejuvenated partnership with reform-oriented social movements as a normatively appealing development.

BIBLIOGRAPHY

Abramson, Paul. 1975. *Generational Change in American Politics*. Lexington, Mass.: Lexington Books.

—— and Ronald Inglehart. 1995. *Value Change in Global Perspective*. Ann Arbor: University of Michigan Press.

—— John H. Aldrich, and David W. Rohde. 1994. *Change and Continuity in the 1992 Elections*. Washington, DC: Congressional Quarterly Press.

Abzug, Bella. 1984. *The Gender Gap*. Boston: Houghton Mifflin.

Acker, Joan. 1973. 'Women and Social Stratification: A Case of Intellectual Sexism'. *American Journal of Sociology* 78: 936–45.

Aldrich, John H. 1995. *Why Parties? The Origins and Transformation of Political Parties in America*. Chicago: University of Chicago Press.

Alford, Robert R. 1963. *Party and Society*. Chicago: Rand-McNally.

Allardt, Erik, and Pertti Pesonen. 1967. 'Cleavages in Finnish Politics'. In *Party Systems and Voter Alignments*, ed. Seymour Martin Lipset and Stein Rokkan, pp. 325–66. New York: Free Press.

Almond, Gabriel, and Sidney Verba. 1965. *The Civic Culture*. Boston: Little Brown.

Alpern, Sara, and Dale Baum. 1985. 'Female Ballots: The Impact of the Nineteenth Amendment'. *Journal of Interdisciplinary History* 26: 43–67.

Alvarez, R. Michael, and John Brehm. 1995. 'American Ambivalence Towards Abortion Policy'. *American Journal of Political Science* 30: 1–25.

—— and Jonathan Nagler. 1995. 'Economics, Issues and the Perot Candidacy: Voter Choice in the 1992 Presidential Election'. *American Journal of Political Science* 39: 714–44.

—— —— 1998. 'Economics, Entitlements, and Social Issues: Voter Choice in the 1996 Presidential Election'. *American Journal of Political Science* 42: 1349–63.

Amenta, Edwin. 1998. *Bold Relief: Institutional Politics and the Origins of Modern American Social Policy*. Princeton: Princeton University Press.

Andersen, Kristi. 1979. *The Creation of a Democratic Majority, 1928–1936*. Chicago: University of Chicago Press.

—— and Elizabeth A. Cook. 1985. 'Women, Work, and Political Attitudes'. *American Journal of Political Science* 29: 606–25.

Anderson, Dewey and Percy Davidson. 1943. *Ballots and the Democratic Class Struggle*. Stanford, Calif.: Stanford University Press.

Asher, Herb. 1995. 'The Perot Campaign'. In *Democracy's Feast*, ed. Herbert F. Weisberg, pp. 153–75. Chatham, NJ: Chatham House Publishers.

Ashford, Douglas. 1987. *The Emergence of the Welfare States*. Oxford: Blackwell.

Axelrod, Robert. 1972. 'Where the Votes Come From: An Analysis of Electoral Coalitions'. *American Political Science Review* 66: 11–20.

—— 1986. 'Presidential Election Coalitions in 1984'. *American Political Science Review* 80: 281–84.

Baltzell, E. Digby. 1964. *The Protestant Establishment*. New York: Random House.

Bancroft, Gertrude. 1958. *The American Labor Force: Its Growth and Changing Composition*. New York: Wiley.

Bartolini, Stefano, and Peter Mair. 1990. *Identity, Competition and Electoral Availability*. New York: Cambridge University Press.

Bass, Harold F. 1987. 'Background to the Debate: A Reader's Guide and Bibliography'. In *The End of Realignment?*, ed. Byron Shafer, pp. 141–78. Madison: University of Wisconsin Press.

Baxter, Sandra, and Marjorie Lansing. 1983. *Women and Politics: The Visible Majority*. Ann Arbor: University of Michigan Press.

Beckhofer, F., and B. Elliott. 1985. 'Persistance and Change: The Petite Bourgeoisie in Industrial Society. *Annual Review of Sociology* 11: 181–207.

Bell, Daniel (ed.). 1963. *The Radical Right*. New York: Doubleday.

—— 1973. *The Coming of Post-Industrial Society*. New York: Basic Books.

—— 1977. 'The Return of the Sacred? The Argument on the Future of Religion'. *British Journal of Sociology* 28: 419–49.

—— 1997 [1967]. *Marxian Socialism in the United States*. Ithaca, NY: Cornell University Press.

Benson, Lee. 1961. *The Concept of Jacksonian Democracy: New York as a Test Case*. Princeton: Princeton University Press.

Berelson, Bernard R., and Paul F. Lazarsfeld. 1945. 'Women: A Major Problem for the P.A.C.' *Public Opinion Quarterly* 9: 79–82.

—— —— and William McPhee. 1954. *Voting: A Study of Opinion Formation in a Presidential Campaign*. Chicago: University of Chicago Press.

Bernard, Jesse. 1982. *The Future of Marriage*. 2nd edn. New Haven, CT: Yale University Press.

Bernhardt, Annette, Martina Morris, and Mark Handcock. 1995. 'Women's Gains, Men's Losses? The Shrinking Gender Gap in Earnings'. *American Journal of Sociology* 101: 302–28.

Bishop, George F., Robert W. Oldendick, and Alfred J. Tuchfarber. 1978. 'Change in the Structure of American Political Attitudes: The Nagging Question of Question Wording'. *American Journal of Political Science* 22: 250–69.

Black, Earl. 1976. *Southern Governors and Political Rights*. Cambridge, Mass.: Harvard University Press.

Blau, Joseph (ed.). 1954. *Social Theories of Jacksonian Democracy: Representative Writings of the Period, 1825–50*. Indianapolis: Bobbs-Merrill.

Bloom, Jack M. 1987. *Class, Race and the Civil Rights Movement*. Bloomington: Indiana University Press.

Bolce, Louis. 1985. 'The Role of Gender in Recent Presidential Elections: Reagan and the Reverse Gender Gap'. *Presidential Studies Quarterly* 15: 372–85.

Bonk, Kathy. 1988. 'The Selling of the "Gender Gap": The Role of Organized Feminism.' In *The Politics of the Gender Gap*, ed. Carol M. Mueller, pp. 82–101. Newbury Park, Calif.: Sage Publications.

Bordo, John. 1954. *The Protestant Clergy and Public Issues, 1812–1848*. Princeton: Princeton University Press.

Bourquez, Julio, Edie N. Goldenberg, and Kim F. Kahn. 1988. 'Press Portrayals of the Gender Gap'. In *The Politics of the Gender Gap*, ed. Carol M. Mueller, pp. 124–47. Newbury Park, Calif.: Sage Publications.

Briggs, B. Bruce (ed.). 1979. *The New Class?* San Diego: Harcourt, Brace.

Brint, Steven. 1984. '"New Class" and Cumulative Trend Explanations of the Liberal Political Attitudes of Professionals'. *American Journal of Sociology* 90: 30–71.

—— 1994. *In an Age of Experts*. Princeton: Princeton University Press.

—— and Susan Kelley. 1993. 'The Social Bases of Political Beliefs in the United States: Interests, Cultures, and Normative Pressures in Comparative-Historical Perspective'. *Research in Political Sociology* 6: 277–317.

Britten, Nicky, and Anthony Heath. 1983. 'Women, Men, and Social Class'. In *Gender, Class, and Work*, ed. Eva Garmarnikow et al., pp. 49–60. London: Heinemann.

Brody, Richard. 1978. 'The Puzzle of Non-Participation'. In *The New American Political System*, ed. Anthony King, pp. 291–99. Washington, DC: American Enterprise Institute.

Brooks, Clem and Jeff Manza. 1994. 'Do Changing Values Explain the New Politics?' *The Sociological Quarterly* 35: 541–70.

—— —— 1997. 'The Social and Ideological Bases of Middle Class Political Realignment in the United States, 1972–1992'. *American Sociological Review* 62: 191–208.

—— —— 1997. 'Class Politics and Political Change in the United States, 1952–1992'. *Social Forces* 79: 379–409.

—— —— 1997. 'Social Cleavages and Political Alignments: U.S. Presidential Elections, 1960–1992', *American Sociological Review* 62: 937–46.

Bruce, Steve. 1988. *The Rise and Fall of the New Christian Right*. New York: Oxford University Press.

—— 1994. 'The Inevitable Failure of the New Christian Right'. *Sociology of Religion* 55: 229–42.

Buell Jr., Emmett H., and Lee Sigelman. 1985. 'An Army that Meets Every Sunday? Popular Support for the Moral Majority in 1980'. *Social Science Quarterly* 66: 426–34.

Buhle, Paul. 1987. *Marxism in the United States*. London: Verso.

Burnham, Walter Dean. 1981. 'The System of 1896: An Analysis'. In *The*

Evolution of American Electoral Systems, ed. Paul Kleppner, pp. 147–202. Westport, Conn.: Greenwood Press.

—— 1981. 'The 1980 Earthquake: Realignment, Reaction, or What?' In *The Hidden Election: Politics and Economics in the 1980 Campaign*, ed. Thomas Ferguson and Joel Rogers, pp. 98–140. New York: Pantheon.

—— 1982. *The Current Crisis in American Politics*. New York: Oxford University Press.

—— 1987. 'The Turnout Problem'. In *Elections American Style*, ed. A. J. Reichley, pp. 97–133. Washington, DC: Brookings Institute.

—— 1997. 'Bill Clinton: Riding the Tiger'. In *The Election of 1996: Reports and Interpretations*, ed. Gerald Pomper et al., pp. 1–20. Chatham, NJ: Chatham House Publishers.

Butler, David, and Dennis Kavanaugh. 1984. *The British General Election of 1983*. New York: St Martin's Press.

Butler, Tim, and Mike Savage (eds.). 1995. *Social Change and the Middle Classes*. London: UCL Press.

Buxton, William. 1985. *Talcott Parsons and the Capitalist Nation-State*. Toronto: University of Toronto Press.

Campbell, Angus, Gerald Gurin, and Warren E. Miller. 1954. *The Voter Decides*. Evanston, Ill.: Row, Peterson.

—— Philip E. Converse, Warren Miller, and Donald E. Stokes. 1960. *The American Voter*. New York: Wiley.

—— —— —— —— (eds.). 1966. *Elections and the Political Order*. New York: Wiley.

Campbell, Bruce A., and Richard J. Trilling (eds.). 1980. *Realignment in American Politics*. Austin: University of Texas Press.

Carmines, Edward G. 1987. 'Unrealized Partisanship: A Theory of Dealignment'. *Journal of Politics* 49: 376–400.

—— and Robert Huckfeldt. 1996. 'Political Behavior: An Overview'. In *The New Handbook of Political Science*, ed. Robert E. Goodin and Hans-Dieter Klingemann, pp. 223–54. New York: Oxford University Press.

—— and Harold W. Stanley. 1992. 'The Transformation of the New Deal Party System: Social Groups, Political Ideology, and Changing Partisanship among Northern Whites, 1972–1988'. *Political Behavior* 14: 213–37.

—— and James Stimson. 1989. *Issue Evolution: Race and the Transformation of American Politics*. Princeton: Princeton University Press.

Carroll, Susan J. 1988. 'Women's Autonomy and the Gender Gap: 1980 and 1982'. In *The Politics of the Gender Gap*, ed. Carol Mueller, pp. 236–57. Newbury Park, Calif.: Sage Publications.

Carter, Stephen. 1993. *The Culture of Disbelief*. New York: Basic Books.

Casanova, Jose. 1994. *Public Religions in the Modern World*. Chicago: University of Chicago Press.

Chaney, Carole, Michael Alvarez, and Jonathan Nagler. 1998. 'Explaining the

Gender Gap in U.S. Presidential Elections, 1980–1992'. *Political Research Quarterly* 51: 311–40.

—— —— 1998. 'Explaining the Gender Gap in the 1992 U.S. Presidential Election'. Unpublished manuscript. Department of Political Science, University of California, Riverside.

Charles, Maria, and David B. Grusky. 1997. 'Models for Describing the Underlying Structure of Sex Segregation'. *American Journal of Sociology* 100: 688–732.

Cherlin, Andrew. 1992. *Marriage, Divorce, Remarriage*. Cambridge, Mass.: Harvard University Press.

Chodorow, Nancy. 1978. *The Reproduction of Mothering*. Berkeley: University of California Press.

Clark, Terry N., Seymour Martin Lipset, and Michael Rempel. 1993. 'The Declining Political Significance of Social Class'. *International Sociology* 8: 293–316.

Clawson, Dan, Alan Neustadtl, and Denise Scott. 1992. *Money Talks: Corporate PACs and Political Influence*. New York: Basic Books.

Coleman, John J. 1996. *Party Decline in America*. Princeton: Princeton University Press.

Collins, Randall. 1979. *The Credential Society*. New York: Academic Press.

Condron, John G., and Joseph B. Tamney. 1985. 'Religious "Nones": 1957 to 1982'. *Sociological Analysis* 46: 415–23.

Conover, Pamela J. 1988. 'The Role of Social Groups in Political Thinking', *British Journal of Political Science* 18: 51–76.

—— 1988. 'Feminists and the Gender Gap'. *Journal of Politics* 50: 985–1010.

Converse, Jean. 1986. *Survey Research in the United States*. Berkeley: University of California Press.

Converse, Philip E. 1964. 'The Nature of Belief Systems in Mass Publics'. In *Ideology and Discontent*, ed. David Apter, pp. 206–61. New York: Free Press.

—— 1974. 'Some Priority Variables in Comparative Electoral Research'. In *Electoral Behavior: A comparative Handbook*, ed. Richard Rose, pp. 727–45. New York: Free Press.

—— Warren Miller, Jerrold G. Rush, and Arthur C. Wolfe. 1969. 'Continuity and Change in American Politics: Parties and Issues in the 1968 Elections'. *American Political Science Review* 63: 1083–1105.

Cook, Elizabeth A. 1989. 'Measuring Feminist Consciousness'. *Women and Politics* 9: 71–88.

—— 1993. 'Feminist Consciousness and Candidate Preference among American Women, 1972–1988'. *Political Behavior* 15: 228–46.

—— and Clyde Wilcox. 1991. 'Feminism and the Gender Gap: A Second Look'. *Journal of Politics* 53: 1111–22.

—— —— 1995. 'Women Voters in the "Year of the Woman"'. In *Democracy's Feast: Elections in America*, ed. Herbert Weisberg, pp. 195–219. Chatham, NJ: Chatham House.

—— Sue Thomas, and Clyde Wilcox (eds.). 1994. *The Year of the Woman.* Boulder, Colo.: Westview Press.

Cook, Rhodes. 1992. 'Democratic Clout is Growing as the Gender Gap Widens'. *Congressional Quarterly Weekly Report* 50: 3265–68.

Crespi, Irving. 1971. 'Structural Sources of the George Wallace Constituency'. *Social Science Quarterly* 52: 115–32.

Dahl, Robert. 1961. *Who Governs?* New Haven: Yale University Press.

—— 1982. *Dilemmas of Pluralist Democracy.* New Haven: Yale University Press.

Dalton, Russell J. 1988. *Citizen Politics in Western Democracies.* Chatham, NJ: Chatham House Publishers.

—— 1996. 'Comparative Politics: Micro-Behavioral Perspectives'. In *A New Handbook of Political Science,* ed. Robert E. Goodin and Hans-Dieter Klingemann, pp. 336–52. New York: Oxford University Press.

—— and Martin P. Wattenberg. 1993. 'The Not So Simple Act of Voting'. In *Political Science: The State of the Discipline II,* ed. Ada Finifter, pp. 193–218. Washington, DC: American Political Science Association.

D'Antonio, Michael. 1992. *Fall from Grace: The Failed Crusade of the Christian Right.* New Brunswick, NJ: Rutgers University Press.

Danziger, Sheldon, and Peter Gottschalk (eds.). 1993. *Uneven Tides: Rising Inequality in America.* New York: Russell Sage.

—— —— 1995. *America Unequal .* Cambridge, Mass.: Harvard University Press.

Davidson, James. 1994. 'Religion among America's Elite: Persistence and Change in the Protestant Establishment'. *Sociology of Religion* 55: 419–40.

—— Ralph E. Pyle, and David V. Reyes. 1995. 'Persistence and Change in the Protestant Establishment, 1930–1992.' *Social Forces* 74: 157–75.

Davis, Nancy, and Robert Robinson. 1996. 'Are the Rumors of War Exaggerated? Religious Orthodoxy and Moral Progressivism in America'. *American Journal of Sociology* 102: 756–87.

Dawson, Michael C. 1994. *Behind the Mule.* Princeton: Princeton University Press.

—— and Ernest J. Wilson. 1991. 'Paradigms and Paradoxes: Political Science and African American Politics'. In *Political Science: Looking to the Future,* volume 1, ed. William P. Crotty, pp. 189–234. Evanston, Ill.: Northwestern University Press.

Deitch, Cynthia. 1988. 'Sex Differences in Support for Government Spending'. In *The Politics of the Gender Gap,* ed. Carol Mueller, pp. 192–216. Newbury Park, Calif.: Sage Publications.

Delli Carpini, Michael, and Scott Keeter. 1996. *What Americans Know about Politics and Why It Matters.* New Haven: Yale University Press.

Delphy, Christine. 1984. *Close to Home: A Materialist Analysis of Women's Oppression.* Amherst: University of Massachusetts Press.

Dennis, Jack. 1987. 'Groups and Political Behavior: Legitimation, Deprivation, and Competing Values'. *Political Behavior* 9: 323–72.

Derber, Charles, William Schwartz, and Yale Magrass. 1990. *Power in the Highest Degree.* New York: Oxford University Press.

DeSipio, Louis. 1996. *Counting on the Latino Vote.* Charlottesville: University of Virginia Press.

Diamond, Sara. 1995. *Roads to Dominion: Right-Wing Movements and Political Power in the United States.* New York: Guilford Press.

Diggins, John P. 1992. *The Rise and Fall of the American Left.* New York: Norton.

Dionne, E. J. 1981. 'Catholics and the Democrats: Estrangement But Not Desertion'. In *Party Coalitions in the 1980s*, ed. Seymour Martin Lipset, pp. 307–25. San Francisco: Institute for Contemporary Studies.

—— 1991. *Why Americans Hate Politics.* New York: Simon and Shuster.

Dogan, Mattei. 1967. 'Political Cleavage and Social Stratification in France and Italy'. In *Party Systems and Voter Alignments*, ed. Seymour Martin Lipset and Stein Rokkan, pp. 129–96. New York: Free Press.

Domhoff, G. William. 1990. *The Power Elite and the State.* New York: Aldine de Gruyter.

Douglas, Mary, and Steven Tipton (eds.). 1982. *Religion and America: Spirituality in a Secular Age.* Boston: Beacon Press.

Downs, Anthony. *An Economic Theory of Democracy.* New York: Harper, 1957.

Dreisbach, Daniel. 1997. 'Introduction: A Debate on Religion and Politics in the Early Republic'. In *Religion and Politics in the Early Republic: Jasper Adams and the Church/State Debate*, ed. Daniel Dreisbach, pp. 1–36. Lexington: University of Kentucky Press.

D'Souza, Dinesh. 1995. *The End of Racism.* New York: Free Press.

Duverger, Maurice. 1955. *The Political Role of Women.* Paris: UNESCO.

Eckstein, Harry. 1966. *Division and Cohesion in Democracy.* Princeton: Princeton University Press.

Edsall, Thomas. 1984. *The New Politics of Inequality.* New York: Norton.

—— with Mary Edsall. 1991. *Chain Reaction: The Impact of Race, Rights, and Taxes on American Politics.* New York: Norton.

Ehrenreich, John, and Barbara Ehrenreich. 1979. 'The Professional-Managerial Class'. In *Between Labor and Capital*, ed. Pat Walker, pp. 5–49. Boston: South End Press.

Elshtain, Jean Bethke. 1984. 'Reclaiming the Socialist-Feminist Citizen'. *Socialist Review* 74: 23–30.

Engels, Friedrich. 1978 [1895]. 'The Tactics of Social Democracy'. In *The Marx/Engels Reader*, ed. Robert W. Tucker, pp. 556–73. New York: Norton.

Erie, Steven P., and Martin Rein. 1988. 'Women and the Welfare State'. In *The Politics of the Gender Gap*, ed. Carol Mueller, pp. 173–91. Newbury Park, Calif.: Sage Publications.

Erikson, Robert, and John H. Goldthorpe. 1993. *The Constant Flux*. Oxford: Clarendon Press.

Erikson, Robert, S. and Kent L. Tedin. 1981. 'The 1928–1936 Partisan Realignment: The Case for the Conversion Hypothesis'. *American Political Science Review* 75: 951–65.

—— Thomas D. Lancaster, and David W. Romero. 1989. 'Group Components of the Presidential Vote, 1952–84'. *Journal of Politics* 51: 337–46.

—— Norman R. Luttbeg, and Kent L. Tedin. 1988. *American Public Opinion: Its Origins, Content and Impact*. New York: MacMillan.

Esping-Andersen, Gosta. 1992. 'Postindustrial Cleavage Structures: A Comparison of Evolving Patterns of Social Stratification in Germany, Sweden and the United States'. In *Labor Parties in Postindustrial Societies*, ed. Frances Fox Piven, pp. 147–68. New York: Oxford University Press.

—— (ed.). 1993. *Changing Classes: Stratification and Mobility in Post-Industrial Societies*. Newbury Park, Calif.: Sage Publications.

Fair, Roy C. 1996. "The Effect of Economic Events on Votes for President: 1992 Update." *Political Behavior*, 18: 119–39.

Fantasia, Rick. 1988. *Cultures of Solidarity*. Berkeley: University of California Press.

Farley, Reynolds. 1984. *Blacks and Whites: Narrowing the Gap?* Cambridge, Mass.: Harvard University Press.

—— and Walter R. Allen. 1987. *The Color Line and the Quality of Life in America*. New York: Russell Sage.

Feltner, Paula, and Leneen Goldie. 1974. 'The Impact of Socialization and Personality on the Female Voter: Speculations Tested with 1964 Presidential Data'. *Western Political Quarterly* 27: 680–92.

Ferguson, Thomas, and Joel Rogers. 1986. *Right Turn: The Decline of the Democrats and the Future of American Politics*. New York: Hill and Wang.

Ferree, Myra Marx. 1980. 'Working Class Feminism: A Consideration of the Consequences of Employment'. *Sociological Quarterly* 21: 173–84.

Finke, Roger, and Rodney Stark. 1992. *The Churching of America, 1776–1980*. New Brunswick, NJ: Rutgers University Press.

Fiorina, Morris. 1981. *Retrospective Voting in American National Elections*. New Haven: Yale University Press.

—— 1994. 'The Electorate at the Polls in the 1990's'. In *The Parties Respond: Changes in American Parties and Campaigns*, 2nd edn., ed. Sandy Maisel, pp. 123–42. Boulder, Colo.: Westview Press.

Fischer, Claude, et al. 1996. *Inequality by Design*. Princeton: Princeton University Press.

Flanigan, William H., and Nancy Zingale. 1994. *Political Behavior of the American Electorate*, 5th edn. Washington, DC: Congressional Quarterly Press.

Forbath, William. 1991. *Law and the Shaping of the American Labor Movement*. Cambridge, Mass.: Harvard University Press.

Form, William. 1985. *Divided We Stand: Working Class Stratification in America*. Urbana: University of Illinois Press.

—— 1995. *Segmented Labor, Fractured Politics*. New York: Plenum.

Formisano, Ronald P. 1971. *The Birth of Mass Political Parties: Michigan, 1827–1891*. Princeton: Princeton University Press.

—— 1983. *The Transformation of Political Culture: Massachusetts Parties, 1790s–1840s*. New York: Oxford University Press.

Fowler, Robert B., and Allen D. Hertzke. 1995. *Religion and Politics in America: Faith, Culture, and Strategic Choices*. Boulder, Colo.: Westview Press.

Frank, Robert H., and Philip J. Cook. 1995. *The Winner-Take-All Society*. New York: Free Press.

Franklin, Mark. 1985. *The Decline of Class Voting in Britain*. New York: Oxford University Press.

—— 1992. 'The Decline of Cleavage Politics'. In *Electoral Change*, ed. Mark Franklin, Thomas Mackie, and Henry Valen, pp. 383–405. New York: Cambridge University Press.

—— Thomas Mackie, and Henry Valen. 1992. 'Introduction'. In *Electoral Change*, ed. Mark Franklin, Thomas Mackie, and Henry Valen, pp. 3–32. New York: Cambridge University Press.

Frankovic, Kathleen. 1982. 'Sex and Politics: New Alignments, Old Issues'. *PS* 15: 439–48.

Fraser, Steve, and Gary Gerstle (eds.). 1989. *The Rise and Fall of the New Deal Order, 1930–1980*. Princeton: Princeton University Press.

Freeman, Jo. 1993. 'Feminism and Family Values: Women at the 1992 Democratic and Republican Conventions.' *PS: Political Science & Politics* 26: 21–28.

—— 1997. 'Forward'. In *Women in Modern American Politics: A Bibliography*, ed. Elizabeth M. Cox, pp. xiii-xiv. Washington, DC: Congressional Quarterly Inc.

Friedson, Eliot. 1986. *Professional Powers*. Chicago: University of Chicago Press.

Gallup Jr., George. 1985. 'Religion in American 50 Years: 1935–1985'. Gallup Report No. 236. Princeton: Gallup.

—— and Jim Castelli. 1989. *The People's Religion*. New York: MacMillan.

Gamm, Gerald. 1986. *The Making of the New Deal Democrats*. Chicago: University of Chicago Press.

Gavin, William. 1975. *Street Corner Conservative*. New Rochelle, NY: Arlington House.

Gerson, Kathleen. 1985. *Hard Choices: How Women Decide about Work, Career, and Motherhood*. Berkeley: University of California Press.

—— 1987. 'Emerging Social Divisions Among Women: Implications for Welfare State Policies'. *Politics and Society* 15: 213–21.

Giddens, A. 1994. *The Next Left*. Stanford, Calif.: Stanford University Press.

—— 1994. *Beyond Left and Right*. Stanford: Stanford University Press.

Gilbert, Christopher P. 1993. *The Impact of Churches on Political Behavior: An Empirical Study.* Westport, Conn.: Greenwood Publishers.

Gilens, Martin. 1988. 'Gender and Support for Reagan: A Comprehensive Model of Presidential Approval'. *American Journal of Political Science* 32: 19–49.

Giles, Michael, and Kaenen Hertz. 1994. 'Racial Threat and Partisan Identification'. *American Political Science Review* 88: 316–26.

Gilligan, Carol. 1982. *In a Different Voice: Psychological Theory and Women's Development.* Cambridge, Mass.: Harvard University Press.

Glaser, James M. 1994. 'Back to the Black Belt: Racial Environment and White Racial Attitudes'. *Journal of Politics* 56: 21–41.

Glenn, Norval D. 1987. 'The Trend in "No Religion" Respondents to U.S. National Surveys, Late 1950s to Early 1980s'. *Public Opinion Quarterly* 51: 293–314.

Glock, Charles Y., and Rodney Stark. 1965. *Religion and Society in Tension.* Chicago: Random House.

Goldfield, Michael. 1989. *The Decline of Organized Labor in the United States,* Chicago: University of Chicago Press.

—— 1997. *The Color of Politics.* New York: New Press.

Goldthorpe, John H. 1982. 'On the Service Class, Its Formation and Future'. In *The New Working Class*, ed. Richard Hyman and Robert Price, pp. 162–85. London: MacMillan.

—— 1983. 'Women and Class Analysis: In Defence of the Conventional View'. *Sociology* 17: 465–88.

—— 1984. 'Women and Class Analysis: A Reply to the Replies'. *Sociology* 18: 491–99.

—— 1987. *Class Structure and Social Mobility in Britain,* New York: Oxford University Press.

—— 1995. 'The Service Class Revisited'. In *Social Change and the Middle Class*, ed. Tim Butler and Mike Savage, pp. 313–29. London: UCL Press.

Goodwyn, L. Democratic Promise: The Populist moment in America. New York: Oxford University Press, 1976.

Gouldner, Alvin. 1979. *The Future of Intellectuals and the Rise of the New Class.* New York: Continuum.

Greeley, Andrew. 1977. *The American Catholic: A Social Portrait.* New York: Basic Books.

—— 1985. *American Catholics since the Council: An Unauthorized Report.* Chicago: Thomas More.

—— 1989. *Religious Change in America.* Cambridge, Mass.: Harvard University Press.

—— 1990. *The Catholic Myth.* New York: Scribner's.

—— 1991. 'American Exceptionalism: The Religious Phenomenon'. In *Is America Different?*, ed. Byron E. Shafer, pp. 94–115. New York: Oxford University Press.

Green, John C., and James L. Guth. 1991. 'The Bible and the Ballot Box: The Shape of Things to Come'. In *The Bible and the Ballot Box*, ed. James Guth and John Green, pp. 207–26. Boulder, Colo.: Westview Press.

Greenberg, Stanley. 1997. 'Popularizing Progressive Politics'. In *The New Majority*, ed. Stanley Greenberg and Theda Skocpol, pp. 279–98. New Haven, Conn.: Yale University Press.

Grusky, David B. (ed.). 1994. *Social Stratification*. Boulder, Colo.: Westview Press.

—— and Jesper B. Sorensen. 1998. 'Can Class Analysis Be Salvaged?' *American Journal of Sociology* 103: 1187–1234.

Guinier, Lani. 1994. *Tyranny of the Majority*. New York: Free Press.

Gurin, Patricia. 1985. 'Women's Gender Consciousness'. *Political Opinion Quarterly* 49: 143–63.

—— Arthur H. Miller, and Gerald Gurin. 1980. 'Stratum Identification and Consciousness', *Social Psychology Quarterly* 43: 30–47.

Hadaway, C. Kirk, Penny L. Marler, and Mark Chaves. 1993. 'What the Polls Don't Show: A Closer Look at U.S. Church Attendance'. *American Sociological Review* 58: 741–52.

—— —— —— 1998. 'Over-reporting Church Attendance in America: Evidence That Demands the Same Verdict'. *American Sociological Review* 64: 122–30.

Hadden, Jeffrey. 1969. *The Gathering Storm in the Churches*. Garden City, NY: Anchor.

Hall, John R. 1997. 'The Reworking of Class Analysis'. In *Reworking Class*, ed. John R. Hall, pp. 1–37. Ithaca, NY: Cornell University Press.

Halle, David. 1984. *America's Working Man*. Chicago: University of Chicago Press.

—— and Frank Romo. 1991. 'The Blue Collar Working Class: Continuity and Change'. In *America at Century's End*, ed. Alan Wolfe, pp. 152–84. Berkeley: University of California Press.

Hamilton, R. *Class and Politics in the United States*. New York: Wiley, 1972.

Harris, Louis. 1954. *Is There a Republican Majority?* New York: Harper & Row.

Hartmann, Heidi. 1981. 'The Family as the Locus of Gender, Class, and Political Struggle'. *Signs* 6: 366–94.

—— 1981. 'The Unhappy Marriage of Marxism and Feminism'. In *Women and Revolution*, ed. Lydia Sargent, pp. 1–38. Boston: South End Press.

Harvey, David. 1989. *The Condition of Postmodernity*. Oxford: Blackwell.

Hattam, Victoria C. 1993. *Labor Visions and State Power*. Princeton: Princeton University Press.

Hays, Samuel P. 1980. *American Political History as Social Analysis: Essays*. Knoxville: University of Tennessee.

Heath, Anthony, Roger Jowell, and John Curtice. 1985. *How Britain Votes*. London: Pergamon.

—— —— —— 1987. 'Trendless Fluctuation: A Reply to Crewe'. *Political Studies* 35: 256–77.

—— et al. 1991. *Understanding Political Change: The British Voter, 1964–87.* London: Pergamon.

—— Bridget Taylor, and Gabor Toka. 1993. 'Religion, Morality and Politics'. In *International Social Attitudes: The Tenth BSA Report*, ed. Roger Jowell, Lindsay Brook, and Lizanne Dowds, pp. 49–80. Aldershot, England: Dartmouth.

Herberg, Will. 1960. *Protestant, Catholic, Jew: An Essay in American Religious Sociology.* Garden City, NY: Doubleday.

Hess, Robert D., and Judith V. Tourney. 1967. *The Development of Political Attitudes in Children.* Chicago: Aldine.

Hibbs, Douglas. 1982. 'The Dynamics of Political Support for American Presidents among Occupational and Partisan Groups'. *American Journal of Political Science* 26: 313–32.

—— 1987. *The American Political Economy.* Cambridge, Mass.: Harvard University Press.

Himmelstein, Jerome L. 1990. *To the Right: The Transformation of American Conservatism.* Berkeley: University of California Press.

Hixon, William B. 1992. *Search for the American Right Wing.* Princeton: Princeton University Press.

Hochschild, Arlie. 1989. *The Second Shift.* New York: Avon.

Hoge, Dean R. 1979. 'A Test of Theories of Denominational Growth and Decline'. In *Understanding Church Growth and Decline, 1950–1978*, ed. Dean Hoge and David A. Roozen. pp. 179–98. New York: Pilgrim Press.

Holden, Karen C., and Pamela J. Smock. 1991. 'The Economic Costs of Marital Dissolution'. *Annual Review of Sociology* 17: 51–78.

Hout, Michael. 1988. 'More Universalism, Less Structural Mobility'. *American Journal of Sociology* 93: 1358–1400.

—— forthcoming. 'The Terms of the Debate: Abortion Politics in the United States, 1972–1996'. *Gender Studies.*

—— Clem Brooks, and Jeff Manza. 1994. 'The Democratic Class Struggle in the United States, 1948–1992'. Paper presented at the World Congress of the International Sociology Association, Bielefeld, Germany, July 18–24.

—— —— —— 1995. 'The Democratic Class Struggle in the United States, 1948–1992'. *American Sociological Review* 60: 805–28.

—— and Andrew Greeley. 1987. 'The Center Doesn't Hold', *American Sociological Review* 52: 325–45.

—— —— 1998. 'What Church Officials' Reports Don't Show'. *American Sociological Review* 64: 113–19.

—— and Robert Hauser. 1992. 'Hierarchy and Symmetry in Social Mobility'. *European Sociological Review* 8: 239–66.

Huckfeldt, Robert, and Carol W. Kohfeld. 1989. *Race and the Decline of Class in American Politics.* Urbana: University of Illinois Press.

—— and John Sprague. 1995. *Citizens, Politics and Social Communication: Information and Influence in an Election Campaign*. New York: Cambridge University Press.

Hunter, James D. 1980. 'The New Class and the Young Evangelicals'. *Review of Religious Research* 22: 155–69.

—— 1982. 'Operationalizing Evangelicalism: A Review, Critique, and Proposal'. *Sociological Analysis* 42: 363–72.

—— 1983. *American Evangelicalism: Conservative Religion and the Quandry of Modernity*. New Brunswick, NJ: Rutgers University Press.

—— 1991. *Culture Wars: The Struggle to Define America*. New York: Basic Books.

Hyman, Herbert, and Charles Wright. 1979. *Education's Lasting Influence on Values* Chicago: University of Chicago Press.

Inglehart, Ronald. 1977. *The Silent Revolution*. Princeton: Princeton University Press.

—— 1990. *Culture Shift in Advanced Industrial Society*. Princeton: Princeton University Press.

—— 1997. *Modernization and Post-Modernization*. Princeton: Princeton University Press.

Jackman, Mary. 1978. 'General and Applied Tolerance: Does Education Increase Commitment to Racial Integration?' *American Journal of Political Science* 22: 302–24.

Jelen, Ted. G. 1987. 'The Effects of Religious Separatism on White Protestants in the 1984 Presidential Election'. *Sociological Analysis* 48: 30–45.

Jenkins, J. Craig, and Kevin Leicht. 1997. 'Class Analysis and Social Movements: A Critique and Reformulation'. In *Reworking Class*, ed. John R. Hall, pp. 369–97. Ithaca, NY: Cornell University Press.

Jennings, M. Kent. 1988. 'Preface'. In *The Politics of the Gender Gap*, ed. Carol Mueller, pp. 7–12. Newbury Park, Calif.: Sage Publications.

Jensen, Richard. 1971. *The Winning of the Midwest: Social and Political Conflict, 1888–1896*. Chicago: University of Chicago Press.

Kalmijn, Matthijs. 1991. 'Shifting Boundaries: Trends in Religious and Educational Homogamy'. *American Sociological Review* 56: 786–800.

Karabel, Jerome. 1979. 'The Failure of American Socialism Reconsidered'. *Socialist Register* 18: 204–27.

Kazin, Michael. 1995. *The Populist Persuasion: An American History*. New York: Basic Books.

Keith, Bruce, et al. 1991. *The Myth of the Independent Voter*. Berkeley: University of California Press.

Kellner, Hansfried, and Frank Heuberger (eds.). 1992. *The Hidden Technocrats*. New Brunswick, NJ: Transaction Publishers.

Kellstedt, Lyman A. 1989. 'Evangelicals and Political Realignment'. In *Contemporary Evangelical Political Evolvement*, ed. Corwin Schmidt, pp. 99–117. Lanham, Md.: University Presses of America.

—— and John C. Green. 1993. 'Knowing God's Many People: Denominational Preference and Political Behavior'. In *Rediscovering the Religious Factor in American Politics*, ed. David Leege and Lyman Kellstedt, pp. 53–71. Armonk, NY: M. E. Sharpe.

—— and Mark. A. Noll. 1990. 'Religion, Voting for President, and Party Identification, 1948–1984'. In *Religion and American Politics: From the Colonial Period to the 1980s*, ed. Mark A. Noll, pp. 355–79. New York: Oxford University Press.

—— John C. Green, James L. Guth, and Corwin E. Schmidt. 1994. 'Religious Voting Blocs in the 1992 Election: Year of the Evangelical?' *Sociology of Religion* 55: 307–26.

Kelly, Dean M. 1972. *Why Conservative Churches Are Growing*. New York: Harper and Row.

Kelly, Rita Mae, and Mary Boutilier. 1974. *The Making of Political Women: A Study of Socialization and Role Conflict*. Chicago: Nelson-Hall.

Kenski, Henry C., and William Lockwood. 1991. 'Catholic Voting Behavior in 1988: A Critical Swing Vote'. In *The Bible and the Ballot Box*, ed. James L. Guth and John C. Green, pp. 173–87. Boulder, Colo.: Westview Press.

Key, V. O. 1949. *Southern Politics*. New York: Knopf.

—— 1955. 'A Theory of Critical Elections', *Journal of Politics* 17: 3–18.

—— 1959. 'Secular Realignments and the Party System'. *Journal of Politics* 21: 198–210.

—— 1964. *Politics, Parties & Pressure Groups*, 5th edn. New York: Crowell.

—— and Frank Munger. 1959. 'Social Determinism and Electoral Decision: The Case of Indiana'. In *American Voting Behavior*, ed. Eugene Burdick and Arthur J. Brodbeck, pp. 281–99. Glencoe, Ill.: The Free Press.

Kiewiet, D. Roderick. 1983. *Macroeconomics and Micropolitics*. Chicago: University of Chicago Press.

Kinder, Donald R., and D. Roderick Kiewiet. 1981. 'Sociotropic Politics: The American Case', *British Journal of Political Science* 11: 129–61.

—— and Lynn Sanders. 1996. *Divided by Color*. Chicago: University of Chicago Press.

King, Gary. 1997. *A Solution to the Ecological Inference Problem*. Princeton: Princeton University Press.

Kingston, Paul W., and Steven E. Finkel. 1987. 'Is There a Marriage Gap in Politics?' *Journal of Marriage and the Family* 49: 57–64.

Klein, Ethel. 1984. *Gender Politics*. Cambridge, Mass.: Harvard University Press.

—— 1985. 'The Gender Gap: Different Issues, Different Answers'. *Brookings Review* Winter: 33–37.

Kleppner, Paul. 1970. *The Cross of Culture: A Social Analysis of Midwestern Politics, 1850–1900*. New York: Free Press.

—— 1979. *The Third Electoral System: 1853–1892*. Chapel Hill: University of North Carolina Press.

Knoke, David. 1976. *The Social Bases of Political Parties*. Baltimore: Johns Hopkins University Press.

Koch, Jeffrey W. 1993. 'Is Group Membership a Prerequisite for Group Identification?' *Political Behavior* 15: 49–60.

—— 1995. *Social Reference Groups and Political Life*. Lanham, Md.: University Press of America.

Kohn, Melvin L. 1969. *Class and Conformity*. Homewood, Ill.: Dorsey Press.

Kuttner, Robert. 1987. *The Life of the Party*. New York: Penguin.

Lacy, Dean, and Barry C. Burden. 1999. 'The Vote-Stealing and Turnout Effects of Ross Perot in the 1992 U.S. Presidential Election'. *American Journal of Political Science* 43: 233–55.

Ladd, Everett C. 1976–77. 'Liberalism Upside Down: The Inversion of the New Deal Order'. *Political Science Quarterly* 91: 577–600.

—— with Charles Hadley. 1975. *Transformations of the American Party System*. New York: Norton.

Lamont, Michele. 1987. 'Cultural Capital and the Liberal Political Attitudes of Professionals: Comment on Brint'. *American Journal of Sociology* 92: 1501–06.

Larson, Magali Sarfetti. 1977. *The Rise of Professionalism*. Berkeley: University of California Press.

Lash, Scott, and John Urry. 1987. *The End of Organized Capitalism*. Madison: University of Wisconsin Press.

Lawrence, David. 1997. *The Collapse of the Democratic Majority*. Boulder, Colo.: Westview Press.

Layman, Geoffrey C. 1997. 'Religion and Political Behavior in the United States: The Impact of Beliefs, Affiliations, and Commitment from 1980 to 1994'. *Public Opinion Quarterly* 61: 288–316.

Lazarsfeld, Paul F., Bernard R. Berelson, and Hazel Gaudet. 1948. *The People's Choice*. New York: Columbia University Press.

Leege, David C. 1988. 'Catholics and the Civic Order: Parish Participation, Politics, and Civic Participation'. *Review of Politics* 50: 704–37.

—— 1993. 'Religion and Politics in Theoretical Perspective'. In *Rediscovering the Religious Factor in American Politics*, ed. David Leege and Lyman Kellstedt, pp. 3–25. Armonk, NY: M. E. Sharpe.

—— 1993. 'The Decomposition of the Religious Vote: A Comparison of White, Non-Hispanic Catholics with Other Ethnoreligious Groups, 1960–1992'. Paper presented at the Annual Meetings of the American Political Science Association, Washington, DC., September 2–5.

—— 1996. 'Religiosity Measures in the National Election Studies: A Guide to their Use, Part 1'. *Votes & Opinions* 2: 6–9, 33–36.

—— and Lyman A. Kellstedt (eds.). 1993. *Rediscovering the Religious Factor in American Politics*. Armonk, NY: M. E. Sharpe.

Leighley, Jan E., and Jonathan Nagler. 1992. 'Socioeconomic Class Bias in

Turnout: The Voters Remain the Same'. *American Political Science Review* 86: 725–36.

—— —— 1992. 'Individual and Systemic Influences on Turnout: Who Votes? 1984'. *Journal of Politics* 54: 718–40.

Lemons, J. Stanley. 1977. *The Woman Citizen: Social Feminism in the 1920s.* 2nd edn. Chicago: University of Chicago Press.

Lenski, Gerhard. 1963. *The Religious Factor.* New York: Doubleday.

Levy, Frank. 1995. 'Incomes and Income Inequality'. In *The State of the Union*, volume I, ed. Reynolds Farley, pp. 1–57. New York: Russell Sage Foundation.

—— 1998. *The New Dollars and Dreams.* New York: Russell Sage.

Lewis-Beck, Michael, and Tom W. Rice. 1992. *Forecasting Elections.* Washington, DC: Congressional Quarterly Press.

Lieberman, Robert C. 1998. *Shifting the Color Line.* Cambridge, Mass.: Harvard University Press.

Liebman, Robert C., John R. Sutton, and Robert Wuthnow. 1988. 'Exploring the Social Sources of Denominationalism: Schisms in American Protestant Denominations, 1890–1980'. *American Sociological Review* 53: 343–52.

Lijphart, Arend. 1979. 'Religious vs. Linguistic vs. Class Voting'. *American Political Science Review* 73: 442–58.

Linder, Marc. 1994. *Farewell to the Self-Employed.* Westport, Conn.: Greenwood Press.

—— and John Houghton. 1990. 'Self-Employment and the Petty Bourgeoisie: Comment on Steinmetz and Wright'. *American Journal of Sociology* 96: 727–34

Lipset, Seymour Martin. 1970. 'Religion and Politics in the American Past and Present'. In *Revolution and Counterrevolution*, pp. 305–73. New York: Anchor Press.

—— 1981 [1960]. *Political Man.* Expanded edition. Baltimore: Johns Hopkins University Press.

—— 1981. 'Party Coalitions and the 1980 Election'. In *Party Coalitions in the 1980s*, ed. Seymour Martin Lipset, pp. 15–46. San Francisco: Institute for Contemporary Studies.

—— 1996. 'Steady Work: An Academic Memoir'. *Annual Review of Sociology* 22: 1–27.

—— 1996. *American Exceptionalism: A Double-Edged Sword.* New York: Norton.

—— Paul Lazarsfeld, Allan Barton, and Juan Linz. 1954. 'The Psychology of Voting: An Analysis of Political Behavior'. In *Handbook of Social Psychology*, ed. Gardiner Lindzey, pp. 1124–75. Cambridge, Mass.: Addison-Wesley.

—— and Earl Raab. 1978. *The Politics of Unreason: Right-Wing Extremism in America, 1790–1970.* Chicago: University of Chicago Press.

—— —— 1995. *Jews and the New American Scene.* Cambridge, Mass.: Harvard University Press.

—— and Stein Rokkan. 1967. 'Cleavage Structures, Party Systems, and Voter

Alignments: An Introduction'. In *Party Systems and Voter Alignments*, ed. S. M. Lipset and Stein Rokkan, pp. 1–64. New York: Free Press.

Lo, Clarence. 1990. *Small Property versus Big Government*. Berkeley: University of California Press.

Lopatto, Paul. 1985. *Religion and the Presidential Election*. New York: Praeger.

Lubell, Samuel. 1965. *The Future of American Politics*. 3rd edn. New York: Harper & Row.

McClosky, Herbert, and Alida Brill. 1983. *Dimensions of Tolerance: What Americans Believe about Civil Liberties*. New York: Russell Sage.

McCormick, Richard P. 1966. *The Second American Part System*. Chapel Hill: University of North Carolina Press.

McKenzie, Robert T., and Allan Silver. 1968. *Angels in Marble: Working Class Conservaties in Urban England*. Chicago: University of Chicago Press.

McLanahan, Sara, and Lynne Casper. 1995. 'Growing Diversity and Inequality in the American Family'. In *The State of the Union*, ed. Reynolds Farley, pp. 1–46. New York: Russell Sage.

Machung, Anne. 1989. 'Talking Career, Thinking Job: Gender Differences in Career and Family Expectations of Berkeley Seniors'. *Feminist Studies* 15: 35–58.

Mann, Michael. 1995. 'Sources of Variation in Working Class Movements in Twentieth-Century Europe'. *New Left Review* 212: 14–54.

Mansbridge, Jane. 1985. 'Myth and Reality: The ERA and the Gender Gap in the 1980 Election'. *Public Opinion Quarterly* 49: 164–78.

Manza, Jeff, and Clem Brooks. 1997.'The Religious Factor in U.S. Presidential Elections, 1960–1992'. *American Journal of Sociology* 103: 38–81.

—— —— 1998. 'The Gender Gap in U.S. Presidential Elections: When? Why? Implications?' *American Journal of Sociology* 103 (1998): 1235–66.

—— Michael Hout, and Clem Brooks. 1995. 'Class Voting in Capitalist Democracies since World War II: Dealignment, Realignment, or Trendless Fluctuation?' *Annual Review of Sociology* 21: 137–63.

Markoff, John. 1996. *Waves of Democracy*. Thousand Oaks, Calif.: Pine Forge Press.

Marshall, Gordon, David Rose, Howard Newby, and Carolyn Vogler. 1988. *Social Class in Modern Britain*. London: Unwin Hyman.

Massey, Douglas, and Nancy Denton. 1993. *American Apartheid*. Cambridge, Mass.: Harvard University Press.

Melich, Tanya. 1996. *The Republican War Against Women*. New York: Bantam Books.

Merriam, Charles E., and H. F. Gosnell. 1924. *Non-Voting: Causes and Methods of Control*. Chicago: University of Chicago Press.

Merton, Robert, K. *Social Theory and Social Structure*. New York: Free Press, 1957.

Miliband, Ralph. 1977. *Marxism and Politics*. New York: Oxford University Press.

Milkman, Ruth, and Eleanor Townsley. 1994. 'Gender and the Economy'. In *The Handbook of Economic Sociology*, ed. Neil Smelser and Richard Swedberg, pp. 600–19. Princeton: Princeton University Press.

Miller, Arthur, H. 1988. 'Gender and the Vote: 1984'. In *The Politics of the Gender Gap*, ed. Carol M. Mueller, pp. 258–82. Newbury Park, Calif.: Sage Publications.

—— Patricia Gurin, Gerald Gurin, and Oksana Malanchuk. 1981. 'Group Consciousness and Political Participation'. *American Journal of Political Science* 25: 494–511.

—— Anne Hildreth, and Grace L. Simmons. 1988. 'The Mobilization of Gender Group Consciousness'. In *The Political Interests of Gender*, ed. Kathleen B. Jones and Anna G. Jonasdottir, pp. 106–34. Newbury Park, Calif.: Sage Publications.

—— and Brad Lockerbie. 1992. 'The United States of America', in *Electoral Change*, ed. Mark Franklin, Thomas Mackie, and Henry Valen, pp. 362–80. New York: Cambridge University Press.

—— and Martin P. Wattenberg. 1984. 'Politics from the Pulpit: Religiosity and the 1980 Elections'. *Public Opinion Quarterly* 48: 301–17.

—— Christopher Wlezien, and Anne Hildreth. 1991. 'A Reference Group Theory of Partisan Coalitions'. *Journal of Politics* 53: 1134–49.

Miller, Warren E., and J. Merrill Shanks. 1996. *The New American Voter*. Cambridge, Mass.: Harvard University Press.

Mills, C. Wright. 1951. *White Collar*. New York: Oxford University Press.

—— 1956. *The Power Elite*. New York: Oxford University Press.

Milton, J. Gordon. 1996. *Encyclopedia of American Religions*. 5th edn. Detroit: Gale Research.

Mishel, Lawrence (comp). 1999. *The State of Working America 1998*. Ithaca, NY: Cornell University Press.

Morris, Martina, and Bruce Western. 1999. 'Inequality in Earnings at the Close of the 20th Century'. *Annual Review of Sociology* 25: in press.

Mueller, Carol. 1991. 'The Gender Gap and Women's Political Influence'. *Annals of the American Academy of Political and Social Sciences* 515: 23–37.

Murrin, John M. 1990. 'Religion and Politics in America from the First Settlements to the Civil War.' In *Religion and American Politics*, ed. Mark Noll, pp. 19–43. New York: Oxford University Press.

Myrdal, Gunnar. 1944. *An American Dilemma: The Negro Problem and Modern Democracy*. New York: Harper.

National Research Council. 1989. *Blacks and American Society*. Washington, DC: National Academy of Sciences Press.

National Urban League. 1997. *The State of Black America 1996*. Washington, DC: National Urban League.

Neuhaus, Richard J. 1984. *The Naked Public Square*. Grand Rapids, Mich.: Eerdmans.

Nie, Norman H., Sidney Verba and John R. Petrocik. 1981. *The Changing American Voter*, 2nd edn. Cambridge, Mass.: Harvard University Press.

Nieuwbeerta, Paul. 1996. 'The Democratic Class Struggle in Postwar Societies: Class Voting in Twenty Countries, 1945–1990'. *Acta Sociologica* 39: 345–84.

—— and Wout Ultee. Forthcoming. 'Class Voting in Western Industrialized Countries, 1945–1990: Systematizing and Testing Explanations'. *European Journal of Political Research*.

Norris, Pippa. 1985. 'The Gender Gap in Britain and America'. *Parliamentary Affairs* 38: 192–201.

—— 1988. 'The Gender Gap: A Cross-National Trend?' In *The Politics of the Gender Gap*, ed. Carol M. Mueller, pp. 217–34. Newbury Park, Calif.: Sage Publications.

Nunn, Clyde Z., Harry J. Crockett, Jr., and J. Allen Williams, Jr. 1978. *Tolerance for Nonconformity*. San Francisco: Jossey-Bass.

Oestreicher, Richard. 1988. 'Urban Working-Class Political Behavior and Theories of American Electoral Politics, 1870–1940'. *Journal of American History* 74: 1257–86.

Offe, Claus. 1985. 'New Social Movements: Challenging the Boundaries of Institutional Politics'. *Social Research* 52: 817–68.

—— 1987. *Disorganized Capitalism*. Cambridge, Mass.: MIT Press.

Ogburn, William F., and Lolagene Coombs. 1940. 'The Economic Factor in the Roosevelt Elections'. *American Political Science Review* 34: 719–27.

—— and Estelle Hill. 1935. 'Income Classes and the Roosevelt Vote in 1932'. *Political Science Quarterly* 50: 186–93.

—— and Delvin Peterson. 1916. 'Political Thought of Social Classes'. *Political Science Quarterly* 31: 300–17.

Orfield, Gary. 1993. *The Growth of Segregation in American Schools*. Alexandria, Va.: NSBA Council of Urban Boards of Education.

Orum, Anthony. 1970. 'Religion and the Rise of the Radical White: The Case of Southern Wallace Support in 1968', *Social Science Quarterly* 51: 674–88.

Parsons, Talcott. 1954. *Essays in Sociological Theory*. New York: Free Press.

—— 1960. 'Social Structure and Political Orientation'. *World Politics* 13: 113–14.

Perkins, Jerry. 1989. 'The Moral Majority as a Political Reference in the 1980 and 1984 Elections'. In *Religion and Political Behavior in the United States*, ed. Ted G. Jelen. pp. 157–68. New York: Praeger.

Perlman, Selig. 1970 [1928]. *A Theory of the Labor Movement*. New York: Augustus M. Kelley.

Perot, Ross. 1992. *United We Stand: How We Can Take Back Our Country*. New York: Hyperion Books.

Persinos, John F. 1994. 'Has the Christian Right Taken Over the Republican Party?' *Campaigns and Elections* 15 (September): 21–24.

Petersen, Trond and Laurie A. Morgan. 'Separate and Unequal: Occupation-

Establishment Sex Segragation and the Gender Wage Gap.' *American Journal of Sociology*, 101 (1995): 329–65.

Petrocik, John. 1981. *Party Coalitions: Realignments and the Decline of the New Deal Party System*. Chicago: University of Chicago Press.

—— 1987. 'Realignment: New Party Coalitions and the Nationalization of the South'. *Journal of Politics* 49: 347–75.

Pettigrew, Thomas, and Roel W. Meetens. 1995. 'Subtle and Blatent Prejudice in Western Europe', *European Journal of Social Psychology* 25: 57–75.

Phillips, Kevin. 1970. *The Emerging Republican Majority*. Garden City, NY: Anchor Books.

—— 1982. *Post-Conservative America*. New York: Random House.

—— 1991. *The Politics of Rich and Poor*. New York: Random House.

—— 1993. *Boiling Point: Democrats, Republicans, and the Decline of Middle Class Prosperity*. New York: Random House.

Pierce, John C., Kathleen M. Beatty, and Paul R. Hagner. 1982. *The Dynamics of Public Opinion*. Glenview, Ill.: Scott Foresman.

Piven, Frances Fox. 1985. 'Women and the State: Ideology, Power and the Welfare State'. In *Gender and the Life Course*, ed. Alice Rossi, pp. 265–87. New York: Aldine.

—— (ed.). 1992. *Labor Parties in Postindustrial Capitalism*. New York: Oxford University Press.

—— and Richard A. Cloward. 1988. *Why Americans Don't Vote*. New York: Pantheon.

—— —— 1998. *The Breaking of the American Social Compact*. New York: New Press.

Plissner, Martin. 1983. 'The Marriage Gap'. *Public Opinion* (February-March): 53.

Plutzer, Eric, and Michael McBurnett. 1991. 'Family Life and American Politics: The "Marriage Gap" Reconsidered.' *Public Opinion Quarterly* 55: 113–27.

Pomper, Gerald R. 1975. *Voter's Choices: Varieties of American Electoral Behavior*. New York: Dodd, Mead.

Poole, Keith T., and Howard Rosenthal. 1997. *Congress: A Political-Economic History of Roll-Call Voting*. New York: Oxford University Press.

—— and Harmon Ziegler. 1985. *Women, Public Opinion and Politics*. New York: Longman.

Popkin, Samuel. 1991. *The Reasoning Voter*. Chicago: University of Chicago Press.

Posner, Gerald. 1996. *Citizen Perot: His Life & Times*. New York: Random House.

Powell, G. Bingham. 1982. *Contemporary Democracies: Participation, Stability and Violence*. Cambridge, Mass.: Harvard University Press.

Przeworski, Adam. 1985. *Capitalism and Social Democracy*. New York: Cambridge University Press.

—— and John Sprague. 1986. *Paper Stones: A History of Electoral Socialism.* Chicago: University of Chicago Press.

Quadagno, Jill. 1988. 'From Old Age Assistance to Supplemental Security Income: The Political Economy of Relief in the South'. In *The Politics of Social Policy in the United States*, ed. Margaret Weir, Ann S. Orloff, and Theda Skocpol pp. 235–64. Princeton: Princeton University Press.

—— 1994. *The Color of Welfare.* New York: Oxford University Press.

Quinley, Harold E. 1974. *The Prophetic Clergy: Social Activism among Protestant Ministers.* New York: Wiley.

Radosh, Ronaold. 1996. *Divided They Fell: The Demise of the Democratic Party 1964–1996.* New York: Free Press.

Rae, Douglas W. 1971. *The Political Consequences of Electoral Laws.* Revised edn. New Haven: Yale University Press.

—— and Michael Taylor. 1970. *The Analysis of Political Cleavages.* New Haven: Yale University Press.

Raftery, Adrian. 1995. 'Bayesian Model Selection in Sociology'. *Sociological Methodology* 25: 111–63.

Reeves, Keith. 1997. *Voting Hopes or Fears?* New York: Oxford University Press.

Reich, Robert. 1991. *The Work of Nations.* New York: Alfred A. Knopf.

Reichley, A. James. 1985. *Religion in American Public Life.* Washington, DC: Brookings Institute.

Reider, Jonathan. 1989. 'The Rise of the Silent Majority'. In *The Rise and Fall of the New Deal Order*, ed. Steven Fraser and Gary Gerstle, pp. 243–68. Princeton: Princeton University Press.

Rempel, Michael, and Terry N. Clark. 1997. 'Postindustrial Politics: A Framework for Interpreting Citizen Politics since the 1960s,' in *Citizen Politics in Post-Industrial Societies*, ed. Terry N. Clark and Michael Rempel, pp. 9–54. Boulder, Colo.: Westview Press.

Reskin, Barbara, and Patricia Roos. 1990. *Job Queues, Gender Queues: Explaining Women's Inroads into Male Occupations.* Philadelphia: Temple University Press.

Ribuffo, Leo. 1989. 'God and Jimmy Carter'. In *Transforming Faith*, ed. M. L. Bradbury and James B. Gilbert, pp. 141–60. Westport, Conn.: Greenwood Press.

Rice, Stuart A. 1969 [1928]. *Quantitative Methods in Politics.* New York: Russell and Russell.

Robinson, William S. 1950. 'Ecological Correlation and the Behavior of Individuals'. *American Sociological Review* 15: 351–57.

Rogin, Michael P. 1967. *The Intellectuals and McCarthy.* Cambridge. Mass.: MIT Press.

Roof, Wade C., and McKinney, William. 1987. *American Mainline Religion: Its Changing Shape and Future.* New Brunswick, NJ: Rutgers University Press.

Rose, Douglas (ed.). 1992. *The Emergence of David Duke and the Politics of Race.* Chapel Hill: University of North Carolina Press.

Rose, Richard. 1974. *The Problem of Party Government*. London: MacMillan.
—— (ed.). 1974. *Electoral Behavior: A Comparative Handbook*. New York: Free Press.
—— Ian McAllister. 1986. *Voters Begin to Choose*. Newbury Park, Calif: Sage Publications.
—— and Derek Unwin. 1969. 'Social Cohesion, Political Parties, and Strains in Regimes'. *Comparative Political Studies* 2: 7–67.
Rosenstone, Steven J., and John M. Hansen. 1993. *Mobilization, Participation, and Democracy in America*. New York: MacMillan.
—— Roy L. Behr, and Edward H. Lazarus. 1996. *Third Parties in America*, 2nd edn. Princeton: Princeton University Press.
Rossi, Alice. 1983. 'Beyond the Gender Gap: Women's Bid for Political Power'. *Social Science Quarterly* 64: 718–33.
Rossi, Peter. 1959. 'Four Landmarks in Voting Research'. In *American Voting Behavior*, ed. Eugene Burdick and Arthur J. Brodbeck, pp. 5–54. Glencoe, Ill.: The Free Press.
Roth, Byron M. 1994. *Prescription for Failure: Race Relations in the Age of Social Science*. New Brunswick, NJ: Transaction Publishers.
Rovere, Richard. 1965. *The Goldwater Caper*. New York: Harcourt.
Rozell, Mark J., and Clyde Wilcox (eds.). 1995. *God at the Grass Roots: The Christian Right in the 1994 Elections*. Lanham, Md.: Rowman and Littlefield.
Ruddick, Sara. 1989. *Maternal Thinking*. Boston: Beacon Press.
Rueschemeyer, Dietrich, Evelyne Stephens, and John Stephens. 1992. *Capitalist Development and Democracy*. Chicago: University of Chicago Press.
Rusher, William A. 1975. *The Making of a New Majority Party*. New York: Sheed and Ward.
Sainsbury, Diane. 1990. 'Party Strategies and Electoral Trade-Off of Class-Based Parties'. *European Journal of Political Research* 18: 29–50.
Sapiro, Virginia. 1983. *The Political Integration of Women*. Urbana: University of Illinois Press.
—— 1991. 'Feminism: A Generation Later'. *Annals of the American Academy of Political and Social Sciences* 515: 10–22.
Scammon, Richard, and Ben Wattenberg. 1970. *The Real Majority*. New York: Coward, McCann and Geoghegan, Inc.
Schneider, Beth E. 1988. 'Political Generations and the Contemporary Women's Movement.' *Sociological Inquiry*, 58: 4–21.
Schuman, Howard, Charlotte Steeh, Lawrence Bobo, and Maria Krysan. 1997. *Racial Attitudes in America: Trends and Interpretations*. Revised edn. Cambridge, Mass.: Harvard University Press.
Sears, David O. 1988. 'Symbolic Racism'. In *Eliminating Racism: Profiles in Controversy*, ed. Phyllis A. Katz and Dalmas A. Taylor, pp. 53–84. New York: Plenum.
—— and Leonie Huddy. 1990. 'On the Origins of Political Disunity among

Women'. In *Women, Politics and Change*, ed. Louise Tilly and Patricia Gurin, pp. 249–77. New York: Russell Sage.

—— and Donald R. Kinder. 1981. 'Prejudice and Politics: Symbolic Racism Versus Racial Threats to the Good Life', *Journal of Personality and Social Psychology* 40: 414–31.

Shafer, Byron (ed.). 1991. *Is America Different? A New Look at American Exceptionalism*. Oxford: Clarendon Press.

Shapiro, Robert Y., and Harpreet Mahajan. 1986. 'Gender Differences in Policy Preferences: A Summary of Trends from the 1960s to the 1980s'. *Public Opinion Quarterly* 50: 42–61.

Shea, Daniel M. and John C. Green (eds.). 1994. *The State of the Parties*. Lanham, Md.: Rowman & Littlefield.

Shelton, Beth A. 1992. *Women, Men, and Time: Gender Differences in Paid Work, Housework, and Leisure Time*. Westport, Conn. Greenwood Press.

Sherman, Richard B. 1973. *The Republican Party and Black America: From McKinley to Roosevelt*. Charlottesville: University of Virginia Press.

Sigelman, Lee. 1991. 'Jews and the 1988 Election: More of the Same?' In *The Bible and the Ballot Box*, ed. James L. Guth and John C. Green, pp. 188–203. Boulder, Colo.: Westview Press.

Silver, Brian D., Barbara Anderson, and Paul Abramson. 1986. 'Who Over-reports Voting?' *American Political Science Review* 80: 613–24.

Singer, Eleanor. 1981. 'Reference Groups and Social Evaluations'. In *Social Psychology: Sociological Perspectives*, ed. Morris Rosenberg and Ralph H. Turner, pp. 66–93. New York: Basic Books.

Skocpol, Theda. 1992. *Protecting Soldiers and Mothers*. Cambridge, Mass.: Harvard University Press.

—— 1995. *Social Policy in the United States*. Princeton: Princeton University Press.

Sleeper, Jim. 1990. *The Closest of Strangers: Liberalism and the Politics of Race in New York*. New York: Norton.

Smeal, Eleanor. 1984. *Why and How Women Will Elect the Next President*. New York: Harper and Row.

Smidt, Corwin. 1989. 'Contemporary Evangelical Political Involvement: An Overview'. In *Contemporary Evangelical Political Involvement*, ed. Corwin Smidt. Lanham, Md.: University Presses of America.

Smith, Eric R. A. N. 1989. *The Unchanging American Voter*. Berkeley: University of California Press.

Smith, Tom W. 1984. 'The Polls: Gender and Attitudes Toward Violence'. *Public Opinion Quarterly* 48: 384–96.

—— 1990. 'Classifying Protestant Denominations'. *Review of Religious Research* 31: 225–45.

Sniderman, Paul, Richard Brody, and Philip Tetlock. 1991. *Reasoning and Choice: Explorations in Political Psychology*. New York: Cambridge University Press.

—— and Thomas Piazza. 1993. *The Scar of Race*. Berkeley: University of California Press.

Sombart, Werner. 1976 [1906]. *Why Is There No Socialism in the United States?* White Plains, NY: M. E. Sharpe.

Sørensen, Annemette. 1992. 'Estimating the Economic Consequences of Separation and Divorce: A Cautionary Tale From the United States.' In *Economic Consequences of Divorce*, ed. Lenore Weitzman and Mavis McLean, pp. 263–82. New York: Oxford University Press.

Spain, Daphne, and Suzanne Bianchi. 1996. *Balancing Act: Motherhood, Marriage, and Employment among American Women*. New York: Russell Sage Foundation.

Stanley, Harold W. 1988. 'Southern Partisan Changes: Dealignment, Realignment or What?' *Journal of Politics* 50: 64–88.

—— and Richard Niemi. 1993. 'Partisanship and Group Support Over Time'. In *Controversies in Voting Behavior*, ed. Richard Niemi, pp. 350–67. Washington, DC: Congressional Quarterly Press.

—— —— 1995. 'The Demise of the New Deal Coalition'. In *Democracy's Feast: Elections in America*, ed. Herbert Weisberg, pp. 220–40. Chatham, NJ: Chatham House Publishers.

Stark, Rodney. 1991. 'Modernization, Secularization, and Mormon Success'. In *In Gods We Trust*, ed. Thomas Robbins and Dick Anthony, pp. 201–18. New Brunswick, NJ: Transaction Publishers.

—— and William S. Bainbridge. 1985. *The Future of Religion*. Berkeley: University of California Press.

—— and Charles Y. Glock. 1968. *American Piety: The Nature of Religious Commitment*. Berkeley: University of California Press.

Steinmetz, George, and Erik Olin Wright. 1989. 'The Fall and Rise of the Petty Bourgeoisie'. *American Journal of Sociology* 94: 973–1018.

Stouffer, Samuel A. 1955. *Communism, Conformity, and Civil Liberties*. Garden City, NY: Doubleday.

—— et al. 1949. *The American Soldier*. Princeton: Princeton University Press.

Sundquist, James. 1983. *Dynamics of the Party System*. Revised edn. Washington, DC: Brookings Institute.

Swierenga, Robert P. 1990. 'Ethnoreligious Political Behavior in the Mid-Nineteenth Century: Voting, Values, Cultures'. In *Religion and American Politics*, ed. Mark A. Noll, pp. 146–71. New York: Oxford University Press.

Szelenyi, Ivan, and Bill Martin. 1988. 'The Three Waves of New Class Theories'. *Theory and Society* 17: 645–667.

Szelenyi, Szonja. 1994. 'Women and the Class Structure'. In *Social Stratification*, ed. David B. Grusky, pp. 577–83. Boulder, Colo.: Westview Press.

Taagepera, Rein, and Matthew S. Shugart. 1989. *Seats and Votes: The Effects and Determination of Electoral Systems*. New Haven: Yale University Press.

Tate, Katherine. 1993. *From Protest to Politics*. Cambridge, Mass.: Harvard University Press.

Teixeira, Ruy. 1992. *The Disappearing American Voter.* Washington, DC: Brookings Institute.
—— 1997. 'Finding the Real Center'. *Dissent* 44: 51–59.
Thernstrom, Stephen, and Abigail Thernstrom. 1997. *America in Black and White: One Nation, Indivisible.* New York: Simon and Shuster.
Thompson, E. P. 1963. *The Making of the English Working Class.* New York: Vintage.
Tingsten, Herbert. 1963 [1937]. *Political Behavior: Studies in Election Statistics.* Totowa, NJ: Bedminster Press.
Tiryakian, Edward. 1993. 'American Religious Exceptionalism: A Reconsideration'. *Annals of the American Academy of Political and Social Science* 527: 40–54.
Tocqueville, Alexis de. 1969 [1835]. *Democracy in America,* ed. J. P. Mayer, trans. George Lawrence. New York: Anchor.
Tomsky, Michael. 1996. *Left for Dead.* New York: Free Press.
Trilling, Richard J., and Bruce A. Campbell. 1980. 'Toward a Theory of Realignment: An Introduction'. In *Realignment in American Politics,* ed. Campbell and Trilling, pp. 3–20. Austin: University of Texas Press.
Truman, David. 1951. *The Governmental Process.* New York: Alfred A. Knopf.
Tuch, Stephen. 1997. 'Metastereotypes: Blacks' Perceptions of Whites Stereotypes of Blacks'. *Public Opinion Quarterly* 61: 87–101
Turner, John C. 1987. *Rediscovering the Social Group.* Oxford: Blackwell.
U.S. Bureau of the Census. 1993. Current Population Reports P20–466. *Voting and Registration in the Election of November 1992.* Washington, DC: Government Printing Office.
van der Eijk, Cees, et al. 1992. 'Cleavages, Conflict Resolution and Democracy'. In *Electoral Change,* ed. Mark Franklin, Thomas Mackie, and Henry Valen, pp. 406–31. New York: Cambridge University Press.
Verba, Sidney, Norman H. Nie, and Jae-On Kim. 1978. *Participation and Political Equality: A Seven Nation Comparison.* New York: Cambridge University Press.
—— —— and John R. Petrocik. 1979. *The Changing American Voter.* Enlarged edn. Cambridge, Mass.: Harvard University Press.
—— Kay Lehman Schlozman and Henry E. Brady. 1997. *Voice and Equality.* Cambridge, Mass.: Harvard University Press.
Vernon, Glenn. 1968. 'The Religious "Nones"'. *Journal for the Scientific Study of Religion* 7: 219–29.
Voss, Kim. 1994. *The Making of American Exceptionalism: The Knights of Labor in the Nineteenth Century.* Ithaca, NY: Cornell University Press.
Wald, Kenneth. D. 1996. *Religion and Politics in the United States.* 3rd edn. Washington, DC: Congressional Quarterly Press.
—— Dennis Owen, and Samuel Hill. 1988. 'Churches as Political Communities'. *American Political Science Review* 82: 531–48.
Walker, Nancy J. 1994. 'What We Know about Women Voters in Britain, France

and West Germany'. In *Different Roles, Different Voices*, ed. Marianne Githens, Pippa Norris, and Joni Lovenduski, pp. 61–70. New York: HarperCollins.

Wallis, Roy, and Steve Bruce. 1992. 'Secularization: The Orthodox Model'. In *Religion and Modernization*, ed. Steve Bruce, pp. 8–30. New York: Oxford University Press.

Wattenberg, Ben. 1995. *Values Matter Most*. New York: Free Press.

Wattenberg, Martin. 1991. *The Rise of Candidate-Centered Politics*. Cambridge, Mass.: Harvard University Press.

—— 1996. *The Decline of American Political Parties, 1952–1994*. Cambridge, Mass.: Harvard University Press.

Weakliem, David L. 1991. 'The Two Lefts? Occupation and Party Choice in France, Italy, and the Netherlands'. *American Journal of Sociology* 96: 1327–61.

—— 1995. 'Two Models of Class Voting'. *British Journal of Political Science* 25: 259–70.

—— 1997. 'Race Versus Class? Racial Composition and Class Voting, 1936–1992'. *Social Forces* 75: 939–56.

—— and Anthony Heath. 1994. 'Rational Choice and Class Voting'. *Rationality and Society* 6: 243–70.

—— —— forthcoming. 'The Secret Life of Class Voting'. In *The End of Class Politics?*, ed. Geoff Evans, pp. 97–136. Oxford: Oxford University Press.

Weber, Max. 1958 [1906]. 'The Protestant Sects and the Spirit of Capitalism'. In *From Max Weber*, ed. H. H. Gerth and C. Wright Mills, pp. 302–22. New York: Oxford University Press.

—— 1978 [1922]. *Economy and Society*. Berkeley: University of California Press.

Weinstein, James. 1975. *Ambiguous Legacy: The Left in American Politics*. New York: New Viewpoints.

Weisberg, Herbert F. 1987. 'The Demographics of a New Voting Gap: Marital Differences in American Voting'. *Public Opinion Quarterly* 51: 335–43.

—— and David Kimball. 1995. 'Attitudinal Correlates of the 1992 Presidential Vote: Party Identification and Beyond'. In *Democracy's Feast: Elections in America*, ed. Herbert Weisberg, pp. 72–111. Chatham, NJ: Chatham House Publishers.

Weiss, Nancy. 1983. *Farewell to the Party of Lincoln*. Princeton: Princeton University Press.

Welch, Michael, and David Leege. 1991. 'Dual Reference Groups and Political Orientations: An Examination of Evangelically Oriented Catholics'. *American Journal of Political Science* 35: 28–56.

Welch, Susan, and John Hibbing. 1992. 'Financial Conditions, Gender, and Voting in American National Elections'. *Journal of Politics* 54: 197–213.

Western, Bruce. 1997. *Between Class and Market: Postwar Unionization in the Capitalist Democracies*. Princeton: Princeton University Press.

Wilcox, Clyde. 1986. 'Fundamentalists and Politics: An Analysis of the Effects of Different Operational Definitions'. *Journal of Politics* 48: 1041–51.

—— 1989. 'The New Christian Right and the Mobilization of the Evangelicals'. In *Religion and Political Behavior in the United States*, ed. Ted Jelen, pp. 139–56. New York: Praeger.

—— 1994. 'Premillennialists at the Millennium: Some Reflections on the Christian Right'. *Sociology of Religion* 55: 243–62.

Willey, Malcolm M., and Stuart A. Rice. 1924. 'A Sex Cleavage in the Presidential Election of 1920'. *Journal of the American Statistical Association* 19: 519–20.

Williams, Rhys (ed.). 1997. *Culture Wars in American Politics*. New York: Aldine de Gruyter.

Wills, Garry. 1990. *Under God: Religion and Politics in America*. New York: Simon and Shuster.

Wilson, Bryan R. (ed.). 1981. *The Social Impact of New Religious Movements*. New York: Rose of Sharon Press.

Wilson, William Julius. 1978. *The Declining Significance of Race*. Chicago: University of Chicago Press.

—— 1987. *The Truly Disadvantaged*. Chicago: University of Chicago Press.

—— 1996. *When Work Disappears*. New York: Alfred A. Knopf.

Winders, William. 1999. 'The Roller Coaster of Class Conflict: Class Segments, Mass Mobilization, and Voter Turnout in the United States, 1840–1996'. *Social Forces*: in press.

Wirls, Daniel. 1986. 'Reinterpreting the Gender Gap'. *Public Opinion Quarterly* 50: 316–30.

Wolff, Edward T. 1996. *Top Heavy: The Increasing Inequalities of Wealth and What Can Be Done About It*. New York: New Press.

Wood, James R. 1970. 'Authority and Controversial Policy: The Churches and Civil Rights'. *American Sociological Review* 35: 1057–69.

Woodard, J. David. 1989. 'Evangelicals and the Media'. In *Contemporary Evangelical Political Involvement*, ed. Corwin Smidt, pp. 119–31. Lanham, Md.: University Presses of America.

Wright, Erik Olin. 1979. *Class Structure and Income Determination*. New York: Academic Press.

—— 1985. *Classes*. London: Verso.

—— 1996. *Class Counts*. New York: Cambridge University Press.

Wuthnow, Robert. 1988. *The Restructuring of American Religion: Society and Faith since World War II*. Princeton: Princeton University Press.

—— 1989. *The Struggle for America's Soul*. Grand Rapids, Mich.: William B. Eerdmans Publishing Company.

—— 1993. *The Future of Christianity*. New York: Oxford University Press.

Yamane, David. 1997. 'Secularization on Trial: In Defense of a Neosecularization Paradigm'. *Journal for the Scientific Study of Religion* 36: 109–22.

Zaller, John R. 1992. *The Nature and Origins of Mass Opinion*. New York: Cambridge University Press.

Zipp, John. 1986. 'Social Class and Social Liberalism'. *Sociological Forum* 1: 301–29.

—— and Eric Plutzer. 1985. 'Gender Differences in Voting for Female Candidates: Evidence from the 1982 Election'. *Public Opinion Quarterly* 60: 30–57.

Zuckerman, Alan. 1975. 'Political Cleavage: A Conceptual and Theoretical Analysis'. *British Journal of Political Science* 5: 231–48.

SUBJECT INDEX

NAME INDEX